THE LABOR &
EMPLOYMENT LAW
PRACTICE GROUP of
DINSMORE &
HOHL, LLP

Michael W. Hawkins, Chair
G. Randall Ayers
April York Berman
Louise S. Brock
Cheryl E. Bruner
Randall M. Comer
Kenneth E. Douthat
Jon L. Fleischaker
Harold S. Freeman
Tammy R. Geiger
Michael S. Glassman
Charles K. Grant
Kimberly K. Greene
Murray K. Griess
C. Mark Kingseed
Stephen J. Kuebbing
Colleen P. Lewis
Michael A. Manzler
R. Kenyon Meyer
Nora S. Morris
Alice J. Neeley
Robert J. Reid
Charles M. Roesch
Terry S. Sallee
Jeffrey S. Shoskin
Holly C. Wallace
Trina M. Walton
Cheryl R. Winn

The HR Survival Guide to Labor & Employment Law

The
**NATIONAL
UNDERWRITER**
Company
PROFESSIONAL PUBLISHING GROUP

P.O. Box 14367 • Cincinnati, Ohio 45250-0367
1-800-543-0874 • www.nationalunderwriter.com

2001 Edition

This publication is designed to provide accurate and authoritative information in regard to the subject matter covered. It is sold with the understanding that the publisher is not engaged in rendering legal, accounting or other professional service. If legal advice or other expert assistance is required, the services of a competent professional person should be sought. — From a Declaration of Principles jointly adopted by a Committee of the American Bar Association and a Committee of Publishers and Associations.

ISBN: 0-87218-293-2

Printed in U.S.A.

Table of Contents

Acknowledgements

We would like to thank our editor, Deborah A. Miner, J.D., CLU, ChFC, associate editors, Deborah Price Rambo, J.D., William J. Wagner, J.D., LL.M., CLU, assistant editor, Joseph F. Stenken, J.D., CLU, ChFC, staff writer, Cynde R. Clausen, J.D., marketing manager, Nancy E. DeZarn, and the staff of the Financial Services and Human Resources Markets Department of The National Underwriter Company for their efforts in making this book a reality.

We would also like to thank the administrative assistants of Dinsmore and Shohl's Labor & Employment Law Practice Group: Connie Arnold, Rosie Kirkpatrick, Anne Mess, Patty Sammons, Danielle Sams, Gina Schneider, Denise Suter, Judy Turner, Cathy Webb, and Debbie Webb.

Foreword

Human Resources professionals are often called upon to be a resource for all employment laws. They are generally the people in the organization (along with inside legal counsel) who are expected to render opinions as to the legality of the company's employment practices. The complexity of employment law, and its constantly changing nature, make this responsibility a real challenge.

This book is intended to ease the HR professional's burden by providing a comprehensive guide to the basic provisions of federal laws related to labor and employment. Our desire was to give the Human Resources professional a handy reference to answer the most frequently asked questions in a straightforward and conversational style. We made the contents more useable by writing it in a question and answer format. We chose the questions based on our broad study of the law involved, as well as the hundreds of years of combined experience of our attorneys. Many of these questions have come up in our practice over the years.

A quick glance at the table of contents will reveal that we cover a broad range of topics. We have included chapters on traditional issues of labor relations, employment discrimination, and wage and hour law. We have also included some less traditional topics, such as workplace violence, and the application of federal civil rights laws to public employers.

On the other hand, no book can answer every unique question of law. Even the most complete volume is no substitute for an attorney experienced in labor and employment law and familiar with a client's operations and culture. There are many "gray areas" in labor and employment law that simply cannot be covered within the confines of even the most comprehensive book. We encourage our readers to develop a relationship with a qualified attorney experienced in labor and employment law, and to consult him or her as questions arise. We also recommend effective training of your supervisors and managers on labor and employment laws, and the development of proactive policies and procedures dealing with Human Resources issues. Along with developing a personal familiarity with the law, these approaches can avoid costly litigation.

We hope you find this book useful and informative.

The Attorneys of the Dinsmore & Shohl
Labor and Employment Law Practice Group

Chapter 1

Employee Status

IN GENERAL

1-1. Why should employers be concerned with whether a worker is an employee or an independent contractor?

1-2. What is an employer's tort liability with respect to an employee, versus an independent contractor?

1-3. What is an employer's tax liability with respect to an employee, versus an independent contractor?

1-4. How can an employer determine whether the person it has hired is an employee or an independent contractor?

1-5. What test does the IRS use to determine employee versus independent contractor status?

1-6. What test does the National Labor Relations Board (NLRB) use for determining which employees must be excluded from the bargaining unit because they are "independent contractors," rather than employees?

1-7. Has the U.S. Supreme Court provided a common law test for determining employee/independent contractor status?

1-8. What common law tests are used to determine employee or independent contractor status in employment discrimination suits?

1-9. What is the "Economic Realities" test?

1-10. What is the "Right to Control" test?

1-11. Are employees who are hired for temporary jobs considered independent contractors?

TEMPORARY WORKERS

1-12. What if an employer utilizes a temporary agency to supplement its workforce? Are employees from a temporary agency considered independent contractors?

1-13. What if an employer hires a subcontractor to perform work, and the subcontractor uses a temporary agency to supplement its workforce? Are the employees from a temporary agency considered employees?

1-14. Do statutes provide specific tests to be used in determining employment status?

STATUTORY TESTS

1-15. What are the specific test(s) to be used when determining employment status under the Family and Medical Leave Act?

1-16. What are the specific tests to be used when determining employment status under the Immigration Reform and Control Act?

1-17. What are the specific tests to be used when determining employment status under the Fair Labor Standards Act?

1-18. What are the specific tests to be used when determining employment status under the Employee Retirement Income Security Act?

1-19. What are the specific tests to be used when determining employment status under the Occupational Health and Safety Act?

1-20. What are the specific tests to be used when determining employment status for purposes of workers' compensation and unemployment compensation claims?

1-21. What tests are used when determining employment status under other statutes?

IN GENERAL

1-1. Why should employers be concerned with whether a worker is an employee or an independent contractor?

The status of a hired individual as either an employee or an independent contractor is critical for three reasons.

First, while employers may find themselves facing tort liability for the negligent actions of their employees, they generally do not assume tort liability for the negligent acts of an independent contractor. Likewise, federal employment discrimination laws, such as Title VII and the Age Discrimination in Employment Act (ADEA) and their state counterparts, prohibit discrimination in employment on the basis of an individual's race, color, religion, sex, national origin or age. Thus, employers are normally liable for the discriminatory actions of their employees; whereas such liability would normally not lie if the discriminating action was that of an independent contractor.

Second, the employee or independent contractor status will ultimately determine the employer's liability for paying various payroll taxes, such as workers' compensation and unemployment compensation.

Third, whether individuals are classified as employees or not has an effect on whether the employer must provide them with benefits, such as health insurance, retirement plans, and stock options. This is especially problematic with regard to temporary workers. See Q 1-12.

In addition, the status of a hired individual can also be important for purposes of determining the ownership of intellectual property[1] and in state sexual harassment claims.[2]

1-2. What is an employer's tort liability with respect to an employee, versus an independent contractor?

As noted, an employer may face tort liability for the negligent actions of its employees. Specifically, an employer is responsible for the negligent acts of its employees when the employee is acting within the scope of his/her employment and is acting in furtherance of the employer's business.[3]

Conversely, an employer is not liable for the torts of an independent contractor over whom the employer has not retained the right to control the manner or means of performing the work.

There are three generally recognized exceptions to the independent contractor rule. First, an employer may be directly liable for injuries resulting from its own negligence in selecting or retaining an independent contractor. Second, an employer may be held vicariously liable for the negligence of an independent contractor performing certain "non-delegable duties," which are imposed by statute, contract, franchise, or charter, or by common law. Third, an employer may be held vicariously liable for the negligence of an independent contractor under the doctrine of agency by estoppel (i.e., the recipient of services reasonably believes they are being provided by the employer).[4]

1-3. What is an employer's tax liability with respect to an employee, versus an independent contractor?

For each employee hired, employers are required to pay workers' compensation, unemployment compensation (state and federal unemployment insurance), social security and Medicare taxes (FICA), and any other applicable payroll taxes.

However, employers generally are not required to pay these taxes for independent contractors.

If an employer misclassifies an employee as an independent contractor, the employer will be responsible for not only the employer's but also the employee's FICA, unemployment compensation taxes, and all other taxes owed by the employee.[5]

1-4. How can an employer determine whether the person it has hired is an employee or an independent contractor?

There are several tests used to determine whether an individual is an employee or an independent contractor. They include tests developed by the Internal Revenue Service and the National Labor Relations Board (NLRB), and various common law tests. These tests are discussed in Q 1-5 through Q 1-8.

1-5. What test does the IRS use to determine employee versus independent contractor status?

The IRS test applies to issues involving the Federal Insurance Contribution Act (FICA), Federal Unemployment Tax Act (FUTA), and personal income tax withholding. Some courts have applied it in other areas of law as well.

The Internal Revenue Code requires employers to deduct withholding taxes and pay FICA and FUTA taxes on employees' wages.[6] An "employer" is defined as "the person for whom an individual performs or performed any service, of whatever nature, as the employee of such person except that... if the person for whom the individual performs or performed the services does not have control of the payment of the wages for such services, the term *employer*... means the person having control of the payment of such wages...."[7]

The determination of the employer-employee relationship involves an analysis of 20 common law factors:

1. Whether the worker must comply with other persons' instructions about when, where, and how to work;

2. Whether the worker is trained by the person for whom services are performed;

3. Whether the worker's services are integrated into the business operations;

4. Whether the services must be rendered personally by the worker;

5. Whether the person for whom the services are performed hires, supervises, and pays assistants;

6. Whether there is a continuing relationship between the worker and the person for whom the services are performed;

7. Whether the person for whom the services are performed establishes set hours of work;

8. Whether the worker must devote substantially full time to the business of the person or persons for whom the services are performed;

9. Whether the work is performed on the premises of the person for whom the services are performed;

10. Whether the person for whom services are performed retains the right to set the order or sequence of tasks;

11. Whether the worker is required to submit oral or written reports;

12. Whether payment is made by hour, week, or month rather than lump sum;

13. Whether the workers' business and/or traveling expenses are paid;

14. Whether the worker must supply tools, materials, and other equipment;

15. Whether the worker makes a significant investment in facilities used to perform services;

16. Whether a worker can realize a profit or suffer a loss as a result of services;

17. Whether a worker performs services for more than one firm at a time;

18. Whether a worker makes services available to the general public;

19. Whether the person for whom services are performed has the right to discharge a worker; and

20. Whether a worker has the right to terminate the working relationship without incurring liability.[8]

1-6. What test does the National Labor Relations Board (NLRB) use for determining which employees must be excluded from the bargaining unit because they are "independent contractors," rather than employees?

The National Labor Relations Act (NLRA) expressly excludes independent contractors as employees, and thus, they cannot be included in bargaining units.[9] To determine whether individuals are employees or independent contractors within the meaning of the NLRA, the National Labor Relations Board (NLRB) applies common law principles of agency.

According to the NLRB, an employer-employee relationship exists when the employer reserves not only the right to control the result to be achieved, but also the means to be used in attaining the result. On the other hand, where the employer has reserved only the right to control the ends to be achieved, an independent contractor relationship exists.[10] The determination of employee status or independent contractor status depends on the facts of each case, and *no one factor is determinative.*[11]

In *Adderley*, the NLRB used the following factors to determine whether an employment relationship existed:

- Whether individuals perform functions that are an essential part of the company's normal operation or operate an independent business;

- Whether they have a permanent working arrangement with the company which will ordinarily continue as long as performance is satisfactory;

- Whether they do business in the company's name with assistance and guidance from the company's personnel and ordinarily sell only the company's products;

- Whether the agreement that contains the terms and conditions under which they operate is promulgated and changed unilaterally by the company;

- Whether they account to the company for the funds they collect under a regular reporting procedure prescribed by the company;

- Whether particular skills are required for the operations subject to the contract;

- Whether they have a proprietary interest in the work in which they are engaged; and

- Whether they have the opportunity to make decisions that involve risks taken by independent businessmen which may result in profit or loss.[12]

In 1998, the NLRB clarified the test that employers and courts must use to determine independent contractor versus employee status. In *Roadway Package System, Inc.*,[13] and *Dial-a-Mattress Operating Corp.*,[14] (both decided on the same day), the NLRB listed the ten restatement factors as the guide to use when assessing employment status. Those restatement factors (which are very similar to those listed in *Adderley*), include:

- The extent of control which, by the agreement, the master may exercise over the details of the work;

- Whether or not the one employed is engaged in a distinct occupation or business;

- The kind of occupation, with reference to whether, in the locality, the work is usually done under the direction of the employer or by a specialist without supervision;

- The skill required in the particular occupation;

- Whether the employer or the workman supplies the instrumentalities, tools, and the place of work for the person doing the work;

- The length of time for which the person is employed;

- The method of payment, whether by the time or by the job;

- Whether or not the work is part of the regular business of the employer;

- Whether or not the parties believe they are creating the relation of master and servant;

- Whether the principal is or is not in the business.

In *Roadway*, the NLRB noted that "the common-law agency test encompasses a careful examination of all factors and not just those that involve a right of control." The *Roadway* and *Dial-a-Mattress* decisions neither overruled *Adderley* nor attempted to discredit any earlier versions of the common law tests of agency. Rather, the NLRB's goal in *Roadway* and *Dial-a-Mattress* was to

reiterate that no single factor weighs more heavily than any other in the independent contractor/employee analysis.

The NLRB also has dealt with a different, but related, issue: dual or joint employees. These are employees who are employed by an independent contractor, but are nonetheless included in the "user" employer's bargaining unit. To assess whether joint employer status is present, the NLRB has developed the following test:

1. The entities must share or codetermine matters governing essential terms and conditions of employment; and

2. The entities must meaningfully affect matters relating to the employment relationship, such as hiring, firing, discipline, supervision, and direction.[15]

1-7. Has the U.S. Supreme Court provided a common law test for determining employee/independent contractor status?

In *Nationwide Mutual Insurance Co. v. Darden*,[16] the Supreme Court approved the following factors in an analysis of whether an individual is an independent contractor or employee:

1. The hiring party's right to control the manner and means by which the product is accomplished;

2. The skill required by the hired party;

3. The source of instrumentalities and tools;

4. The location of the work;

5. The duration of the relationship between the parties;

6. The hiring party's right to assign additional projects;

7. The hired party's discretion over when and how long to work;

8. The method of payment;

9. The hired party's role in hiring the paying assistants;

10. Whether the work is part of the hiring party's regular business;

11. Whether the hiring party is in business;

12. The hired party's employee benefits; and

13. The tax treatment of the hired party's compensation.

1-8. What common law tests are used to determine employee or independent contractor status in employment discrimination suits?

Although there are many similarities in the common law tests states use to determine employee/independent contractor status, they vary enough that the exact test to use when assessing employee versus independent contractor status should be researched for the specific state or states where the relationships are being created.

The "economic realities" test (Q 1-9) and the "right to control" test (Q 1-10) are, however, the two common law tests typically used for determining employee versus independent contractor status in employment discrimination suits. There may, however, be different tests and/or results depending on which state law is applicable. For example, some states may have specific tests to assess employee/independent contractor status in unemployment compensation cases, but a different test to determine employment status in workers' compensation cases. Employers should consult with legal counsel in their state to determine the applicable law and the correct test to utilize. See also, Q 1-14, which addresses some of these concerns.

1-9. What is the "economic realities" test?

The "economic realities" test has been described as "a loose formulation, leaving the determination of employment status to case-by-case resolution based on the totality of the circumstances."[17] The economic realities test considers whether the hired individual is economically dependent upon the principal or is instead in business for himself. There are five factors courts generally consider in applying this test:

1. The degree of control exerted by the alleged employer over the worker;

2.   The worker's opportunity for profit or loss;

3.   The worker's investment in the business;

4.   The permanence of the working relationship; and

5.   The degree of skill required to perform the work.[18]

1-10. What is the "right to control" test?

In some states, an employer-employee relationship is characterized by the high level of control that the employer exercises over the mode and manner of the employee's work.[19] Courts have held that the "right to control is the hallmark of an employer-employee relationship" or that "the principal test of an employer and employee relationship is control."[20] The "right to control" test includes not just the control of the result to be accomplished by the work, but also control of the means and method utilized in accomplishing that result.[21]

Courts may also adopt a "hybrid" test. The test incorporates common law principles of agency, and requires a determination of:

- Whether an individual is economically dependent for his or her livelihood upon his employer; and

- Whether the employer maintains the right to control the means and manner of the individual's performance.

Under the second prong of this hybrid test, if the employer has the right to control the manner and means by which the work is completed, then the worker is an employee. However, if the employer is merely interested in the result and does not retain the right to direct the manner in which the work is completed, the worker is an independent contractor.[22] Some factors used to make the determination of whether the employer has the "right to control" the employee's performance include:

- The degree to which the employer controls the details of the work;

- Whether the individual is employed in a distinct occupation or business;

- Whether the individual's occupation is usually done under the supervision of someone else;

- Whether a high level of skill is required by the occupation;

- Whether the worker provides the supplies and tools or the place of work;

- The length of time service is provided;

- Method of payment (i.e., by the job or by time);

- Whether work is part of the regular business of the employer;

- Whether the parties intend to create an independent contractor relationship; and

- Whether the hiring agency is not in business.

1-11. Are employees who are hired for temporary jobs considered independent contractors?

Generally, if an employer hires a employee to perform a temporary job (i.e., the employee is hired for seasonal work), that employee is treated as a regular employee of the employer, for payroll taxes and otherwise.

TEMPORARY WORKERS

1-12. What if an employer utilizes a temporary agency to supplement its workforce? Are employees from a temporary agency considered independent contractors?

There is some ambiguity as to whether workers hired through a temporary agency are also considered employees of the employer. It appears that the employee status is determined on a case-by-case basis.

For example, courts have determined that even if an employee's contract with his/her employment agency describes the employee as an independent contractor, it is the nature of the work performed that dictates the employment status.[23] In *Walker*, the plaintiff (Walker) contracted with Genny's Home Health Care

(Genny's) to find her a job as an in-home health care provider. The defendant, Ben Lahoski (Lahoski), hired Genny's to provide twenty-four hour home-based health care services to his ailing wife. Genny's placed Walker on the Lahoski job, and Walker began working at the Lahoski home in shifts assigned by Genny's. Mr. Lahoski paid Genny's for the work performed by Walker. Walker was injured in the Lahoski's home while she was mopping the kitchen floor. She filed a claim with the Ohio Bureau of Workers' Compensation (OBWC), naming the Lahoskis as her employer. The OBWC denied her claim on the basis that Genny's, not the Lahoskis, was her employer. Even though there was a contract in place between Genny's and Walker, and even though Lahoski paid Genny's directly for services rendered by Walker, the court declared that Lahoski had sufficient "control [of] the manner or means of the work performed" to present a question to a jury, to decide whether Walker was, in fact, an employee of Lahoski. The court held that "court[s] must look to the substance of the [employment] relationship, not merely to a label attached to the relationship." Yet, despite the foregoing, even courts in the same state have determined that the contract was "primary evidence" of the parties' employment relationship.[24]

A similar rationale is followed in determining whether workers are employees for benefits purposes. Federal law contains many complex rules about who must participate in employee benefit plans, including stock option plans. "Temps" and independent contractors have been deemed to be employees for this purpose, as in the 1999 "Microsoft" decision.[25]

Microsoft had long supplemented its workforce with independent contractors and temporary workers, who performed the same duties as Microsoft's "common law" employees (see Q 1-8). Microsoft used this strategy not only to meet unexpected demands, but also to reduce the cost of benefits. A class action was brought by "all persons employed by Microsoft Corporation...who are denied employee benefits because they are considered independent contractors or employees of third-party employment agencies, but who meet the definition of employees of Microsoft Corporation under the common law."[26] Microsoft denied liability because (1) the individuals alleged to be independent contractors had signed an "independent contractor agreement," which expressly provided that independent contractors were responsible for their own benefits; and (2) temporary workers were employed by a temporary staffing agency. The appeals court rejected Microsoft's arguments,

finding that Microsoft either exercised, or retained the right to exercise, direction over the services performed, and that this control served to override both the independent contractor agreement and the relationship with the temporary staffing agency to form an employer-employee relationship between Microsoft and the class members. Accordingly, the court held that the class members were entitled to benefits to the same extent as Microsoft's full-time employees, which included stock options, believed to be worth millions of dollars.[27]

Because other cases have upheld a specific exclusion of temporary workers or "leased employees" in a plan document,[28] employers should ascertain that their plan documents are properly drafted to exclude applicable groups.

Likewise, employers should avoid any actions that would tend to confer employee status on these individuals or groups. For example, employers should not provide non-employees with business cards or company cars, and should not include them in employee events, whether formal (e.g., orientation) or informal (e.g., company picnics).

Employers should also make sure that the temporary staffing agency is taking steps that would reinforce its position as the employer of temporary workers. For example, the temporary staffing agency should (1) recruit the workers; (2) make the employment offer; (3) provide training or other orientation; (4) expressly inform the workers that they are employed by the temporary staffing agency and not the employer receiving the worker's services; (5) retain the right to remove and/or reassign the worker; (6) retain the right to discipline the worker, up to and including termination.

1-13. What if an employer hires a subcontractor to perform work, and the subcontractor uses a temporary agency to supplement its workforce? Are the employees from a temporary agency considered employees?

Generally, when an employer hires an independent contractor, if the original employer has no control over safety or any operative detail or method of work of the employees hired by the independent contractor, those employees are not employees of the original employer.[29]

STATUTORY TESTS

1-14. Do statutes provide specific tests to be used in determining employment status?

Yes, the Family and Medical Leave Act (FMLA), the Immigration Reform and Control Act, the Fair Labor Standards Act (FLSA), the Employee Retirement Income Security Act (ERISA), and the Occupational Health and Safety Act (OSHA), provide the factors to be considered when assessing employment status.

Most states have tests that are used in the context of workers' compensation and unemployment compensation claims.

Other statutes, however, have been subject to the common law approach to assessing employment status. The tests that are applicable to various statutes affecting employers are discussed in Q 1-15 to Q 1-21.

1-15. What are the specific test(s) to be used when determining employment status under the Family and Medical Leave Act?

The Family and Medical Leave Act (FMLA) looks to the Fair Labor Standards Act (FLSA) in determining the definition of employee. Under the FMLA, a determination of the employment relationship is not based on "isolated factors" or upon a single characteristic or "technical concepts," but depends "upon the circumstances of the whole activity" including the underlying "economic reality."

An employee, as distinguished from an independent contractor who is engaged in a business of his or her own, is one who "follows the usual path of an employee" and is dependent upon the business which he or she serves.[30]

1-16. What are the specific tests to be used when determining employment status under the Immigration Reform and Control Act?

The Immigration Reform and Control Act contains a definition of "independent contractor." Included in the definition are individuals or entities who carry on independent business, contract to do a piece of work according to their own means and methods, and are subject to control only as to results. Whether an individual or entity is an independent contractor, regardless of what the individual or entity calls itself, will be determined on a case-by-case basis. Factors to be considered in that determination include, but are not limited to, whether the individual or entity: (1) supplies the tools or materials; (2) makes services available to the general public; (3) works for a number of clients at the same time; (4) has an opportunity for profit or loss as a result of labor or services provided; (5) invests in the facilities for work; (6) directs the order or sequence in which the work is to be done; or (7) determines the hours during which the work is to be done.[31]

1-17. What are the specific tests to be used when determining employment status under the Fair Labor Standards Act?

At least one court has determined that the relevant test for assessing employment status under the Fair Labor Standards Act (FLSA) is the "economic realities" test.[32] *Dole* held that the "ultimate determination" is the degree to which the employee is dependent for his livelihood upon the employer. In performing its analysis, *Dole* focused on the following six criteria:

1. The nature and degree of the alleged employer's control as to the manner in which the work is to be performed;

2. The alleged employee's opportunity for profit or loss depending upon his/her managerial skill;

3. The alleged employee's investment in equipment or materials required for his/her task, or his employment of workers;

4. Whether the service rendered requires a special skill;

5. The degree of permanency and duration of the working relationship; and

6. The extent to which the service rendered is an integral part of the alleged employer's business.

Another court noted that "[these] factors are not exhaustive, nor can they be applied mechanically to arrive at a final determination of employee status."[33]

1-18. What are the specific tests to be used when determining employment status under the Employee Retirement Income Security Act?

The Employee Retirement Income Security Act (ERISA) defines "employee" simply as "any individual employed by an employer." But the Supreme Court has held that whether an individual was an "employee" for purposes of an ERISA benefits claim is subject to an analysis of common law agency principles.[34] See Q 1-7.

1-19. What are the specific tests to be used when determining employment status under the Occupational Health and Safety Act?

Courts typically apply the *Darden*[35] (see Q 1-7) analysis to the definition of an "employee" in an OSHA claim.[36] The *Loomis* court determined that the "[c]entral inquiry in determining whether common-law employment relationship exists is: who controls work environment."

1-20. What are the specific tests to be used when determining employment status for purposes of workers' compensation and unemployment compensation claims?

Most states employ a right to control test (see Q 1-10) in workers' compensation and unemployment compensation cases.[37] ("the entity possessing the right to control the manner of the performance of the servant's work is the employer, irrespective of whether the control is actually exercised; other factors which may be relevant include the right to select and discharge the employee and the skill or expertise required for the performance of the work.")

1-21. What tests are used when determining employment status under other statutes?

When a statute does not expressly articulate the relevant test to apply, courts will infer that the common law principles of agency are applicable. In *Nationwide Mut. Ins. Co. v. Darden*,[38] the Supreme Court noted that:

"[w]here Congress uses terms that have accumulated settled meaning under... the common law, a court must infer, unless the statute otherwise dictates, that Congress means to incorporate the established meaning of these terms.... In the past, when Congress has used the term 'employee' without defining it, we have concluded that Congress intended to describe the conventional master-servant relationship as understood by common-law agency doctrine."

CHAPTER ENDNOTES

1. See, e.g., *Community for Creative Non-Violence v. Reid*, 490 U.S. 730 (1989).
2. See, e.g., *NME Hospitals, Inc. v. Rennels*, 994 S.W. 2d 142 (Tx. S. Ct. 1999).
3. See. e.g., *Gulla v. Straus*, 154 Ohio St. 193, 93 N.E.2d 662 (1950); *Kuhn v. Youlten*, 118 Ohio App. 3d 168, 692 N.E.2d 226 (1997).
4. See, e.g., *Mutual Ins. Co. of Eagle Township v. Hunt*, 2000 Ohio App. LEXIS 4038.
5. *303 West 42nd Street Enterprise, Inc. v. IRS*, 181 F. 3d 272 (2nd Cir. 1999).
6. IRC §§3402, 3102, and 3301.
7. IRC §3401(d), emphasis supplied.
8. Rev. Rul. 87-41, 1987-1 C.B. 296.
9. 29 U.S.C. §152(3).
10. *NLRB v. Adderley Industries, Inc.*, 322 NLRB 1016, 155 LRRM 1223 (1997).
11. *NLRB v. United Insurance Co. of America*, 390 U.S. 254 (1968).
12. *Adderley*, 322 NLRB 1016 at 1022 (citing *Standard Oil Co.*, 230 NLRB 967, 968 (1977)).
13. 326 NLRB No. 72, 1998 WL 547959 (1998).
14. 326 NLRB No. 75, 1998 WL 574957 (1998).
15. *M.B. Sturgis Inc.*, 331 NLRB No. 173, 165 LRRM 1017 (2000).
16. *Nationwide Mut. Ins. Co. v. Darden*, 503 U.S. 318 (1992).
17. *Lilley v. BTM Corporation*, 958 F.2d 746, 750 (6th Cir.), cert. denied, 506 U.S. 940 (1992).
18. *Dole v. Snell*, 875 F.2d 802 (10th Cir. 1989) (cited in *Lilley*, supra, 958 F.2d at 749).
19. See, e.g., *Councell v. Douglas*, 163 Ohio St. 292, 126 N.E.2d 597 (1955) (syllabus). See also, *Gillum v. Industrial Commission of Ohio*, 141 Ohio St. 373, 48 N.E.2d 234 (1943).
20. See, e.g., *Third Federal Savings and Loan Association of Cleveland v. Fireman's Fund Insurance Co.*, 548 F.2d 166, 171 (6th Cir. 1977), and *William H. Sill Mortgages v. Ohio Casualty Insurance Co.*, 412 F.2d 341, 344 (6th Cir. 1969) (both applying Kentucky law).
21. See *Glenn v. Standard Oil Co.*, 148 F.2d 51 (6th Cir. 1945), and *Glenn v. Beard*, 141 F.2d 376 (6th Cir. 1944) (both applying Kentucky law).
22. See, e.g., *Lancaster Colony Corp. v. Limbach*, 37 Ohio St. 3d 198, 524 N.E.2d 1389 (1988).
23. See, e.g., *Walker v. Lahoski*, 1999 Ohio App. LEXIS 3435.
24. See, e.g., *McDonald v. Canton Free Press*, 1997 Ohio App. LEXIS 1033.
25. *Vizcaino v. Microsoft*, 173 F.3d 713 (9th Cir. 1999), cert. denied, 528 U.S. 1105 (2000).
26. *Vizcaino*, supra.

27. See also, *Herman v. Time Warner, Inc.*, 56 F. Supp. 2d 411 (S.D.N.Y. 1999).
28. See *Casey v. Atlantic Richfield Co.*, 2000 U.S. Dist. Lexis 6836; *Clark v. E.I. DuPont de Nemours & Co., Inc.*, 1997 U.S. App. LEXIS 321.
29. See, e.g., *Hittel v. WOTCO, Inc.*, 996 P.2d 673 (Wyoming 2000).
30. 29 CFR §825.105(a).
31. 8 CFR 274a.1(j).
32. *Dole v. Amerilink Corp.*, 729 F.Supp. 73 (E.D. Mo. 1990).
33. *Brock v. Mr. W Fireworks, Inc.*, 814 F.2d 1042, 1043 (5th Cir. 1987).
34. See *Nationwide Mut. Ins. Co. v. Darden*, 503 U.S. 318 (1992).
35. *Nationwide Mut. Ins. Co. v. Darden*, 503 U.S. 318 (1992).
36. See e.g., *Loomis Cabinet Co. v. Occupational Safety & Health Review Comm'n*, 20 F.3d 938 (9th Cir. 1994).
37. See, e.g., *JFC Temps, Inc. v. W.C.A.B.*, 545 Pa. 149, 153, 680 A.2d 862, 864 (Pa. 1996).
38. *Nationwide Mut. Ins. Co. v. Darden*, 503 U.S. 318 (1992).

Chapter 2

Workplace Violence

GENERALLY

2-1. How serious a problem is workplace violence?

2-2. Can an employer be legally liable for acts of violence by its employees?

2-3. Can an employer be legally liable with respect to an employee accused of violence or threatened violence?

PREVENTATIVE MEASURES

2-4. How can an employer avoid liability for acts of workplace violence?

2-5. What steps can the employer take in the hiring process to avoid liability?

2-6. What policies and procedures can the employer use in the workplace to avoid liability?

2-7. How should the employer plan for the termination of an employee who has engaged in workplace violence?

2-8. Are there ways to predict workplace violence?

GENERALLY

2-1. How serious a problem is workplace violence?

Prominent news stories of employees assaulting and murdering co-workers have raised management awareness of workplace violence. The legal and psychological fallout from a serious incident of violence in the workplace can be devastating to an organization and its community. Employers must be prepared to prevent violent acts, and to deal with emergency situations should they arise.

Government studies have shed light on the extent of the workplace violence problem in the United States.

NATIONAL INSTITUTE OF OCCUPATIONAL SAFETY AND HEALTH

A landmark study on workplace violence was conducted by the National Institute of Occupational Safety and Health (NIOSH) in 1996. According to that study, a reasonable working definition of workplace violence is as follows: violent acts, including physical assaults and threats of assault, directed toward persons at work or on duty.

NIOSH states that violence is a substantial contributor to occupational injury and death. Homicide has become the second leading cause of occupational injury death. NIOSH estimated that each week, an average of 20 workers are murdered, and 18,000 are assaulted while at work or on duty. Most of these assaults occur in service settings, such as hospitals, nursing homes, and social service agencies.

DEPARTMENT OF JUSTICE

In July, 1998, the U.S. Department of Justice (DOJ) issued a special report on workplace violence. This report estimated that each year between 1992 and 1996, more than two million U.S. residents were victims of a violent crime while they were at work or on duty. This number is more than double the estimate given by NIOSH. More than 160,000 workers in medical occupations, including an estimated 70,000 nurses, 24,000 technicians, and about 10,000 physicians, were victimized each year between 1992 and 1996.

Additional DOJ statistics for the years 1992 through 1996 include the following:

- More than 1,000 workplace homicides occurred annually.

- The most common type of workplace victimization was simple assault, with an estimated 1.5 million occurring each year; aggravated assaults numbered 395,000.

- Among the people victimized while working, male victims outnumbered females by about 2:1.

- Almost 60% of victims were attacked by a stranger; 35% of victims were attacked by an acquaintance or co-worker.

2-2. Can an employer be legally liable for acts of violence by its employees?

Yes.

OSHA LIABILITY

While there is no federal law specifically covering employer liability for workplace violence by employees, The Occupational Safety and Health Act of 1970 (OSHA) mandates that, in addition to compliance with hazard specific guidelines, employers have a general duty to provide employees with a safe working environment. This general duty clause requires employers to keep the workplace free of recognized hazards likely to cause death or serious physical harm. OSHA has indicated that it will rely on the general duty clause to cite employers for violations. There is no private right of action under OSHA.[1]

Among federal agencies, the Occupational Safety and Health Administration (OSHA) seems to have taken the lead in attempting to provide guidance to employers. In addition to the particular problems of health care workers, the agency has issued guidance for preventing violence to taxi drivers and night retail workers.[2]

STATE LAW LIABILITY FOR EMPLOYERS

Most cases holding employers liable for acts of workplace violence are based on state laws. State law claims by victims are generally tort law claims, and come under several general theories of liability.

WORKERS' COMPENSATION

Employees injured by violence in the course of their employment may have a compensable workers' compensation claim. In fact, employers often argue that state worker's compensation programs are intended to be the exclusive remedy for all workplace injuries, including those arising from violence.

For an injury to be exclusively compensable under workers' compensation, the injury must:

1. Arise out of the employment;

2. Be in the course of employment; and

3. Not fall within the intentional tort exemption (i.e., not the type of injury that the employer knew or should have known would happen).

RESPONDEAT SUPERIOR

If an employee commits a violent act within the scope of his employment, then the doctrine of respondeat superior may be invoked to make the employer liable for the damages caused by the violence. Courts will focus on whether the act is committed by an employee while in the scope of his or her employment, or while he or she is doing anything that is reasonably incidental to the employment. When an employee departs from his job responsibilities to engage in conduct that has purely personal ends, the employer is generally not be held liable for resulting injuries to other employees or third parties.

NEGLIGENT HIRING

The tort of negligent hiring is based on the concept that, under certain circumstances, the law will impose a duty on employers to protect potential victims from the criminal acts of others. Plaintiffs in these cases claim that the employer's hiring process was unreasonably lax, so that the violent employee was hired when a reasonable process would have discovered his violent tendencies.

NEGLIGENT RETENTION

After an employee is hired, if the employer becomes aware of his or her violent tendencies and takes no action to curb them, the employer may be liable for negligent retention or supervision of the employee when injuries result from such tendencies.

NEGLIGENT FAILURE TO PROVIDE A SAFE WORKPLACE

In some states, an employer has a statutory duty to provide a safe work environment for its employees. Thus, an employer may be independently liable for failing to take corrective action against an employee who poses a threat of harm to fellow employees. Like negligent retention actions, these suits usually allege that the employer was aware of the individual's violent nature. The main difference is that the employer's duty arises out of statute instead of a common law tort theory.

2-3. Can an employer be legally liable with respect to an employee accused of violence or threatened violence?

Yes, under certain circumstances.

DEFAMATION

An employer can be sued for defamation if three elements are met. First, the employer must make a false statement about an employee. Second, the false statement must be "published" to a third party. Finally, the false statement must tend to injure the employee's reputation or deter others from associating with him or her.

WRONGFUL DISCHARGE

An employee fired due to anticipated but not yet manifested violence may sue under a variety of wrongful discharge theories. For instance, he may claim that the employer violated a general public policy in discharging him. This general heading also includes cases where plaintiffs claim that the employer intentionally inflicted emotional distress on them by discharging them in an outrageous manner.

DISABILITY DISCRIMINATION

Both state and federal disability discrimination laws must be considered when dealing with a workplace violence issue. Employers cannot ignore their responsibility, under the Americans With Disabilities Act (ADA), to accommodate mental impairments that qualify as "disabilities." See Chapter 6. Under the ADA (and some state counterparts), a "disability" is any physical or mental impairment that substantially limits a "major life activity." If a person has a past record of a disability, or is regarded by the employer as being disabled, then he or she also is protected under the ADA. Of particular concern regarding workplace violence is the statutory protection for mental disabilities. They include any mental or

psychological disorder, emotional, or mental illness that significantly restricts a major life activity, such as working.

It is significant to the issues of workplace violence that some state and federal laws allow employers to reject an applicant that poses a "direct threat" to himself or to others. This direct threat is strictly defined, however, to require a showing of "a significant risk (i.e., a high probability) of substantial harm to the health or safety of the individual or others that cannot be eliminated or reduced by reasonable accommodation."[3] This determination cannot be based on mere speculation; rather it must be based on an individualized assessment involving reasonable medical judgment about the person's current ability to perform the job's essential functions safely. The determination must account for the duration of the risk, the nature and severity of the potential harm, and the likelihood that it will occur.

PREVENTATIVE MEASURES

2-4. How can an employer avoid liability for acts of workplace violence?

Most of the strategies for avoiding violence, and therefore avoiding liability, revolve around strong fundamental Human Resources practices in hiring, managing, and terminating employees, as discussed in Q 2-5, Q 2-6, and Q 2-7.

2-5. What steps can the employer take in the hiring process to avoid liability?

A careful hiring process, which finds out as much as possible (within legal bounds) about an applicant before he or she is hired will help to avoid many future problems.

INTERVIEWS

Employers should always require that applicants fill out application forms, not merely submit resumes. The application form provides the employer with background information, and releases the employer from the need to make further inquiry.

Employers should screen the applications and select those that meet the employer's legitimate requirements before beginning interviews. Employers should develop a written interview guide, based upon job requirements.

The applicant should be required to explain in detail any criminal convictions (felonies and misdemeanors) listed. "Conviction" should be defined, for this purpose, to encompass pleading guilty, pleading no contest, or a finding of guilt. Employers should account for the applicant's activities for all periods for at least the past ten years—gaps in time may be the result of jail sentences.

REFERENCE AND BACKGROUND CHECKS

Employers should thoroughly check all listed references. Notes should be taken on separate sheets of paper, not on the application form.

Employers should ask an applicant's references for other references.

If a job requires a specific degree or professional license, employers should not take the applicant's word, but should call the school or licensing agency to verify the information.

An application form should contain the necessary language to allow the employer to investigate the applicant's personal history and financial and credit record, and employers should follow through and check these items.

CREDIT REPORTS

Employers who intend to obtain credit reports on applicants must comply with the Fair Credit Reporting Act, which is discussed in detail in Chapter 14.

Failure to comply with the Fair Credit Reporting Act can result in state or federal enforcement actions, as well as private lawsuits by the applicant or employee. Additionally, any person who knowingly and willfully obtains a consumer credit report under false pretenses may face criminal prosecution.

THE OFFER LETTER

After selecting an applicant to hire, the employer should document the reasons for selecting the applicant, and then write an offer letter. The letter should indicate that the offer is contingent upon a medical examination. Employers should be careful to avoid making any "promises" in the offer letter, which could be construed as undermining the at-will employment relationship. The offer letter should clearly state that the employment relationship is at will, and can be terminated by either party, with or without reason, and with or without notice.

MEDICAL EXAMINATION

A thorough medical examination provides an employer with a baseline description of the employee's physical and mental condition, so that later claims that a condition arose as a result of employment can be evaluated.

This post-offer phase is also the time to require that the applicant submit to a psychological examination, although this is an extreme and expensive measure.

Since psychological disorders are not as easy to identify as medical ones, the analysis under disability laws becomes more complex. Defending psychological testing and the use of its results in the workplace may be worthwhile, but requires even more planning and consideration than medical evaluations.

Employers should bear in mind, however, that they cannot refuse to hire an individual because of a mental (or physical) disability, unless the disability prevents the person, even with reasonable accommodation, from performing the essential functions of the job, or the person poses a direct threat to the safety of him or herself or others in the workplace. See Chapter 6.

Finally, employers should make sure the medical examination includes a test for drugs, performed by a laboratory that follows National Institute for Drug Abuse procedures.

2-6. What policies and procedures can the employer use in the workplace to avoid liability?

POLICIES

Employers should develop and implement policies that clearly state that violence, intimidation, or harassment by or against employees will not be tolerated, and consistently back up those policies with appropriate discipline, up to and including discharge.

Employers should inform all employees that they are required to contact human resources personnel, or other designated management, regarding any threats or questionable behavior by co-workers, customers, or others coming into the workplace.

EMERGENCY PROCEDURES

It is important for employers to develop an emergency procedure that will go into effect if violence erupts in the workplace. This plan should include a list of the company officials to be contacted, evacuation plans, and telephone numbers for emergency personnel. The employer should provide training to its employees and supervisors concerning violence in the workplace, and the manner in which such acts should be addressed.

EMPLOYEE ASSISTANCE PROGRAMS

Many employers use Employee Assistance Programs (EAPs) to provide their employees with help and counseling for personal and psychological problems.

An EAP contract should be carefully drafted to provide that the EAP indemnifies the employer against any claims based on the conduct of the EAP.

Employers should require participating employees to sign a disclosure form, in which they state that they understand and agree that some limited information may be shared with an HR professional, on a "need-to-know" basis.

PSYCHIATRIC EXAMINATIONS

Under the ADA (the Americans with Disabilities Act, discussed in Chapter 6), employers can require employees to submit to a medical examinations if it is job-related and necessary for the business. If the employer believes, based upon an employee's behavior, that he or she has a mental problem that may require an accommodation, or that he or she poses a threat to the safety of himself or others, the employer may require a psychiatric examination.

INVESTIGATION AND DISCIPLINE

Employers should promptly and thoroughly investigate any questionable situations as soon as they are reported, document the investigative steps, and take consistent, appropriate action. If the alleged misconduct is serious, the employer should suspend the employee pending investigation.

INVESTIGATION

All witnesses should be interviewed, and thereafter sign written statements.

A representative of the employer should meet with the employee, in order to get his or her complete version of the facts.

DISCIPLINE

If discipline short of discharge is the appropriate remedy, the employer should consider requiring the employee to obtain counseling or successfully complete an Employee Assistance Program as a condition of continued employment.

Discipline should be determined in light of work rules, contractual restrictions, company policies and practices, employee handbooks, etc.

If no discipline is warranted, and the employee was suspended pending the investigation, he or should be reinstated with back pay.

If the investigation reveals that discharge of the potentially dangerous employee is the proper disciplinary action, the employer must plan appropriately for the process of terminating the employee. See Q 2-7.

2-7. How should the employer plan for the termination of an employee who has engaged in workplace violence?

An employer should plan to add extra security coverage, and should take extra care to avoid offending the employee in the termination process. The termination should occur in a way that causes as little embarrassment to the employee as possible.

THE TERMINATION NOTIFICATION MEETING

Employers should not conduct termination meetings while the individuals involved are still angry. The termination notification meeting should be business-like and calm.

WHO SHOULD ATTEND THE MEETING

In addition to the employee being discharged, two individuals should generally be present at the termination meeting. These may include a union representative or the employee's immediate supervisor, and a representative from Human Resources. An individual should be present who can answer the employee's questions.

LOCATION OF THE MEETING

The meeting should be held in a management office or similarly formal atmosphere.

CONDUCTING THE MEETING

The employee should be given an opportunity to talk, but no one should argue with the employee during this meeting.

TIMING OF THE MEETING

The meeting should be held at the end of the day, or during the lunch hour, in order to allow the employee the opportunity to exit discreetly.

ESCORTING THE EMPLOYEE FROM THE WORKPLACE

While it may be prudent to escort an employee off the premises or to have a security guard accompany the employee while he packs personal belongings, care should be taken to be discreet and avoid unnecessary attention, embarrassment or humiliation to the employee.

EXTREME MEASURES

In extreme cases, the employer should obtain a restraining order or injunction preventing the employee from returning to the workplace and its immediate surroundings.[4]

Figure 2.1

WORKPLACE VIOLENCE CHECKLIST		
	True	False
This industry frequently confronts violent behavior and assaults of staff.		
Violence occurs regularly where this facility is located.		
Violence has occurred on the premises or in conducting business.		
Customers, clients, or coworkers assault, threaten, yell, push, or verbally abuse employees or use racial or sexual remarks.		
Employees are NOT required to report incidents or threats of violence, regardless of injury or severity, to employer.		
Employees have NOT been trained by the employer to recognize and handle threatening, aggressive, or violent behavior.		

Figure 2.1 Continued

	True	False
Violence is accepted as "part of the job" by some managers, supervisors, and/or employees.		
Access and freedom of movement within the workplace are NOT restricted to those persons who have a legitimate reason for being there.		
The workplace security system is inadequate — e.g., door locks malfunction, windows are not secure, and there are no physical barriers or containment systems.		
Employees or staff members have been assaulted, threatened, or verbally abused by clients and patients.		
Medical and counseling services have NOT been offered to employees who have been assaulted.		
Alarm systems such as panic alarm buttons, silent alarms, or personal electronic alarm systems are NOT being used for prompt security assistance.		
There is no regular training provided on correct response to alarm sounding.		
Alarm systems are NOT tested on a monthly basis to assure correct function.		
Security guards are NOT employed at the workplace.		
Closed circuit cameras and mirrors are NOT used to monitor dangerous areas.		
Metal detectors are NOT available or NOT used in the facility.		
Employees have NOT been trained to recognize and control hostile and escalating aggressive behaviors, and to manage assaultive behavior.		
Employees CANNOT adjust work schedules to use the "Buddy system" for visits to clients in areas where they feel threatened.		
Cellular phones or other communication devices are NOT made available to field staff to enable them to request aid.		
Vehicles are NOT maintained on a regular basis to ensure reliability and safety.		
Employees work where assistance is NOT quickly available.		

2-8. Are there ways to predict workplace violence?

OSHA has published the following Workplace Violence Checklist, which may be used and modified by employers. The checklist may help to identify present or potential violence problems. A response of "true" indicates a risk factor for security hazards.

In addition to the above factors related to the workplace itself, experts have suggested a profile of individuals prone to workplace violence. Employers should be aware of these individual tendencies, and take particular care in dealing with employees who exhibit them. Some profile factors are:

1. Few interests outside of work;

2. A fascination with guns or the military;

3. A history of family problems;

4. A possible history of violence;

5. A tendency to hold grudges and blame others for problems;

6. Drug and/or alcohol abuse;

7. A violent influence on the workforce;

8. Chronically discontented;

9. An unstable work record;

10. Often violates company policies; and/or

11. Withdrawn, loner.

Experts also note some behavioral tendencies that give clues that an employee may be becoming volatile:

1. Verbal threats, especially implied or express warnings that "something" will or may happen;

2. Physical acts of intimidation or harassment of other workers;

3. Attempts to gain access to unauthorized areas;

4. Bizarre thoughts, paranoia, or indications that the individual's perception is skewed;

5. A perception that he or she has been unjustly denied an entitlement, or humiliated by a seemingly insignificant act; and

6. A focus on a specific target or revenge or an escalating grudge against another employee or supervisor.

Employers should pay attention when an employee exhibits any of these tendencies, and where the employee exhibits two or more, the employer should take the behavior very seriously.

CHAPTER ENDNOTES

1. See *Guidelines for Preventing Workplace Violence for Health Care and Social Service Workers*, found at: www.osha-slc.gov/SLTC/workplaceviolence/guideline.html.
2. See www.osha-slc.gov/SLTC/workplaceviolence/index.html.
3. See 29 CFR §1630.2(r).
4. For more information on handling such terminations, see the discussion on workplace violence in Gavin De Becker, *The Gift of Fear: Survival Signals That Protect Us from Violence*, 1st ed. New York, NY: Little Brown & Company; 1997.

Chapter 3

Worker Privacy

THE RIGHT TO PRIVACY

3-1. Are employees entitled to privacy in the workplace?

3-2. What are the sources of employees' right to privacy in the public sector?

3-3. What are the sources of employees' right to privacy in the private sector?

POTENTIAL CLAIMS

3-4. What claims can employees bring against their employers for violating their privacy?

TORT OF INVASION OF PRIVACY

3-5. What is the tort of invasion of privacy?

3-6. What are the elements of a claim of unreasonable intrusion upon the seclusion of another?

3-7. What are the elements of a claim of appropriation of another's name or likeness for one's own commercial advantage?

3-8. What are the elements of a claim of unreasonable public disclosure of the private facts of another?

3-9. What are the elements of a claim of publication of facts placing another in a false light?

3-10. What types of activities might constitute invasion of privacy?

THE ELECTRONIC COMMUNICATIONS PRIVACY ACT OF 1986

3-11. What is the ECPA?

3-12. What is a "wire communication"?

3-13. What is an "oral communication"?

3-14. What is an "electronic communication"?

3-15. What does not constitute an "electronic communication"?

3-16. What does "intercept" mean?

3-17. What does "electronic storage" mean?

3-18. What is the relationship between the ECPA and state law?

LIMITATIONS ON MONITORING EMPLOYEES

3-19. What types of activities does the ECPA limit?

EXCEPTIONS TO THE ECPA

3-20. Are there any exceptions to the ECPA?

3-21. What is the service provider exception to the ECPA?

3-22. What is the prior consent exception to the ECPA?

3-23. What is the ordinary course of business exception to the ECPA?

ENFORCEMENT, REMEDIES AND DEFENSES UNDER THE ECPA

INTERCEPTING COMMUNICATIONS

3-24. Who enforces the ECPA's prohibition against intercepting a communication?

3-25. To what relief is the injured party entitled for a violation of the prohibition against intercepting communications?

3-26. How does the court assess damages when the prohibition against intercepting communications is violated?

3-27. Are there any defenses to a civil or criminal action brought for violation of the prohibition against intercepting communications?

3-28. What is the statute of limitations for a violation of the prohibition against intercepting communications?

ACCESSING COMMUNICATIONS WHILE IN ELECTRONIC STORAGE

3-29. Who enforces the ECPA's prohibition against accessing communications while in electronic storage?

3-30. To what relief is the injured party entitled for a violation of the prohibition against accessing communications while in electronic storage?

3-31. How does the court assess damages when a violation of the prohibition against accessing communications while in electronic storage occurs?

3-32. Are there any defenses to a civil or criminal action brought for a violation of the prohibition against accessing communications while in electronic storage?

3-33. What is the statute of limitations for a violation of the prohibition against accessing communications while in electronic storage?

PREVENTATIVE MEASURES

3-34. What preventative measures can an employer take to avoid violating the ECPA?

3-35. What provisions should an electronic communications policy contain?

THE RIGHT TO PRIVACY

3-1. Are employees entitled to privacy in the workplace?

Yes, but the nature and extent of the right to privacy depends on whether the employee is employed in the public or private sector. This chapter will briefly address worker privacy in the public sector, but will focus on federal statutory law pertaining to worker privacy in the private sector.

3-2. What are the sources of employees' right to privacy in the public sector?

A public sector employer's ability to monitor or search an employee is limited by the Fourth Amendment to the United States Constitution. The Fourth Amendment protects individuals from unreasonable searches and seizures by government actors. A search is unreasonable if "the invasion of the employees' legitimate expectations of privacy [outweighs] the government's need for supervision, control, and the efficient operation of the workplace."[1]

Public sector employers also need to be cognizant of state constitutions, federal and state statutes, and common law torts that might provide additional limitations on their ability to monitor employees. Common law torts and federal statutory law are discussed below.

3-3. What are the sources of employees' right to privacy in the private sector?

The Fourth Amendment generally does *not* limit a private employer's ability to monitor its employees because, in order to be applicable, there must be state action. State action may be found, however, when a private sector employer engages in an essential government function, receives a specified amount of government financing, or acts in concert with a state actor.[2]

Under common law, in the area of workplace privacy, the primary source of liability for an employer is the tort of invasion of privacy. Invasion of privacy encompasses four separate causes of action which are described below.

With respect to federal statutory law, Title III of the Omnibus Crime Control and Safe Streets Act of 1968, as amended by the Electronic Communications Privacy Act of 1986, limits an employer's

ability to monitor an employee's wire, oral or electronic communications.[3]

POTENTIAL CLAIMS

3-4. What claims can employees bring against their employers for violating their privacy?

PUBLIC SECTOR

Employees of state and local governments may enforce their Fourth Amendment rights by bringing an action under 42 U.S.C. §1983 against their employers. This statute provides:

> Every person who, under color of any statute, ordinance, regulation, custom, or usage, of any State or Territory or the District of Columbia, subjects, or causes to be subjected, any citizen of the United States or other person within the jurisdiction thereof to the deprivation of any rights, privileges, or immunities secured by the Constitution and laws, shall be liable to the party injured in an action at law, suit in equity, or other proper proceeding for redress.

Employees of the federal government may enforce their right to privacy against the federal government directly under the Fourth Amendment by bringing a Bivens-type action.[4]

PRIVATE SECTOR

Under common law, employees may bring a variety of torts against their employers for violating their privacy. The most common, however, is the tort of invasion of privacy (see Q 3-5).

With respect to federal statutory claims, the Electronic Communications Privacy Act of 1986 provides a private right of action against an entity or individual who intercepts or accesses another's wire, oral or electronic communications without the other's consent. The applicability of the statute is not restricted to the employer-employee context, however, this chapter will focus on the statute's impact on the workplace and the employer-employee relationship. It must be noted, however, that the statute does not define the term "employer" or "employee."[5]

TORT OF INVASION OF PRIVACY

3-5. What is the tort of invasion of privacy?

Under common law, the tort of invasion of privacy comprises the following four separate claims:

1. Unreasonable intrusion upon the seclusion of another (see Q 3-6).

2. Appropriation of another's name or likeness for one's own commercial advantage (see Q 3-7).

3. Unreasonable public disclosure of the private facts of another (see Q 3-8).

4. Publication of facts placing another in a false light (see Q 3-9).

3-6. What are the elements of a claim of unreasonable intrusion upon the seclusion of another?

In order to establish a prima facie case, an employee must establish that:

1. the employer intentionally pried or intruded upon the affairs or seclusion of the employee;

2. the employer's conduct would be highly objectionable to a reasonable person; and

3. the matter pried or intruded upon is private.

For example, an employee may have a claim when an employer places surveillance cameras in the restroom or another area where an employee has a reasonable expectation of privacy, even if the employee signed a form consenting to random searches.[6]

3-7. What are the elements of a claim of appropriation of another's name or likeness for one's own commercial advantage?

In order to establish a prima facie case, an employee must establish that:

1. the employer's use of the employee's picture or name was unauthorized; and

2. the employer used the employee's picture or name for the employer's own commercial advantage.[7]

For example, using an employee's picture on a product for sale without the employee's permission constitutes appropriation of another's name or likeness for one's own commercial advantage.

3-8. What are the elements of a claim of unreasonable public disclosure of the private facts of another?

In order to establish a prima facie case, an employee must establish that:

1. the employer published or publicly disclosed private information about the employee;

2. a reasonable person would find disclosure of the information highly offensive; and

3. the matter disclosed was not of legitimate public interest.[8]

For example, in *Greenwood v. Taft, Stettinius & Hollister,*[9] the court held that a homosexual employee stated a claim based on his allegations that his employer disclosed that he listed his male partner as the beneficiary of his insurance and pension benefits to people unassociated with the administration of the employer's benefits plan.

3-9. What are the elements of a claim of publication of facts placing another in a false light?

In order to establish a prima facie case, an employee must establish that:

1. the employer published facts about the employee to the general public that placed the employee in a false light (i.e., attributed to the employee views that the employee does not hold or actions that the employee did not take);

2. a reasonable person would be highly offended by being placed in such a false light; and

3. the employer had knowledge of or acted in reckless disregard as to the falsity of the publicized matter.[10]

For example, an attorney stated a claim for false light invasion of privacy by alleging that a newspaper article implied to the public that he was unethical and dishonest and that such article placed him in a false light before the public.[11]

3-10. What types of activities might constitute invasion of privacy?

Other than those covered under the Electronic Communications Privacy Act (see Q 3-11), employers can be found liable for searching an employee's work area or personal belongings if the court finds the employee had a reasonable expectation of privacy. In order to minimize liability, employers should inform employees that the employees' work area is subject to searches without notice.[12]

Drug testing is another potential source of liability for employers. Nonetheless, private employers, not subject to the Fourth Amendment's limitations on searches and seizures, are generally free to conduct random drug tests, particularly when the tests are motivated by a concern for employees' safety. As in the case of physical searches, employers should inform employees that they are subject to random drug tests without notice. Employees, who had signed an agreement providing that they were subject to drug tests at any time, and who were fired for refusing to take a drug test, were found to have failed to state a claim.[13]

THE ELECTRONIC COMMUNICATIONS PRIVACY ACT OF 1986

3-11. What is the ECPA?

The Electronic Communications Privacy Act of 1986 ("ECPA") prohibits the unlawful, intentional interception of wire, oral and electronic communications, including intercepting e-mail.[14] The ECPA also prohibits the unlawful intentional access to wire, oral and electronic communications while they are in electronic storage.[15]

3-12. What is a "wire communication"?

A "wire communication" is any audio transfer made through the use of facilities for the transmission of communications by the aid of wire, cable, or other like connection furnished or operated by any person engaged in providing or operating such facilities for the transmission of interstate or foreign communications or communications affecting interstate or foreign commerce and such term includes any electronic storage of such communication.[16] For example, a telephone conversation transmitted over telephone lines is a "wire communication."[17]

In contrast, the surreptitious taping of an individual's statements into the mouthpiece of a phone was not an interception of a "wire communication" because the defendant did not tape statements that were actually transmitted over the telephone wires, hence there was no "wire communication."[18]

3-13. What is an "oral communication"?

An "oral communication" is any oral communication uttered by a person exhibiting an expectation that such communication is not subject to interception under circumstances justifying such expectation, but such term does not include any electronic communication.[19] In other words, a conversation between people under circumstances in which the participants have a reasonable expectation of privacy is an "oral communication." The reasonable expectation of privacy requirement is unique to "oral communications." "Wire communications" and "electronic communications" do not have this requirement.[20]

3-14. What is an "electronic communication"?

An "electronic communication" is any transfer of signs, signals, writing, images, sounds, data or intelligence of any nature transmitted by a wire, radio, electromagnetic, photoelectronic or photooptical system that affects interstate or foreign commerce. For example, messages sent via a computerized paging system constitute "electronic communications." E-mail messages are another example of "electronic communications."[21]

3-15. What does not constitute an "electronic communication"?

Examples of items that are not "electronic communications" include any communication from a tracking device that permits the tracking of the movement of a person or object, electronic funds transfer information stored by a financial institution in a communications system used for the electronic storage and transfer of funds, or a paging system that only permits the pager to enter his or her telephone number, as opposed to a message.[22]

3-16. What does "intercept" mean?

"Intercept" means the acquisition of the contents of any wire, electronic, or oral communication through the use of any electronic, mechanical, or other device.[23] The unauthorized taping of a telephone conversation is an "interception," for example, whereas the mere retrieval of a message from a digital display pager, after the completion of the transmission of the message, is not. Hidden microphones used to tape conversations and duplicate pagers "cloned" to receive messages intended for another also constitute "interceptions."[24]

3-17. What does "electronic storage" mean?

"Electronic storage" means:

1. any temporary, intermediate storage of a wire or electronic communication incidental to the electronic transmission thereof; and

2. any storage of such communication by an electronic communication service for purposes of backup protection of such communication.[25]

The temporary storage of an e-mail message, which is incidental to the transmission of the message, by the sender's Internet service provider is an example of electronic storage.

3-18. What is the relationship between the ECPA and state law?

The ECPA preempts state laws that are less protective of employees' privacy rights, but allows states to determine their own level of privacy protection, as long as the provisions are at least as protective as the ECPA.[26]

LIMITATIONS ON MONITORING EMPLOYEES

3-19. What types of activities does the ECPA limit?

SURVEILLANCE

The audio portion of a videotape is governed by the ECPA. Employers, therefore, must be careful to comply with the statute when conducting video surveillance of their employees.[27]

The use of video cameras that do not capture sound is not governed by the ECPA. Under the express language of the statute, the ECPA governs wire, oral or electronic communications. Silent video surveillance is not within the scope of the statute; nonetheless, such surveillance by an employer could subject the employer to an invasion of privacy claim.[28]

LISTENING TO OR RECORDING PRIVATE CONVERSATIONS

The ECPA generally prohibits wiretapping and tape recording of private conversations, including telephone conversations. A private conversation is one in which the parties have a reasonable expectation of privacy. The ECPA does not generally prohibit the interception of a telephone conversation over a cordless phone, for example, because a cordless phone utilizes radio waves that are broadcast for all to hear. The parties, therefore, cannot be said to have a reasonable expectation of privacy.[29]

ACCESSING VOICE MAIL

The ECPA prohibits the unauthorized access of voice mail messages. For this reason, an employer should inform its employees that their voice mail messages are not private and are subject to monitoring. Preferably, the employer should have the employee sign a statement that clearly describes the employer's policy with regard to voice mail messages. By so doing, the employer can argue

that the employees consented to having their voice mail messages monitored.[30]

INTERCEPTING OR ACCESSING E-MAIL

The ECPA prohibits the unauthorized interception of e-mail as well as the unauthorized access of stored e-mail messages. In order to protect itself, an employer should follow the same procedures as listed above under "Accessing Voice Mail."[31]

EXCEPTIONS TO THE ECPA

3-20. Are there any exceptions to the ECPA?

Yes, there are three exceptions that are applicable in the employer-employee context: the service provider exception; prior consent; and monitoring activities conducted within the ordinary course of business.

3-21. What is the service provider exception to the ECPA?

A switchboard operator, or an officer, employee, or agent of a provider of wire or electronic communication services, whose facilities are used in the transmission of a wire or electronic communication, may intercept, disclose, or use that communication in the normal course of his or her employment while engaged in any activity that is a necessary incident to the rendition of his or her services, except that a provider to the public shall not utilize service observing or random monitoring except for mechanical or service quality control checks.[32]

The prohibition against accessing wire or electronic communications while in electronic storage does not apply to a person or entity providing a wire or electronic communications service.[33]

3-22. What is the prior consent exception to the ECPA?

A wire, oral or electronic communication may be intercepted when one of the parties to the communication consents.[34] However, the consent exception was not applicable where the employee was not informed of the manner in which the telephone calls would be monitored, or that he personally would be monitored.[35]

A wire or electronic communication may be accessed while in electronic storage if the recipient or author of the communication consents.[36]

Courts have not reached a consensus on whether implied consent is sufficient to shield a defendant from liability. One circuit court has held that an employee's acceptance of employment with knowledge of the company's telephone monitoring policy created a partial implied consent for limited purposes only.[37] But another circuit court held that there was no implied consent where an employee was only informed of the "possibility" or "threat" that monitoring might take place.[38]

3-23. What is the ordinary course of business exception to the ECPA?

An employer does not violate the ECPA by intercepting a wire, oral or electronic communication by using any equipment or facility that was furnished to it by a provider of wire or electronic communication services in the ordinary course of its business, as long as the employer is also using the equipment in the ordinary course of its business.[39] The employer must also disclose the nature of the monitoring activities to its employees. The exception is not applicable where a person surreptitiously records telephone conversation.[40]

For example, where a manager monitored a conversation between an employee and a former employee because the manager believed the employee was disclosing confidential business information, the manager did qualify for the ordinary course of business exception. In contrast, where an employer taped twenty-two hours of an employee's personal conversations, the employer exceeded the scope of the ordinary course of business exception.[41]

ENFORCEMENT, REMEDIES AND DEFENSES UNDER THE ECPA

INTERCEPTING COMMUNICATIONS

3-24. Who enforces the ECPA's prohibition against intercepting a communication?

Any person whose wire, oral, or electronic communication is intercepted, disclosed, or intentionally used in violation of the ECPA may in a civil action recover from the person or entity that engaged in the violation.[42]

3-25. To what relief is the injured party entitled for a violation of the prohibition against intercepting communications?

The injured party is entitled to appropriate relief which may include:

1. such preliminary and other equitable or declaratory relief as may be appropriate;

2. damages and punitive damages;

3. costs and attorneys' fees.[43]

3-26. How does the court assess damages when the prohibition against intercepting communications is violated?

The court may assess the greater of:

1. the sum of the actual damages suffered by the plaintiff and any profits made by the violator as a result of the violation; or

2. statutory damages of whichever is the greater of $100 a day for each day of violation or $10,000.[44]

"[I]f violations occur on 100 days or less, then the minimum statutory award of $10,000 must be paid. If, on the other hand, violations occur on more than 100 days, then of course the higher statutory award of $100 per day must be paid."[45]

3-27. Are there any defenses to a civil or criminal action brought for violation of the prohibition against intercepting communications?

Yes, a good faith reliance:

1. on a court warrant or order, a grand jury subpoena, a legislative authorization, or a statutory authorization;

2. on a request of an investigative or law enforcement officer in compliance with the statute; or

3. by a person or entity providing electronic communication service to the public that it was acting in compliance with a statutory exception.[46]

3-28. What is the statute of limitations for a violation of the prohibition against intercepting communications?

A civil action may not be commenced later than two years after the date upon which the claimant first had a reasonable opportunity to discover the violation.[47]

ACCESSING COMMUNICATIONS WHILE IN
ELECTRONIC STORAGE

3-29. Who enforces the ECPA's prohibition against accessing communications while in electronic storage?

Any provider of electronic communication services, subscriber, or other person aggrieved by a violation of the statute may bring a claim against another who acted with a knowing or intentional state of mind.[48]

3-30. To what relief is the injured party entitled for a violation of the prohibition against accessing communications while in electronic storage?

The injured party is entitled to appropriate relief which may include:

1. such preliminary and other equitable or declaratory relief as may be appropriate;

2. damages and punitive damages;

3. costs and attorneys' fees.[49]

3-31. How does the court assess damages when a violation of the prohibition against accessing communications while in electronic storage occurs?

The court may assess as damages the sum of the actual damages suffered by the plaintiff and any profits made by the violator as a result of the violation, but in no case shall a person entitled to recover receive less than the sum of $1,000. If the violation is willful or intentional, the court may assess punitive damages.[50]

3-32. Are there any defenses to a civil or criminal action brought for a violation of the prohibition against accessing communications while in electronic storage?

Yes, a good faith reliance:

1.   on a court warrant or order, a grand jury subpoena, a legislative authorization, or a statutory authorization;

2.   on a request of an investigative or law enforcement officer in compliance with the statute; or

3.   by a person or entity providing electronic communication service to the public that it was acting in compliance with a statutory exception.[51]

3-33. What is the statute of limitations for a violation of the prohibition against accessing communications while in electronic storage?

A civil action may not be commenced later than two years after the date upon which the claimant first had a reasonable opportunity to discover the violation.[52]

PREVENTATIVE MEASURES

3-34. What preventative measures can an employer take to avoid violating the ECPA?

There is no one particular action that employers can take to guarantee that they will avoid liability under the ECPA. That being said, employers would be wise to adopt an electronic communications policy and distribute it to their employees. Employers should explain the policy to their employees and have the employees sign a form acknowledging that they have received a copy of the policy, reviewed it, and agree to abide by its terms. See Q 3-35. By making adherence to the electronic communications policy a condition of the employees' employment, the employees may be characterized as having consented to the employers' monitoring of their communications.

Similarly, if an employer intends to engage in video surveillance, monitor employees' telephone calls or voice mail, or engage in other monitoring activities, the employer should disclose this information to the employees and draft a policy statement, similar

to the electronic communications policy described in Q 3-35, and disseminate it to all employees for their review and signature.

3-35. What provisions should an electronic communications policy contain?

An electronic communications policy should contain, at a minimum, the following provisions:

1. A provision that the company's electronic communications systems are the property of the company and that by using company property the employee consents to monitoring.

2. A provision that the contents of the electronic communications systems are business records and owned by the company.

3. A provision that electronic communications are to be used for business purposes only, not employees' personal interests.

4. A provision that the employees should not consider their electronic communications private and that the company may monitor the use of its electronic communications system at any time at its sole discretion.

5. A provision setting forth guidelines for storage and retention of electronic communication messages.

6. A provision for training on the proper use of electronic communications.

7. A provision stating that a violation of the employer's electronic communications policy will result in discipline, up to and including termination.

CHAPTER ENDNOTES

1. See *O'Connor v. Ortega*, 480 U.S. 709, 719-20 (1987).
2. See, e.g., *Vector Research, Inc. v. Howard & Howard Attorneys, P.C.*, 76 F.3d 692 (6th Cir. 1996).
3. See 18 U.S.C. §§2510-22, 2701-11.
4. See *Bivens v. Six Unknown Named Agents of Federal Bureau of Narcotics*, 403 U.S. 388 (1971).
5. See 18 U.S.C. §§2510-22, 2701-11.
6. Restatement (Second) of Torts §652B (1977); *Speer v. Ohio Department of Rehabilitation and Corrections*, 624 N.E.2d 251 (Ohio Ct. App. 1993).
7. Restatement (Second) of Torts §652C (1977).
8. Restatement (Second) of Torts §652D (1977).
9. 663 N.E.2d 1030 (Ohio Ct. App. 1995).
10. Restatement (Second) of Torts §652E (1977).
11. *McCall v. Courier-Journal & Louisville Times*, 623 S.W.2d 882 (Ky. 1981).
12. See, e.g., *K-Mart Corp. Store No. 7441 v. Trotti*, 677 S.W.2d 632 (Tex. App. 1984) (plaintiff stated a claim for invasion of privacy where employer searched her locker and her purse therein, plaintiff had provided her own lock for the locker, and the employer did not have the key or combination to the lock).
13. *Hart v. Seven Resorts, Inc.*, 947 P.2d 846 (Ariz. Ct. App. 1997).
14. See 18 U.S.C. §2511(1)(a).
15. See 18 U.S.C. §2701(a).
16. 18 U.S.C. §2510(1).
17. *Ali v. Douglas Cable Communications*, 929 F. Supp. 1362 (D. Kan. 1996).
18. *Siripongs v. Calderon*, 35 F.3d 1308 (9th Cir. 1994).
19. 18 U.S.C. §2510(2).
20. See 18 U.S.C. §§2510(1), 2510(12).
21. See 18 U.S.C. §2510(12); *Bohach v. City of Reno*, 932 F. Supp. 1232 (D. Nev. 1996).
22. 18 U.S.C. §2510(12).
23. 18 U.S.C. §2510(4).
24. See *Platt v. Platt*, 951 F.2d 159 (8th Cir. 1989); cf. *U.S. v. Meriwether*, 917 F.2d 955 (6th Cir. 1990).
25. 18 U.S.C. §2510(17).
26. *Roberts v. Americable International, Inc.*, 883 F. Supp. 499 (E.D. Cal. 1995).
27. See *United States v. Foster*, 985 F.2d 466 (9th Cir. 1993).
28. See *United States v. Koyomejian*, 970 F.2d 536 (9th Cir. 1992).
29. See 18 U.S.C. §2511(1)(a).
30. See 18 U.S.C. §2701; see also *United States v. Moriarty*, 962 F. Supp. 217 (D. Mass. 1997).
31. See 18 U.S.C. §§2511(1)(a), 2701(a); see also *United States v. Moriarty*, 962 F. Supp. 217 (D. Mass. 1997).
32. See 18 U.S.C. §2511(2)(a)(i).
33. See 18 U.S.C. §2701(c)(1).
34. See 18 U.S.C. §2511(2)(d); see also *Griggs-Ryan v. Smith*, 904 F.2d 112 (1st Cir. 1990).
35. *Williams v. Poulos*, 11 F.3d 271 (1st Cir. 1993).
36. See 18 U.S.C. §2701(c)(2); see also *American Computer Trust Leasing v. Jack Farrell Implement Co.*, 763 F. Supp. 1473 (D. Minn. 1991).
37. *Watkins v. L.M. Berry & Co.*, 704 F.2d 577 (11th Cir. 1983).
38. *Deal v. Spears*, 980 F.2d 1153 (8th Cir. 1992).
39. See 18 U.S.C. §2510(5)(a).

40. See *George v. Carusone*, 849 F. Supp. 159, 164 (D. Conn. 1994).

41. See *Briggs v. American Air Filter Co., Inc.*, 630 F.2d 414 (5th Cir. 1980); cf. *Deal v. Spears*, 980 F.2d 1153 (8th Cir. 1992).

42. See 18 U.S.C. §2520(a).

43. 18 U.S.C. §2520(b).

44. 18 U.S.C. §2520(c)(2).

45. *Desilets v. Wal-Mart Stores, Inc.*, 171 F.3d 711, 714 (1st Cir. 1999).

46. 18 U.S.C. §2520(d).

47. 18 U.S.C. §2520(e).

48. 18 U.S.C. §2707(a).

49. 18 U.S.C. §2707(b).

50. 18 U.S.C. §2707(c).

51. 18 U.S.C. §2707(e).

52. 18 U.S.C. §2707(f).

Chapter 4

Family and Medical Leave Act of 1993

In General

4-1. What is the Family and Medical Leave Act of 1993?

4-2. What employers are covered by the FMLA?

4-3. What employees are eligible to take leave under the FMLA?

4-4. When must employers grant leave under the FMLA?

4-5. What is a "serious health condition?"

4-6. When is an employee entitled to FMLA leave to care for a family member?

4-7. How much leave may an employee take?

4-8. When may an employee take intermittent leave or a reduced leave schedule?

4-9. Is FMLA leave paid or unpaid?

4-10. What entitlement does an employee have to benefits while on FMLA leave?

4-11. What are an employee's rights upon returning to work from FMLA leave?

4-12. What are the limitations on an employer's obligation to reinstate an employee after the completion of FMLA leave?

4-13. What protections do employees have against retaliation?

NOTICE REQUIREMENTS

4-14. What requirements do employers have to notify employees of their FMLA rights?

4-15. Do employees have obligations to give employers notice of FMLA leave?

4-16. What are the notice rules when the need for FMLA leave is foreseeable?

4-17. What is the notice requirement if the need for FMLA leave is unforeseeable?

4-18. What is the employer's recourse when an employee fails to provide the required FMLA notice?

MEDICAL CERTIFICATION

4-19. How do employers utilize medical certifications?

4-20. When should an employer request a medical certification?

4-21. What information may be requested in a medical certification form?

4-22. What procedures exist for an employer to challenge an employee's medical certification?

4-23. When may a second or third opinion be required of an employee?

4-24. When may subsequent medical recertification be required?

4-25. How can an employee enforce his or her rights under the FMLA?

In General

4-1. What is the Family and Medical Leave Act of 1993?

On February 5, 1993, President Clinton signed the Family and Medical Leave Act of 1993 (FMLA) into law. The FMLA provides up to twelve weeks of unpaid, job-protected leave in a twelve-month period to eligible employees for covered family or medical needs. The purpose of the FMLA is to help balance the demands of the workplace with the needs of families, to promote stability and economic security of families, and to promote national interests in preserving family integrity.[1]

4-2. What employers are covered by the FMLA?

The FMLA applies to all federal, state, or local governmental employers as well as any individual or entity employing fifty or more employees for each working day during each of twenty or more calendar workweeks in the current or preceding calendar year. When determining whether fifty or more employees are employed by an employer, the legal entity is the employer, not divisions within the entity.[2]

When one corporation has an ownership interest in another corporation, it is a separate employer unless it meets the "joint employment" test or the "integrated employer" test.

The "joint employment" test must be applied when two or more businesses exercise some control over the work or working conditions of an employee. When an employee performs work which simultaneously benefits two or more employers, a joint employment relationship exists in situations such as:

1. where the employers have an arrangement to share an employee's services or to interchange employees;

2. where one employer acts in the interest of the other employer in relation to the employee; and

3. where the employers are not completely disassociated with respect to the employee's employment and may be deemed to share control of the employee because one employer is under common control with the other employer.

Employees jointly employed by two employers must be counted by both employers in determining whether the FMLA applies.[3]

The "integrated employer" test is met when the entire relationship between two entities in its totality indicates that separate entities are an integrated employer. Factors to consider in determining whether two or more entities are an integrated employer include:

1.　common management;

2.　interrelation between operation;

3.　centralized control of labor relations; and

4.　degree of common ownership/financial control.

The employees of all entities making up the integrated employer will be counted in determining whether the entities are covered employers under the FMLA.[4]

4-3. What employees are eligible to take leave under the FMLA?

An "eligible employee" is an employee of a covered employer who:

1.　has been employed by the employer for at least 12 months;

2.　has been employed for at least 1,250 hours of service during the 12-month period immediately preceding the commencement of the leave; and

3.　is employed at a worksite where 50 or more employees are employed by the employer within 75 miles of that worksite.

The 12 months an employee must have been employed by the employer need not be consecutive months. If an employee is maintained on the payroll for any part of a week, including any periods of paid or unpaid leave during which other benefits or compensation are provided by the employer (e.g., workers' compensation, group health plan benefits, etc.), the week counts as a week of employment.

Whether an employee has worked the minimum 1,250 hours of service is determined according to the principles established under the Fair Labor Standards Act (FLSA) for determining compensable hours of work (see Chapter 19). Any accurate accounting of actual hours worked under FLSA's principles may be used. In the event an employer does not maintain an accurate record of hours worked by an employee, including for employees who are exempt from FLSA's requirement that a record be kept for their hours worked (e.g., bona fide executive, administrative, and professional employees), the employer has the burden of showing that the employee has not worked the requisite hours. In the event the employer is unable to meet this burden the employee is treated as meeting this test.

The determinations of whether an employee has worked for the employer for at least 1,250 hours in the past 12 months and has been employed by the employer for a total of at least 12 months must be made as of the date a leave commences. If an employee notifies the employer of the need for FMLA leave before the employee meets these eligibility criteria, the employer must either confirm the employee's eligibility based upon a projection that the employee will be eligible on the date leave would commence, or must advise the employee when the eligibility requirement is met. If the employer confirms eligibility at the time the notice for leave is received, the employer may not subsequently challenge the employee's eligibility. If the employer does not advise the employee whether the employee is eligible as soon as practicable (which is considered two business days absent any extenuating circumstances) after the date employee eligibility is determined, the employee will have satisfied the notice requirements, and the notice of leave is considered current and outstanding until the employer does advise. If the employer fails to advise the employee whether the employee is eligible prior to the date the requested leave is to commence, the employee will be considered eligible and the employer may not deny the leave. Where the employee does not give notice of the need for leave more than two business days prior to commencing leave, the employee will be treated as eligible if the employer fails to advise the employee that the employee is not eligible within two business days of receiving the employee's notice.

Whether fifty employees are employed within seventy-five miles is determined when the employee gives notice of the need for leave. Once an employee is determined eligible in response to that notice of the need for leave, the employee's eligibility is not affected by any subsequent change in the number of employees employed at or within seventy-five miles of the employee's worksite, for that specific notice of the need for leave. Similarly, an employer may not terminate an employee leave that has already started if the employee count drops below fifty.[5]

4-4. When must employers grant leave under the FMLA?

Employers covered by the FMLA are required to grant leave to eligible employees for any of the following reasons:

1.   the birth of a child and to care for a newborn child;

2.   the placement with the employee of a child for adoption or foster care;

3.   to care for the employee's spouse, son, daughter, or parent with a serious health condition; or

4.   the employee's own serious health condition makes the employee unable to perform the functions of his or her job.

Both male and female employees are entitled to FMLA leave for the birth, placement for adoption, or placement for foster care of a child. An expectant mother may take FMLA leave when her pregnancy or prenatal care makes her unable to work because pregnancy qualifies as a serious health condition.

An employee's entitlement to leave for birth or placement for adoption or foster care of a child expires at the end of the twelve-month period commencing on the date of birth or placement.

Employers are required to grant FMLA leave for the placement of a child for adoption or foster care before the actual adoption or placement if an absence from work is necessary for the adoption or placement to proceed.[6]

4-5. What is a "serious health condition?"

A "serious health condition" is an illness, injury, impairment, or physical or mental condition involving:

1.   an overnight stay at a hospital, hospice, or residential medical care facility including any period where the

employee cannot work or perform regular daily activities due to the condition and any subsequent treatment connected with the inpatient care; or

2.   continuing treatment by a health care provider.

A serious health condition involving continuing treatment by a health provider includes:

1.   a period of incapacity of more than three consecutive calendar days (and any subsequent treatment or period of incapacity relating to the same condition). It must also involve treatment by: (a) a health care provider on at least one occasion which results in a regimen of continuing treatment, such as a course of prescription medication or therapy utilizing special equipment; or (b) that involves treatment two or more times by a health care provider, by a nurse or physician's assistant under direct supervision of a health care provider, or by a therapist or other provider of health care services under orders of a health care provider;

2.   any period of incapacity due to pregnancy or prenatal care;

3.   any period of incapacity or treatment due to a chronic serious health condition. A chronic serious health condition is one: (a) that requires periodic visits for treatment by a health care provider or by a nurse or physician's assistant under direct supervision of a health care provider, (b) continues over an extended period of time (including recurring episodes of a single underlying condition), and (c) may cause episodic rather than a continuing period of incapacity (e.g., asthma, diabetes, epilepsy, etc.);

4.   a long-term period of incapacity for which treatment may not be effective. The employee or family member must be under the continuing supervision of a health care provider, but need not be receiving active treatment (e.g., Alzheimer's, severe stroke, or terminal disease);

5.   a period of absence to receive multiple treatments by a health care provider or as a result of the order of a

health-care provider for restorative surgery after an accident or other injury or for a condition that would likely result in a period of incapacity of more than three consecutive calendar days in the absence of medical intervention;

Cosmetic treatment is generally not a "serious health condition" unless inpatient hospital care is required or complications develop. Substance abuse may be a serious health condition if the tests above are met. However, absence because of the employee's use of a substance, rather than for treatment, does not qualify for FMLA leave.[7]

4-6. When is an employee entitled to FMLA leave to care for a family member?

An employee is entitled to FMLA leave when needed to care for a family member with a serious health condition. This encompasses both physical and psychological care. It includes situations where, for example, because of a serious health condition, the family member is unable to care for her own basic medical, hygienic, or nutritional needs or safety, or is unable to transport herself to the doctor. Leave may also be granted to provide psychological comfort and reassurance that would be beneficial to a child, spouse, or parent with a serious health condition who is receiving inpatient or home care.

An employee may take FMLA leave in situations where the employee may be needed to fill in for others who are caring for the family member, or to make arrangements for changes in care, such as transfer to a nursing home. An employee may take intermittent leave or a reduced leave schedule where the family member's condition itself is intermittent and also where the employee is needed intermittently—such as where other care is normally available, or care responsibilities are shared with another member of the family or a third party.[8]

4-7. How much leave may an employee take?

The FMLA provides up to twelve workweeks of leave in any twelve-month period for any one or more of the following reasons:

1.   the birth of the employee's child and to care for the newborn child;

2.   the placement with the employee of a child for adoption or foster care and to care for the newly-placed child;

3.   to care for the employee's spouse, child, or parent with a serious health condition; or

4.   because of a serious health condition that makes the employee unable to perform one or more of the essential functions of his job.

An employer may use any one of the following methods for determining the twelve-month period in which the twelve-week limit on FMLA leave is imposed:

1.   the calendar year;

2.   any fixed twelve-month period;

3.   the twelve-month period measured from the date of any employee's first day of FMLA leave; or

4.   a rolling twelve-month period measured backward from the date an employee uses any FMLA leave.

Employers may choose any of these methods as long as they apply the same method to all employees. If an employer wishes to change to another method, it must give at least sixty days notice to all employees. However, the effect of a change in method cannot be to avoid the FMLA's leave requirement. If an employer fails to designate one of these methods, the method which is most beneficial to the employee will be applied. If the employer wishes to then implement a method, it must meet the sixty-day notice requirement.

If a holiday falls within a week of leave, it has no effect—the week counts as a week of leave. However, if an employer's business activity ceases for a week or more, that week will not count against the twelve-week maximum.[9]

If leave is taken for a birth or placement for adoption or foster care, it must be completed by the end of the twelve-month period beginning on the date of the birth or placement.[10]

If a husband and wife are employed by the same employer and are both eligible under the FMLA, their leave may be limited to a combined total of twelve weeks of leave during any twelve-month period if the leave is taken:

1. for the birth of the employee's child or to care for the child after birth;

2. for placement of a child with the employee for adoption or foster care or to care for the child after placement; or

3. to care for the employee's parent with a serious health condition.

If a husband and wife both utilize a portion of the total twelve-week leave for one of these reasons, each spouse would be entitled to the difference between twelve weeks and the leave actually taken by that individual for other FMLA-qualifying reasons.[11]

4-8. When may an employee take intermittent leave or a reduced leave schedule?

Intermittent leave is FMLA leave taken in separate blocks of time due to a qualifying reason. A reduced leave schedule is a leave schedule that reduces an employee's usual number of working hours per workweek or hours per workday.[12]

An employee is entitled to take intermittent or reduced schedule leave when there is a medical need for the leave (as opposed to voluntary treatments and procedures) and when the medical need can best be accommodated through an intermittent or reduced leave schedule. Such leave may also be taken to provide care or psychological comfort to an immediate family member with a serious health condition. Employees needing intermittent FMLA leave or leave on a reduced leave schedule must attempt to schedule their leave so as not to disrupt the employer's operations. An employee may not be required to take more leave than necessary to address the circumstance that precipitated the need for leave, except that an employer can require that leave increments be at least as long as the shortest period that the employer's payroll system uses to account for absences or use of leave, provided it is one hour or less. Only the amount of leave actually taken may be counted toward the twelve-week limit. For example, if an employee who normally works five days per week takes one day off, the employee would use one-fifth of a week of FMLA leave. Similarly, a reduced leave schedule of four hours per day would use one-half of a week every week if the employee normally works eight-hour days. If an employee's schedule varies from week to week, a weekly average of the hours worked over the twelve weeks prior to the leave is used to calculate the normal workweek.

An employer is entitled to assign an employee on intermittent leave or a reduced leave schedule to an alternative position with equivalent pay and benefits that better accommodates the schedule.

When leave is taken after the birth or placement for adoption or foster care of a child, an employee may take leave intermittently or on a reduced leave schedule only if the employer agrees. This does not apply to leave resulting from a serious health condition in connection with the birth of a child or if the newborn has a serious health condition.

4-9. Is FMLA leave paid or unpaid?

Generally, FMLA leave is unpaid. However, if an employer gives paid leave to its employees as a benefit and if an employee has accrued such paid leave, the employee may choose to take the paid leave at the same time the employee is taking FMLA leave. The employer also has the option of requiring the use of the paid leave at the same time an employee is on FMLA leave. Of course, in order for an employee or the employer to require use of the paid leave, the leave must qualify for the paid leave under the employer's policies.[13]

4-10. What entitlement does an employee have to benefits while on FMLA leave?

During any leave under the FMLA, an employer must maintain the employee's coverage under any group health plan as if the employee had been continuously employed during the entire leave period.[14]

If an employer provides a new health plan or benefits, or changes health benefits or plans while an employee is on leave, the employee is entitled to the new or changed plan or benefits to the same extent as if he were not on leave. Notice of any opportunity to change plans or benefits must also be given to an employee on leave. If the plan permits an employee to change from single to family coverage upon the birth of a child or otherwise add new family members, such a change in benefits must be made available while an employee is on leave.

An employee is obligated to pay health plan premiums while on leave to the same extent as when not on leave. An employer's obligation to maintain health insurance coverage ceases if an employee's premium payment is more than thirty days late when the employee has been advised of possible coverage loss. An employer may recover the employee's share of any premium payments missed by the employee if the employer maintains health coverage by paying the employee's share after the premium payment is missed.

Such employer contribution payments may be wise. If coverage lapses because an employee has not made required premium payments, upon the employee's return from leave, the employer must nevertheless restore the employee to coverage or benefits equivalent to those the employee would have had if leave had not been taken. In such a case, an employee may not be required to meet a new preexisting condition waiting period of any other qualification requirements imposed by the plan.

An employer may recover its portion of health plan premiums paid during an employee's period of unpaid leave if the employee fails to return to work after the FMLA leave entitlement is exhausted or expires, unless the reason for not returning is the continuation, recurrence, or onset of a serious health condition that would entitle the employee to leave under FMLA, or other circumstances beyond the employee's control.

An employer may require medical certification of the employee's or the family member's serious health condition in these circumstances. The employee is required to provide medical certification within thirty days of the date of the employer's request. If the employee does not provide certification in a timely manner, the employer may recover the health benefit premiums it paid during the period of unpaid FMLA leave.

The employer's right to recover its share of health premiums paid during periods of unpaid leave extends to the entire period of unpaid FMLA leave taken by the employee. However, when an employee elects or an employer requires the substitution of paid leave for FMLA leave, the employer may not recover its share of health insurance premiums for any period of FMLA leave covered by paid leave. In some cases, an employer may need to sue the employee to recover these premiums or costs.

An employee's entitlement to benefits other than group health benefits during a period of FMLA leave is to be determined by the employer's established policy for providing benefits when the employee is on other forms of leave.

4-11. What are an employee's rights upon returning to work from FMLA leave?

On return from FMLA leave, an employee is entitled to return to the same position the employee held when leave commenced or to an equivalent position with equivalent benefits, pay, and other terms and conditions of employment. An equivalent position is one that is virtually identical to the employee's former position in terms of pay, benefits, and working conditions. An employee is entitled to reinstatement even if the employer has replaced the employee or if the position has been restructured to accommodate the absence of the employee.[15]

Under the FMLA, the employee has no right to be employed in another position upon completion of leave if the employee is unable to perform an essential function of the position he or she previously held. However, the employer may have some obligations in that regard under the Americans with Disabilities Act (see Chapter 6).

In a joint employment situation, job restoration is the primary responsibility of the primary employer. The secondary employer is responsible for accepting the employee returning from FMLA leave in place of the replacement employee if the secondary employer has continued to use an employee from the primary employer (usually a temporary employee or employee leasing company) and the primary employer chooses to place the returning employee with the secondary employer. A secondary employer cannot retaliate against an employee who exercises FMLA rights even if the secondary employer is not covered by the FMLA. Nor can such a secondary employer interfere with the employee's ability to exercise rights under the FMLA.

To determine which joint employer is primary and which is secondary, the following factors must be applied: (1) the authority or responsibility to hire, fire, and assign the employee; (2) the responsibility to make payroll; and (3) the responsibility to provide benefits. For employees of temporary help or leasing agencies, the placement agency most commonly will be the primary employer.[16]

4-12. What are the limitations on an employer's obligation to reinstate an employee after the completion of FMLA leave?

An employee has no greater right to reinstatement than if the employee had been actively employed during his or her FMLA leave. In other words, if an employee would have been laid off had the employee not been on FMLA leave, the employer is permitted to treat the employee as if the employee were actively employed and to deny reinstatement to the employee.

An employer may deny job restoration to salaried eligible "key employees" if the employer determines the denial of restoration is necessary to prevent "substantial and grievous economic injury" to the operations of the employer. The determination may not be made based on whether the absence of a key employee will cause "substantial and grievous economic injury."[17]

A "key employee" is a salaried FMLA-eligible employee who is among the highest paid ten percent of all employees employed by the employer within seventy-five miles of the employee's worksite. There is no precise test for measuring the level of hardship which must be sustained before denial of restoration can be safely asserted without legal liability. Federal regulations suggest the standard is more stringent that the already stringent "undue hardship" test under the Americans with Disabilities Act. Employers must be prepared to show that restoration would threaten the economic viability of the company.

In determining whether restoration will cause substantial and grievous injury, an employer may take into account its ability to replace on a temporary basis. If permanent replacement is unavoidable, the cost of reinstating the employee can be considered in evaluating whether substantial and grievous economic injury will occur from restoration.

An employee who qualifies as a key employee must receive written notice at the time the employee gives notice of the need for FMLA leave (or when FMLA begins, if earlier) in person or by certified mail of the following:

1. the employee's status as a key employee;

2. the potential for denial of reinstatement; and

3.   the potential consequences concerning health benefits if reinstatement is denied.

As soon as the employer makes a good-faith determination that reinstatement will cause substantial and grievous economic injury, the employer shall notify the employee in person or by certified mail:

1.   of the determination that substantial and grievous economic injury precludes reinstatement; and

2.   of the basis for its determination that substantial and grievous economic injury will result if the employee is reinstated.

If the employee has already begun leave, the employee must be given reasonable time and opportunity to return to work in light of the circumstances. A key employee's rights under the FMLA continue unless or until the employee either gives notice that he or she no longer wishes to return to work or the employer actually denies reinstatement. The key employee is still entitled to maintenance of health benefit premiums during leave.

Even if the employee does not return to work upon receiving notice, the employee is still entitled to request reinstatement at the end of the leave. Any decision must then be made on the facts existing at the time the request for reinstatement is made. Denial of reinstatement must then be given in writing in person or by certified mail.[18]

4-13. What protections do employees have against retaliation?

The FMLA prohibits interference with an employee's FMLA rights. These rights include the rights to file a legal proceeding and to inquire regarding his or her rights. Employers may not discharge or retaliate in any way against someone for opposing or complaining about any unlawful practice under the FMLA, because he has filed a charge or instituted a proceeding under the FMLA, or because he has participated in any other way with such a proceeding. Employers are prohibited from improperly refusing to authorize FMLA leave, discouraging an employee from using such leave, and any other manipulation to avoid responsibility under the FMLA. Likewise, employers may not discriminate or retaliate against employees or prospective employees who have used FMLA leave. Employees may not waive their rights under the FMLA.

NOTICE REQUIREMENTS

4-14. What requirements do employers have to notify employees of their FMLA rights?

The FMLA imposes many notice requirements on employers to inform employees of their rights and obligations under the FMLA. Employers must post a notice informing employees of their FMLA rights and provide employees a written notice of these rights every time the employee takes FMLA leave. (See Appendix B.) Additionally, if an employer has any written guidance to employees concerning employee benefits, or leave rights, such as an employee handbook, information concerning FMLA entitlement and employee obligations must be included in the handbook.[19]

When an employee requests leave under the Act, the employer must also explain any employee obligations and the consequences for failing to meet those obligations. The employer should:

1. state that the leave will be counted against the employee's annual FMLA leave entitlement;

2. outline any requirements for the employee to furnish a medical certification of a serious health condition and the consequences of failing to do so;

3. indicate whether the employee has the right to substitute paid leave and whether the employer will require the substitution of paid leave;

4. list the conditions relating to any substitution;

5. describe any requirement for the employee to make premium payments to maintain health benefits, and the arrangements for making such payments during the leave period;

6. indicate whether a fitness-for-duty certificate will be required;

7. state the employee's status as a "key employee;"

8. note that restoration may be denied following FMLA leave, explaining the conditions for such denial;

9. describe the employee's right to restoration to the same or an equivalent job upon return from leave; and

10. indicate the employee's potential liability for payment of health insurance premiums paid by the employer during the leave if the employee fails to return to work after taking leave.

4-15. Do employees have obligations to give employers notice of FMLA leave?

Employees have certain obligations to provide notice to the employer of the need for leave. How much advance notice an employee must give depends on whether the leave is foreseeable or not.

4-16. What are the notice rules when the need for FMLA leave is foreseeable?

Where FMLA leave is foreseeable (such as with the birth, adoption, or foster placement of a child, or the planned medical treatment for a serious health condition) the employee must give at least thirty days notice of the need for leave. Also, an employee taking leave for planned medical treatment must make a reasonable effort to schedule treatment to minimize the disruption to the employer's business operations. If disruption to the employer's business operations is expected from a planned leave of absence, the employer may require the employee to reschedule treatment, depending on the health care provider's schedule and the employee's medical needs.[20]

However, exceptions to the thirty-day notice requirement for planned leaves exist. If thirty days notice is "not practicable" due to lack of knowledge of when the leave will begin, a change in circumstances, or a medical emergency, the employee must provide the employer with notice of the need for leave "as soon as practicable." What constitutes notice takes into account all of the facts and circumstances of each case. Notice ordinarily means at least verbal notification to the employer within two days of when the employee knows of the need for leave.

While employees must provide at least verbal notice that is sufficient to make the employer aware that leave is needed for an FMLA qualifying reason, along with the anticipated timing and duration of the leave, the employee need not expressly mention the FMLA. The employee need only state that leave is required for a potentially FMLA qualifying reason, and the employer then has the burden to inquire and to obtain more information to determine whether the leave is FMLA leave.

Employers may request that employees comply with their regular notice policies for requesting leaves, such as written notice setting forth the reasons for leave, the anticipated start date, and the anticipated duration of the leave. However, if an employee fails to comply with an employer's notice policy but otherwise complies with the FMLA's notice provisions, the employer may not deny or delay the employee's FMLA leave.

Where an employer's own leave policy allows for less advance notice, the employer may not require employees to comply with the FMLA's stricter notice requirements. For example, if an employee substitutes paid vacation leave for unpaid FMLA leave and the employer's paid vacation policy requires less than thirty days notice, the vacation policy's shorter notice provisions apply.

4-17. What is the notice requirement if the need for FMLA leave is unforeseeable?

When the employee's need for leave is not foreseeable, the employee must provide as much notice as is practicable under the facts and circumstances of the particular situation. Once an employee learns of the need for leave, the employee is expected to notify the employer within two working days, except in extraordinary circumstances where notice is not feasible.

Notice may be given to the employer by an employee representative, such as a spouse or family member, if the employee is unable to do so. As with foreseeable leaves, the employee need not expressly mention the FMLA but must state only that leave is needed for a potentially qualifying reason. The employer then has the duty to obtain additional information regarding whether the leave is FMLA qualifying.

4-18. What is the employer's recourse when an employee fails to provide the required FMLA notice?

When an employee fails to give thirty days notice for foreseeable leave and no reasonable excuse exists for the delay, the employer may delay the start of the leave for thirty days from the date the employee provides notice. However, employers may not often have the opportunity to invoke this statutory right, and once the employer takes this type of action against an employee who failed to give adequate notice of the need for leave, the employer must apply the policy uniformly in similar circumstances. If the employee fails to provide notice of an unforeseeable leave within two business days after the need for leave became apparent, the employer may consider the absences unexcused and take action in accordance with its absence-control policy.

MEDICAL CERTIFICATION

4-19. How do employers utilize medical certifications?

When an employee is taking leave for his own serious health condition, the employer may request a medical certification from a health care provider. The certification should say that the employee is unable to perform the essential functions of the position. The employer must give written notification that such certification is required. A description of the employee's essential functions may be provided by the employer for the employee to submit to the health care provider in obtaining this medical certification. Similarly, where an employee seeks leave to care for an ill family member, the employer may require the health care provider to certify that third-party care is required or that the employee's presence would be beneficial or desirable for the care of the patient.

It is important for employers to exercise this right to obtain medical certification, as the employee's own belief as to whether he is incapacitated and would qualify for FMLA leave is not determinative of whether the individual has a "serious health condition."

4-20. When should an employer request a medical certification?

In most cases, the employer should ask for medical certification at the same time the employee asks for leave or within two business days thereafter. When the FMLA leave is foreseeable and at least thirty days notice has been provided, the employer may request that the employee furnish the medical certification before the leave period starts. When this is not possible, the employee must provide the requested certification to the employer within the time frame requested by the employer, which must allow at least fifteen calendar days after the employer's request. However, the employee who needs additional time to complete the medical certification may still be protected, as the Regulations state that the employee may have more than fifteen days to obtain the certification if "it is not practicable under the particular circumstances to do so" despite the employee's good faith efforts.[21]

In the case of unforeseen leave, the employer should request certification within two business days after the commencement of the leave. The employer may request certification at some later date but only if it has reason to question the appropriateness or length of the leave time. Employer's should take the time when an employee requests leave to advise the employee of the consequences of not providing the proper medical certification. When the employer finds the certification furnished by the employee to be inadequate, the employee should be informed and provided with the opportunity to remedy the certification.

If an employee uses general paid time off for an absence caused by illness and the employer does not typically require medical certification, then the employer may not require medical certification for an FMLA absence for which paid time off is used. The same certification policy must apply whether the absence is FMLA or non-FMLA. Thus, employers should consider implementing certification requirements for non-FMLA medical leave.

4-21. What information may be requested in a medical certification form?

Employers should use their own Medical Certification Form to verify the need for medical leave rather than relying on the employee or the health care provider to submit the relevant information needed to determine whether there is a serious health condition.

The information on the form must relate only to the serious health condition for which the current need for leave exists. The form should include a space to identify the health care provider and type of medical practice, as well as the following entries:

1.　　A certification as to which part of the definition of "serious health condition," if any, applies to the patient's condition, and the medical facts that sustain the certification, including a brief synopsis as to how the medical facts meet the criteria of the serious health condition definition.

2. The approximate date the serious health condition began and its likely duration, including the probable length of the patient's present incapacity, if different.

3. Whether intermittent or reduced leave schedules will be necessary due to the serious health condition, and if so, the likely durations of such schedules.

4. If the condition is pregnancy or chronic, whether the patient is currently incapacitated, and the likely duration and frequency of episodes of incapacity.

5. If additional treatments will be necessary and the probable number of treatments.

6. If the patient's incapacity will be intermittent or require a reduced leave schedule, an estimate of the number and interval between such treatments, actual or estimated dates of treatment, and period of recovery, if any.

7. If any of the treatments referred to above will be provided by another health services provider, the nature of these treatments.

8. If a regimen of continuing treatment of the patient is required under the supervision of the health care provider, a general explanation of the regimen.

9. If medical leave is required due to the employee's own condition, the form should indicate whether the employee is unable to perform work of any kind, is unable to perform any one or more of the essential functions of the employee's job, including a statement of the essential functions the employee is not able to perform, based on either information provided on a statement from the employer of the essential functions of the position or, if not supplied, discussion with the employee about the employee's job functions, or must be absent from work for treatment.

10. If leave is needed to care for a family member of the employee, whether the patient mandates assistance for basic medical or personal needs or safety, or for transportation; or if not, whether the employee's presence to provide psychological comfort would be beneficial to the patient to assist in the patient's recovery. The employee is required to indicate on the form the care that will be provided and an estimate of the time period.

11. If the employee's family member will need only intermittent care or care on a reduced leave schedule basis, the likely duration of the need.

By requesting all of this information, the employer is in a better position to make a determination as to whether the employee or family member has a medical condition that is covered by the FMLA, rather than simply relying on whatever information the employee or the employee's physician decides to provide.

4-22. What procedures exist for an employer to challenge an employee's medical certification?

While medical certifications are an important part of implementing an FMLA policy, a certification from the employee's own health-care provider is not necessarily the final word on whether the employee has an FMLA covered medical condition.

If an employee submits a complete medical certification signed by the health care provider, the employer may not request additional information from the health care provider. However, a health care provider representing the employer (not any representative of the employer), may contact the employee's health care provider, with the employee's permission, to clarify the information and confirm that the information was provided by the employee's health care provider. The employer's health care provider may not seek additional information. The circumstances under which an employer may obtain additional information about the medical certification are limited to protect employee privacy, but an employer may utilize other procedures to verify the medical necessity for FMLA leave.

4-23. When may a second or third opinion be required of an employee?

An employer who has reason to doubt the validity of an employee's medical certification may require the employee to obtain a second opinion by a health care provider selected by the employer, at the employer's expense. The Regulations do not elaborate on the circumstances under which the employer may have a "reason to doubt" the certification of the employee's health-care provider. Presumably, defects in the certification documents itself could raise sufficient doubt to permit the employer to require a second opinion. In addition, reason may exist to doubt the validity of a medical certification when an employee submits medical documentation from a general practitioner for a psychological condition. Under those circumstances, the employer may require the employee to be evaluated for a second opinion by a specialist.[22]

The health-care provider furnishing the second opinion must not be a provider who is regularly employed by the employer, unless the employer is located in an area with limited access to health care. While the Regulations are not clear on this point, an employer who uses insurance companies for disability plans or workers' compensation should not use the same health care providers to perform second opinion examinations under the FMLA who the employer regularly employs for medical evaluations under those plans.

Another limitation on the second opinion is that the employee may not be required to travel outside normal commuting distance, except in unusual circumstances. Even for examinations in the local area, the employer must pay the employee's reasonable travel expenses incurred to obtain the second opinion.

If the second opinion differs from the first, the employer may require a third opinion. The health care provider for the third opinion must be one who is mutually agreed upon by both the employer and the employee and the examination is again at the employer's expense. This third medical opinion is binding.

Pending receipt of the second or third opinion, the employee provisionally is entitled to the benefits of the FMLA (e.g., maintenance of health benefits). If it turns out the employee is not entitled to leave, then the time off may not be designated as FMLA time off and may be treated as paid or unpaid leave, as appropriate, under the employer's established leave policies.

4-24. When may subsequent medical recertification be required?

Employers may require subsequent recertification of a medical condition on a "reasonable basis." The Regulations define "reasonable basis" as no more than every thirty days, unless one of the following conditions is met:

1. The employee requests an extension of leave;

2. Circumstances in the original certification have changed significantly;

3. The employer receives information to doubt the continuing validity of the original certification; or

4. The employee is unable to return to work at the end of the leave because of the continuation, recurrence, or onset of a serious health condition.[23]

If the original certification was for a period of incapacity of more than thirty days, an employer may not request a recertification until the original certification period expires. This does not apply, however, if the individual's circumstances change significantly or information is received casting doubt on the original certification.

Controlling the employee's choice of physician is difficult given the limitations in the FMLA. The employer may not compel an employee to see a certain physician for purposes of obtaining the initial medical certification, but may direct the employee to a selected physician (whose services are not regularly utilized by the employer) for purposes of obtaining a second opinion under appropriate circumstances. The employer may also have a health care provider contact the employee's health care provider to seek clarification. The employer may even require a third opinion in certain circumstances. By implementing these procedures into an FMLA policy, the employer may then be in a better position to verify the need for medical leave.

PERIODIC REPORTS

Employers may require an employee on FMLA leave to report periodically on the employee's status and intent to return to work. Employers should be reasonable in their reporting requests (e.g. once per week).

4-25. How can an employee enforce his or her rights under the FMLA?

An employee who believes his or her rights under the FMLA have been violated has a choice of:

1. filing, or having another person file on his or her behalf, a complaint with the Secretary of Labor, or

2. filing a private lawsuit under the FMLA.

The statute of limitations on filing a complaint or private lawsuit is two years from the date of the last action which the employee contends was in violation of the FMLA or three years if the violation was willful.[24]

If an employee is successful in demonstrating that his rights under the FMLA have been violated, the employee may receive wages, employment benefits, or other compensation lost by reason of the violation or, where no such tangible loss has occurred, any actual monetary loss sustained by the employee as a direct result of the violation, such as the cost of providing care, up to the sum equal to twelve weeks of wages for the employee. In addition, the employee may be entitled to interest on this sum. An employee may also be awarded as liquidated damages an amount equal to the actual monetary loss sustained unless the court determines that the violation was in good faith and that the employer had reasonable grounds for believing the employer had not violated the act. If this is the case, the court may reduce the liquidated damages. An employee may also obtain appropriate equitable relief such as reinstatement or promotion. Finally, the employee may recover attorney's fees, reasonable expert witness fees, and other costs of a lawsuit in a successful lawsuit.

CHAPTER ENDNOTES

1. 29 U.S.C. §2601(b).
2. 29 CFR §825.104.
3. 29 CFR §825.106.
4. 29 CFR §825.104(c)(2).
5. 29 CFR §825.110.
6. 29 CFR §825.112.
7. 29 CFR §825.114.
8. 29 CFR §825.116.
9. 29 CFR §825.200.
10. 29 CFR §825.201.
11. 29 CFR §825.202.
12. 29 CFR §825.203.
13. 29 CFR §825.207.
14. 29 CFR §825.209.
15. 29 CFR §825.214.
16. 29 CFR §825.106(c).
17. 29 CFR §825.216.
18. 29 CFR §825.219.
19. 29 CFR §825.301.
20. 29 CFR §825.302.
21. 29 CFR §825.305(b).
22. 29 CFR §825.307.
23. 29 CFR §825.308.
24. 29 CFR §825.400.

Chapter 5

Sexual Harassment

GENERALLY

5-1. Generally, what is sexual harassment?

5-2. What does Title VII prohibit?

5-3. Who enforces Title VII?

5-4. Who is protected from sexual harassment under Title VII?

5-5. Who must comply with Title VII?

5-6. Are there any posting or record-keeping requirements related to sexual harassment?

5-7. Specifically, what is sexual harassment?

5-8. What is an actionable "hostile work environment?"

5-9. When is an employer legally responsible for sexual harassment?

5-10. Who qualifies as a "supervisor" for purposes of employer liability?

5-11. What is a "tangible employment action?"

5-12. How might harassment culminate in a tangible employment action?

5-13. What should employers do to prevent and correct harassment?

5-14. Do employees who are experiencing sexual harassment have any responsibilities?

5-15. Is an employer legally responsible for its supervisor's harassment if the employee failed to use the employer's complaint procedures?

PROCEDURAL REQUIREMENTS FOR FILING A SEXUAL HARASSMENT CLAIM

5-16. Is a plaintiff required to file a charge with the EEOC before filing a sexual harassment suit?

5-17. What is the statute of limitations for filing an EEOC charge?

5-18. What is a "right-to-sue" letter?

5-19. What is the statute of limitations for filing suit against the federal government under Title VII?

LITIGATING A SEXUAL HARASSMENT CLAIM

5-20. What are the elements of a sexual harassment claim?

5-21. What are the elements of a hostile work environment claim?

5-22. What are the elements of a "quid pro quo" claim?

5-23. What is the standard of proof in a sexual harassment lawsuit?

5-24. Who can be named as a defendant in a sexual harassment lawsuit?

DEFENSES TO SEXUAL HARASSMENT CLAIMS

5-25. What procedural or statutory defenses exist to sexual harassment claims?

5-26. What judicial or legal defenses exist to sexual harassment claims?

5-27. If the employer is liable for sexual harassment, are there defenses that will limit the amount of its damages?

REMEDIES FOR SEXUAL HARASSMENT UNDER TITLE VII

5-28. What remedies exist under Title VII for successful claims of sexual harassment?

GENERALLY

5-1. Generally, what is sexual harassment?

Sexual harassment is a form of gender discrimination in employment and is prohibited by Title VII of the Civil Rights Act of 1964.[1]

5-2. What does Title VII prohibit?

Title VII is a broad federal statute that prohibits many forms of discrimination, including discrimination on the basis of race, color, religion, sex, or national origin.[2] For detailed information about the applicability, enforcement and record-keeping requirements of Title VII, which necessarily includes sexual harassment, please see Chapter 9, Title VII of the Civil Rights Act of 1964.

Title VII also prohibits retaliation against any individual who opposes any unlawful practice, such as sexual harassment, or participates in protecting rights under Title VII. The statute provides that it shall be an unlawful employment practice for an employer to discriminate against any of its employees or applicants for employment because the employee or applicant has opposed any practice made an unlawful employment practice under Title VII, or because the individual has made a charge, testified, assisted, or participated in any manner in an investigation, proceeding, or hearing under Title VII.[3] Similar prohibitions apply to employment agencies and labor management committees involved in training programs.[4]

5-3. Who enforces Title VII?

EQUAL EMPLOYMENT OPPORTUNITIES COMMISSION

The Equal Employment Opportunities Commission (EEOC) is charged with the enforcement of Title VII.[5] The EEOC receives,

processes, and investigates charges of employment discrimination, including sexual harassment, under Title VII. If the EEOC determines that a charge is untimely or otherwise fails to state a claim, it will dismiss the charge.[6] If, after completing its investigation, the EEOC finds that there is not reasonable cause to believe that the law has been violated, it will issue a Notice of Right to Sue (also called a "right-to-sue letter") to the charging party.[7] On the other hand, if the EEOC determines after investigation that there is reasonable cause to believe that the law has been violated, it attempts conciliation.[8] If conciliation efforts fail, the EEOC may either file a lawsuit in federal court, or dismiss the charge and issue a Notice of Dismissal and a right-to-sue letter to the charging party.[9]

Individual Plaintiffs

Aggrieved individuals also may file and prosecute civil actions for sexual harassment under Title VII.[10] Prior to doing so, however, the individual must file a charge of unlawful discrimination with the EEOC and must obtain a right-to-sue letter.

Employers should be aware that most states have also enacted civil rights legislation that prohibits discrimination, including sexual harassment. While individual state laws are not covered in this text, employers are encouraged to become familiar with any state civil rights legislation in states in which they are doing business, as employees may rely on state law and state courts to avoid the procedural restrictions of Title VII and the EEOC.

5-4. Who is protected from sexual harassment under Title VII?

Title VII protects all employees of covered entities (see Q 5-5), both male and female, from sexual harassment. It prohibits sexual harassment by members of the same sex or by members of the opposite sex.[11]

5-5. Who must comply with Title VII?

Title VII applies to public and private employers that have at least 15 employees for each working day in at least 20 calendar weeks in the current or preceding calendar year. It also applies to employment agencies and labor organizations that serve such employers, unions with 15 or more members, and unions that represent employees of covered employers.

The term "employer" does not include:

1. the United States or any corporation owned by the United States;

2. an Indian tribe;

3. any department or agency of the District of Columbia; or

4. a bona fide private membership club (other than a labor organization).[12]

For a more detailed explanation of coverage, see Chapter 9, Title VII of the Civil Rights Act of 1964.

5-6. Are there any posting or record-keeping requirements related to sexual harassment?

Because sexual harassment is prohibited by Title VII, all of the notice and record-keeping provisions of Title VII apply. For a detailed explanation of these provisions, see Chapter 9, Title VII of the Civil Rights Act of 1964.

NOTICE REQUIREMENTS

Employers must post conspicuous notices stating the rights afforded under Title VII, including the right to a workplace free of sexual harassment. (See Appendix A.) The notices should be prepared or approved by the EEOC and should set forth excerpts from or summaries of the pertinent provisions of Title VII and information pertinent to the filing of a complaint with the EEOC.[13]

RECORD-KEEPING REQUIREMENTS

Every employer or other entity covered by Title VII is required to:

1. make and keep records relevant to the determinations of whether sexual harassment has been or is being committed;

2. preserve such records for periods prescribed by the EEOC; and

3. make reports as required by the EEOC.[14]

Personnel or employment records, including application forms and records concerning hiring, promotion, demotion, transfer, layoff or termination, rates of pay or other terms of compensation, and selection for training or apprenticeship must be retained for one year from the date the record was made or personnel action taken, whichever is later.[15] For example, if an employee is fired, records on that individual must be kept for one year after the termination.

When a sexual harassment or other discrimination charge has been filed, records relating to the complainant as well as to all others seeking or holding positions similar to that sought or held by the complainant must be preserved until final disposition of the charge.

5-7. Specifically, what is sexual harassment?

Sexual harassment is a form of discrimination on the basis of sex. Unwelcome sexual advances, requests for sexual favors, and other verbal or physical conduct of a sexual nature constitute sexual harassment when:

1.   submission to such conduct is made either explicitly or implicitly a term or condition of employment;

2.   submission to or rejection of such conduct by an individual is used as the basis for employment decisions; or

3.   such conduct has the purpose or effect of unreasonably interfering with an individual's work performance or creating an intimidating, hostile, or offensive working environment.[16]

Sexual harassment of the type described in (1) and (2) above is frequently called "quid pro quo" sexual harassment. Sexual harassment of the type described in (3) above is typically called "hostile work environment" sexual harassment. While the term "quid pro quo" does not appear in Title VII and has little actual legal significance after the Supreme Court's decision in *Burlington Industries, Inc. v. Ellerth*,[17] it remains a frequently used term of art describing sexual harassment where employment decisions are based upon the employee's submission to or rejection of sexual advances.

5-8. What is an actionable "hostile work environment?"

A "hostile work environment" exists where there is a sexually objectionable environment so severe and pervasive that it alters the terms or conditions of employment.[18] In order to be actionable, this environment must be both objectively and subjectively offensive. That is, the environment must be such that a reasonable person would find it hostile or abusive, *and* the alleged victim must in fact perceive it to be so.[19]

Whether an environment is sufficiently hostile or abusive to be actionable is determined by looking at all of the circumstances, including, for example, the frequency and severity of the conduct at issue, whether the conduct is physically threatening or humiliating or merely offensive, and whether the conduct interferes with an employee's work performance. Generally, simple teasing, off-hand comments, and isolated incidents, unless extremely serious, will not amount to actionable discriminatory changes in the "terms and conditions" of employment. Because Title VII is not "a general civility code," all employees are expected to tolerate "the ordinary tribulations of the workplace, such as the sporadic use of abusive language, gender-related jokes, and occasional teasing."[20]

5-9. When is an employer legally responsible for sexual harassment?

CO-WORKER HARASSMENT

With respect to conduct between co-workers, an employer is legally responsible for sexual harassment in the workplace where the employer, or its agents or supervisory employees, knew or should have known of the conduct and failed to take immediate and appropriate corrective action.[21]

NON-EMPLOYEE HARASSMENT

An employer may also be responsible for the behavior of non-employees who sexually harass employees in the workplace. This may occur if the employer, its agents, or supervisors, knew or should have known of the harassment, but failed to take immediate and appropriate corrective action, to the extent possible given the amount of control that the employer had over the non-employee harasser.[22] For example, if a restaurant customer sexually harasses a server and the owners or managers knew or should have known, but did nothing to stop the customer or prevent that behavior in the future, the restaurant may be liable for the harassment, because the restaurant has sufficient control over its customers to intervene, and, if necessary, eject them from the property.

SUPERVISOR HARASSMENT

With respect to the harassment of an employee by a supervisor or manager, the employer is always responsible for harassment that culminated in a tangible employment action against the employee.[23] If the harassment by the supervisor did not lead to a tangible employment action, the employer is liable unless it proves that:

1.   it exercised reasonable care to prevent and promptly correct any harassment; and

2.   the employee unreasonably failed to complain to management or to avoid harm otherwise.

5-10. Who qualifies as a "supervisor" for purposes of employer liability?

An individual qualifies as an employee's "supervisor" if the individual has immediate or successively higher authority over the employee.[24] An individual further qualifies as an employee's "supervisor" if:

1.   the individual has the authority to recommend tangible employment decisions affecting the employee; or

2.   the individual has the authority to direct the employee's daily work activities.[25]

In some limited circumstances, an employer may be liable for sexual harassment by a supervisor who does not have any actual authority over the employee.[26] This result is only appropriate if the employee reasonably believed that the harasser had such power, because, for example, the chain of command is unclear or the harasser has broad powers that would cause the employee to believe the harasser could influence employment decisions. If the harasser has no actual authority over the employee, and the employee did not reasonably believe the harasser had such authority, then the standard of liability for co-worker harassment applies. That is, the employer is responsible for acts of sexual harassment where the employer knows or should have known of the conduct and fails to take immediate and appropriate corrective action.

5-11. What is a "tangible employment action"?

A "tangible employment action" is a significant change in employment status, including, for example, hiring, firing, promotion, demotion, reassignment, and significant changes in benefits, compensation, or work assignments. While a tangible employment action usually inflicts direct economic harm, such harm is not always required. For instance, changes in work assignments or schedules may have no economic consequences, but may significantly lower an employee's prestige or responsibilities. These are tangible employment actions, despite the lack of economic impact, because they effectively constitute demotion. On the other hand, relatively insignificant changes, such as changes in title that do not affect compensation, benefits, responsibilities or duties, are not tangible employment actions, nor are unfulfilled threats.[27]

The distinction is crucial for liability determinations. If a supervisor causes an employee to suffer a tangible employment action because of the supervisor's sexual harassment of the employee, the employer is automatically liable and there is no defense. If there is no tangible employment action in a supervisor harassment case, then the employer may raise a complete defense by proving:

1.   that it took reasonable measures to prevent and correct harassment; and

2.   that the employee unreasonably failed to complain or otherwise avoid harm.

5-12. How might harassment culminate in a tangible employment action?

Tangible employment actions resulting from harassment may occur, for example, if a supervisor fires or demotes an employee for refusing requests for sexual favors, or if a supervisor promotes an employee who submitted to the supervisor's sexual demands.

5-13. What should employers do to prevent and correct harassment?

Employers should establish and enforce a policy, preferably written, prohibiting sexual harassment and setting out a procedure for making complaints. The policy should be disseminated to all employees and should provide that retaliation for making

complaints will not be tolerated. It should also provide that employees can bypass a harassing supervisor in making the complaint.

Upon receiving a complaint, the employer should conduct a prompt, thorough, and impartial investigation and undertake swift and appropriate corrective action where indicated. Disciplinary measures taken against the harasser should be proportionate to the offense. Remedial measures should be designed to stop the harassment, correct its effects on the complaining employee, and ensure that the harassment does not recur. The remedial measures need not be those that the complaining employee requests or prefers, as long as they are effective.[28] Care should be used to ensure that the corrective actions, such as transfers or schedule changes, do not burden the complaining employee, because such actions can constitute unlawful retaliation. Also, the employer should correct the effects of the harassment on the complaining employee. For example, negative evaluations of the employee that arose from the harassment should be expunged from the employee's personnel file.

An employer who consistently implements these measures will generally have fulfilled its responsibility under the law to effectively prevent and correct sexual harassment.

5-14. Do employees who are experiencing sexual harassment have any responsibilities?

Yes. Employees have a duty to use reasonable care to avoid harm to themselves arising from the sexual harassment. Typically, employees are expected to fulfill this duty by using the employer's complaint procedures to report the harassment.[29]

5-15. Is an employer legally responsible for its supervisor's harassment if the employee failed to use the employer's complaint procedures?

No, if there was no tangible employment action and if the complaint procedures were reasonable and were disseminated to employees. There is an exception if it was reasonable for the employee not to complain. An employee's failure to complain may be reasonable, for instance, if the complaint procedure was such that the employee could only complain to the harasser and to no one else. If the failure to complain was reasonable, the employer may be liable for the harassment. Generally, embarrassment and

fear of retaliation are insufficient to make a failure to complain reasonable.

However, if the harassment was by a supervisor and resulted in a tangible employment action, there is no defense and the employer *will* be liable.

PROCEDURAL REQUIREMENTS FOR FILING A SEXUAL HARASSMENT CLAIM

5-16. Is a plaintiff required to file a charge with the EEOC before filing a sexual harassment suit?

Yes. Before an individual can file a civil suit against an employer for sexual harassment under Title VII (as opposed to a suit in state court filed under state civil rights laws), the individual must first exhaust her administrative remedies by filing a charge with the EEOC. A charge must be in writing under oath or affirmation.[30] Each charge should contain the full name, address, and telephone number of the person making the charge. Additionally, it must contain a clear and concise statement of the facts, including pertinent dates, constituting the alleged unlawful sexual harassment.[31]

If the alleged sexual harassment occurs in a state which has a state or local law prohibiting sexual harassment or sex discrimination and a state or local authority to enforce that law, no charge may be filed with the EEOC before 60 days after proceedings have been commenced under the state or local law, unless those proceedings have been terminated.[32] Note, however, that a particular state or local agency may waive this 60-day deferral period by entering into a "Worksharing Agreement" with the EEOC.

5-17. What is the statute of limitations for filing an EEOC charge?

An individual must file a charge of unlawful discrimination with the EEOC within 180 days of the alleged act of sexual harassment. However, if the aggrieved individual has filed a charge with a state or local agency comparable to the EEOC, the individual can file an EEOC charge within 300 days after the alleged sexual harassment, or within 30 days after receiving notice that the state or local agency has terminated its proceedings, whichever is earlier.[33] In many states, a charge filed with the state agency is automatically simultaneously filed with the EEOC.

5-18. What is a "right-to-sue" letter?

Following the filing of an EEOC charge, the EEOC conducts an investigation to determine if there exists probable cause to believe that sexual harassment has occurred. If the EEOC determines that there is probable cause, the EEOC will attempt conciliation. If conciliation fails, and if the EEOC elects not to file a lawsuit on behalf of the individual, the EEOC will issue a "probable cause" finding and a Notice of Right to Sue, also known as a "right-to-sue" letter. If the EEOC's investigation shows no probable cause to believe that sexual harassment occurred, it will dismiss the charge and issue a right-to-sue letter. The right-to-sue letter gives the individual notice that the EEOC has terminated its investigation and permits the individual to file a private civil suit.

It is also common for individuals to request a right-to-sue letter prior to the EEOC completing its investigation. When the aggrieved person requests, in writing, that a notice of right to sue be issued, the EEOC will issue a notice of right to sue at any time after expiration of 180 days from the date the charge was filed.[34] The EEOC may issue the notice of right to sue prior to the expiration of 180 days provided that a specified EEOC official has determined that it is probable that the EEOC will be unable to complete its administrative processing within 180 days from the filing of the charge. A written certificate stating this conclusion must be attached to the notice of right to sue.[35]

Generally, the right-to-sue letter is required before filing a lawsuit. Even so, many courts will not dismiss a lawsuit in the absence of a right-to-sue letter but instead will stay the case and allow the plaintiff to obtain the letter.

5-19. What is the statute of limitations for filing suit against the federal government under Title VII?

An individual has 90 days after receipt of a Notice of Right to Sue to file a lawsuit against the federal government.[36] Because there is no set amount of time within which the EEOC must complete its investigation, the lawsuit may ultimately be filed years after the events at issue in the case.

LITIGATING A SEXUAL HARASSMENT CLAIM

5-20. What are the elements of a sexual harassment claim?

Every individual plaintiff claiming sexual harassment under Title VII must prove, by direct or indirect evidence, certain elements. These elements depend upon the type of claim that the plaintiff is asserting. The types of claims are "hostile work environment" and "quid pro quo" claims. However, plaintiffs may, and many do, assert more than one type of claim.

5-21. What are the elements of a hostile work environment claim?

If the plaintiff's claim is for a "hostile work environment," she must prove that:

1. the plaintiff is a member of a protected class;

2. the plaintiff was subjected to unwelcome harassment;

3. the unwelcome harassment was based on sex;

4. the harassment was sufficiently severe or pervasive so as to alter the conditions of the plaintiff's employment and create an abusive work environment; and

5. the sexually objectionable conduct was both objectively and subjectively offensive, such that a reasonable person would find it hostile or abusive and the plaintiff did in fact perceive it to be so.

In addition, there must be some basis for employer liability. If the accused harasser is a co-worker of the plaintiff's, then the basis for liability is established when the plaintiff shows that the employer knew or should have known of the harassment, but failed to take prompt remedial action.

If the accused harasser is a supervisor of the plaintiff, then the basis for liability is established by the principles of agency law. Because a supervisor is an agent of the employer, the employer is liable for the actions of a harassing supervisor if the employee suffered a tangible employment action because of the harassment. If there was no tangible employment action, the employer can avoid liability by proving that it exercised reasonable care to prevent and correct harassment, and that the employee unreasonably failed to complain or otherwise act to prevent harm.[37]

5-22. What are the elements of a "quid pro quo" claim?

If the plaintiff's claim is for "quid pro quo" sexual harassment, she must prove that:

1.   the plaintiff is a member of a protected class;

2.   the plaintiff was subjected to unwelcome harassment;

3.   the unwelcome harassment was based on sex; and

4.   submission to the unwelcome sexual conduct was made either explicitly or implicitly a term or condition of plaintiff's employment or was used as the basis for employment decisions affecting the plaintiff.

In every "quid pro quo" case, the accused harasser will be a supervisor, as only a supervisor can make employment decisions affecting an employee or impacting the terms or conditions of employment. In supervisor harassment cases, once the plaintiff establishes the prima facie case, the next step is a determination of whether the plaintiff experienced some tangible employment action. (See Q 5-11 for the definition of a tangible employment action.) If the plaintiff was subjected to a tangible employment action, then the employer is liable to the employee for damages stemming from the harassment. If, however, there was no tangible employment action, the employer may then try to establish a complete affirmative defense. The employer will not be liable if it proves that:

1.   it exercised reasonable care to prevent and promptly correct any harassment; and

2.   the employee unreasonably failed to complain to management or to avoid harm otherwise.[38]

5-23. What is the standard of proof in a sexual harassment lawsuit?

Each element of the claim must be proven by a preponderance of the evidence. This means that the evidence demonstrates that it is more likely than not true that the element is met. For example, the plaintiff must prove by a preponderance of the evidence that there was unwelcome sexual conduct. She must therefore put on enough evidence to at least make it probable that such conduct occurred and that she considered it to be unwelcome. Likewise, the employer has the burden of proving by a preponderance of the

evidence that its actions were taken for legitimate, non-discriminatory reasons.

5-24. Who can be named as a defendant in a sexual harass-
ment lawsuit?

The employer is the appropriate defendant in a sexual harassment action. The individual accused of harassment, whether it be
a supervisor or co-worker, cannot be held individually liable for the
alleged harassment under Title VII.[39]

DEFENSES TO SEXUAL HARASSMENT CLAIMS

5-25. What procedural or statutory defenses exist to sexual
harassment claims?

NOT A COVERED ENTITY

At the outset, a defendant in any Title VII case, including one
for sexual harassment, can raise a defense that it is not an
"employer" (or other covered entity) as that term is defined under
Title VII. (See Q 5-5 for the definition of an employer.)

STATUTE OF LIMITATIONS

An individual must file a charge of unlawful discrimination
with the EEOC within 180 days of the alleged act of sexual
harassment. However, if the individual has filed a charge with a
state or local agency comparable to the EEOC, the individual can
file an EEOC charge within 300 days after the alleged sexual
harassment, or within 30 days after receiving notice that the state
or local agency has terminated its proceedings, whichever is
earlier.[40]

Generally this means that plaintiffs cannot sue for conduct
that occurred outside of the 180/300 day statute of limitations for
filing a charge. However, most courts recognize a limited exception
called a "continuing violation," which allows claims for otherwise
untimely unlawful behavior where the sexual harassment (or other
discriminatory behavior) is part of an ongoing and connected
pattern.[41] Courts differ on the actual requirements for successfully
using a continuing violation theory to bypass the statute of
limitations. However, most courts require that:

1. at least one discriminatory act occurred within the
limitations period;

2.   the discriminatory or harassing behavior occurred as part of a related and continuous pattern; and

3.   the harassment was such that the plaintiff did not immediately recognize that her civil rights were being violated by the harassing conduct.[42]

Where the plaintiff fails in the attempt to use the continuing violation theory, she will be unable to collect any damages based on untimely sexual harassment, i.e., conduct that occurred outside of the 180/300 day limitation period. However, the vast majority of courts will allow testimony and other evidence to be admitted at trial about some or all of the untimely events, as this evidence is typically viewed as "relevant background evidence" for the plaintiff's remaining claims.

5-26. What judicial or legal defenses exist to sexual harassment claims?

FAILURE OF PLAINTIFF'S PROOF

When defending any discrimination claim, the defendant may be able to challenge one or more of the basic elements of the plaintiff's claim. (See Q 5-20 for the elements of the different claims.) The plaintiff is required to prove these elements to establish her case. Failure to do so is grounds for judgment in the defendant's favor and dismissal of the lawsuit. For example, the employer can argue that the plaintiff failed to prove that the alleged harassment was based on sex, rather than on some unprotected quality, such as hair color.

LEGITIMATE, NON-DISCRIMINATORY REASON

In any case where the accused harasser is a supervisor, once the plaintiff has established the basic elements of the claim, the question becomes whether the plaintiff was subjected to a tangible employment action. This is a critical point for the employer, because a tangible employment action, such as hiring, firing, promotion or demotion, that was based upon the harassment makes the employer liable for the harassment without defense or exception.[43]

The employer can defend this point two ways. First, if possible, the employer can demonstrate that there was no tangible employment action at all. This defense is appropriate if the plaintiff neither lost nor gained anything of any real value, economic or otherwise, because of the supervisor's conduct.

Second, if there was a tangible employment action, the employer can articulate a legitimate, non-discriminatory reason for its action or decision. For example, if the plaintiff was terminated and claims the termination was because she refused a supervisor's sexual demands, the employer may assert that the employee was in fact terminated because of poor attendance. The burden then shifts to the plaintiff to establish that the employer's reason was not the real reason, but a pretext for discrimination.[44]

AFFIRMATIVE DEFENSE FOR SUPERVISOR SEXUAL HARASSMENT CASES

In a case where the accused harasser is a supervisor, if the plaintiff has established the basic elements of the claim, but has failed to show that there was a tangible employment action because of the alleged harassment, the employer may then raise a complete affirmative defense that will, if successful, absolve it of liability. The defense has two elements, both of which the employer has the burden of proving:

1. that the employer exercised reasonable care to prevent and promptly correct any harassment; and

2. that the employee unreasonably failed to complain to management or to otherwise avoid harm.[45]

As for the first element, generally proof that the "employer had promulgated an anti-harassment policy with complaint procedure" is sufficient to show reasonable care to prevent harassment. Proof that the employers acts promptly to correct any existing problems is also important.

The second element makes it clear that employees have a duty to use reasonable care to avoid harm to themselves. Demonstration by the employer that the plaintiff failed to use its complaint procedures to address the alleged harassment is generally sufficient to prove this element of the defense.[46]

5-27. If the employer is liable for sexual harassment, are there defenses that will limit the amount of its damages?

AFTER-ACQUIRED EVIDENCE DEFENSE

One defense that affects the plaintiff's remedy is the "after-acquired evidence" defense. This defense was recognized by the Supreme Court in *McKennon v. Nashville Banner Publishing Co.*.[47]

The defense applies when the plaintiff alleges she was discharged because of sexual harassment (or for some other discriminatory reason), and subsequent to the discharge the employer discovers wrongdoing by the plaintiff that occurred during the plaintiff's employment. This evidence of the plaintiff's wrongdoing may even turn up during the litigation itself. To use this defense, the employer must prove that the discovered wrongdoing was of such severity that the employee would have been terminated for that conduct alone if the employer had known about it before or at the time of the termination. The defense does not relieve the employer of liability, however, because the employer could not have been motivated by knowledge it did not have at the time of the termination. But wrongdoing by the employee, although not discovered until after the discharge, must be taken into account in determining the plaintiff's remedy, such as the amount of back pay and front pay. This defense can be a highly effective way to limit the amount of the plaintiff's damage award.

PLAINTIFF'S FAILURE TO MITIGATE DAMAGES

Another defense that may limit the plaintiff's remedy involves the plaintiff's duty to mitigate damages. The plaintiff may not recover damages for any harm that she could have avoided or minimized with reasonable effort. The employer has the burden of showing that the plaintiff failed to exercise reasonable diligence to mitigate damages.[48] For example, if the plaintiff proves that she was terminated because of sexual harassment, the employer is entitled to provide proof the plaintiff failed to exercise reasonable diligence in finding comparable employment. If the plaintiff failed to make reasonable efforts, the damage award related to back pay and front pay may be limited accordingly.

REMEDIES FOR SEXUAL HARASSMENT UNDER TITLE VII

5-28. What remedies exist under Title VII for successful claims of sexual harassment?

Statutory damages for violations of Title VII include: (1) an injunction to prevent future violations; (2) back pay; (3) attorney's fees; and (4) costs.[49]

Back pay is routinely awarded as a remedy where the plaintiff was terminated from employment because of sexual harassment. However, there are limitations on back pay. For example, back pay liability does not accrue from a date more than two years prior to the filing of a charge with the EEOC. Also, interim earnings or amounts the plaintiff could have earned through reasonable diligence operate to reduce the back pay award.

Trial courts also award front pay when appropriate. Front pay may extend until the plaintiff fails to make reasonable efforts to secure substantially equivalent employment or until the plaintiff obtains or is offered such employment.

In addition, the plaintiff may recover compensatory and punitive damages. Compensatory damages include future pecuniary losses, emotional pain and suffering, inconvenience, mental anguish, loss of enjoyment of life and other non-monetary losses. Punitive damages may be recovered for sexual harassment if the plaintiff demonstrates that the defendant acted with malice or with reckless indifference to the individual's rights. These damages are subject to a statutory cap, however, the amount of which depends upon the size of the employer. The sum of the amount of compensatory damages and the amount of punitive damages shall not exceed the following for each plaintiff: $50,000 for defendants with 15 to 100 employees; $100,000 for defendants with 101 to 200 employees; $200,000 for defendants with 201 to 500 employees; and $300,000 for defendants with more than 500 employees.[50]

CHAPTER ENDNOTES

1. 42 U.S.C. §2000e, et seq.
2. 42 U.S.C. §2000e-2.
3. 42 U.S.C. §2000e-3(a).
4. 42 U.S.C. §2000e-3(a).
5. 42 U.S.C. §2000e-5.
6. 29 CFR §1601.18.
7. 29 CFR §1601.19.
8. 29 CFR §1601.24.
9. 42 U.S.C. §2000e-5(f); 29 CFR §§1601.27 and 1601.28(b)(1).
10. 42 U.S.C. §2000e-5(f).
11. *Oncale v. Sundowner Offshore Services, Inc.*, 523 U.S. 75 (1998).
12. 42 U.S.C. §2000e.
13. 42 U.S.C. §2000e-10.
14. 42 U.S.C. §2000e-8(c).
15. 29 CFR §1602.14.
16. 29 CFR §1604.11.
17. 524 U.S. 742 (1998).
18. *Meritor Savings Bank, FSB v. Vinson*, 477 U.S. 57 (1986).
19. *Harris v. Forklift Systems, Inc.*, 510 U.S. 17 (1993).
20. *Faragher v. City of Boca Raton*, 524 U.S. 775 (1998).
21. 29 CFR §1604.11(d).

22. 29 CFR §1604.11(e).
23. *Faragher v. City of Boca Raton*, 524 U.S. 775 (1998).
24. *Burlington Industries, Inc. v. Ellerth*, 524 U.S. 742 (1998).
25. See *Vicarious Employer Liability for Unlawful Harassment by Supervisors* §III(A) (EEOC June 18, 1999).
26. *Burlington Industries, Inc. v. Ellerth*, 524 U.S. 742 (1998).
27. *Burlington Industries, Inc. v. Ellerth*, 524 U.S. 742 (1998); *Vicarious Employer Liability for Unlawful Harassment by Supervisors* §IV(B) (EEOC June 18, 1999).
28. *Vicarious Employer Liability for Unlawful Harassment by Supervisors* §V(C) (EEOC June 18, 1999).
29. *Burlington Industries, Inc. v. Ellerth*, 524 U.S. 742 (1998).
30. 42 U.S.C. §2000e-5(b).
31. 29 CFR §1601.12(a).
32. 42 U.S.C. §2000e-5(c).
33. 42 U.S.C. §2000e-5(e).
34. 29 CFR §1601.28(a)(1).
35. 29 CFR §1601.28(a)(2).
36. 42 U.S.C. §2000e-16(c).
37. *Faragher v. City of Boca Raton*, 524 U.S. 775 (1998); *O'Rourke v. City of Providence*, 235 F.3d 713 (1st Cir. 2001).
38. *Faragher v. City of Boca Raton*, 524 U.S. 775 (1998).
39. *Indest v. Freeman Decorating, Inc.*, 164 F.3d 258 (5th Cir. 1999).
40. 42 U.S.C. §2000e-5(e).
41. See *O'Rourke v. City of Providence*, 235 F.3d 713 (1st Cir. 2001).
42. *O'Rourke v. City of Providence*, 235 F.3d 713 (1st Cir. 2001).
43. *Faragher v. City of Boca Raton*, 524 U.S. 775 (1998).
44. *Newton v. Cadwell Laboratories*, 156 F.3d 880 (8th Cir. 1998).
45. *Faragher v. City of Boca Raton*, 524 U.S. 775 (1998).
46. *Burlington Industries, Inc. v. Ellerth*, 524 U.S. 742 (1998).
47. 513 U.S. 352 (1995).
48. *Weaver v. Casa Gallardo, Inc.*, 922 F.2d 1515 (11th Cir. 1991); *Fleming v. County of Kane*, State of Ill., 898 F.2d 553 (7th Cir. 1990).
49. 42 U.S.C. §2000e-5.
50. 42 U.S.C. §1981a.

Chapter 6

The ADA and The Rehabilitation Act

THE AMERICANS WITH DISABILITIES ACT

6-1. What is the Americans with Disabilities Act?

6-2. Who must comply with Title I of the ADA?

6-3. Does the ADA apply to states and state agencies?

6-4. Does the ADA apply to foreign employers or foreign operations of U.S. employers?

6-5. Who is protected under the ADA?

6-6. Who enforces the ADA?

DEFINITIONS OF KEY ADA TERMS

6-7. What is meant by the term "qualified individual with a disability"?

6-8. What is a "disability" under the ADA?

6-9. Are there any conditions expressly excluded from the definition of the term "qualified individual with a disability"?

6-10. What is a "major life activity"?

6-11. What is required in order for an employee to demonstrate that he or she is "substantially limited" with respect to one of the major life activities?

6-12. What is a "record of an impairment"?

6-13. What does "regarded as having an impairment" mean?

6-14. What are the "essential functions" of a job?

6-15. What is a "direct threat"?

REASONABLE ACCOMMODATION

6-16. What does "reasonable accommodation" mean?

6-17. How does an employer determine what is a reasonable accommodation in a particular situation?

6-18. Must an employer provide a qualified individual with a disability with the particular accommodation that the individual requests?

6-19. Must an individual accept the reasonable accommodation offered by the employer?

6-20. When does a proposed accommodation constitute an "undue hardship" such that the employer is not required to provide that accommodation?

EMPLOYER CONDUCT PROHIBITED BY THE ADA

6-21. What specifically does the ADA prohibit?

6-22. What is meant by the term "qualification standards"?

6-23. Does the ADA also prohibit retaliation against an employee for exercising rights under the ADA?

Medical Examinations

6-24. Does the ADA allow medical examinations of applicants for employment?

6-25. When is an employer permitted to require a medical examination of an applicant?

6-26. Does the ADA place restrictions on access to an applicant's medical files?

6-27. Does the ADA permit covered entities to require medical examinations of current employees?

6-28. Does the ADA permit an employer to offer voluntary medical examinations?

6-29. Do drug tests constitute medical examinations under the ADA?

Notice and Recordkeeping Requirements

6-30. Does the ADA require employers to post notices of its provisions?

6-31. Does the ADA impose recordkeeping requirements upon employers?

6-32. What are the recordkeeping requirements when a discrimination charge has been filed?

Procedures for Filing an ADA Claim

6-33. What are the procedures for filing an ADA claim?

6-34. Does the ADA require that an individual file a "charge of discrimination" with the EEOC before filing a civil lawsuit in federal court against a covered entity?

6-35. What is the time limit for filing an EEOC charge?

6-36. What is a "right to sue" letter?

LITIGATING AN ADA CLAIM

6-37. What are the different types of ADA claims?

6-38. What is a disparate treatment disability discrimination claim?

6-39. How will the courts analyze a disparate treatment claim?

6-40. How does a plaintiff establish a prima facie case of disability discrimination?

6-41. How does an ADA plaintiff demonstrate that the employer's stated legitimate business reason for the adverse employment action was a pretext for disability discrimination?

6-42. What is a "mixed motive" discrimination claim?

6-43. What is the most important difference between the McDonnell Douglas/Burdine framework and the mixed motive framework?

6-44. What is a hostile environment harassment claim?

6-45. What is a disparate impact claim?

6-46. How will the courts analyze a disparate impact claim?

DEFENSES TO ADA CLAIMS

6-47. What are some of the defenses that an employer generally may assert against an ADA discrimination claim?

6-48. How else can an employer defend against a "disparate treatment" claim?

6-49. How can an employer defend against a claim that it applied qualification standards to screen out qualified individuals with disabilities?

6-50. How can an employer defend against a disparate impact claim?

6-51. How can an employer defend against a claim that it failed to make reasonable accommodation for the known disability of an employee?

6-52. Do religious entities have any special defenses under the ADA?

REMEDIES PROVIDED BY THE ADA

6-53. What remedies exist under the ADA?

THE REHABILITATION ACT OF 1973

6-54. Are there any other federal laws addressing disability discrimination in employment?

6-55. Who is protected under the Rehabilitation Act?

6-56. What does the Rehabilitation Act require with respect to federal executive branch agencies?

6-57. Who enforces Section 501 of the Rehabilitation Act?

6-58. What does the Rehabilitation Act require of entities contracting with the federal government?

6-59. Who enforces Section 503 of the Rehabilitation Act?

6-60. What does the Rehabilitation Act require of recipients of federal financial assistance?

6-61. Who enforces Section 504 of the Rehabilitation Act?

THE AMERICANS WITH DISABILITIES ACT

6-1. What is the Americans with Disabilities Act?

The Americans with Disabilities Act (ADA) is a federal law enacted in 1990 "to provide a clear and comprehensive national mandate for the elimination of discrimination against individuals with disabilities."[1]

The ADA does not, however, guarantee equal results, establish quotas, or require preferences favoring individuals with disabilities over those without disabilities.

The ADA includes three principal subchapters, or "titles," prohibiting discrimination against individuals with disabilities in (1) employment; (2) "public services" (such as transportation); and (3) "public accommodations" (such as hotels, restaurants, places of entertainment, exhibition, recreation, or transportation, malls, retail stores, offices and other places of business, schools, libraries, and agencies).

This chapter covers only Title I of the ADA, the subchapter that addresses employment.

6-2. Who must comply with Title I of the ADA?

Employers who employ 15 or more employees on each working day during 20 or more calendar weeks in the current or preceding calendar year must comply with Title I, the employment portion of the ADA.

The term "employer" does not include (1) the United States government or any corporation wholly owned by the United States; (2) Indian tribes; or (3) bona fide private membership clubs, other than labor organizations, that are exempt from taxation under Internal Revenue Code Section 501(c).[2]

The ADA also covers employment agencies, labor organizations, and joint labor-management committees (collectively referred to as "covered entities").[3]

The terms "employer" and "covered entity" will be used interchangeably throughout this chapter.

6-3. Does the ADA apply to states and state agencies?

No. Although the employment provisions of the ADA purport to apply to states and state agencies,[4] the U.S. Supreme Court recently ruled that Congress exceeded its Constitutional authority and violated the 11th Amendment by attempting to apply the ADA to the States.[5] (The Eleventh Amendment to the United States Constitution provides States with immunity from federal laws except under certain circumstances.)

6-4. Does the ADA apply to foreign employers or foreign operations of U.S. employers?

The ADA covers the foreign operations of U.S. employers, the U.S. operations of a foreign employer, and any foreign corporation that is "controlled" by a U.S. employer.[6]

The determination of "control," for this purpose, is based upon four factors: (1) the interrelation of operations; (2) common management; (3) centralized control of labor relations; and (4) common ownership or financial control.[7]

The ADA does not apply to foreign operations of foreign corporations not controlled by a U.S. employer.[8]

6-5. Who is protected under the ADA?

The ADA provides protection to any employee or applicant who is a "qualified individual with a disability" (see Q 6-7).

The term "employee" is defined simply as any individual employed by an employer.[9]

The definition of employee includes former employees, but does not include independent contractors.[10]

With respect to employment in a foreign country, the term employee includes only citizens of the United States.[11]

6-6. Who enforces the ADA?

The Equal Employment Opportunity Commission (EEOC) is charged with the enforcement of Title I of the ADA.[12] The EEOC investigates charges of disability discrimination filed with it, has the power to subpoena evidence, and, if it finds "probable cause" to believe that discrimination has occurred, will attempt "conciliation" to settle the matter. It may also pursue a civil action against the employer on behalf of the disabled employee in federal court. The EEOC also has authority to create (and has created) regulations interpreting the various provisions of the ADA.[13] While these regulations do not have the force of law, courts will generally— although not always—defer to the EEOC's interpretations of the statute.

The ADA also authorizes individual plaintiffs to file action in civil court, which is the most common method by which the ADA is enforced. Prior to filing a civil court action, however, the disabled employee must first have filed a charge of discrimination with the EEOC.[14] For the procedures to be followed in filing an ADA Claim, see Q 6-33.

DEFINITIONS OF KEY ADA TERMS

6-7. What is meant by the term "qualified individual with a disability"?

A "qualified individual with a disability" is a person with a disability (see Q 6-8) who satisfies the requisite skill, experience, education, and other job-related requirements of the employment position such individual holds or desires to hold. In addition, such person must be able to perform the "essential functions" of that position, with or without "reasonable accommodation."[15]

6-8. What is a "disability" under the ADA?

The ADA defines the term "disability" in three alternative ways: (1) a "physical or mental impairment" that "substantially limits" one or more of an individual's "major life activities"; (2) a record of such an impairment; or (3) being regarded (by the employer) as having such an impairment.[16]

As outlined by EEOC regulations, the term "physical or mental impairment" includes:

1.   Any physiological disorder or condition, cosmetic disfigurement, or anatomical loss affecting one (or more) of the following body systems:

    a) neurological,

    b) musculoskeletal,

    c) special sense organs,

    d) respiratory (including speech organs),

    e) cardiovascular,

    f) reproductive,

    g) digestive,

    h) genito-urinary,

    i) hemic and lymphatic,

    j) skin, and

    k) endocrine; or

2. Any mental or psychological disorder, such as:

a) mental retardation,

b) organic brain syndrome,

c) emotional or mental illness, and

d) specific learning disabilities.[17]

6-9. Are there any conditions expressly excluded from the definition of the term "qualified individual with a disability"?

Yes.

Drugs. Individuals "currently engaging in the illegal use of drugs" are excluded from the term "qualified individual with a disability."[18] However, an individual who is either (1) participating in a supervised rehabilitation program and is no longer engaging in the illegal use of drugs; or (2) who has successfully completed drug rehabilitation and is no longer engaging in such use may qualify as an individual with a disability, because of having a record of impairment.[19]

An employee who is *erroneously* regarded as engaging in the illegal use of drugs may also be a qualified individual with a disability.[20]

Psychoactive substance disorders resulting from current illegal use of drugs are also excluded from the definition of disability.[21]

Conditions Related to Sex and Gender . Also specifically excluded from the definition of a disability are the following conditions:

1. Transvestism;

2. Transsexualism;

3. Pedophilia;

4. Exhibitionism;

5. Voyeurism;

6. Gender identity disorders not resulting from physical impairments;

7. Homosexuality;

8. Bisexuality; and

9. other sexual behavior "disorders."[22]

Excluded Psychological Conditions. Compulsive gambling, kleptomania, and pyromania are also specifically excluded from the definition of a disability.[23]

Pregnancy. Several courts have also held that, absent complicating factors, pregnancy is not a disability under the ADA.[24]

Other Excluded Conditions. The EEOC has also explained that temporary, non-chronic impairments of short duration, with little or no long term or permanent impact, such as broken limbs, sprained joints, concussions, appendicitis, and influenza, are usually not disabilities.[25]

Similarly, except in extreme cases ("i.e. morbid") obesity, obesity is not considered a disabling impairment.[26]

6-10. What is a "major life activity"?

Under the first prong of the ADA's definition of disability, the term "major life activity" means functions such as caring for oneself, performing manual tasks, walking, seeing, hearing, speaking, breathing, learning, and working.[27]

Other activities that the EEOC considers and/or courts have found to be "major life activities" include, for example: sitting, standing, lifting, and reaching.[28]

Some functions that courts have ruled are not "major life activities" include: climbing, kneeling, twisting, bending, crawling, squatting, and general mobility.[29]

6-11. What is required in order for an employee to demonstrate that he or she is "substantially limited" with respect to one of the major life activities?

The term "substantially limited" means either (1) unable to perform a major life activity that the average person in the general population can perform; or (2) significantly restricted as to the condition, manner, or duration under which an individual can perform a particular major life activity, as compared to the condition, manner, or duration under which the average person in the general population can perform that same major life activity.[30]

Factors that may be considered in determining whether an individual is "substantially limited" with respect to a major life activity include: (1) the nature and severity of the impairment; (2) the duration or expected duration of the impairment; and (3) the permanent or long term impact resulting from the impairment.[31]

Specifically, with respect to the major life activity of "working," substantially limited means significantly restricted with respect to the ability to perform either a class of jobs or a broad range of jobs in various classes, as compared to the average person having comparable training, skills, and abilities. The inability to perform a particular job does not constitute a "substantial limitation."[32]

The analysis of whether an employee is "substantially limited" in a major life activity must take into account corrective measures that reduce or eliminate the effects of the impairment, such as eyeglasses or medication.[33]

6-12. What is a "record of an impairment"?

Under the second prong of the ADA's definition of disability, a "record of an impairment" means that the individual "has a history of, or has been misclassified as having, a mental or physical impairment that substantially limits one or more major life activities."[34]

6-13. What does "regarded as having an impairment" mean?

Under the third prong of the ADA's definition of disability, an employee may show that he or she is "regarded as having such an impairment" by showing either that he or she: (1) has a physical or mental impairment that does not, in fact, substantially limit any major life activity, but is treated by the employer as constituting such a limitation; (2) has a physical or mental impairment that substantially limits major life activities only as a result of the attitudes of others toward such impairment; or (3) does not in fact have an impairment as defined above, but is treated by a covered entity as having a substantially limiting impairment.[35]

6-14. What are the "essential functions" of a job?

The term "essential functions" means the fundamental job duties of a given employment position. A job function may be considered essential because: (1) the reason that the position exists is to perform that function; (2) there are a limited number of employees available to perform that function; or (3) the function is highly specialized and the employee was hired for his or her expertise and ability to perform that particular function.[36]

Evidence of whether a particular job duty is an essential function includes such factors as: (1) the employer's judgment as to which functions are essential; (2) written job descriptions; (3) the amount of time spent performing the function; and (4) the consequences of not requiring the employee in the position to perform the function.[37]

6-15. What is a "direct threat"?

The term "direct threat" means a significant risk to the health or safety of the disabled individual or others (e.g., coworkers, customers) that cannot be eliminated by reasonable accommodation.[38]

An employer's conclusion that an individual poses a "direct threat" must be based on an individualized medical assessment of the individual's present ability to safely perform the essential functions of the job. The medical judgment must rely on the most current medical knowledge and/or on the best available objective evidence. Factors to be considered include: (1) the duration of the risk; (2) the nature and severity of the potential harm; and (3) the likelihood that the potential harm will occur.[39]

REASONABLE ACCOMMODATION

6-16. What does "reasonable accommodation" mean?

Reasonable accommodation may consist of many different types of actions on the part of the covered entity that enable the employee to perform the essential functions of the position.

The types of reasonable accommodations may include:

1. Making existing facilities more accessible to individuals with disabilities;

2.   Job restructuring;

3.   Part-time or modified work schedules;

4.   Acquisition or modification of equipment or devices;

5.   Adjustment of examinations, training materials, or policies; and

6.   Reassignment to a vacant position for which the employee is qualified and/or a leave of absence (these are usually considered accommodations of last resort).[40]

An accommodation is not "reasonable" if the employer can show that such accommodation would impose an "undue hardship" on the employer.[41] See Q 6-20.

Requiring a disabled employee's co-workers to assist him/her in performing essential duties of his/her position is not a reasonable accommodation required by the ADA.[42]

6-17. How does an employer determine what is a reasonable accommodation in a particular situation?

The burden is on the employee needing the accommodation to raise the issue with his or her employer. If and when necessary, in order to determine an appropriate reasonable accommodation, employers must engage in an "informal, interactive process" with the qualified individual with a disability to determine the nature of the needed accommodation. This process should identify the precise limitations resulting from the disability and the potential reasonable accommodations that could overcome those limitations.[43]

6-18. Must an employer provide a qualified individual with a disability with the particular accommodation that the individual requests?

No. An employer must provide reasonable accommodation to a qualified individual with a disability, but the accommodation need not be the particular accommodation requested by the qualified individual with a disability, as long as the accommodation of the employer's choosing is, in fact, sufficient to allow the individual to perform the essential functions of the job.[44]

6-19. Must an individual accept the reasonable accommodation offered by the employer?

No. A qualified individual with a disability is not required to accept an employer's offered accommodation.[45] However, if such individual rejects a reasonable accommodation that is necessary to enable—and in fact would have enabled—him to perform the essential functions of the position, and as a result he cannot perform the essential functions of the position, then the individual will not be considered a qualified individual with a disability.[46]

6-20. When does a proposed accommodation constitute an "undue hardship," such that the employer is not required to provide that accommodation?

The ADA does not require employers to provide any accommodation that would create an undue hardship on the employer.[47]

Factors that will be considered in determining whether an accommodation would impose an undue hardship generally include: (1) the nature and net cost of the accommodation; (2) the overall financial resources of the facility and/or employer; (3) the number of employees and number of facilities; (4) the composition, structure, and functions of the employer's workforce; and (5) the impact of the accommodation upon the operation of the facility, including the impact on the ability of other employees to perform their duties.[48]

Undue hardship cannot, however, be based upon coworkers' or customers' fears or prejudices toward the individual's disability, nor upon a claim that the requested accommodation would have a negative impact on employee morale.[49]

An accommodation that would require the employer to violate a term of a collective bargaining agreement with a union (e.g., seniority, work jurisdiction, etc.) constitutes an undue burden according to several courts.[50]

The EEOC has taken the position in published guidance addressing reasonable accommodation and undue hardship that employers may not use a "cost-benefit analysis" as a basis for claiming undue hardship. Several federal courts of appeals, however, have rejected the EEOC's position on this issue and ruled that employers may use a cost-benefit analysis as grounds for claiming that a requested accommodation would constitute an undue hardship for the employer.[51]

EMPLOYER CONDUCT PROHIBITED BY THE ADA

6-21. What specifically does the ADA prohibit?

The ADA makes it unlawful for a covered entity to discriminate against a qualified individual with a disability because of such disability with respect to:

1. Recruitment or job application procedures;

2. The hiring, advancement, training, promotion, transfer, demotion, layoff, discharge, or rehiring of employees;

3. Employee pay, fringe benefits, or other compensation;

4. Job assignments, classifications, or descriptions;

5. Leaves of absence, sick leave, or any other leave;

6. Selection and financial support for training, including apprenticeships, professional meetings, conferences, and other related activities, and selection for leaves of absence to pursue such activities;

7. Covered entity-sponsored activities, including social and recreational programs; and

8. Any other term, condition, or privilege of employment.[52]

The ADA also prohibits covered entities from:

1. Limiting, segregating, or classifying applicants or employees based upon their disability in a way that adversely affects their opportunities or status;

2. Participating in contractual or other arrangements or relationships, (for example, with employment referral agencies, labor unions, benefits providers, or training or apprenticeship organizations) that have the effect of subjecting to discrimination the covered entity's own qualified applicant or employee with a disability;

3. Using standards, criteria, or methods of administration that either have the effect of discriminating on the basis of disability, or perpetuate the discrimination of others who are subject to common administrative control;

4. Denying equal jobs or benefits to a qualified individual because of the known disability of another person with whom the qualified individual is known to have a family, business, social, or other relationship or association;

5. Failing or refusing to make reasonable accommodation for the known limitations of a qualified individual with a disability who is an employee or applicant (unless the covered entity can show that the desired accommodation would impose an undue hardship, see Q 6-20), or denying employment opportunities to a qualified individual with a disability because of the need to make reasonable accommodation for such individual;

6. Using qualification standards, employment tests, or other selection criteria for jobs or benefits that screen out or tend to screen out individuals with disabilities (unless the employer can show that the standard, test, or criterion is job-related for the position in question and consistent with business necessity); or

7. Failing to use tests in the most effective manner so as to ensure that such test results reflect the skills, aptitude, or whatever other factor such test is intended to measure, rather than reflecting the employee's or applicant's impaired sensory, manual, or speaking skills (except where such skills are the factors that the test is intended to measure).[53]

6-22. What is meant by the term "qualification standards"?

The term "qualification standards" means the personal and professional attributes including the skill, experience, education, physical, medical, safety, and other requirements established by a covered entity as requirements that an individual must meet in order to be eligible for the position held or desired.

Qualification standards may include a requirement that the individual shall not pose a "direct threat" (see Q 6-15) to the health or safety of himself/herself or other individuals in the workplace.[54]

6-23. Does the ADA also prohibit retaliation against an employee for exercising rights under the ADA?

Yes. It is unlawful to retaliate against any individual because that individual has opposed any act or practice made unlawful by the ADA. It is also unlawful to retaliate against an individual who has made a charge, testified, assisted, or participated in an investigation, proceeding, or hearing to enforce the ADA.

The ADA also prohibits coercion, intimidation, threats, harassment, or interference with respect to any individual's exercise or enjoyment of the ADA.

The ADA protects any individual who has aided or encouraged any other individual in the exercise of any right under the ADA.[55]

MEDICAL EXAMINATIONS

6-24. Does the ADA allow medical examinations of applicants for employment?

With the exceptions noted below, the ADA generally prohibits employers from: (1) conducting medical examinations of applicants; (2) asking them if they have a disability; or (3) inquiring as to the nature or severity of such disability.[56]

Employers may, however, make pre-employment inquiries into the ability of an applicant to perform job-related functions. Employers may also ask the applicant to demonstrate how, with or without reasonable accommodation, he will be able to perform such functions.[57]

6-25. When is an employer permitted to require a medical examination of an applicant?

The ADA permits employers to require a medical examination and/or make medical inquiries after making an offer of employment to a job applicant and before the applicant begins working.

The employer may condition the offer of employment on the results of such examination. However, the medical examination should be specifically tailored to assess whether the employee can perform the essential functions of the job, which means that the doctor conducting the exam must be provided with a detailed description of the job's requirements.

For example, in *Holiday v. City of Chattanooga*,[58] the court ruled that the defendant employer had acted improperly under the ADA when it relied upon a doctor's conclusion that the applicant was not qualified for the job, because the doctor who performed the post-offer physical examination did not specifically inquire into the applicant's ability to perform particular functions of the job.

Employers may require such post-offer medical examinations only if: (1) all entering employees in the same job category are subjected to such an examination and/or inquiry (i.e., an employer cannot require medical examinations only of applicants who appear to have some type of disability); and (2) any medical information obtained is collected and maintained on separate forms and in separate medical files and is treated as a confidential medical record (see Q 6-26).[59]

6-26. Does the ADA place restrictions on access to an applicant's medical files?

Yes. Any medical information that an employer collects regarding an applicant must be maintained in a separate, confidential file.

Once an applicant has been hired, exceptions to this confidentiality requirement allow employers to: (1) inform supervisors and managers regarding necessary restrictions on the work or duties of the employee and necessary accommodations; (2) inform first aid and safety personnel, when appropriate, if the disability might require emergency treatment; and (3) provide government officials investigating compliance with the ADA relevant information on request.[60]

6-27. Does the ADA permit covered entities to require medical examinations of current employees?

Employers may require a medical examination of a current employee or make inquiries as to whether such employee has a disability, or the nature and extent of such disability, only if the examination/inquiry is job-related and consistent with business necessity.[61]

Just as with post-offer, pre-employment medical examinations/inquiries (see Q 6-26), any medical information obtained regarding the medical condition or history of any employee must be maintained in separate files and treated as a confidential. Employers are permitted to: (1) inform supervisors and managers regarding necessary restrictions on the work or duties of the employee and necessary accommodations; (2) inform first aid and safety personnel, when appropriate, if the disability might require emergency treatment; and (3) provide government officials investigating compliance with the ADA relevant information on request.[62]

6-28. Does the ADA permit an employer to offer voluntary medical examinations?

Yes. Employers may conduct voluntary medical examinations, including voluntary medical histories, which are part of an employee health program available to employees at the work site. Information obtained from such examinations is subject to the same confidentiality requirements (and exceptions) as noted in Q 6-26 and Q 6-27.[63]

6-29. Do drug tests constitute medical examinations under the ADA?

No. Drug tests do not constitute medical exams or inquiries under the ADA, and thus are not affected by the restrictions discussed in Q 6-26 through Q 6-28.[64]

The ADA also specifically allows that employers may prohibit the illegal use of drugs and the use of alcohol (or being under the influence of same) at the workplace, and may hold an employee who engages in the illegal use of drugs or who is an alcoholic to the same standards of performance and behavior as other employees.[65]

Prohibitions on smoking are also specifically permitted.[66] Employers should be aware that some state laws protect the rights of smokers.

NOTICE AND RECORDKEEPING REQUIREMENTS

6-30. Does the ADA require employers to post notices of its provisions?

Yes. The ADA provides that all covered entities must post notices in conspicuous places upon its premises, where notices to employees and applicants are customarily posted. The notices must set forth summaries of the ADA's provisions in an "accessible format," approved by the EEOC.[67] See the model ADA notice continued in Appendix A.

6-31. Does the ADA impose recordkeeping requirements upon employers?

Yes, the ADA imposes the same recordkeeping requirements as Title VII of the Civil Rights Act of 1964 (see Chapter 9).

Specifically, every covered entity subject to the ADA is required to:

1.   Make and keep records relevant to the determinations of whether unlawful employment practices have been or are being committed;

2.   Preserve such records for periods prescribed by the EEOC; and

3.   Make reports as required by the EEOC.[68]

The EEOC has prescribed that the following records must be retained for one year from the date when the record was made or personnel action taken, whichever is later:

1.   Personnel or employment records;

2.   Application forms;

3.   Records concerning hiring, promotion, demotion, transfer, layoff or termination, rates of pay, or other terms of compensation; and

4.   Records concerning selection for training or apprenticeship.[69]

Every covered entity that controls an apprenticeship program must maintain a chronological list of the names and addresses of all persons who have applied to participate in the apprenticeship program.[70] The list must contain the sex and race or ethnic group of each applicant. In lieu of the chronological list, a file of written applications may be kept, as long as the information on sex, race, and ethnicity is provided. The applicant list or application file must be kept for a period of two years from the date the application was received, or the period of a successful applicant's apprenticeship, whichever is longer.[71]

6-32. What are the recordkeeping requirements when a discrimination charge has been filed?

When a discrimination charge has been filed, records relating to the person making the complaint must be preserved until the final disposition of the discrimination charge. Likewise, records relating to all other persons seeking or holding similar positions must be kept until the final disposition of the charge. The final disposition of the charge means the date when the statutory period within which the aggrieved person may bring an action in a U.S. District Court expires. Whether an action is brought against an employer by the aggrieved person, the EEOC, or by the Attorney General, final disposition of the charge means the date on which such litigation is terminated.[72]

PROCEDURES FOR FILING AN ADA CLAIM

6-33. What are the procedures for filing an ADA claim?

The procedures for filing a claim of disability discrimination under the ADA are discussed in Q 6-34 through Q 6-36, and are the same as those for filing claims of discrimination (race, sex, religion, national origin, etc.) under Title VII.[73]

6-34. Does the ADA require that an individual file a "charge of discrimination" with the EEOC before filing a civil lawsuit in federal court against a covered entity?

Yes. Before an individual can file a civil lawsuit in federal court against a covered entity under the ADA, the individual must first exhaust his or her administrative remedies by filing a "charge of discrimination" with the EEOC.

A charge of discrimination filed with the EEOC must be made in writing and under oath or affirmation.[74] Each charge should contain the full name, address, and telephone number of the aggrieved person or the person making the charge on behalf of the aggrieved person. Additionally, it must contain a clear and concise statement of the facts that constitute the alleged unlawful employment practice, including pertinent dates.[75]

6-35. What is the time limit (statute of limitations) under the ADA?

FILING AN EEOC CHARGE

Generally, an individual must file a charge of disability discrimination with the EEOC within 180 days of the alleged discrimination.

If, however, the aggrieved individual has filed a charge with a state or local agency comparable to the EEOC, then the individual can file an EEOC charge within the earlier of: (1) 300 days after the alleged unlawful employment practice occurred; or (2) 30 days after receiving notice that the state or local agency has terminated its proceedings.[76]

It should be noted that in many states, a charge filed with the state agency is automatically and simultaneously filed with the EEOC.

PRIVATE CIVIL SUIT

The private civil suit must be filed in federal court within 90 days of receipt of the "right to sue" letter (See Q6-36).[77]

6-36. What is a "right to sue" letter?

Following the filing of an EEOC charge, the EEOC conducts an investigation to determine if "probable cause" exists to believe that discrimination has occurred.

If the EEOC determines that there is probable cause, the EEOC will attempt conciliation (settlement) of the matter.[78] If conciliation fails, but the EEOC elects not to file a lawsuit on behalf of the individual, the EEOC will issue a Notice of Right to Sue letter.

If the EEOC's investigation reveals no probable cause to believe that discrimination occurred, the EEOC will dismiss the charge and issue a "right to sue" letter.

The "right to sue" letter gives notice to the individual who filed the charge that the EEOC has terminated its investigation, and permits the individual to file a private civil suit.

The EEOC has a large backlog of cases, which means that it often takes over a year for the EEOC to complete its investigation of a charge. For this reason, it is not uncommon for charging parties to request a "right to sue" letter prior to the EEOC completing its investigation.

If such a request is made, the EEOC will issue the notice of right to sue once 180 days have passed since the date when the charge was filed.[79]

The EEOC may also issue the notice of right to sue prior to the expiration of the 180-day period if it determines that it will be unable to complete its investigation within 180 days of the date when the charge was filed.[80]

LITIGATING AN ADA CLAIM

6-37. What are the different types of ADA claims?

There are several different theories under which a qualified individual with a disability can pursue an ADA lawsuit, including disparate treatment, mixed motive, hostile environment (harassment), and disparate impact. Each type of claim will be discussed in turn.

6-38. What is a disparate treatment disability discrimination claim?

A lawsuit alleging disparate treatment because of an individual's disability is the most common type of claim under the ADA. Under this theory, the plaintiff asserts that the defendant employer intentionally treated him differently than non-disabled employees, because of his disability.

6-39. How will the courts analyze a disparate treatment claim?

In disparate treatment cases, the courts apply a three stage burden-shifting framework that was established by the Supreme Court in *McDonnell Douglas Corp. v. Green*,[81] and *Texas Dept. of Community Affairs v. Burdine*.[82]

Under the *McDonnell Douglas/Burdine* framework, a plaintiff must first establish a prima facie case of discrimination (see Q 6-40). If the plaintiff can produce such evidence, the burden of production shifts to the defendant employer to articulate a legitimate, nondiscriminatory reason for its actions (e.g., lack of qualifications, poor performance, violation of a company policy, financial considerations, etc.).

The defendant is not required to prove its nondiscriminatory reason; it need only produce evidence, which, if believed by the jury, would support a finding that unlawful discrimination was not the cause of the adverse employment action. Once the employer produces such evidence, then the burden shifts back to the plaintiff to prove that the legitimate reason put forth by the employer was not its true reason but rather a *pretext* for discrimination.

If the plaintiff is able to present evidence sufficient to establish all elements of the prima facie case and come forward with evidence that the employer's articulated legitimate business reason for its actions is merely a pretext for disability discrimination, then the case will proceed to trial before a jury.

The Supreme Court has held that evidence that casts doubt on the employer's explanation is enough to establish pretext and put the case before a jury.[83]

Although the burden of *production* may shift to the employer, at all times the burden of *proof* remains with the plaintiff.

6-40. How does a plaintiff establish a prima facie case of disability discrimination?

To establish the first stage, prima facie case of disability discrimination, a plaintiff can present either "direct" or "circumstantial" evidence.

Direct or "smoking gun" evidence is evidence, which, if believed, would demonstrate without inference that the defendant employer was in fact motivated by the plaintiff's disability in making the challenged employment decision. Direct evidence is rare.

For example, a decision maker's alleged statement that "John was demoted because he has diabetes and I didn't think he'd be able to meet the demands of the job" would be direct evidence. Contrast this with *Hopkins v. Electronic Data Systems Corporation*,[84] which held that a supervisor's reference to a plaintiff as "the mentally ill guy on Prozac that's going to shoot the place up" was not direct evidence of disability discrimination in the later decision to eliminate plaintiff's position.

Lacking direct evidence, a plaintiff must attempt to establish a prima facie case of disability discrimination through circumstantial evidence.

Though different courts have characterized the elements of a prima facie case of disability discrimination somewhat differently, a plaintiff is generally required to show that:

1. He or she is disabled, as defined by the ADA;

2. He or she is otherwise qualified for the position in question;

3. He or she suffered an adverse employment decision;

4. The employer knew or had reason to know of his or her disability; and

5. After rejection or termination, the position remained open or the disabled individual was replaced by a non-disabled individual.[85]

The fifth element may also be satisfied by showing that one or more "similarly situated" non-disabled employees were treated more favorably than the plaintiff.[86]

6-41. How does an ADA plaintiff demonstrate that the employer's stated legitimate business reason for the adverse employment action was a pretext for disability discrimination?

Assuming that a plaintiff is able to produce evidence sufficient to establish all elements of the prima facie case, and that the employer then articulates a legitimate business reason for the challenged decision, a plaintiff can raise an issue of *pretext*. This entitles the plaintiff to a jury trial, rather than having the case dismissed by the judge. The plaintiff must present evidence demonstrating that the employer's stated reason either: (1) had no basis in fact; (2) did not actually motivate the actions; or (3) was insufficient to motivate the actions.

6-42. What is a "mixed motive" discrimination claim?

Mixed motive claims are a subcategory of disparate treatment claims, in which the disabled employee claims that the employer's alleged discriminatory actions were based on mixed motives; that is, both lawful and unlawful factors played a role in the challenged employment decision.

The framework for mixed motive cases was originally established by the Supreme Court for cases under Title VII (see Chapter 9) and was subsequently altered by the Civil Rights Act of 1991.[87] Numerous courts have since held that the mixed motive analysis is applicable to ADA claims as well.[88]

In a case based on a mixed motive theory, the plaintiff must prove that his or her disability was a motivating part of the employer's decision. If a plaintiff demonstrates that an unlawful discriminatory reason was a motivating factor, then the employer is liable.[89]

On the other hand, if the employer demonstrates that it would have made the same decision regardless of the plaintiff's disability, the plaintiff's remedy will be limited.[90]

6-43. What is the most important difference between the McDonnell Douglas/Burdine framework and the mixed motive framework?

The difference between the *McDonnell Douglas/ Burdine* framework and the mixed motive framework is that the defendant in a mixed motive case bears the burden of persuasion on the issue of whether it would have reached the same decision absent consideration of the plaintiff's disability. Under the *McDonnell Douglas/ Burdine* framework, the defendant does not bear the burden of proving its legitimate business reason, but is merely required to articulate its legitimate business reason.

6-44. What is a hostile environment harassment claim?

Individual plaintiffs may bring claims for harassment on the basis of disability. The legal framework that governs disability harassment claims is generally the same as the framework created for sexual harassment claims under Title VII. See Chapter 5.

6-45. What is a disparate impact claim?

Disparate *impact* claims involve employer policies, practices, standards, and job qualifications that appear to be facially neutral but have a disproportionately large negative impact on disabled individuals as a group. Thus, to prove a disparate impact claim, plaintiffs must rely on statistical evidence.

By contrast, in a disparate treatment claim (see Q 6-38), the plaintiff must produce at least circumstantial evidence that the employer was in fact motivated by the plaintiff's disability to take the adverse action, which intentionally singled out or treated the plaintiff differently because of his or her disability.

6-46. How will the courts analyze a disparate impact claim?

The Supreme Court first recognized the disparate impact framework in the Title VII context.[91] Like disparate treatment claims, disparate impact claims are also subject to a three stage burden-shifting analysis.

To make out a prima facie case of disparate impact, the plaintiff must (1) identify a specific employment policy, standard, or practice of the employer; and (2) produce reliable statistical evidence of deficiencies sufficiently substantial to show that the identified policy, standard, or practice has caused the exclusion of employees or applicants because of their disabilities.[92]

If a plaintiff produces evidence sufficient to establish a prima facie case, then the defendant employer must state its legitimate, nondiscriminatory reason for the employment policy or practice, such as business necessity or job-relatedness. To qualify as serving a legitimate business interest, the challenged employment policy, standard, or practice need not be essential or indispensable to the employer's business, but must substantially promote the efficient operation of the business.

Once the employer has explained the business necessity or job-relatedness of the challenged practice, then the burden shifts back to the plaintiff to demonstrate either: (1) that the employer's explanation is a pretext for discrimination; or (2) that there exists an alternative employment practice that would also serve the employer's legitimate interests without the disparate impact.

A key component to the employer's defense to a disparate impact claim is to validate any test the employer is using that allegedly causes a disparate impact. Tests can be validated by demonstrating:

1. Content validity (they properly measure the skills needed for the job);

2.   Construct validity (they measure subjective qualities that are related to performance); or

3.   Criterion-related validity (there is a statistical relationship between the test scores and job performance).

DEFENSES TO ADA CLAIMS

6-47. What are some of the defenses that an employer generally may assert against an ADA discrimination claim?

There are numerous potential defenses to a claim that an employer or other covered entity has discriminated against an individual because of his or her disability.

The employer may be able to show that the individual asserting the ADA claim is not a "qualified individual with a disability." This may be demonstrated by showing that the individual (1) is not disabled enough (i.e., he or she does not have an impairment, has an impairment but it does not affect a major life activity, or has an impairment that may affect, but does not "substantially limit," a major life activity); or (2) is so disabled that he or she is unable to perform the essential functions of the job, even with any accommodation that would be reasonable.

The employer may also defend against an accusation of discrimination by demonstrating a nondiscriminatory reason for its actions. For example, if an employer is alleged to have discriminated against a qualified individual with a disability by terminating or demoting that individual, the employer could defend against the accusation by showing that it acted not because of the individual's disability but, because of such as the individual's unsatisfactory performance or violation of the employer's rules or policies (which are equally applied to all employees). Alternatively, the employer could claim that it had to eliminate the individual's position due to a reorganization of job functions or a reduction in force.

6-48. How else can an employer defend against a "disparate treatment" claim?

An employer can defend against a "disparate treatment" claim (i.e., a claim that it treated a qualified individual with a disability differently than a non-disabled employee or applicant) by showing that the challenged action was justified by a legitimate, nondiscriminatory business reason.[93]

6-49. How can an employer defend against a claim that it applied qualification standards to screen out qualified individuals with disabilities?

An employer can defend against a claim that its application of qualification standards, tests, or selection criteria screened out or tended to screen out, or otherwise denied a job or benefit to, individuals with disabilities by showing such qualification standards to be job-related and consistent with business necessity, and that such standards cannot be satisfied with reasonable accommodation.[94]

The term "qualification standards" may include a requirement that an individual not pose a "direct threat" to the health or safety of himself or herself or any other individuals in the workplace.[95] See Q 6-15.

6-50. How can an employer defend against a disparate impact claim?

An employer can defend against a disparate impact claim (a claim that some employment policy, practice, or requirement, while not intentionally discriminatory against qualified individuals with disabilities, is having an unintentional effect of adversely affecting them) by showing that the challenged policy, practice, or requirement (1) is job related; (2) is consistent with business necessity; and (3) cannot be accomplished with reasonable accommodation or some other policy that would still satisfy the employer's legitimate business need without having the discriminatory effect.[96]

6-51. How can an employer defend against a claim that it failed to make reasonable accommodation for the known disability of an employee?

An employer can defend against a claim of failure to accommodate by showing that the requested or necessary accommodation would impose an undue hardship on the operation of the employer's business.[97] See Q 6-20.

6-52. Do religious entities have any special defenses under the ADA?

Yes. Although religious entities are not exempt from ADA coverage, the ADA specifically notes that it does not prohibit a religious corporation, association, educational institution, or society from giving preference in employment to individuals of a particular religion. For example, a religious organization may require that all applicants and employees conform to the religious tenets of such organization.[98]

REMEDIES PROVIDED BY THE ADA

6-53. What remedies exist under the ADA?

As under Title VII, if an ADA plaintiff proves that the defendant employer intentionally engaged in or is intentionally engaging in unlawful discrimination, he or she may be awarded an injunction, reinstatement or hiring, and/or back pay.[99]

The prevailing party in ADA litigation, whether it be the plaintiff or the defendant employer, may be allowed, at the trial court's discretion, reasonable attorneys' fees and costs.[100]

In a mixed motive case, the plaintiff's remedies may be limited to declaratory or injunctive relief, attorney's fees, and costs if the employer proves that it would have taken the same action even in the absence of the impermissible motivating factor.[101]

BACK PAY

Back pay is routinely awarded as a remedy where the plaintiff was terminated from employment for an unlawful discriminatory reason. However, there are limitations on back pay. For example, back pay liability does not accrue from a date more than two years prior to the filing of a charge with the EEOC. Also, the back pay award is reduced by the amount of interim earnings or other amounts that the plaintiff could have earned through reasonable diligence.

FRONT PAY

Trial courts may also award front pay when appropriate. Front pay may extend until the plaintiff has failed to make reasonable efforts to secure substantially equivalent employment, or until the plaintiff obtained or was offered such employment. In some cases, front pay may extend until the plaintiff would have retired, if the court determines that the plaintiff cannot obtain comparable employment.

COMPENSATORY AND PUNITIVE DAMAGES

In addition, in cases involving unlawful intentional discrimination (i.e., not disparate impact), the plaintiff may recover compensatory and punitive damages under amendments made pursuant to the Civil Rights Act of 1991.[102]

Compensatory damages include future pecuniary losses, emotional pain, suffering, inconvenience, mental anguish, loss of enjoyment of life, and other non-pecuniary losses.[103]

Punitive damages may be recovered for intentional discrimination if the plaintiff demonstrates that the defendant engaged in a discriminatory practice with "malice or reckless indifference to the individual's rights."[104]

There are caps on compensatory and punitive damages, however, depending upon the size of the defendant employer. The sum of the amount of compensatory damages and the amount of punitive damages may not exceed the following (for each individual plaintiff): $50,000 for defendants with 15 to 100 employees; $100,000 for defendants with 101 to 200 employees; $200,000 for defendants with 201 to 500 employees; and $300,000 for defendants with more than 500 employees.[105]

THE REHABILITATION ACT OF 1973

6-54. Are there any other federal laws addressing disability discrimination in employment?

Yes. Title V of the Rehabilitation Act of 1973[106] prohibits disability discrimination in employment by (1) federal executive branch departments, agencies and instrumentalities, including the United States Postal Service; (2) private sector contractors and subcontractors who annually do more than $10,000 in business with the federal government; and (3) private sector recipients of federal financial assistance.[107]

Since the passage of the ADA, however, claims brought under the Rehabilitation Act against private sector employers are relatively rare.

6-55. Who is protected under the Rehabilitation Act?

Like the ADA, the Rehabilitation Act provides protections for "qualified individuals with disabilities." Because the ADA was patterned on some of the provisions of the Rehabilitation Act, the definition of qualified individual with a disability is the same under the two acts.[108] Likewise, court decisions interpreting the employment provisions of the Rehabilitation Act generally apply to the ADA, and vice versa.[109]

6-56. What does the Rehabilitation Act require with respect to federal executive branch agencies?

Section 501 of the Rehabilitation Act requires federal executive branch departments, agencies, and instrumentalities, including the U.S. Postal Service, to establish and annually update affirmative action program plans for the hiring, placement, and advancement of individuals with disabilities in each such agency, department, or instrumentality. Each such agency, department, or instrumentality must make annual reports concerning same to Congress.[110] Each federal agency must also maintain a complaint procedure, and must investigate complaints.[111]

6-57. Who enforces Section 501 of the Rehabilitation Act?

If, after filing a complaint with the employing federal agency, a federal employee is unsatisfied with the agency's investigation and resolution of the matter, the employee may request a hearing before an administrative law judge (ALJ) from the EEOC.[112] The employee may appeal the ALJ's ruling to the EEOC and/or to federal court.[113]

6-58. What does the Rehabilitation Act require of entities contracting with the federal government?

Section 503 of the Rehabilitation Act requires that any contract in excess of $10,000 entered into by any federal department or agency for the procurement of personal property and/or nonpersonal services, including construction, must contain a provision stating that the party contracting with the federal government will not discriminate against any qualified employee or applicant because of physical or mental disability, and will take affirmative action to employ, advance in employment, and otherwise treat qualified individuals with disabilities without discrimination in all employment practices.[114] Note that there is no threshold number of employees that the contractor must have in order to be covered by Section 503.

Section 503 of the Rehabilitation Act also requires that government contractors who have:

1.   50 or more employees; and

2.   A contract with the federal government of $50,000 or more to prepare and maintain an affirmative action program within 120 days of the commencement of a contract. Such affirmative action program must be reviewed and updated annually.[115]

The contents of such affirmative action programs are set forth in regulations promulgated by the Department of Labor's Office of Federal Contract Compliance Programs (OFCCP).[116]

6-59. Who enforces Section 503 of the Rehabilitation Act?

Any individual with a disability who believes that a contractor has failed or refused to comply with the nondiscrimination or affirmative action requirements under a contract with the federal government, as required by Section 503, may file a complaint with the Office of Federal Contract Compliance Programs (OFCCP). The complaint must be filed within 300 days of the date of the alleged violation.[117] The OFCCP may also initiate compliance reviews on its own to determine if a contractor is complying with Section 503.[118]

If an OFCCP investigation discovers an alleged violation of Section 503, the OFCCP will attempt conciliation with the contractor to resolve the matter.[119]

If conciliation fails, the OFCCP may refer the matter to the Solicitor of Labor for enforcement proceedings before an Administrative Law Judge.[120]

Penalties may include back pay and other make-whole relief for aggrieved individuals, withholding of contract payments from the government to the contractor, termination of the contract, and debarment from receiving future contracts.[121]

6-60. What does the Rehabilitation Act require of recipients of federal financial assistance?

Section 504 of the Rehabilitation Act provides that no qualified individual with a disability may, solely because of his or her disability, be excluded from participation in, be denied the benefits of, or be subjected to discrimination, under any "program or activity" receiving federal financial assistance.[122]

The term "program or activity" is defined to include corporations, partnerships, sole proprietorships, and other private organizations that receive federal financial assistance, as well as state and local governments, agencies, and institutions of higher education.[123]

Section 504 specifically states that "the standards used to determine whether this section has been violated in a complaint alleging employment discrimination under this section shall be the standards applied under Title I of the Americans with Disabilities Act."[124]

Section 504 also imposes certain requirements with respect to filing reports with the Department of Labor.[125] Again, there is no threshold number of employees that an entity must have in order to be covered by Section 504.

6-61. Who enforces Section 504 of the Rehabilitation Act?

The Department of Labor's regulations implementing Section 504 require recipients of federal financial assistance to adopt internal review procedures to address complaints of disability discrimination under the Rehabilitation Act.[126]

Such complaints must be raised within 180 days of the alleged discrimination.[127] If the matter is not resolved to the complaining party's satisfaction within 60 days, the complainant may proceed to file a written complaint with the Assistant Secretary of the Department of Labor's Employment and Training Administration (ETA).[128] The ETA will investigate the matter, and, if necessary, attempt conciliation.

If conciliation fails, the ETA may refer the matter to the Department of Justice for enforcement or seek a hearing before the Secretary of Labor.[129]

Remedies for violations of Section 504 may include suspension, termination, or refusal to grant or continue federal financial assistance, as well as remedies available under state or local law.[130]

CHAPTER ENDNOTES

1. 42 U.S.C. §12101(b).
2. 42 U.S.C. §12111(5).
3. 42 U.S.C. §12111(2).
4. See 42 U.S.C. §12202.
5. See *Board of Trustees of University of Alabama v. Garrett*, 531 U.S. 356 (2001).
6. 42 U.S.C. §12112(c).
7. 42 U.S.C. §12112(c)(2)(C).
8. 42 U.S.C. §12112(c)(2)(B).
9. 42 U.S.C. §12111(4).
10. See, e.g., *Birchem v. Knights of Columbus*, 116 F.3d 310, 312-13 (8th Cir. 1997); *Johnson v. City of Saline*, 151 F.3d 564, 567 (6th Cir. 1998); *Aberman v. J. Abouchar & Sons, Inc.*, 160 F.3d 1148, 1150 (7th Cir. 1998).
11. 42 U.S.C. §12111(4).
12. 42 U.S.C. §12117(a).
13. 42 U.S.C. §12116.
14. 42 U.S.C. §12117(a).
15. 42 U.S.C. §12111(8); 29 CFR §1630.2(m).
16. 42 U.S.C. §12102 (2).
17. 29 CFR §1630.2(h).
18. 42 U.S.C. §12114(a); 29 CFR §1630.3(a).
19. 42 U.S.C. §12114(b); 29 CFR §1630.3(b)(1), 29 CFR §1630.3(b).
20. 42 U.S.C. §12114(b)(3); 29 CFR §1630.3(b)(3), emphasis supplied.
21. 29 CFR §1630.3(d)(3).
22. 29 CFR §1630.3(d)(1), 29 CFR §1630.3(e).
23. 29 CFR §1630.3(d)(2).
24. *Minott v. Port Authority of N.Y.*, 116 F.Supp.2d 513, 525 (S.D.N.Y. 2000); *Conley v. United Parcel Service*, 88 F.Supp.2d 16, 19-20 (E.D.N.Y. 2000); *Gudenkauf v. Stauffer Communications, Inc.*, 922 F.Supp. 465, 474 (D. Kan. 1996).
25. Appendix to 29 CFR Part 1630 at § 1630.2(j)(2)(ii).
26. Appendix to 29 CFR Part 1630 at § 1630.2(j).
27. 29 CFR §1630.2(i).
28. See, e.g., *McKay v. Toyota Motor Mfg., U.S.A., Inc.*, 110 F.3d 369 (6th Cir. 1997) (lifting); *Lowe v. Angelo's Italian Foods, Inc.*, 87 F.3d 1170 (10th Cir. 1996) (lifting); *Oesterling v. Walters*, 760 F.2d 859, 861 (8th Cir. 1985) (standing).
29. See, e.g., *Robinson v. Global Marine Drilling Co.*, 101 F.3d 35 (5th Cir. 1996) (climbing not a major life activity); *Matthews v. Reno*, 92 F.3d 1193 (9th Cir. 1996) (kneeling, twisting, and making rapid movements not major life activities); *Reeves v. Johnson Controls World Serv., Inc.*, 140 F.3d 144 (2d Cir. 1998) (general mobility, in context of mental disorder, not major life activity); *Miller v. Airborne Express*, 1999 U.S. Dist. LEXIS 811 (N.D. Tex. 1998) (crawling, kneeling, squatting, climbing not major life activities).
30. 29 CFR §1630.2(j)(1).
31. 29 CFR §1630.2(j)(2).
32. 29 CFR §1630.2(j)(3).
33. *Sutton v. United Air Lines, Inc.*, 527 U.S. 471; *Murphy v. United Parcel Service, Inc.*, 527 U.S. 516.
34. 29 CFR §1630.2(k).
35. 29 CFR §1630.2(l). See, e.g., *Pritchard v. Southern Co. Services*, 92 F.3d 1130 (11th Cir. 1996) (the fact that employer placed employee on one month disability leave created genuine issue of material fact regarding whether plaintiff had record of impairment and/or was regarded as impaired).

36. 29 CFR §1630.2(n).
37. 42 U.S.C. §12111(8); 29 CFR §1630.2(n)(3).
38. 42 U.S.C. §12111(3); 29 CFR §1630.2(r).
39. 29 CFR §1630.2(r).
40. 42 U.S.C. §12111(9); 29 CFR §1630.2(o).
41. 42 U.S.C. §12112(b)(5)(A).
42. See, e.g., *Bratten v. SSI Services, Inc.*, 185 F.3d 625 (6th Cir. 1999).
43. 29 CFR §1630.2(o)(3).
44. 29 CFR §1630.9.
45. 42 U.S.C. §12201(d).
46. 29 CFR §1630.9(d).
47. 42 U.S.C. §12112(b)(5)(A).
48. 42 U.S.C. §12111(10); 29 CFR §1630.2(p).
49. Appendix to 29 CFR Part 1630 at Sec. 1630.2(r).
50. *Kralik v. Durbin*, 130 F.3d 76, 83 (3rd Cir. 1997); *Eckles v. Consolidated Rail Corp.*, 94 F.3d 1041, 1048 (7th Cir. 1996); *Burns v. Coca-Cola Enterprises, Inc.*, 222 F.3d 247, 257 (6th Cir. 2000).
51. EEOC Compliance Manual, Vol. II, Section 902 (issued 3/01/99).
52. 42 U.S.C. §12112(a); 29 CFR §1630.4.
53. 42 U.S.C. §12112(b); 29 CFR §1630.5 through 29 CFR §1630.11.
54. 42 U.S.C. §12113(b); 29 CFR §1630.2(q).
55. 42 U.S.C. §12203; 29 CFR §1630.12.
56. 42 U.S.C. §12112(d)(2); 29 CFR §1630.13.
57. 42 U.S.C. §12112(d)(2); 29 CFR §1630.14(a).
58. 2000 U.S. App. LEXIS 3660 (6th Cir. March 10, 2000).
59. 42 U.S.C. §12112(d)(3); 29 CFR §1630.14(b).
60. 42 U.S.C. §12112(d)(3)(B); 29 CFR §1630.14(b)(1).
61. 42 U.S.C. §12112(d)(4); 29 CFR §1630.14(c).
62. 29 CFR §1630.14(c)(1).
63. 42 U.S.C. §12112(d)(4)(B); 29 CFR §1630.14(d).
64. 42 U.S.C. §12114(d); 29 CFR §1630.16(c).
65. 42 U.S.C. §12114(c); 29 CFR §1630.16(b).
66. 29 CFR §1630.16(d).
67. 42 U.S.C. §12115.
68. See 42 U.S.C. §12117, referencing 42 U.S.C. §2000e-8(c).
69. 29 CFR §1602.14.
70. 29 CFR 1602.20(b).
71. 29 CFR 1602.21(a).
72. 29 CFR §1602.14.
73. See 42 U.S.C. §12117(a).
74. 42 U.S.C. §2000e-5(b); 29 CFR §1601.9.
75. 29 CFR §1601.12(a).
76. 42 U.S.C. §2000e-5(e).
77. 42 U.S.C. §2000e-5(b).
78. 42 U.S.C. §2000e-16(c).
79. 29 CFR §1601.28(a)(1).
80. 29 CFR §1601.28(a)(2).
81. 411 U.S. 792 (1973).
82. 450 U.S. 248 (1981).
83. *Reeves v. Sanderson Plumbing Products, Inc.*, 530 U.S. 133, 120 S.Ct. 2097 (2000).
84. 196 F.3d 655 (6th Cir. 1999).

85. See, e.g., *Hopkins v. Electronic Data Systems Corp.*, 196 F.3d 655, 660 (6th Cir. 1999); *Monette v. Electronic Data Systems Corp.*, 90 F.3d 1173 (6th Cir. 1996).

86. Id. See also, *Parker v. Columbia Pictures Industries*, 204 F.3d 326 (2nd Cir. 2000) (alternatively describing final element of prima facie case as requiring evidence that the defendant employer either refused to make a reasonable accommodation needed by the plaintiff or took the adverse action because of the plaintiff's disability).

87. See *Price Waterhouse v. Hopkins*, 490 U.S. 228 (1989).

88. See, e.g., *Parker v. Columbia Pictures Industries*, 204 F.3d 326 (2nd Cir. 2000) (cataloging such cases).

89. 42 U.S.C. §2000e-2(m).

90. 42 U.S.C. §2000e-5(g)(2)(B).

91. *Griggs v. Duke Power Co.*, 401 U.S. 424 (1971).

92. *Wards Cove Packing Co., Inc. v. Atonio*, 490 U.S. 642 (1989); *Watson v. Fort Worth Bank and Trust*, 487 U.S. 977 (1988); see also, 42 U.S.C. §2000e-2(k).

93. 29 CFR §1630.15(a).

94. 42 U.S.C. §12113(a); 29 CFR §1630.15(b).

95. 42 U.S.C. §12113(b); 29 CFR §1630.15(b)(2).

96. 29 CFR §1630.15(d).

97. 29 CFR §1630.15(d).

98. 42 U.S.C. §12113(c); 29 CFR §1630.16(a).

99. 42 U.S.C. §12117(a), referencing 42 U.S.C. §2000e-5(g)(1).

100. 42 U.S.C. §12205.

101. 42 U.S.C. §2000e-5(g)(2)(B).

102. See 42 U.S.C. §1981a(a)(1).

103. 42 U.S.C. §1981a(b)(3).

104. 42 U.S.C. §1981a(b)(1).

105. 42 U.S.C. §1981(b)(3).

106. 29 U.S.C. §§701-796.

107. 29 U.S.C. §§791, 793, 794.

108. 29 U.S.C. §§705(9), 705(20).

109. 29 U.S.C. §§791(g), 793(d), 794(d).

110. 29 U.S.C. §§791(b), (d).

111. 29 CFR §§1614.104 through 1614.104.108.

112. 29 CFR §§1614.108 to 1614.108.109.

113. 29 CFR §1614.110.

114. 29 U.S.C. §793(a); 41 CFR §60-741.5(a).

115. 41 CFR §§60-741.40.

116. See 41 CFR §60-741.44.

117. 29 U.S.C. §793(b); 41 CFR §60-741.61.

118. 41 CFR §60-741.60.

119. 41 CFR §60-741.62.

120. 41 CFR §§60-741.61, 60-741.61.65.

121. 41 CFR §§60-741.65 through 60-741.66.

122. 29 U.S.C. §794(a).

123. 29 U.S.C. §794(b).

124. 29 U.S.C. §794(d); 29 CFR §§32.12 32.15.

125. 29 CFR §32.44.

126. 29 CFR §32.45(b).

127. 29 CFR §32.45(b).

128. 29 CFR §32.45(c).

129. 29 CFR §§32.46 to 32.47.

130. 29 CFR §32.46.

Chapter 7

Affirmative Action

GENERALLY

7-1. What is affirmative action?

7-2. When was affirmative action mandated by law?

7-3. What government agency has enforcement authority for affirmative action?

7-4. Does the OFCCP have the same authority as the Equal Employment Opportunity Commission to investigate discrimination claims?

7-5. What is the scope of the OFCCP's authority?

7-6. Are all companies required to comply with Executive Order 11246, Section 503 of the Rehabilitation Act and VEVRA?

REQUIREMENTS

7-7. What is required of federal contractors and subcontractors who meet the basic jurisdictional threshold under Executive Order 11246?

7-8. What is required of federal contractors and subcontractors who meet the basic jurisdictional threshold under Section 503 of the Rehabilitation Act and VEVRA?

7-9. Must all government contractors develop a written affirmative action plan (AAP) for minorities and women and for disabled individuals and veterans?

7-10. Must all subcontractors that do business with federal government contractors comply with the affirmative action obligations?

7-11. If only one facility of a large corporation with several facilities enters into a covered federal contract, must all of the company's facilities develop and maintain a written affirmative action plan?

7-12. What are the requirements for a written Affirmative Action Program under Executive Order 11246?

7-13. What are the requirements for a written Affirmative Action Program under Section 503 of the Rehabilitation Act and VEVRA plans?

GENERALLY

7-1. What is affirmative action?

Affirmative action connotes positive steps a company takes to identify and eliminate impediments to equal employment opportunity.

7-2. When was affirmative action mandated by law?

In 1965, President Johnson issued Executive Order 11246 prohibiting federal contractors and subcontractors (covered contractors) from discriminating on the basis of race, religion, color and national origin. The Executive Order also required covered contractors to engage in "affirmative action" to employ and advance minorities in employment. The Executive Order was amended in 1967 to include the protection of women.

A few years later, similar protection was afforded to disabled individuals and Vietnam-era veterans. Section 503 of the Rehabilitation Act of 1973 (Section 503) prohibits covered contractors from discriminating against disabled individuals and requires them to take affirmative action to employ, advance, and make reasonable accommodation for the disabled.[1]

The Vietnam Era Veterans' Readjustment Assistance Act of 1974 (VEVRA) applies the affirmative action obligations of federal

contractors and subcontractors to qualified disabled veterans and veterans of the Vietnam era.[2] In 1998, the Veterans Employment Opportunity Act (VEOA) amended VEVRA to expand the protected class to include any "veterans who served on active duty during a war or in a campaign or expedition for which a campaign badge has been authorized."[3] Thus, veterans of the Persian Gulf War, among other campaigns, are protected. (Note, however, that the Office of Federal Contract Compliance Programs (OFCCP) still accepts affirmative action programs that address only disabled and Vietnam-era veterans because, to date, no regulations have been finalized requiring a change in the VEVRA affirmative Action programs.)

7-3. What government agency has enforcement authority for affirmative action?

The United States Department of Labor's Office of Federal Contract Compliance Programs (OFCCP). The OFCCP's regulatory authority to enforce Executive Order 11246 with respect to minorities and women is found at 41 CFR §60-1 et seq. The Agency's authority to enforce VEVRA can be found at 41 CFR §60-250 et seq., and its authority to enforce Section 503 can be found at 41 CFR §60-741 et seq.

7-4. Does the OFCCP have the same authority as the Equal Employment Opportunity Commission to investigate discrimination claims?

Yes. However, employers are cautioned not to confuse the Equal Employment Opportunity Commission's (EEOC) enforcement powers with those of the OFCCP. The EEOC enforces several federal non-discrimination laws. Either the EEOC or an individual may enforce his rights under these laws. In contrast, individuals do not have a right to bring a private cause of action under Executive Order 11246. However, an individual may file a complaint alleging discrimination with the OFCCP within 180 days of the alleged violation.[4] The complaint can be filed with the OFCCP in Washington, D.C. or with any regional or area office. The OFCCP's authority also allows it to accept complaints under VEVRA and Section 503 as well.[5] Typically, if a complaint is filed by only one individual, the OFCCP will refer it to the EEOC to be processed under Title VII. Significantly, the OFCCP is not required to wait for an individual to file a complaint to investigate discrimination. Once a company becomes a covered federal contractor or subcontractor, it is subject to the OFCCP's investigatory authority.

7-5. What is the scope of the OFCCP's authority?

INVESTIGATE AND AUDIT

The OFCCP is an investigatory agency that has authority to audit any covered non-exempt contractor's employment practices and policies and during such audit determine that the contractor has discriminated against applicants and/or employees. If the OFCCP believes that discrimination has occurred, it will first try to resolve the matter through informal means.[6] If informal means of resolution fail, the regulations authorize the OFCCP to recommend that the contractor be prosecuted. The OFCCP will recommend to the Solicitor of Labor that a complaint be issued. If the Solicitor confirms that a violation has occurred, the OFCCP files an Administrative Complaint before an Administrative Law Judge (ALJ). A hearing is held and the ALJ will issue "Recommended Findings, Conclusions and Decision."[7] Ultimately, the contractor may appeal the administrative decision to federal court.[8]

The OFCCP also has authority to review a contractor's written affirmative action program (AAP), assuming the contractor is required to draft a written AAP. If the OFCCP finds the AAP not in compliance with the regulations it will attempt to resolve the matter by informal means. If those means do not succeed, the OFCCP can refer the case to the Office of the Solicitor of Labor to proceed with enforcement through the administrative process as outlined above.

REMEDIES

The OFCCP has no authority to seek compensatory damages or punitive damages. Rather the OFCCP has authority to seek only actual damages, such as back pay, front pay, and reinstatement.[9] In addition to the authority to seek actual damages, the OFCCP has authority to seek the imposition of sanctions such as declaring a contractor ineligible to receive further government contracts and to interrupt progress payments on existing contracts.[10]

7-6. Are all companies required to comply with Executive Order 11246, Section 503 of the Rehabilitation Act, and VEVRA?

No. Only certain government contractors and subcontractors are covered.

Contractors or subcontractors that have contracts with the federal government (including any federally assisted construction

contracts or subcontracts) in any 12-month period having an aggregate value exceeding $10,000 are subject to the non-discrimination mandates of Executive Order 11246 and Section 503 of the Rehabilitation Act. In addition, those covered contractors are required to engage in affirmative action. Also covered is a contractor or subcontractor that has Government bills of lading, which serves as a depository of federal funds in any amount, or is a financial institution which is an issuing and paying agent for United States savings bonds and saving notes in any amount.

Federal contractors and subcontractors that have federal contracts in excess of $25,000 during any 12-month period are subject to the nondiscrimination and affirmative action obligations set forth in 41 CFR §60-250.

REQUIREMENTS

7-7. What is required of federal contractors and subcontractors who meet the basic jurisdictional threshold under Executive Order 11246?

Covered contractors and subcontractors must include in each of their covered federal subcontracts the equal opportunity clause set forth at 41 CFR §60-1.4(a). The clause itself contains 7 clauses which can be incorporated by reference rather than quoted verbatim.[11]

All covered contractors and subcontractors with 50 or more employees annually must file a Standard Form 100 (EEO-1) with the Joint Reporting Committee on or before September 30.[12]

All covered contractors and subcontractors must "ensure that facilities provided for employees are provided in such a manner that segregation on the basis of race, color, religion, sex or national origin cannot result."[13] Prior to the regulatory amendments effective on September 18, 1997, a contractor also had to submit a written certification that it did not currently and would not in the future maintain segregated facilities. The certification is no longer required.

Contractors and subcontractors are required to keep any personnel or employment record made or kept by a contractor for a period of not less than two years from the date of making the record or the personnel action involved, whichever occurs later.[14] Note, however, that the record retention period is reduced to one

year if the contractor or subcontractor has fewer than 150 employees or does not have a government contract of at least $150,000.

Also, contractor establishments required to develop a written
affirmative action program (AAP) must maintain its current AAP
and supporting documentation as well as its preceding AAP and
documentation. For any such record maintained, the contractor
must be able to identify the gender, race, and ethnicity of each
employee and, where possible, the gender, race, and ethnicity of
each applicant.[15]

Covered contractors must expressly state in solicitations or
advertisements for employees placed by or on behalf of the covered
contractor that "all qualified applicants will receive consideration
for employment without regard to race, color, sex or national
origin."[16]

Covered contractors and subcontractors are required to post
in conspicuous places, available to employees and applicants for
employment, notices containing very specific language.[17] The
OFCCP has available a "combined" poster which contains all of the
language necessary to meet both the requirements of the OFCCP
and the EEOC. The poster can be obtained by going to www.dol.gov/
dol/esa/public/regs/compliance/posters/eeo.htm, or by calling
one of OFCCP's regional or area offices or the national office in
Washington, D.C. (See Appendix A.)

7-8. What is required of federal contractors and subcontractors who meet the basic jurisdictional threshold under Section 503 of the Rehabilitation Act and VEVRA?

Contractors and subcontractors subject to the affirmative
action obligations under Section 503 of the Rehabilitation Act
must include in all of their covered subcontracts or purchase
orders six affirmative action clauses.[18] Similarly, VEVRA requires
covered contractors and subcontractors to include 13 affirmative
action clauses concerning veterans in their subcontracts.[19] Contractors, however, are not required to quote the clauses verbatim,
but instead can incorporate them into a contract of purchase order
by citing to 41 CFR §60-741.5(a) and 41 CFR §60-250.4.[20]

Both VEVRA and Section 503 require contractors to invite
applicants and employees to self identify as an individual with a
disability and/or as a veteran. The invitation to self identify given
to applicants must be given post-offer but before the applicant

begins work. (Model VEVRA and Section 503 identification invitation forms can be found at Appendix A and B to OFCCP's regulations.)

Covered contractors must notify each labor union or representative of workers with which the contractor has a contract or collective bargaining agreement that it is bound by the terms of the Rehabilitation Act and VEVRA and, moreover, that the contractor is committed to take affirmative action in the employment and advancement of physically and mentally disabled individuals and veterans.[21]

Contractors must post in conspicuous places a notice that the contractor is obligated to take affirmative action to employ and advance in employment qualified employees and applicants who are veterans and/or have disabilities.[22] This obligation includes a requirement that contractors take action to insure that applicants and employees are informed of the posting's content. (For example, a contractor may need to lower a notice so that it may be read by someone in a wheelchair.)

Covered contractors and sub-contractors must keep any personnel or employment record made or kept by the contractor for a period of not less than two years from the date of making the record or the personnel action involved, whichever occurs later. However, the record retention period is reduced to one year if the contractor has fewer than 150 employees or does not have a government contract of at least $150,000.[23]

Covered contractors required to develop a written affirmative action plan (AAP) for individuals with disabilities and veterans must make available for inspection to any employee or applicant the full AAP upon request. (Note that the contractor is not obligated to provide a copy of the AAP.) As part of this obligation a contractor must post a notice identifying the location and hours during which employees and applicants may have access to the written AAP.[24]

Contractors subject to the VEVRA regulations have two additional obligations. Contractors must list "all employment openings" with the State Unemployment Security Commission. The only positions exempt from this requirement are: positions which are to be filled exclusively from internal sources; positions lasting three days or less; executive and top management positions; or positions that have referral arrangements.

Finally, all covered contractors must annually file a Federal Contractor Veteran's Employment Report (VETS-100) with the Department of Labor's Office of Veterans Employment and Training. In this report contractors provide the number of current employees who are Vietnam era or special disabled veterans, the number of new employees who are special disabled veterans or veterans of the Vietnam era as well as the total number of new employees hired during the annual period covered by the VETS-100 Report. (The Labor Department is revising the VETS-100 regulations to reflect the changes resulting from the 1998 Veterans Employment Opportunities Act to require the reporting of all "other eligible veterans.")

7-9. Must all government contractors develop a written affirmative action plan (AAP) for minorities and women and for disabled individuals and veterans?

No. Only non-construction (supply and service) contractors with 50 or more employees and with a government contract of $50,000 or more must develop a written AAP within 120 days of commencement of a federal contract. In addition, a contractor with 50 or more employees that serves as a depository of federal government funds in any amount or that is a financial institution which is an issuing and paying agent for U.S. savings bond in any amount must develop a written AAP.

Construction contractors and subcontractors that hold any federal or federally assisted construction contracts in excess of $10,000 have different affirmative action obligations. There is no requirement for a construction contractor to prepare a written AAP. However, covered contractors must follow 16 "affirmative action steps" outlined at 41 CFR Part 60-4. Thereafter the AAP annually must be updated so long as the contract continues.[25]

7-10. Must all subcontractors that do business with federal government contractors comply with the affirmative action obligations?

No. The regulations only cover subcontractors if they are "necessary" to the performance of the federal contract.[26]

7-11. If only one facility of a large corporation with several facilities enters into a covered federal contract, must all of the company's facilities develop and maintain a written affirmative action plan?

Yes. A covered contractor or subcontractor must develop a written affirmative action program (AAP) for "each of its establishments."[27] Although the term "establishment" is not defined in the regulations, contractors traditionally have prepared separate AAPs for "establishments" (i.e., plants or offices) located in different geographical areas.

Each employee in a covered contractors' workforce must be included in an AAP. Each employee must be included in the AAP of the establishment at which he works. The only exceptions are as follows:

1. Employees who work at establishments other than that of the manager to whom they report must be included in the AAP of their manager.

2. Employees who work at an establishment where the contractor employs fewer than 50 employees may be included under one of the following three options: (a) in an AAP which covers just that establishment; (b) in the AAP which covers the location of the personnel function which supports the establishment; or (c) in the AAP which covers the location of the official to whom they report.

3. Employees for whom selection decisions are made at a higher level establishment within the organization must be included in the AAP of the establishment where the selection decision is made.

4. If a contractor wishes to establish an AAP other than by establishment, the contractor may reach agreement with OFCCP on the development and use of AAPs based on functional or business units.[28]

7-12. What are the requirements for a written Affirmative Action Program under Executive Order 11246?

A complaint Affirmative Action Program (AAP) under Executive Order 11246 consists of two primary statistical analyses sections. The first step in preparing a complaint AAP is for the contractor to prepare an "organizational profile." The profile is "a depiction of the staffing pattern within the establishment." To prepare the profile a contractor must either use the "organizational display" or the "workforce analysis."[29]

WORKFORCE ANALYSIS

A workforce analysis is defined as a "listing for each job title as appears in . . . collective bargaining agreements or payroll records ranked from the lowest paid to the highest paid within each department."

ORGANIZATIONAL DISPLAY

The organizational display "is a detailed graphical or tabular chart, text, spreadsheet or similar presentation of the contractor's organizational structure." The display must include: (1) the name of the organizational unit; (2) the job title, race, ethnicity and gender of the unit supervisor (assuming the unit has a supervisor); (3) the total number of male and female incumbents and; (4) the total number of male and female incumbents in each of the following groups: Blacks, Hispanics, Asians/Pacific Islanders, and American Indians/Alaskan Natives. A sample organizational display can be found in the Federal Register.[30]

JOB GROUP ANALYSIS

The second step in preparing a complaint AAP is to perform a job group analysis. To perform the analysis, a contractor must begin by identifying and grouping together job titles within the contractor's establishment with similar content, wage rates, and promotional opportunities. Note that these "job groups" are different from the job titles that are used in the contractor's payroll records. Identifying job groups requires a contractor to analyze each job title according to the criteria set forth above and then group together the titles that share similar content, wage rates, and opportunities. For example, if "scientists" and "researchers" have similar job content (duties and responsibilities), wage rates, and opportunities, they should be grouped together into a job group called "researchers" or "scientists." Smaller employers (contractors with fewer than 150 employees) may prepare a job group analysis that utilizes the EEO-1 categories as their job groups (i.e., officials and managers, professionals, technicians, sales, office and clerical, craft workers (skilled) operatives (semi-skilled), laborers (unskilled), and service workers).[31]

PLACEMENT OF INCUMBENTS IN JOB GROUPS

After the contractor has completed its job group analysis by providing the job titles within the establishment, it must "separately state the percentage of minorities and the percentage of women it employees in each job group."[32]

Two-Factor Availability Analysis

Contractors must determine the availability of minorities and women qualified to be employed in each job group.[33]

To determine the availability of minorities and women for each job group, the contractor must consider the following two factors:

1. The percentage of minorities or women with requisite skills in the reasonable recruitment area (the geographical area from which the contractor normally seeks or reasonably could seek to fill the jobs in question). This analysis requires the contractor to gather data from external sources, such as the Bureau of the Census, U.S. Department of Commerce, Consumer Information. Each state also has information available at the State Unemployment Security Commission.

2. The percentage of minorities or women among those promotable, transferable, and trainable within the contractor's organization. This analysis requires the contractor to analyze its own workforce by calculating the availability of employees promotable, transferable or trainable for movement in the coming year from other job groups within the establishment into the particular job group under review.

Comparing Incumbency to Availability

The contractor must compare the percentage of minorities and women in each job group determined under 41 CFR §60-2.13 with the availability of those job groups as determined by 41 CFR §60-2.14. If the percentage of minorities or women employed in a particular job group "is less than would reasonably be expected given their availability percentage in that particular job group, the contractor must establish a placement goal." This exercise traditionally has been referred to as underutilization analysis.[34]

Placement Goals

Where "underutilization" is identified (i.e., when the percentage of minorities or women employed in a particular job group is less than reasonably expected given their availability percentage) placement goals must be established. "Placement goals serve as objectives or targets reasonably attainable by means of applying every good faith effort to make all aspects of the entire Affirmative Action Program work."[35]

It should be noted that the regulations specifically state that "placement goals may not be rigid and inflexible quotas, which must be met, nor are they to be considered as either a ceiling or a floor for the employment of particular groups. Quotas are expressly forbidden."

REQUIRED NARRATIVE SECTIONS FOR EXECUTIVE ORDER 11246 AAPs

A compliant AAP must also contain the following narrative portions.[36]

1. *Designation of responsibility.* The contractor must assign responsibility for the implementation of the AAP to an individual in the organization who has the "authority, resources, support of and access to top management to ensure the effective implementation of the affirmative action program."

2. *Identification of problem areas.* The contractor must perform "analysis of its total employment process to determine whether and where impediments to equal employment opportunity exist." At a minimum the contractor must evaluate:

    (a) The workforce by organizational units and job group to determine whether there are problems of minority or female utilization;

    (b) Personnel activity to determine whether there are selection disparities;

    (c) Compensation systems to determine whether there are gender, race, or ethnicity-based disparities;

    (d) Selection, recruitment, referral, and other personnel procedures to determine whether they result in disparities in the employment or advancement of minorities or women; and

    (e) Any other areas that might impact the success of the affirmative action program.

3. *Action-oriented programs.* The contractor must develop and execute programs designed to correct any problem areas identified and to attain established placements goals.

4. *Internal audit and reporting system.* The contractor must develop and implement a system that periodically measures the effectiveness of the total affirmative action program.

EQUAL OPPORTUNITY SURVEY

Regulations require the OFCCP, each year, to designate a substantial portion of all non-construction contractors to prepare and file an Equal Opportunity Survey (Survey). The Survey requires contractors to provide data by race and gender on its applicants, hires, promotions, terminations, compensation, and tenure. The stated purpose for requiring contractors to prepare and file the Survey is to allow "the agency to more effectively identify contractor establishments for further evaluation."[37]

7-13. What are the requirements for a written Affirmative Action Program under Section 503 of the Rehabilitation Act and VEVRA plans?

Covered contractors are required to develop written affirmative action programs (AAPs) with 10 major parts.[38] A contractor can combine its VEVRA and Section 503 AAPs.[39]

The 10 major components of a complaint AAP under VEVRA and Section 503 are as follows:

1. The AAP must contain an Equal Employment Opportunity Policy that sets forth the company's obligation to provide equal employment and advancement opportunities to all individuals. The company must also state that it is obligated to make reasonable accommodations for qualified individuals with known disabilities and that it prohibits harassment.

2. The contractor must state that it ensures its personnel processes provide for careful and systematic consideration of the job qualifications of applicants and employees with known disabilities and for veterans. The company periodically must review its processes and

make necessary modifications to insure that the obligations are carried out.

3. The company must state that it reviews all physical and mental job qualification requirements with management supervisors to ensure that, to the extent qualification requirements screen out qualified disabled individuals or veterans, they are job-related and consistent with business necessity and the safe performance of the job. The contractor must also indicate a time schedule used to review the qualifications (i.e., annually, or as a new job qualification requirement is established, or when new equipment is installed, or any other time schedule stated by the contractor).

4. A contractor must state that it makes reasonable accommodations to the known physical or mental limitations of all otherwise qualified individuals with a disability (unless it can demonstrate the accommodation would impose an undue hardship). A contractor must also set forth the name, title, address, and phone number of the person at the company an employee may contact to request an accommodation.

5. The contractor must develop and implement procedures to ensure that its employees with disabilities and veterans are not harassed because of a disability or veterans status.

6. Contractors must set forth the steps taken to disseminate its policy on equal opportunity and affirmative action to external sources. For example, the company may state that it enlists the assistance of recruiting sources in seeking qualified individuals with disabilities and/or veterans.

7. The company must take steps to ensure greater employee cooperation and participation in the company's efforts with respect to disabled individuals and veterans. For example, a company may state that it publicizes its equal opportunity policy and anti-harassment policy in its company newspaper.

8. The company must design and implement an audit and reporting system that: (a) measures the effective-

ness of the company's AAP; (b) indicates any need for remedial action; (c) determines the degree to which the company's objectives are being attained; (d) determines whether individuals with known disabilities and veterans have had the opportunity to participate in all company-sponsored educational training, recreational and social activities; and (e) measures the company's compliance with the AAP's specific obligations.

9. The company must designate a person having overall responsibility for the affirmative action program.

10. Finally, the company must state that it trains all personnel involved in the recruitment, selection, screening, discipline, and promotion processes to insure that the commitments set forth in the company's AAP are implemented as to disabled persons and veterans.

CHAPTER ENDNOTES

1. 29 U.S.C. §793.
2. 38 U.S.C. §4212.
3. P.L. 105-339.
4. See 41 CFR §§60-1.21-24.
5. See 41 CFR §60-250.61 and 41 CFR §60-741.61.
6. 41 CFR §60-1.24; 41 CFR §§60-741.61-62; 41 CFR §§60-250.61-62.
7. See 41 CFR §60-1.26 and 41 CFR §60-30.
8. 41 CFR §60-30.30.
9. 41 CFR §60-1.26; 41 CFR §60-250.65; 41 CFR §60-741.62.
10. 41 CFR §60-1.27.
11. See 41 CFR §60-1.4.
12. 41 CFR §60-1.7
13. 41 CFR §60-1.8.
14. 41 CFR §60-1.12.
15. 41 CFR §60-1.12(c).
16. 41 CFR §60-1.41.
17. 41 CFR §60-1.42.
18. See 41 CFR §60-741.5.
19. 41 CFR §60-250.4.
20. See 41 CFR §60-741.5(d) and 41 CFR §60-250.22.
21. See 41 CFR §§60-250.4 and 60-741.5(a).
22. 41 CFR §§60-250.4 and 60-741.5(a).
23. 41 CFR §§60-250.52, 60-741.80, and 60-741.23.
24. 41 CFR §§60-250.5(c) and 60-741.41.
25. 41 CFR §§60-1.40, 60-250.40, and 60-741.40.
26. See 41 CFR §§60-1.3, 60-250.2, and 60-741.2.
27. 41 CFR §§60-1.40, 60-250.40, and 60-741.40.
28. 41 CFR §60-2.1.
29. See 41 CFR §60-2.11.

30. 65 Fed. Reg. 68028 (11-13-00).
31. 41 CFR §60-2.12.
32. 41 CFR §60-2.13.
33. 41 CFR §60-2.14.
34. 41 CFR §60-2.15.
35. 41 CFR §60-2.16.
36. 41 CFR §60-2.17.
37. 41 CFR §60-2.18.
38. 41 CFR §60-741.44; 41 CFR §60-250.
39. 41 CFR §60-741.40(b).

Chapter 8

The Age Discrimination in Employment Act (ADEA)

GENERALLY

8-1. What is the Age Discrimination in Employment Act?

8-2. Who enforces the ADEA?

8-3. Who is protected under the ADEA?

8-4. Who must comply with the ADEA?

8-5. Who is not protected under the ADEA?

8-6. Under the ADEA, what constitutes age discrimination by an employer?

8-7. Under the ADEA, what constitutes age discrimination by an employment agency?

8-8. Under the ADEA, what constitutes age discrimination by a labor organization?

8-9. Is retaliation by an employer, employment agency, or labor organization prohibited under the ADEA?

8-10. What is discriminatory advertising under the ADEA?

8-11. Under the ADEA, what constitutes hostile environment and/or harassment?

8-12. Does the ADEA have any notice requirements for employers?

8-13. Does the ADEA have any recordkeeping requirements for employers?

8-14. Does the ADEA have any record keeping requirements for employment agencies?

8-15. Does the ADEA have any record keeping requirements for labor organizations?

8-16. Does the ADEA have any other record keeping requirements?

Procedure for Filing an ADEA Claim

8-17. Does a plaintiff have to file an EEOC charge?

8-18. What is the statute of limitations for filing an EEOC charge?

8-19. What is a "right to sue" letter under the ADEA?

8-20. What is the time limit (statute of limitations) for filing suit under the ADEA?

Litigating an ADEA Claim

8-21. What are the elements of a prima facie case under the ADEA?

8-22. How are ADEA claims litigated?

8-23. What is the burden-shifting mechanism under McDonnell Douglas v. Green?

8-24. What is a the burden-shifting mechanism in mixed motive cases?

8-25. How are pattern and practice claims litigated?

8-26. What is the difference between individual and representative actions under the ADEA?

8-27. Does the ADEA permit disparate impact claims?

8-28. What is meant by a disparate impact claim?

8-29. How are disparate impact claims litigated under the ADEA?

DISCRIMINATION BETWEEN PROTECTED INDIVIDUALS

8-30. Can a plaintiff establish a claim when the employer favors a person younger than the plaintiff but who is also over 40?

DEFENSES TO ADEA CLAIMS

8-31. What procedural defenses exist for ADEA claims?

8-32. What statutory defenses exist for ADEA claims?

8-33. What is the bona fide occupational qualification defense?

8-34. What is the reasonable factors other than age defense?

8-35. What is the bona fide seniority system defense?

8-36. What is the bona fide employee benefit plan defense?

8-37. What is meant by discharge or discipline for good cause?

8-38. What judicial defenses exist for ADEA claims?

8-39. Are state employers immune from ADEA lawsuits under the Eleventh Amendment?

REMEDIES UNDER THE ADEA

8-40. What remedies exist under the ADEA?

OLDER WORKERS BENEFIT PROTECTION ACT

8-41. What is the Older Workers Benefit Protection Act?

8-42. What age discrimination in employee benefits is prohibited under the OWBPA?

8-43. Can an employee waive his rights under the OWBPA?

8-44. What elements must a waiver contain?

8-45. Can an employee waive rights or claims that arise following the execution of the initial waiver?

8-46. What is the meant by the requirement that a waiver be "knowing and voluntary"?

8-47. What are the mandatory time periods for making a waiver?

GENERALLY

8-1. What is the Age Discrimination in Employment Act?

The Age Discrimination in Employment Act (ADEA) is a federal law passed by Congress in 1967 to prohibit employment discrimination based upon age as it relates to hiring, job retention, compensation, conditions, and privileges of employment.[1]

8-2. Who enforces the ADEA?

EQUAL EMPLOYMENT OPPORTUNITIES COMMISSION

The Equal Employment Opportunities Commission (EEOC) is charged with the enforcement of the ADEA. Additionally, the EEOC has the authority to create rules and regulations to further carry out the purpose of the ADEA.[2] The EEOC investigates claims of age discrimination, attempts conciliation, and prosecutes civil actions.

INDIVIDUAL PLAINTIFFS

The EEOC also authorizes individual plaintiffs to file and prosecute civil actions under the ADEA.[3] Civil lawsuits brought by individual plaintiffs are the most common means by which the ADEA is enforced. However, prior to filing a civil suit, an aggrieved individual must file a charge of unlawful discrimination with the EEOC (see Q 8-17).[4]

8-3. Who is protected under the ADEA?

Except for a few, relatively minor exceptions, the ADEA covers individuals who are 40 years of age or older.[5] Among these individuals are employees, job applicants, former employees, members of labor organizations, and individuals placed by employment agencies.[6] Note that, generally, a plaintiff under the ADEA must be at least 40 at the time of the alleged discrimination.

Additionally, United States citizens employed in foreign countries by American-owned companies are protected under the ADEA.[7]

8-4. Who must comply with the ADEA?

The ADEA applies to employers, both private and public, that have 20 or more employees for 20 or more weeks in the current or preceding year.[8]

The ADEA also applies to employment agencies serving such employers.[9]

Labor organizations (i.e., unions) that have 25 or more members are also subject to the ADEA.[10]

The ADEA applies to the federal government as an employer, albeit through a separate section.[11]

8-5. Who is not protected under the ADEA?

Clearly, individuals under age 40 are not protected by the ADEA. However, in addition to those under 40, the ADEA excludes certain other individuals from its protected class.

The ADEA does not protect independent contractors from employment discrimination based upon age.[12]

Generally, the ADEA does not protect bona fide general partners in a partnership.[13]

Elected officials, both at the state and lesser political subdivision levels, are not protected under the ADEA.[14] Although Section 630(f) appears to also exclude the appointees and personal staff of elected officials from "employee" status under the ADEA, they are, in fact, protected against age discrimination by the Civil Rights Act of 1991.[15]

The ADEA does not protect firefighters or law enforcement officers from mandatory retirement policies instituted by state or local governments.[16]

Bona fide executives and high policy-makers are not protected from mandatory retirement at age 65 under the ADEA.[17] A bona fide executive or policy-maker is an individual who has, for a two-year period prior to retirement, been employed in such a position and is entitled to an immediate, non-forfeitable, annual retirement benefit from a pension, profit-sharing, savings, or deferred compensation plan equal to at least $44,000.[18]

8-6. Under the ADEA, what constitutes age discrimination by an employer?

The ADEA makes it unlawful for an employer to:

1. Fail or refuse to hire, or discharge any individual or otherwise discriminate against any individual because of such individual's age with respect to his compensation, terms, conditions, or privileges of employment;

2. Limit, segregate, or classify employees in any way that would deprive or tend to deprive any individual of employment opportunities or otherwise adversely affect his status as an employee, because of such individual's age; or

3. Reduce the wage rate of any employee to comply with this statute.[19]

Specific employer actions that run afoul of the ADEA include:

1. Hiring and recruitment based upon age;

2. Compensation differentials based upon age;

3. Transfers (or refusal to transfer) based upon age;

4. Promotions practices based upon age;

5. Demotions and discharges based upon age; and

6. Mandatory retirement policies based upon age.

8-7. Under the ADEA, what constitutes age discrimination by an employment agency?

The ADEA makes it unlawful for an employment agency to fail or refuse to refer for employment, or otherwise to discriminate against, any individual because of such individual's age.[20]

It is also unlawful under the ADEA to classify or refer for employment any such individual on the basis of such individual's age.[21]

8-8. Under the ADEA, what constitutes age discrimination by a labor organization?

The ADEA makes it unlawful for a labor organization to:

1. Exclude or to expel from its membership, or otherwise discriminate against, any individual because of his age;

2. Limit, segregate, or classify its membership, or to classify or fail or refuse to refer for employment any individual, in any way that would deprive or tend to deprive any individual of employment opportunities, or would limit such opportunities or otherwise adversely affect his status as an employee or as an applicant for employment, because of age; or

3. Cause or attempt to cause an employer to discriminate against an individual in violation of the forgoing.[22]

8-9. Is retaliation by an employer, employment agency, or labor organization prohibited under the ADEA?

Yes. Under the ADEA, it is unlawful for an employer to discriminate against any of its employees or applicants, for an employment agency to discriminate against any individual, or for a labor organization to discriminate against any member thereof, because such individual has opposed any practice made unlawful by the ADEA or because such individual has made a charge, testified, or participated in any manner in an investigation, proceeding, or litigation under the ADEA.[23]

Former employees, in particular those who have been discharged, are among the "employees" protected from retaliation by Section 29 U.S.C. §623(d).

Moreover, an employer need not have affected the terms or conditions of the former employment; withholding letters of recommendation or providing negative references to prospective employers might also constitute retaliation.[24]

8-10. What is discriminatory advertising under the ADEA?

The ADEA prohibits an employer, labor organization, or employment agency from printing or publishing any notice or advertisement relating to employment or membership that indicates any preference, limitation, specification, or discrimination, based upon age.[25]

The two most common areas where legal matters have arisen are "help wanted" advertisements and job application forms. The EEOC has published regulations providing guidance as to what is prohibited under the ADEA.[26]

HELP WANTED NOTICES OR ADVERTISEMENTS

When help wanted notices or advertisements contain terms or phrases such as "age 25 to 35," "young," "college student," "recent college graduate," "boy," "girl," or others of a similar nature, such a term or phrase deters the employment of older persons and is a violation of the ADEA, unless one of the exceptions applies.[27]

Such phrases as "age 40 to 50," "age over 65," "retired person," or "supplement your pension" discriminate against others within the protected group, and therefore, are prohibited unless one of the exceptions apply.[28]

EMPLOYMENT APPLICATIONS

An employer's request for information such as "Date of Birth" or "State Age" on an employment application is not, in itself, a violation of the ADEA. But because the request that an applicant state his age may tend to deter older applicants or otherwise indicate discrimination based upon age, employment application forms that request such information will be closely scrutinized, in order to assure that the request is for a permissible purpose and not for purposes proscribed by the ADEA.[29]

8-11. Under the ADEA, what constitutes hostile environment and/or harassment?

Courts have recognized age-based harassment as a cognizable legal wrong under the ADEA.[30] Relying on Title VII (see Chapter 9) precedent regarding sexual and racial harassment, courts have determined that the ADEA affords employees the right to work in an environment free from discriminatory intimidation, ridicule, and insult.[31]

To establish a claim for a hostile work environment theory created by age-based harassment, a plaintiff must show the following: (1) he was a member of a protected class; (2) he was subject to unwelcome harassment; (3) the harassment was prompted because of his age; (4) the harassment affected a term, condition, or privilege of his employment; and (5) the existence of respondeat superior liability.[32] The burden imposed on a plaintiff bringing a hostile-environment claim is somewhat higher, requiring a plaintiff to show that the harassment was sufficiently "severe" and "pervasive" to alter the employee's employment and create a hostile working environment.[33]

8-12. Does the ADEA have any notice requirements for employers?

Yes. Entities subject to the ADEA (employers, employment agencies, and labor organizations) must post notices as to the rights afforded under the ADEA. The notice must be prepared by, or approved by, the EEOC.[34] It must be posted in a prominent and accessible place where it can be readily seen by individuals who are protected, or may be protected, under the statute.[35] See Appendix A.

A covered entity's failure to post such a notice will provide a sufficient basis for a court to excuse a late-filing grievant (i.e., an individual who had not timely filed a charge of unlawful discrimination with the EEOC) from the adverse consequences of that late filing.[36]

8-13. Does the ADEA have any recordkeeping requirements for employers?

Yes. In order to comply with the ADEA, employers are required by the EEOC to keep the following information for three years: (1) the employee's name; (2) his address; (3) his date of birth; (4) his occupation; (5) his rate of pay; and (6) his compensation earned each week.[37]

In addition, the following information must be retained by employers for one year from the date of the personnel action to which any records relate:

1. Job applications, resumes, or any other form of employment inquiry that was submitted to the employer in response to an advertisement or other notice of existing or anticipated job openings, including records pertaining to the failure or refusal to hire any individual;

2. Promotions, demotions, transfers, selections for training, layoffs, recalls, or discharges of any employee;

3. Job orders submitted by the employer to an employment agency or labor organization for recruitment of personnel for job openings;

4. Test papers completed by applicants or candidates considered by the employer in connection with any personnel action;

5. Results of any physical examinations that are required by the employer in connection with any personnel action; and

6. Any advertisements or notices to the public or to employees relating to job openings, promotions, training programs, or opportunities for overtime work.[38]

Lastly, employers must retain certain records regarding employee benefit plans and application forms for temporary positions.

Every employer must keep on file any documents relating to employee benefit plans, such as pension and insurance plans, as well as copies of any seniority systems and merit systems that have been reduced to writing. Such records must be retained for the full period during which the plan or system is in effect, and for at least one year after its termination.

If the plan or system has not been reduced to writing, a memorandum fully outlining the terms of such plan or system and the manner in which it has been communicated to the affected employees, together with notations relating to any changes or revisions, must be kept on file for the full period during which the plan or system is in effect, and for at least one year after its termination.[39]

Employers must also keep on file application forms and other pre-employment records of applicants for positions that are, and are known by applicants to be, of a temporary nature, must be kept for a period of 90 days from the date of the personnel action to which the record relates.

8-14. Does the ADEA have any record keeping requirements for employment agencies?

Employment agencies must retain records regarding placements, referrals, job orders, job applications, resumes, employment inquiries, test papers, and advertisements for one year.[40]

8-15. Does the ADEA have any record keeping requirements for labor organizations?

Labor organizations are required to maintain current records of the names, addresses, and dates of birth of their members.[41]

Labor organizations are also required to retain for one year the names, addresses, and ages of any persons seeking membership.[42]

8-16. Does the ADEA have any other record keeping requirements?

Yes. Covered entities are not required to use any special forms for record keeping. If the information required is available in records kept for other purposes, or can be obtained readily by recomputing or extending data recorded in some other form, no further records need be made or kept on a routine basis.[43]

An entity that is required to maintain records can petition the EEOC for an exemption from a record-keeping requirement, which will be granted if the exemption will not interfere with enforcement of the statute.[44]

The records maintained in accordance with the EEOC's regulations are to be kept in a safe and accessible place at the place of business or employment of the individual to whom they relate, or where such individual has applied for employment or membership, or at one or more established central record-keeping offices.[45]

The records must be available for inspection and transcription by authorized representatives of the EEOC during the business hours observed by the office at which they are located or in the community generally.[46]

Covered entities must make such extensions, recomputations, or transcriptions of records and submit such reports regarding actions taken and limitations and classifications of individuals set forth in its records, as the EEOC or its authorized representative may request in writing.[47]

Lastly, when an enforcement action is pending, the EEOC may require a covered entity to keep its records until the action is concluded.[48]

PROCEDURE FOR FILING AN ADEA CLAIM

8-17. Does a plaintiff have to file an EEOC charge?

Yes. Before an individual can file a civil suit against an employer or other entity for age discrimination, the plaintiff must first use his or her administrative remedies. Specifically, the aggrieved individual must file a charge of unlawful discrimination with the EEOC. This charged must be filed at least 60 days prior to filing suit.[49]

A complete failure to file, or a failure to file an adequate or timely charge, will result in a dismissal of the plaintiff's case or a grant of summary judgment for the defendant.

The regulations define a charge as "a statement filed with the Commission by or on behalf of an aggrieved person which alleges that the named prospective defendant has engaged in or is about to engage in actions in violation of the Act[.]"[50]

If the aggrieved individual resides in a state that has a statute prohibiting age discrimination and an agency charged with the authority to enforce that statute, then the individual must also file a complaint of discrimination with the state agency. The individual need not pursue his state claims in order to satisfy that ADEA's requirement of state filing. Note that an ADEA claimant can file charges with the EEOC and the state agency simultaneously. Note also that if an individual opts to pursue his or her age discrimination claims in state court, he or she might be foreclosed from pursuing those claims later in federal court.[51]

8-18. What is the statute of limitations for filing an EEOC charge?

If the claim is being asserted in a state that has a statute prohibiting age discrimination and an agency charged with the authority to enforce that statute, an aggrieved individual has 300 days following the occurrence of the alleged discrimination in which to file a charge, or must file within 30 days after receipt of a notice of termination of state law proceedings.[52]

In contrast, if the claim is being asserted in a state that does not have a statute prohibiting age discrimination, an aggrieved individual has 180 days following the occurrence of the alleged discrimination.[53]

8-19. What is a "right to sue" letter under the ADEA?

After the plaintiff files a charge, the EEOC conducts an investigation to determine whether there is reasonable cause to believe that discrimination has occurred.[54] If the EEOC determines that there is reasonable cause to believe that discrimination occurred and conciliation efforts have failed, the EEOC may elect to file a lawsuit in federal court on behalf of the aggrieved individual.[55]

In contrast, if the EEOC's investigation shows no reasonable cause to believe that discrimination occurred, or if the EEOC decides not to file a lawsuit, the aggrieved individual will receive notice that the EEOC has terminated its investigation and will issue a "right to sue" letter, permitting him or her to file a private civil suit.[56]

Note that, under the ADEA, an aggrieved individual need not wait to receive a "right to sue" letter before filing suit. Instead, the claimant, after filing a charge with the EEOC for age discrimination, need only wait 60 days before filing a private lawsuit.[57]

8-20. What is the time limit (statute of limitations) for filing suit under the ADEA?

The ADEA, as amended by the Civil Rights Act of 1991, provides that a claimant has 90 days after receipt of a "right to sue" letter in which to file a lawsuit under the ADEA.[58] There is, however, no requirement that the EEOC act within any particular time period. Therefore, an EEOC notice (i.e., "right to sue" letter) issued any number of years after the alleged discrimination will, upon its receipt, start the running of the 90-day statute of limitations. So long as the claimant files suit within that 90 days, the action will be timely.[59]

LITIGATING AN ADEA CLAIM

8-21. What are the elements of a prima facie case under the ADEA?

Generally, an individual plaintiff establishes a claim for age discrimination under the ADEA with direct or indirect evidence showing that the plaintiff:

1. Is in the protected age group (age 40 or older);

2. Was performing his job satisfactorily;

3. Suffered a materially adverse employment action; and

4. Was replaced by a younger employee (or that younger employees were treated more favorably).[60]

8-22. How are ADEA claims litigated?

In general, the manner in which an ADEA claim is litigated depends largely upon the type of claim brought by the plaintiff. By far the greatest number of ADEA claims concern discriminatory treatment, where the plaintiff relies on circumstantial evidence to establish his or her claim. Such claims of age discrimination based upon circumstantial evidence are litigated using a burden-shifting mechanism first devised by the Supreme Court in the Title VII case *McDonnell Douglas Corp. v. Green.*[61]

A second, growing body of claims arises out of situations where the employer's alleged discriminatory actions were based upon mixed motives (i.e., both lawful and unlawful factors played a role in the challenged employment actions). Mixed motive cases are litigated under the paradigm set forth by the Supreme Court in another Title VII case—*Price Waterhouse v. Hopkins.*[62]

A third, smaller body of cases consists of "pattern and practice" claims, which deal with systemic discrimination. Such cases are litigated using either the *McDonnell Douglas* or the *Price Waterhouse* paradigms; however, they are representative actions maintained by a named plaintiff or a suit involving several named plaintiffs.

8-23. What is the burden-shifting mechanism under McDonnell Douglas v. Green?

The most common mode of proof in ADEA cases is the burden-shifting mechanism set forth by the Supreme Court in *McDonnell Douglas v. Green*. Although *McDonnell Douglas* was a Title VII case, lower courts have uniformly applied its principles to the ADEA.[63]

Under *McDonnell Douglas*: (1) the plaintiff must establish a prima facie case of discrimination by a preponderance of the evidence; (2) the burden then shifts to the defendant to provide evidence of a legitimate, nondiscriminatory reason for its action; and (3) the plaintiff must then prove by a preponderance of the evidence that the legitimate reasons offered by the defendant were not its true reasons, but were a *pretext* for discrimination.

Once a plaintiff establishes a prima facie case, the defendant is not required to prove its non-discriminatory reason. Rather, the defendant need only produce evidence, which, if believed by the trier of fact, would support the finding that unlawful discrimination was not the cause of the adverse employment action.

8-24. What is a the burden-shifting mechanism in mixed motive cases?

In *Price Waterhouse v. Hopkins*, the Supreme Court set forth the burdens of proof for Title VII claims where the plaintiff's evidence shows lawful as well as unlawful factors for the employer's conduct.[64]

Like *McDonnell Douglas*, lower courts have applied the principles of *Price Waterhouse* to the ADEA. Under Price Waterhouse, where the plaintiff's evidence establishes a mixed motive on the part of the employer, the ADEA plaintiff must generally prove, by a preponderance of the evidence, that age was a determinative motivating factor in the challenged employment decision.

Once the plaintiff satisfies its burden, the defendant must then prove, by a preponderance of the evidence, that it would have made the same employment decision independent of the unlawful factor of age.

The chief difference between the *McDonnell Douglas* paradigm and the *Price Waterhouse* paradigm is that the defendant in a mixed motive case bears a burden of persuasion (i.e., the defendant in the mixed motive case must prove its position by a preponderance of the evidence), whereas the defendant under the *McDonnell Douglas* scheme merely needs to satisfy a burden of production.

Clearly, from a plaintiff's perspective, it is advantageous to litigate an ADEA claim as a mixed motive case.

8-25. How are pattern and practice claims litigated?

Pattern and practice claims typically involve multiple alleged acts of wrongdoing in violation of the ADEA. Such claims are usually brought either as a representative action maintained by a named plaintiff where other identified individuals opt in, or as a suit brought by multiple named plaintiffs.

The claimant or claimants in such suits will seek to prove unlawful discrimination in the same manner as an individual plaintiff suing on his or her own behalf. That is, the named representative plaintiff or the group of named plaintiffs will litigate their claims under either the *McDonnell Douglas* burden shifting paradigm or the *Price Waterhouse* mixed motive paradigm.

The plaintiff's task in a pattern and practice case is to prove, by a preponderance of the evidence, that discrimination is the defendant's standard operating procedure rather than the unusual practice. Often times, plaintiffs will attempt to establish a pattern or practice of discrimination by a defendant by using statistical evidence. Of course, the adequacy of such statistical evidence is subject to argument in any given case.

8-26. What is the difference between individual and representative actions under the ADEA?

In an action brought by multiple named plaintiffs, each plaintiff will have to prove that the defendant discriminated against him or her individually, and each will have to prove his or her individual damages.

However, in a representative action, if the named plaintiff is successful in establishing age discrimination by the defendant, then the defendant will be held liable with regard to each of the plaintiffs, leaving the question of remedy to be addressed on an individual basis.

8-27. Does the ADEA permit disparate impact claims?

Yes. Although the Supreme Court has not directly addressed the issue, numerous lower courts have held that the ADEA, like Title VII (see Chapter 9), permits plaintiffs to bring claims based upon a theory of disparate impact.

8-28. What is meant by a disparate impact claim?

A disparate impact claim alleges that an employer's facially neutral policy (i.e., a policy that does not take into consideration an unlawful factor such as age) is unlawful, because such a policy has a disproportionate impact on individuals who are protected under a statute (e.g., individuals age 40 and over under the ADEA).

Note that discriminatory intent is irrelevant in a disparate impact claim. For example, a hiring policy providing that only teachers with fewer than five years experience are eligible for a position is a facially neutral policy, because, as it is written, it does not take into consideration the teachers' age. However, the fact that such a policy disqualifies 90% of teachers age 40 and older makes the policy susceptible to attack via a disparate impact claim. Clearly, such a policy, although not taking age into consideration and not motivated by discriminatory intent, has a disproportionate adverse impact on those applicants age 40 and older.

8-29. How are disparate impact claims litigated under the ADEA?

To establish a claim for disparate impact under the ADEA, a plaintiff must prove, by a preponderance of the evidence, that the policy or practice of the employer in question has a disproportionately adverse impact on individuals age 40 and older.

Typically, plaintiffs rely heavily on statistical evidence to prove their cases. In response, defendants typically either: (1) attack the statistical data relied upon by plaintiffs; or (2) establish a legitimate business justification for the employment policy or practice.

If a defendant produces evidence of a legitimate business justification for the employment policy in question, the plaintiff can still prevail on the claim if he or she proves, by a preponderance of the evidence, that there were alternative employment policies or practices that reduced the adverse impact on the protected class, and the defendant refused to adopt such alternative policies. However, such alternatives must be equally effective in attaining the defendant's legitimate employment goals.

DISCRIMINATION BETWEEN PROTECTED INDIVIDUALS

8-30. Can a plaintiff establish a claim when the employer favors a person who is younger than the plaintiff but who is also over 40?

Yes. The Supreme Court has held that an ADEA plaintiff need not show that he or she was replaced by someone younger than 40 in order to establish a prima facie case. A plaintiff need only produce evidence from which it may be inferred that the employer relied on the younger person's age in making the challenged employment decision. However, such an inference cannot be drawn where the age difference between the two workers is insignificant.[65]

The ADEA does not generally prohibit reverse age discrimination favoring an older worker. Thus, an employee aged 40 or over is generally foreclosed from bringing an ADEA claim against an employer for hiring an older individual over the plaintiff.[66]

DEFENSES TO ADEA CLAIMS

8-31. What procedural defenses exist for ADEA claims?

An employer can raise a number of procedural defenses to defeat a plaintiff's claim of age discrimination under the ADEA.

Specifically, a defendant can claim that it is not a covered entity (an "employer," "employment agency," or "labor organization") as defined by the statute. For example, if a defendant can show that it did not have 20 or more employees for 20 or more weeks in the current or preceding year, then it will not be considered an "employer" under the ADEA and thus not subject to suit.[67]

Conversely, a defendant can defend itself procedurally by establishing that the plaintiff is not protected under the ADEA. For example, if the defendant can establish that the plaintiff is a "bona fide executive" or an elected official, the plaintiff's claim will be dismissed.[68]

Additionally, a defendant can attack a plaintiff's claim on a number of procedural grounds related to the filing of an EEOC charge and the statute of limitations thereto. For example, a plaintiff must file an EEOC charge prior to filing a lawsuit. If a plaintiff fails to do so, the complaint will likely be dismissed. Likewise, if a plaintiff fails to file its complaint within 90 days following the issuance of an EEOC "right to sue" letter, the plaintiff's case will be dismissed.[69]

8-32. What statutory defenses exist for ADEA claims?

The ADEA provides several affirmative defenses, such as:

1.   The *bona fide occupational qualification* defense (see Q 8-33);

2.   he *reasonable factors other than age* defense (see Q 8-34);

3.   The *bona fide seniority system* defense (see Q 8-35);

4.   he *bona fide employee benefit plan* defense (see Q 8-36); and

5.   The *discharge or discipline for good cause* defense (see Q 8-37).

8-33. What is the bona fide occupational qualification defense?

The bona fide occupational qualification (BFOQ) defense is one of the key affirmative defenses under the ADEA. It provides that it shall not be unlawful for an employer, employment agency, or labor organization to take any action otherwise prohibited under the statute where age is a bona fide occupational qualification reasonably necessary to the normal operation of the particular business.[70]

A defendant that invokes the BFOQ defense admits, in effect, that it engaged in an action, or made a decision, that ordinarily would constitute unlawful age discrimination under the statute.

However, if the BFOQ defense is successful, it will insulate the defendant from liability. It is important to note that the EEOC has expressly stated that the BFOQ defense is to be narrowly construed.[71]

Since the BFOQ defense is an affirmative defense, the defendant must prove the defense by a preponderance of the evidence. A defendant invoking the BFOQ defense has the burden of proving that: (1) the age limit is reasonably necessary to the essence of the business; and either (2) that all or substantially all individuals excluded from the job involved are in fact disqualified; or (3) that some of the individuals so excluded possess a disqualifying trait that cannot be ascertained except by reference to age.

If the employer's objective in asserting a BFOQ is the goal of public safety, the employer must prove that the challenged practice does indeed effectuate that goal and that there is no acceptable alternative that would better or equally advance the goal with less discriminatory impact.[72]

8-34. What is the reasonable factors other than age defense?

The ADEA sets forth an exception for differentiations based upon "reasonable factors other than age" (RFOA). The ADEA states that it shall not be unlawful for an employer, employment agency, or labor organization to take any action otherwise prohibited where the differentiation is based upon reasonable factors other than age.[73]

Thus, for example, when an employment decision is based upon reasonable factor other than age, such as the use of stringent physical requirements necessitated by the nature of the work, the ADEA prohibitions do not apply.

However, when an employment policy or practice uses age as a limiting criterion, the RFOA defense is unavailable.[74]

Although courts differ over whether the RFOA defense is an affirmative defense, the EEOC regulations indicate that the RFOA defense is affirmative and thus requires the defendant to prove the defense by a preponderance of the evidence.[75]

8-35. What is the bona fide seniority system defense?

The ADEA makes lawful the actions or decisions of covered entities (employers, employment agencies, and labor organizations) that would otherwise violate the statute where such actions or decisions are based upon the terms of a bona fide seniority system that is not intended to evade the purposes of the ADEA.[76]

However, in no event may a seniority system require or permit the involuntary retirement of any individual protected under the ADEA based upon his or her age.[77]

A seniority system may be qualified by such factors as merit, capacity, or ability; however, any bona fide seniority system must be based upon length of service as the primary criterion for the equitable allocation of available employment opportunities and prerogatives among younger and older workers.[78]

In addition, adoption of a purported seniority system that gives those with longer service lesser rights may be deemed a subterfuge to evade the statute by the EEOC.[79]

Lastly, unless the essential terms and conditions of an alleged seniority system have been communicated to the affected employees and can be shown to be applied uniformly to all of those affected, regardless of age, it will not be considered a bona fide seniority system within the meaning of the ADEA.[80] As an affirmative defense, the burden is on the defendant to establish, by a preponderance of the evidence, that its actions or decisions were based upon a bona fide seniority system.[81]

8-36. What is the bona fide employee benefit plan defense?

The ADEA makes lawful the actions or decisions of covered entities (employers, employment agencies, and labor organizations) that would otherwise violate the statute where such actions or decisions are based upon the terms of a bona fide benefit plan (retirement, insurance, pension, etc.) that is not intended to evade the purposes of the ADEA.[82]

A benefit plan will be considered in compliance with the ADEA where the actual amount of payment expended, or cost incurred, on behalf of an older worker is equal to that expended or incurred on behalf of a younger worker, even though the older worker may receive a lesser amount of benefits or insurance coverage.[83]

Also, a voluntary early retirement incentive plan that is consistent with the purposes of the statute will be in compliance with the ADEA as a bona fide benefit plan.[84]

However, it is important to note that no employee benefit plan or voluntary retirement incentive plan shall excuse the failure to hire any individual or require or permit the involuntary retirement of any individual protected under the ADEA based upon his or her age.[85]

8-37. What is meant by discharge or discipline for good cause?

The ADEA codifies good cause as a defense to a plaintiff's claims of unlawful discharge or discipline based upon age.[86] In other words, a plaintiff's ADEA claim can be defeated if the defendant can show that he or she had good cause to take the course of action that he or she followed.

8-38. What judicial defenses exist for ADEA claims?

In deciding ADEA cases, courts have created a number of defenses.

For example, in the context of a disparate impact claim, a defendant can raise the defense that a neutral policy that incidentally has an adverse impact upon persons protected under the statute is justified by business necessity.[87]

With regard to mixed motive cases, a defendant can avail itself of the "same decision" defense, whereby it has the burden of proving that it would have made the same employment decision even had it not taken into account the forbidden factor of age.[88]

When defending against an individual age discrimination claim, a defendant need only produce evidence that its challenged actions or decisions were based upon legitimate, non-discriminatory factors.[89]

8-39. Are state employers immune from ADEA lawsuits under the Eleventh Amendment?

Yes. Under a Supreme Court ruling, state employers are immune from suit under the ADEA by virtue of the Eleventh Amendment.[90] Thus, state employers have an extra defense in their arsenal to defeat plaintiffs' claims of age discrimination brought under the ADEA. Note that states, however, can be sued under state laws proscribing age discrimination.

REMEDIES UNDER THE ADEA

8-40. What remedies exist under the ADEA?

A plaintiff may be awarded injunctive relief, back pay, statutory "liquidated" damages equal to the amount of back pay, attorney's fees, and costs.[91]

BACK PAY

As under Title VII, back pay is routinely awarded as a remedy for a proven violation of the ADEA; however, limitations on its availability apply. See Chapter 9.

For example, back pay will be denied for the period beginning after an employer eliminates the position from which the plaintiff was terminated, provided it has not created a comparable position.

FRONT PAY

Lower courts generally award front pay when necessary. Generally, its duration extends until the plaintiff fails to make reasonable efforts to secure substantially equivalent employment or until he/she obtains or is offered such employment.

LIQUIDATED DAMAGES

"Liquidated" damages are equal to twice the amount of compensatory back pay. Liquidated damages are available under the ADEA where the defendant's violations are willful.

Liquidated damages are available when the employer knows that its employment practices are in violation of the ADEA or recklessly disregards whether its conduct will violate the statute. However, it is not enough that the employer knows that the ADEA is potentially applicable to the practice in question. In other words, an employer's conduct must be more than merely voluntary and negligent in order to constitute a willful violation. It is important to point out that lower courts have uniformly held that compensatory and punitive damages are not available to a successful ADEA plaintiff.

ATTORNEYS' FEES

The ADEA authorizes attorneys' fees only to plaintiffs, not prevailing parties. Thus, even a prevailing ADEA defendant who makes the extraordinary showing of frivolousness will not be awarded attorneys' fees from the plaintiff.

OLDER WORKERS BENEFIT PROTECTION ACT

8-41. What is the Older Workers Benefit Protection Act?

In 1990, Congress enacted the Older Workers Benefit Protection Act (OWBPA), amending the ADEA in two important respects.

First, the OWBPA makes clear that discrimination on the basis of age, in virtually all forms of employee benefits, is unlawful.[92]

Second, the OWBPA creates safeguards to ensure that older workers are not coerced or manipulated into waiving their rights to seek legal relief under the ADEA.[93]

8-42. What age discrimination in employee benefits is prohibited under the OWBPA?

With the OWBPA, Congress clarified and restored one of the original purposes of the ADEA—the eradication of age discrimination in employee benefits.

In the OWBPA, Congress reaffirmed the "equal benefit or equal cost principle" so as to ensure that productive older workers, an ever-growing segment of the labor force, are not discouraged from remaining actively employed.

Essentially, the OWBPA requires that employers provide equal benefits to, or to incur equal cost for benefits on behalf of, all employees. For example, if a $100 contribution purchases $50,000 of coverage for an employee age 35 and only $25,000 for an employee age 60, that difference in coverage is considered lawful under the ADEA.

The ADEA sets forth several exceptions to this "equal benefit or equal cost" requirement, but they are severely limited.

One such exception involves defined benefit pension plans, in which case there is a safe harbor provided for three specified practices.[94]

Another exception involves instances in which there is benefit coordination (e.g., retirement health benefits and severance pay).

Finally, in the case of early retirement incentive plans, the law will allow them, provided that they: (1) are truly voluntary; (2) are made available for a reasonable period of time; and (3) do not result in arbitrary age discrimination.[95]

Under the OWBPA, employees eligible for early retirement incentive plans must be given sufficient time to consider their options, particularly in circumstances when no previous retirement counseling has been provided. Eligible employees must be provided with complete and accurate information regarding the benefits available under the plan.

If subsequent layoffs or terminations are contemplated or discussed, employees should be advised of the criteria by which those decisions will be made. The critical question involving an allegation of an involuntary retirement is whether, under the circumstances, a reasonable person would have concluded that there was no choice but to accept the offer.

8-43. Can an employee waive his rights under the OWBPA?

Yes. The ADEA expressly provides that waivers may be valid and enforceable under the ADEA so long as the waiver is "knowing and voluntary."[96]

The ADEA provides, as part of the minimum requirements for a knowing and voluntary waiver, that the waiver be part of an agreement between the individual and the employer that is written in a manner calculated to be understood by such individual, or by the average individual eligible to participate.[97]

8-44. What elements must a waiver contain?

In 1998, the EEOC provided new guidelines on how to prepare a waiver.

The entire waiver agreement must be in writing. Waiver agreements must be drafted in plain language geared to the level of understanding of the individual party to the agreement or individuals eligible to participate. Employers should take into account such factors as the level of comprehension and education of typical participants. The individual must be advised in writing to consult with an attorney prior to executing the agreement.

The waiver agreement must not have the effect of misleading, misinforming, or failing to inform participants and affected individuals, and any advantages or disadvantages described shall be presented without either exaggerating the benefits or minimizing the limitations.

The exit incentive or other employment termination programs offered should be in writing in a manner calculated to be understood by the average participant.

The waiver should specifically refer to rights or claims under the ADEA by name in connection with the waiver. It must refer to the ADEA by name.

An employer is not required to give a person age 40 or older a greater amount of consideration than is given to a person under the age of 40, solely because of that person's membership in the protected class under the ADEA.

There is an informational requirement to provide an employee with enough information regarding the program to allow the employee to make an informed choice whether or not to sign a waiver agreement. Thus, employers must disclose the job titles and ages of employees affected by a program in an easy-to-understand format that compares them to unaffected employees in the same job classification. This ensures that affected employees will have enough information to decide if they want to sign a waiver agreement.

The rule prohibits employers from supplying age-related information in bands broader than one year (for example, describing a group as "age 20 to 30").

The EEOC has issued regulations that restate this Supreme Court ruling that an individual may retain severance benefits, even if he or she subsequently challenges the validity of the waiver under the ADEA. Any covenant not to sue or any action taken to adversely affect any individual's right to challenge a waiver is invalid under the ADEA. The regulations do permit, in appropriate circumstances, that an employer may assert a setoff claim against an employee who does recover damages in a lawsuit; however, the restitution cannot be greater than the amount paid to the employee. Finally, the EEOC rules require an employer to honor its agreement with other employees, even when the validity of a waiver is successfully challenged by an employee.[98]

8-45. Can an employee waive rights or claims that arise following the execution of the initial waiver?

No. The waiver of rights or claims that arise following the execution of a waiver is prohibited. However, the ADEA does not bar, in an otherwise valid waiver, the enforcement of agreements to perform future employment-related actions such as the employee's agreement to retire or otherwise terminate employment at a future date.[99]

8-46. What is the meant by the requirement that a waiver be "knowing and voluntary"?

A waiver may not be considered knowing and voluntary, unless, at a minimum: (1) the individual is given a period of at least 21 days within which to consider the agreement; or (2) if a waiver is requested in connection with an exit incentive or other employment termination program offered to a group or class of employees, the individual is given a period of at least 45 days within which to consider the agreement.

The term "exit incentive or other employment termination program" includes both voluntary and involuntary programs.

A waiver may not be considered knowing and voluntary unless the individual waives rights or claims only in exchange for consideration. Such consideration must be in addition to anything of value to which the individual already is entitled in the absence of a waiver.

In circumstances where there is retention of money given in exchange for a waiver, the Supreme Court has ruled that this did not amount to a ratification when the waiver did not meet the "knowing and voluntary" standard.[100] Indeed, the employee is not required to tender back the money in order to challenge a waiver under the ADEA.

An employer seeking to establish the validity of a waiver agreement has the burden of proving that it was knowingly and voluntarily executed. The required information must be given to each person in the decisional unit who is asked to sign a waiver agreement.

8-47. What are the mandatory time periods for making a waiver?

The employee must be given at least 21 days to consider the waiver agreement. If a waiver is requested in connection with an exit incentive or other employment termination program offered to a group or class of employees (see Q 8-44), then the employee must be given a period of at least 45 days to consider the waiver agreement.

THE 21-DAY AND 45-DAY TIME PERIODS

The 21-day or 45-day periods run from the date of the employer's final offer. Material changes to the final offer restart the running of the 21-day or 45-day periods; however, changes made to the final offer that are not material do not restart the running of the 21-day or 45-day periods. The parties may agree that changes, whether material or immaterial, do not restart the running of the 21-day or 45-day periods.

An employee may sign a release prior to the end of the 21-day or 45-day time periods, thereby commencing the mandatory 7 days revocation period discussed below. This is permissible as long as the employee's decision to accept such shortening of time is knowing and voluntary and is not induced by the employer through fraud, misrepresentation, or threat to withdraw or alter the offer prior to the expiration of the 21-day or 45-day time periods. The employer may expedite the processing of the consideration provided in exchange for the waiver.

7-DAY PERIOD

A waiver may not be considered knowing and voluntary (see Q 8-46) unless, at a minimum, the waiver agreement provides that, for a period of at least seven days following the execution of such agreement, the employee may revoke the waiver agreement. The waiver agreement must not become effective or enforceable until the 7-day revocation period has expired. The 7-day revocation period cannot be shortened by the parties, by agreement or otherwise.

CHAPTER ENDNOTES

1. 29 U.S.C. §621.
2. 29 U.S.C. §628.
3. 29 U.S.C. §626(c)(1).
4. 29 U.S.C. §626(d).
5. 29 U.S.C. §631(a).
6. 29 U.S.C. §§623, 630.
7. 29 U.S.C. §623(h)(1).
8. 29 U.S.C. §630(b).
9. 29 U.S.C. §630(c).
10. 29 U.S.C. §§630(d) and 630(e).

11. 29 U.S.C. §§630(a), 633(a).
12. See, e.g., *Cobb v. Sun Papers Inc.*, 673 F.2d 337 (11th Cir. 1982).
13. See e.g., *Fountain v. Metcalf, Zima & Co.*, P.A., 925 F.2d 1398 (11th Cir. 1991).
14. 29 U.S.C. §630(f).
15. See 42 U.S.C. §325.
16. See 29 U.S.C. §623(j)(1).
17. 29 U.S.C. §631(c)(1).
18. 29 U.S.C. §631(c)(1).
19. 29 U.S.C. §623(a).
20. 29 U.S.C. §623(b).
21. Id.
22. 29 U.S.C. §623(c).
23. 29 U.S.C. §623(d).
24. *Passer v. American Chemical Society*, 935 F.2d 322 (DC Cir. 1991).
25. 29 U.S.C. §623(e).
26. See 29 CFR §§1625.4, 1625.5.
27. See 29 CFR §1625.4.
28. See 29 CFR §1625.4.
29. See 29 CFR §1625.5.
30. See *Crawford v. Medina General Hospital*, 96 F.3d 830 (6th Cir. 1996); *Young v. Will County Dept. of Public Aid*, 882 F.2d 290 (7th Cir. 1989).
31. See *Drez v. E.R. Squibb & Sons, Inc.*, 674 F.Supp. 1432 (D. Kan. 1987).
32. See *Spence v. Maryland Casualty Co.*, 803 F.Supp. 649 (W.D. N.Y. 1992).
33. See *Drez*, supra.
34. 29 U.S.C. §627.
35. 29 CFR §1627.10.
36. *Kephart v. Institute of Gas Technology*, 581 F.2d 1287 (7th Cir. 1978).
37. See 29 CFR §1627.3(a); see also 29 U.S.C. §626(a).
38. 29 CFR §1627.3(b)(1).
39. See 29 CFR §1627.3(b)(2).
40. See 29 CFR §1627.4(a)(1).
41. See 29 CFR §1627.5(a).
42. See 29 CFR §1627.5(b).
43. See 29 CFR §1627.2.
44. See 29 CFR §1627.11.
45. 29 CFR §1627.6(a).
46. 29 CFR §1627.6(b).
47. 29 CFR §1627.7.
48. See 29 CFR §§1627.3(b)(3), 1627.4(a)(2), 1627.5(c).
49. 29 U.S.C. §626(d).
50. 29 CFR §1626.3.
51. See *Kremer v. Chemical Constr. Corp.*, 456 U.S. 461 (1982); *Hogue v. Royse City, Tex.*, 939 F.2d 1249 (5th Cir. 1991).
52. 29 U.S.C. §626(d)(2).
53. 29 U.S.C. §626(d)(1).
54. 29 CFR §1626.15.
55. 29 CFR §1626.15.
56. 29 CFR §1626.12.
57. See 29 U.S.C. §626(d).
58. 29 U.S.C. §626(e).
59. See, e.g, *Browning v. AT&T Paradyne*, 120 F.3d 222 (11th Cir. 1997).
60. See *Sirvidas v. Commonwealth Edison Co.*, 60 F.3d 375, 378 (7th Cir. 1995).
61. See 411 U.S. 792 (1973).

62. See 490 U.S. 228 (1989).
63. See, e.g., *Fisher v. Wayne Dalton Corp.*, 139 F.3d 1137 (7th Cir. 1998).
64. See 490 U.S. 228 (1989).
65. See *O'Connor v. Consolidated Coin Caterers Corp.*, 517 U.S. 308 (1996).
66. See *Hamilton v. Caterpillar, Inc.*, 966 F.2d 1226 (7th Cir. 1992).
67. *Feit v. Biosynth Intl., Inc.*, 1999 WL 99726 (N.D. IL 1996).
68. *Koprowski v. Wistar Institute of Anatomy and Biology*, 819 F.Supp. 410 (E.D. PA 1992).
69. See *Martin v. Henderson*, 2000 U.S. Dist. LEXIS 11066 (D. Kan. 2000).
70. See 29 U.S.C. §623(f)(1).
71. See 29 CFR §1625.6(a).
72. See 29 CFR §1625.6(b).
73. See 29 U.S.C. §623(f)(1).
74. See 29 CFR §1625.6(c).
75. See *Iervolino v. Delta Air Lines, Inc.*, 796 F.2d 1408 (11th Cir. 1986) (holding that RFOA is *not* an affirmative defense); cf. *Criswell v. Western Airlines, Inc.*, 709 F.2d 544 (9th Cir. 1983) (holding that RFOA *is* an affirmative defense).
76. See 29 U.S.C. §623(f)(2)(A).
77. See 29 U.S.C. §623(f)(2)(A).
78. See 29 CFR §1625.8(a).
79. See 29 CFR §1625.8(b).
80. See 29 CFR §1625.8(c).
81. See U.S.C. §623(f)(2)(B)(ii).
82. See U.S.C. §623(f)(2)(B).
83. See U.S.C. §623(f)(2)(B)(i); 29 CFR §1625.10(a)(1).
84. See U.S.C. §623(f)(2)(B)(ii).
85. Id.
86. Id.
87. See *Wards Cove Packing Co., Inc. v. Atonio*, 490 U.S. 642 (1989).
88. See *Price Waterhouse v. Hopkins*, 490 U.S. 228 (1989).
89. See *McDonnell Douglas v. Green*, 411 U.S. 792 (1973).
90. See *Kimel v. Florida Board of Regents*, 528 U.S. 62 (2000).
91. See 29 U.S.C. §626(b)(incorporating by reference the remedies authorized under the Fair Labor Standards Act).
92. See 29 U.S.C. §623(j).
93. See 29 U.S.C. §626(f)(1).
94. 29 U.S.C. §623(l).
95. 29 U.S.C. §623 (f)(1)(B)(ii).
96. See 29 U.S.C. §626(f)(1).
97. See 29 U.S.C. §626(f)(1)(A).
98. 29 CFR §1625.22.
99. 29 CFR §1625.22(c)(2).
100. See *Oubre v. Entergy Operations, Inc.*, 522 U.S. 422 (1998).

Chapter 9

Title VII

GENERALLY

9-1. What is Title VII of the Civil Rights Act of 1964?

9-2. Who enforces Title VII?

9-3. Who is protected under Title VII?

9-4. Who must comply with Title VII?

9-5. Who is not protected under Title VII?

9-6. What specifically does Title VII prohibit?

9-7. What are the rules regarding race and color discrimination?

9-8. What are the rules regarding religious discrimination?

9-9. What are the rules regarding sex discrimination?

9-10. What are the rules regarding national origin discrimination?

9-11. What are the rules regarding retaliation?

9-12. What are the notice requirements of Title VII?

9-13. What are the record-keeping requirements of Title VII?

PROCEDURE FOR FILING A TITLE VII CLAIM

9-14. Is a person required to file a claim with the EEOC before filing suit under Title VII?

9-15. What is the statute of limitation for filing an EEOC charge?

9-16. What is a "right-to-sue" letter?

9-17. What is the statute of limitations for filing suit under Title VII?

LITIGATING A TITLE VII CLAIM

9-18. What are the elements that need to be proven in a case under Title VII?

9-19. In general, how are Title VII claims litigated?

9-20. How are disparate treatment claims litigated?

9-21. How are mixed motive cases litigated?

9-22. How are pattern or practice claims litigated?

9-23. How are disparate impact claims litigated?

DEFENSES TO TITLE VII CLAIMS

9-24. What general defenses exist for Title VII claims?

9-25. What defenses exist to disparate treatment claims?

9-26. What is the bona fide occupational qualification defense?

9-27. What additional defenses are available to religious discrimination claims?

9-28. What additional defense may be used in a mixed motive case?

9-29. What is the after-acquired evidence defense?

9-30. How will a plaintiff's failure to mitigate damages be a defense?

9-31. What defenses exist to disparate impact claims?

REMEDIES UNDER TITLE VII

9-32. What remedies exist under Title VII?

GENERALLY

9-1. What is Title VII of the Civil Rights Act of 1964?

Title VII of the Civil Rights Act of 1964 is a federal law that prohibits discrimination in employment on the basis of race, color, religion, sex, pregnancy, and national origin.[1] Title VII relates to hiring, firing, compensation, and any terms, conditions, or privileges of employment. It prohibits discrimination against employees as well as job applicants.

Title VII most recently was amended by the Civil Rights Act of 1991 to provide that individuals who file lawsuits under Title VII are entitled to a jury trial. Plaintiffs who prevail may be entitled to compensatory and punitive damages, but there are caps on damages depending on the number of employees employed by the defendant. It also altered the method of proving certain claims of discrimination under Title VII. These amendments are discussed in detail in the questions that follow.

9-2. Who enforces Title VII?

EQUAL EMPLOYMENT OPPORTUNITIES COMMISSION

The Equal Employment Opportunities Commission (EEOC) is charged with the enforcement of Title VII.[2] The EEOC receives, processes, and investigates charges of employment discrimination under Title VII. If the EEOC determines that a charge is not timely filed or otherwise fails to state a claim under Title VII, the EEOC will dismiss the charge.[3] If, after completing its investigation, the EEOC finds that there is not reasonable cause to believe the law has been violated, it will issue a notice of right to sue to the charging party.[4] On the other hand, if the EEOC determines after investigation that there is reasonable cause to believe that the law has been violated, it attempts conciliation.[5] If conciliation efforts fail, the EEOC may file a lawsuit in federal district court.[6] Or the EEOC may simply

dismiss the charge and issue a notice of dismissal and right to sue to the charging party.[7] In addition, there are procedures whereby the charging party can obtain a right-to-sue letter before the EEOC completes its investigation. See Q 9-16.

INDIVIDUAL PLAINTIFFS

Aggrieved individuals also may file and prosecute civil actions under Title VII.[8] Prior to doing so, however, the individual must file a charge of unlawful discrimination with the EEOC and must obtain a right-to-sue letter.

9-3. Who is protected under Title VII?

Title VII is perhaps the broadest of all federal employment laws because it protects "any individual." Persons of any sex, race, religion, or ethnic group may potentially have protection under Title VII. Under Title VII, the term employee means an individual employed by an employer. United States citizens employed in foreign countries by American-owned or controlled companies are considered "employees" under Title VII.[9] The law also protects applicants for employment because it extends to an employer's failure or refusal to hire "any individual."[10]

9-4. Who must comply with Title VII?

Title VII applies to employers, both private and public, that have 15 or more employees for each working day in each of 20 or more calendar weeks in the current or preceding calendar year. It also applies to employment agencies serving such employers, labor organizations that service such employers, unions with 15 or more members, and unions that represent employees of such employers.[11]

The "payroll method" is used to determine whether an employer meets the "15 or more employees" requirement for Title VII coverage.[12] Under the payroll method, an individual is counted as an employee for each day that the individual appears on the employer's payroll, regardless of whether the individual is physically present in the office or on paid leave. As a result, part-time employees are counted under Title VII, whether they work part of each day or part of each week, so long as they are on the employer's payroll.

In some circumstances, nominally separate business entities may be consolidated to reach the required 15 or more employees. The EEOC and the courts consider four factors when deciding if two entities should be consolidated: (1) interrelation of operations; (2) common management; (3) centralized control of labor operations; and (4) common ownership.[13] A parent and subsidiary corporation are regarded as a single employer under Title VII if the parent exercises a degree of control beyond the normal control exercised by a parent corporation. The terms employer, employment agency, and labor organization include agents of those entities.[14] Employers, for example, can be held liable for the acts of their agents, i.e., supervisors and managers.

9-5. Who is not protected under Title VII?

The definition of "employer" under Title VII specifically excludes the following:

- the United States;

- corporations wholly owned by the government of the United States;

- departments or agencies of the District of Columbia;

- bona fide private membership clubs that are exempt from taxation; and

- Indian tribes or businesses near an Indian reservation that give preferential treatment to Indians.[15]

In addition, there are exclusions for religious corporations, associations, educational institutions, or societies that employ individuals of a particular religion, and for employers that employ aliens outside any state.[16]

9-6. What specifically does Title VII prohibit?

Title VII prohibits discrimination by employers, employment agencies, and labor organizations against "any individual" because of that individual's race, color, religion, sex, or national origin.[17] Each of these categories is addressed in the questions that follow.

9-7. What are the rules regarding race and color discrimination?

The following categories have been recognized as "races" by the United States Census Bureau: White; Black; African-American or Negro; American Indian or Alaskan Native; Asian Indian; Chinese; Filipino; other Asian: Japanese, Korean, Vietnamese; Native Hawaiian; Guamanian or Chamorro; Samoan; and other Pacific Islander. Persons of mixed racial backgrounds are covered and do not need to prove their exact heritage to be protected. Generally, "color" is viewed as synonymous with race or as a basis for defining a subclass within a race. All people are protected from discrimination on the basis of race or color, regardless of their race. Courts have also recognized claims of race discrimination based on association. For example, a white employee who is discharged because his child is biracial is discriminated against on the basis of his race, even though the root animus for the discrimination is prejudice against the biracial child.[18]

In addition to traditional discrimination claims, courts have recognized claims for racial harassment. Such claims are analyzed using the framework developed for sexual harassment claims. Racially oriented harassment that creates a hostile or offensive work environment is illegal under Title VII. Employers must maintain an atmosphere free of racial intimidation. Such things as racial slurs, graffiti, and ethnic jokes can show a consistent pattern of harassment. As with sexual harassment, the individual must show either an unreasonably abusive or offensive work environment or that the harassment adversely affected a reasonable employee's ability to perform the job. (For additional information regarding harassment claims, see Chapter 5, Sexual Harassment.)

9-8. What are the rules regarding religious discrimination?

Title VII defines "religion" to include all aspects of religious observance and practice, as well as belief.[19] The EEOC's guidelines on religious discrimination define religious practices to include moral or ethical beliefs as to what is right and wrong that are sincerely held with the strength of traditional religious views.[20]

Title VII's prohibition against discrimination on the basis of religion includes the requirement that employers, employment agencies, and labor organizations take reasonable steps to accommodate an individual's religious practices. It is unlawful for an employer to fail to reasonably accommodate the religious practices of an employee or prospective employee, unless the employer demonstrates that accommodation would result in an undue

hardship on the conduct of the employer's business.[21] The most common need for religious accommodation involves a conflict between work schedules and religious practices, *e.g.*, an employee who cannot work on Saturday or Sunday in observance of the Sabbath.

According to the EEOC, a mere assumption that many more people, who engage in the same religious practices as the person being accommodated, may also need accommodation is not evidence of undue hardship.[22] An employer may assert undue hardship if the employer can demonstrate: (1) that the accommodation would require more than a de minimus cost, or (2) that the accommodation would require variance from a bona fide seniority system whereby another employee would be denied a shift preference guaranteed by that system.[23]

As an accommodation, the EEOC requires employers to facilitate the securing of a voluntary substitute where the employee's religious beliefs conflict with a work schedule. Flexible scheduling may be another reasonable accommodation. When an employee cannot be accommodated either as to the entire job or an assignment within the job, the employer should consider whether a possible change in job assignment or lateral transfer is available as an accommodation.[24]

In addition to traditional discrimination claims, courts have recognized claims for religious harassment. Such claims are analyzed using the framework developed for sexual harassment claims.[25] (For additional information regarding harassment claims, see Chapter 5, Sexual Harassment.)

9-9. What are the rules regarding sex discrimination?

Title VII's prohibition against sex discrimination protects both men and women. Two subcategories of sex discrimination include sexual harassment and pregnancy discrimination. Although Title VII does not specifically prohibit sexual harassment, the EEOC and the Supreme Court have recognized that sexual harassment is a type of sex discrimination. (See Chapter 5, Sexual Harassment.) In 1978, Title VII was amended by the Pregnancy Discrimination Act to prohibit discrimination on the basis of pregnancy. (See Chapter 11, Pregnancy Discrimination.)

Courts have also recognized a theory called "sex-plus" discrimination. Under such a theory, an individual can claim dis-

crimination because of sex *plus* some other facially neutral quali-
fication. Consider, for example, an employer who hires mostly
women and even has a preference for women employees. A woman
employee could state a claim for sex discrimination if she could
prove that her employer discriminated against a certain subclass
of women. For example, it would be unlawful to discriminate
against women with school-aged children as compared to men with
school-aged children.[26]

9-10. What are the rules regarding national origin discrimination?

The EEOC defines national origin discrimination to include
the denial of equal employment opportunity because of an
individual's (or ancestor's) place of origin. A claim for national
origin discrimination can also be established if an individual is
discriminated against for having certain physical, cultural, or
linguistic characteristics of a national origin group.[27] According to
its guidelines, the EEOC will examine with particular concern
charges alleging discrimination based on the following: (1) marriage to, or association with, persons of a national origin group; (2)
membership in, or association with, an organization identified with
or seeking to promote the interests of national origin groups; (3)
attendance or participation in schools, churches, temples, or
mosques, generally used by persons of a national origin group; and
(4) because an individual's name or spouse's name is associated
with a national origin group.[28]

Citizenship requirements also may be an issue in a claim of
national origin discrimination. In those circumstances where
citizenship requirements have the purpose or effect of discriminating against an individual on the basis of national origin, they are
prohibited by Title VII.[29]

National origin discrimination claims may also involve "En-
glish-only" rules. The EEOC takes the position that a rule requiring
employees to speak English at all times in the workplace disadvantages an individual's employment opportunities on the basis of
national origin. The primary language of an individual is often an
essential national origin characteristic.[30] On the other hand, an
employer is entitled to implement a rule requiring employees to
speak only in English at certain times provided that the employer
can show that the rule is justified by business necessity.[31] It is
imperative for employers to inform employees of the rule and the
consequences of violating the rule.[32]

Claims for harassment on the basis of national origin are also prohibited under Title VII. An employer has an affirmative duty to maintain a working environment free of harassment on the basis of national origin. Ethnic slurs and other verbal or physical conduct relating to an individual's national origin constitute harassment when this conduct: (1) has the purpose or effect of creating an intimidating, hostile or offensive working environment; (2) has the purpose or effect of unreasonably interfering with an individual's work performance; or (3) otherwise adversely affects an individual's employment opportunities.[33] (For additional information regarding harassment claims, see Chapter 5, Sexual Harassment.)

9-11. What are the rules regarding retaliation?

Title VII prohibits retaliation against an individual who opposes unlawful practices or participates in protecting another individual's rights under Title VII. Title VII provides that it shall be an unlawful employment practice for an employer to discriminate against any of its employees or applicants for employment because the employee or applicant has opposed any unlawful employment practice under Title VII, or because the individual has made a charge, testified, assisted, or participated in any manner in an investigation, proceeding, or hearing under Title VII.[34] Similar prohibitions apply to employment agencies and labor management committees involved in training programs.

9-12. What are the notice requirements of Title VII?

Employers that are required to comply with Title VII must post notices stating the rights that are afforded under Title VII (see Appendix A). Every employer, employment agency, and labor organization must post and keep posted in conspicuous places at its premises where notices to employees, applicants, and members are customarily posted, a notice to be prepared or approved by the EEOC setting forth excerpts from or summaries of the pertinent provisions of Title VII and information pertinent to the filing of a complaint with the EEOC.[35]

9-13. What are the record-keeping requirements of Title VII?

Every employer, employment agency, and labor organization subject to Title VII is required to: (1) make and keep records relevant to the determinations of whether unlawful employment practices have been or are being committed, (2) preserve such

records for periods prescribed by the EEOC, and (3) make reports as required by the EEOC.[36] Personnel or employment records, including application forms and records concerning hiring, promotion, demotion, transfer, layoff, or termination, rates of pay or other terms of compensation, and selection for training or apprenticeship must be retained for one year from the date the record was made or personnel action taken, whichever is later.[37] For example, if an employee is fired, records on that individual must be kept for one year after the termination.

When a discrimination charge has been filed, records relating to the complainant as well as to all others seeking or holding positions similar to that sought or held by the complainant must be preserved until final disposition of the charge.

Every entity subject to Title VII that controls an apprenticeship program must maintain a chronological list of the names and addresses of all persons who have applied to participate in the apprenticeship program.[38] The list must contain the sex and race or ethnic group of each applicant. In lieu of the chronological list, a file of written applications may be kept, as long as the information on sex, race, and ethnicity is provided.[39] The applicant list or application file must be kept for a period of two years from the date the application was received or the period of a successful applicant's apprenticeship, whichever is longer.

Employers covered by Title VII that have 100 or more employees must file an EEO-1 form annually on or before September 30 using data from any pay period in July through August.[40] The information required by the EEO-1 form on racial and ethnic identity may be acquired by a visual survey of the workforce or by keeping post-employment records. The EEOC recommends that records on an employee's race or ethnic identity be kept separate from the employee's personnel file or from other records available to those responsible for personnel decisions.[41]

PROCEDURE FOR FILING A TITLE VII CLAIM

9-14. Is a person required to file a claim with the EEOC before filing suit under Title VII?

Yes. Before an individual can file a civil suit against an employer or other entity covered under Title VII, the individual must first exhaust his administrative remedies by filing a charge with the EEOC. A charge must be in writing under oath or

affirmation.[42] Each charge should contain the full name, address, and telephone number of the aggrieved person or the person making the charge on behalf of the aggrieved person. Additionally, it must contain a clear and concise statement of the facts, including pertinent dates, constituting the alleged unlawful employment practice.[43]

In the case of an alleged unlawful employment practice occurring in a state that has a state or local law prohibiting the unlawful employment practice alleged and establishing or authorizing a state or local authority to enforce that law, no charge may be filed before the expiration of 60 days after proceedings have been commenced under the state or local law, unless such proceedings have been earlier terminated.[44] Note, however, that a particular state or local agency may waive this 60-day deferral period by entering into a "Worksharing Agreement" with the EEOC.

9-15. What is the statute of limitation for filing an EEOC charge?

An individual must file a charge of unlawful discrimination with the EEOC within 180 days after the alleged unlawful employment practice occurred. However, if the aggrieved individual has filed a charge with a state or local agency comparable to the EEOC, the individual can file an EEOC charge within 300 days after the alleged unlawful employment practice occurred, or within 30 days after receiving notice that the state or local agency has terminated its proceedings, whichever is earlier.[45] In many states, a charge filed with the state agency is automatically simultaneously filed with the EEOC.

9-16. What is a "right-to-sue" letter?

Following the filing of an EEOC charge, the EEOC conducts an investigation to determine if there exists probable cause to believe that discrimination has occurred. If the EEOC determines that there is probable cause, the EEOC will attempt conciliation. If conciliation fails, and if the EEOC elects not to file a lawsuit on behalf of the individual, the EEOC will issue a "probable cause" finding and a Notice of Right to Sue, also known as a "right-to-sue" letter. If the EEOC's investigation shows no probable cause to believe that discrimination occurred, it will dismiss the charge and issue a right-to-sue letter. The right-to-sue letter gives the individual notice that the EEOC has terminated its investigation and

permits the individual to file a private civil suit. The private civil suit must be filed within 90 days of receipt of the right-to-sue letter.

It is also common for individuals to request a right-to-sue letter prior to the EEOC completing its investigation. When the aggrieved person requests, in writing, that a notice of right to sue be issued, the EEOC will issue a notice of right to sue at any time after expiration of 180 days from the date the charge was filed.[46] The EEOC may issue the notice of right to sue prior to the expiration of 180 days provided that a specified EEOC official has determined that it is probable that the EEOC will be unable to complete its administrative processing within 180 days from the filing of the charge. A written certificate stating this conclusion must be attached to the notice of right to sue.[47] Such a practice has become more common with an increase in the volume of charges filed with the EEOC.

Generally, the right-to-sue letter is required before filing a lawsuit, however, many courts will not dismiss a lawsuit in the absence of a right-to- sue letter but instead stay the case and allow the plaintiff to obtain such a letter.

9-17. What is the statute of limitations for filing suit under Title VII?

A suit must be filed within 180 days after the alleged unlawful employment practice occurred, except that if the person initially instituted proceedings with a State or local agency, the charge must be filed within 300 days after the alleged unlawful employment practice occurred, or within 30 days after receiving notice that the State or local agency has terminated the proceedings, whichever is earlier.[48]

LITIGATING A TITLE VII CLAIM

9-18. What are the elements that need to be proven in a case under Title VII?

DISCRIMINATION CLAIMS

Generally, an individual plaintiff establishes a claim for discrimination under Title VII by showing that the person:

1.   is in a protected group (particular race, color, religion, sex, national origin);

2. is qualified for the job at issue;

3. suffered adverse employment action; and

4. was replaced by someone outside the protected class, or individuals outside the protected class were treated more favorably than the aggrieved individual.

This is the most common way to establish a case of discrimination.

HARASSMENT CLAIMS

Individual plaintiffs may bring claims for harassment on the basis of any category protected under Title VII. The framework for sexual harassment cases is generally applied to other harassment claims. (See Chapter 5, Sexual Harassment.)

9-19. In general, how are Title VII claims litigated?

The most common Title VII claim is a disparate treatment claim. Under this approach, an individual asserts that he was discriminated against on the basis of a protected trait by comparing himself to an individual outside the protected class. A subcategory of disparate treatment cases are mixed motive cases in which the employee claims that the employer's alleged discriminatory actions were based on mixed motives, i.e., lawful and unlawful factors played a role in the challenged employment actions. Another subcategory, pattern or practice cases, are disparate treatment claims involving multiple alleged acts of wrongdoing committed over a period of time and often with multiple named plaintiffs.

Unlike disparate treatment claims, which involve claims that an individual was in some way singled out or treated differently because of sex, race, etc., disparate impact claims involve facially neutral job qualifications. In a disparate impact case, the plaintiff alleges that a job qualification or requirement has a disproportionately large negative impact on a particular protected group of individuals.

9-20. How are disparate treatment claims litigated?

Plaintiffs can prove disparate treatment through direct or circumstantial evidence. Direct evidence, also known as "smoking gun" evidence, suffices to establish a case of discrimination.

More common are cases in which the plaintiff has only circumstantial evidence of discrimination. In such a case, the courts apply a burden-shifting framework established by the Supreme Court in *McDonnell Douglas Corp. v. Green.*[49] Under *McDonnell Douglas*, the plaintiff must establish a case of discrimination by a preponderance of the evidence. Then the burden of production shifts to the defendant, i.e., the employer must then come forward with evidence of a legitimate, non-discriminatory reason for its actions. If the employer produces such evidence, the burden shifts back to the plaintiff to prove by a preponderance of the evidence that the employer's legitimate reasons were not its true reasons but instead were a pretext for discrimination. Note that even if a plaintiff establishes a case of discrimination, the defendant is not required to prove its non-discriminatory reason. It need only produce evidence that, if believed by the jury, would support a finding that unlawful discrimination was not the cause of the adverse employment action. If the plaintiff is able to come forward with evidence of pretext, the case will be submitted to a jury. The Supreme Court has held that evidence which casts doubt on the employer's explanation is enough to establish pretext and put the case before a jury.[50] Although the burden of production may shift to the employer, at all times the burden of proof remains with the plaintiff.

9-21. How are mixed motive cases litigated?

Mixed motive cases are litigated under a framework first established by the Supreme Court in *Price Waterhouse v. Hopkins,*[51] and subsequently altered by the Civil Rights Act of 1991. In a Title VII case based on a mixed motive theory, the plaintiff must prove that the protected trait (sex, race, etc.) was a motivating part of the employer's decision. If a plaintiff demonstrates that an unlawful discriminatory reason was a motivating factor, then the employer is liable under Title VII.[52] If the employer, however, demonstrates that it would have made the same decision regardless of the illegal factor, the plaintiff's remedy will be limited.[53] An important difference between the *McDonnell Douglas* framework, discussed in Q 9-20, and the mixed motive framework is that the defendant in a mixed motive case bears the burden of persuasion, whereas the defendant under the *McDonnell Douglas* framework must simply satisfy a burden of production.

9-22. How are pattern or practice claims litigated?

Pattern or practice claims typically involve multiple alleged acts of wrongdoing occurring over a period of time. In addition to single plaintiff claims, pattern or practice claims often are brought either as a class action maintained by a named plaintiff where other identified individuals opt in or as a suit brought by multiple named plaintiffs. Such suits seek to prove unlawful discrimination in the same manner as an individual plaintiff suing on his own behalf. That is, the named representative plaintiff or the group of named plaintiffs litigate their claims under either the *McDonnell Douglas* burden shifting paradigm (see Q 9-20) or the mixed motive paradigm (see Q 9-21). The plaintiff's task in a pattern or practice case is to prove by a preponderance of the evidence that discrimination is the defendant's standard operating procedure—the regular rather than the unusual practice. The evidence in such cases often involves a combination of statistics and anecdotal evidence of disparate treatment.

In an action brought by multiple named plaintiffs, each plaintiff must prove that the defendant discriminated against him individually, and each will be required to prove individual damages. By contrast, if the named plaintiff in a class action is successful in establishing unlawful discrimination by the defendant, then the defendant will be held liable with regard to each of the plaintiffs, leaving the question of remedy to be addressed on an individual basis.

The U.S. Attorney General is empowered to bring a civil action where it finds a "pattern or practice" of unlawful intentional discrimination.[54]

9-23. How are disparate impact claims litigated?

The disparate impact framework was first recognized by the Supreme Court in *Griggs v. Duke Power Co.*.[55] An unlawful employment practice based on a disparate impact theory is established if the plaintiff demonstrates that the employer uses a particular neutral employment practice that causes a disparate impact on the basis of race, color, religion, sex, or national origin, and the employer fails to demonstrate that the challenged practice is job related for the position in question and consistent with business necessity.[56] Disparate impact claims are proven using statistical evidence. Once a disparate impact is proven, the employer has the burden to prove job relatedness and business necessity. If the plaintiff demonstrates another, less discriminatory way to meet

the business needs, the employer may have the obligation to adopt that alternative.

A key component to the employer's defense to a disparate impact claim is to validate any test the employer is using that allegedly causes a disparate impact. Tests can be validated by showing content validity (they properly measure the skills needed for the job), construct validity (they measure subjective qualities that are related to performance), or criterion-related validity (there is a statistical relationship between the test scores and job performance).

DEFENSES TO TITLE VII CLAIMS

9-24. What general defenses exist for Title VII claims?

At the outset, a defendant in a Title VII case can raise a defense that it is not an "employer" (or other covered entity) as that term is defined under Title VII. The defendant also can challenge the plaintiff's claims as untimely. The defendant also may attempt to raise specific exclusions under Title VII, such as a claim that it is a religious corporation or a bona fide private club, as those terms are defined under the statute.

9-25. What defenses exist to disparate treatment claims?

NO PROVEN CASE

When defending a disparate treatment claim, the defendant may be able to challenge any one of the four factors the plaintiff is required to prove to establish a case (see Q 9-18). For example, if the plaintiff claims he was not hired because of his race, the employer can argue that the plaintiff failed to prove he was qualified for the particular job. If the plaintiff claims she was discharged because of her sex, the employer can argue that she was replaced by another woman, or the employer can argue that all the employees in the plaintiff's department (men as well as women) were terminated thereby undermining the plaintiff's ability to prove that men were treated more favorably than the plaintiff.

LEGITIMATE, NON-DISCRIMINATORY REASON

In a disparate treatment case, once the plaintiff has established a case, the defendant has the burden of articulating a legitimate, non-discriminatory reason for its action or decision. For example, if an employee was terminated and the employee claims his termination was because of his race, the employer may assert

that the employee was terminated because of poor attendance. The burden then shifts to the plaintiff to establish that the employer's reason was not the real reason but a pretext for discrimination.

9-26. What is the bona fide occupational qualification defense?

The bona fide occupational qualification (BFOQ) defense is applicable only to claims involving discrimination on the basis of sex, national origin, or religion. There is no BFOQ defense for race and color. Title VII provides that it is not an unlawful employment practice for an employer to hire any individual on the basis of his religion, sex, or national origin in those certain instances in which religion, sex, or national origin is a bona fide occupational qualification reasonably necessary to the normal operation of that particular business or enterprise.[57] The BFOQ defense is an affirmative defense for which the defendant has the burden of persuasion. A defendant that invokes the BFOQ defense in essence admits that it engaged in action, or made a decision, that ordinarily would constitute unlawful discrimination under Title VII. If the BFOQ defense is successfully proven, however, the defendant is insulated from liability. Note that the EEOC has expressly stated that the BFOQ defense is to be narrowly construed.

The BFOQ defense has been recognized in situations involving safety. For example, the Supreme Court has found that being male was a BFOQ for certain positions in Alabama state penitentiaries.[58] The BFOQ defense also can be valid in cases of authenticity or genuineness, where the entity or business is trying to portray a particular atmosphere. For example, actors and actresses may need to be male or female for a particular part, or a restaurant may want to portray a genuine ethnic atmosphere, such as in a Chinese restaurant.

9-27. What additional defenses are available to religious discrimination claims?

In addition to the defenses discussed in the questions above, there are two defenses specific to religious discrimination claims. Title VII does not apply to religious corporations, associations, educational institutions, or societies with respect to employment of individuals of a particular religion to perform work connected with the carrying on of its activities.[59] Similarly, Title VII provides that it is not an unlawful employment practice for a school, college,

university, or other educational institution or institution of learning to hire and employ employees of a particular religion if the educational institution is in whole or in substantial part owned, supported, controlled, or managed by a particular religious corporation, association, or society, or if the curriculum of the educational institution is directed toward the propagation of a particular religion.[60]

Also, in cases in which the plaintiff alleges that the defendant failed to accommodate his or her religious beliefs, the employer can raise a defense that such an accommodation would be an undue hardship.[61]

9-28. What additional defense may be used in a mixed motive case?

To establish a mixed motive case, the plaintiff must demonstrate that an unlawful discriminatory reason was a motivating factor in the employer's decision. If successful on such a theory, the employer is liable under Title VII.[62] However, the plaintiff's remedy will be limited if the employer demonstrates that it would have made the same decision regardless of the illegal factor.[63]

9-29. What is the after-acquired evidence defense?

A defense that may affect a plaintiff's remedy is the "after-acquired evidence" defense. This defense was recognized by the Supreme Court in *McKennon v. Nashville Banner Publishing Co.*[64] The defense applies when the plaintiff alleges he was discharged for a discriminatory reason, and subsequent to the discharge (perhaps during the litigation itself) the employer discovers wrongdoing that occurred during the plaintiff's employment. The employer must prove that the discovered wrongdoing was of such severity that the employee would have been terminated for that conduct alone if the employer had known about it at the time of the termination. The defense does not relieve the employer of liability, however, because the employer could not have been motivated by knowledge it did not have at the time of the termination. Consequently, the plaintiff will still be able to prove that his employer was motived by discrimination. But wrongdoing by the employee, although not discovered after the discharge, must be taken into account in determining the remedy (such as the amount of back pay and front pay).

9-30. How will a plaintiff's failure to mitigate damages be a defense?

Another defense that may limit the plaintiff's remedy involves the duty to mitigate damages. The plaintiff may not recover damages for any harm that could have been avoided or minimized with reasonable effort. The employer has the burden of showing that the plaintiff failed to exercise reasonable diligence to mitigate damages.[65] For example, if the plaintiff proves he was terminated because of race and the employer proves that the plaintiff failed to exercise reasonable diligence in finding comparable employment, the plaintiff's ability to recover back pay and front pay may be limited.

9-31. What defenses exist to disparate impact claims?

GENERAL DEFENSES

When the plaintiff's claim is based on a disparate impact theory, the defendant may challenge the plaintiff's statistical data. For example, the comparison group used by the plaintiff might not be appropriate, or the size of the disparity might not be statistically significant. If the sample group is too small, the court may find that the alleged statistical disparity is not relevant. In a disparate impact case, the plaintiff must demonstrate that each employment practice causes a disparate impact. But if the plaintiff can demonstrate that the elements of the employer's decision-making process are not capable of separation for analysis, the decision-making process may be analyzed as one employment practice.[66]

Even if the plaintiff establishes a statistically significant disparate impact, the employer can defend the case by demonstrating that a specific employment practice is job related for the position in question and consistent with business necessity.[67] The employer has the burden of proving job relatedness and business necessity.

BONA FIDE SENIORITY SYSTEMS

Under Title VII, it is not an unlawful employment practice for an employer to apply different standards of compensation, or different terms, conditions, or privileges of employment pursuant to a bona fide seniority or merit system, or a system that measures earnings by quantity or quality of production or to employees who work in different locations, provided that differences are not the result of an intention to discriminate because of race, color,

religion, sex, or national origin.[68] Consequently, even if a bona fide seniority or merit-based system has a disparate impact on a protected group, the employer is not liable.

REMEDIES UNDER TITLE VII

9-32. What remedies exist under Title VII?

Under Title VII, if the plaintiff proves that the defendant intentionally engaged in or is intentionally engaging in unlawful discrimination, she may be awarded an injunction, reinstatement or hiring with or without back pay, attorney's fees, and costs.[69] In a mixed motive case, the plaintiff's remedies may be limited to declaratory or injunctive relief, attorney's fees, and costs if the employer proves that it would have taken the same action even in the absence of the impermissible motivating factor.[70]

Back pay is routinely awarded as a remedy where the plaintiff was terminated from employment for an unlawful discriminatory reason. However, there are limitations on back pay. For example, back pay liability does not accrue from a date more than two years prior to the filing of a charge with the EEOC. Also, interim earnings or amounts the plaintiff could have earned through reasonable diligence operate to reduce the back pay award.

Trial courts also award front pay when appropriate. Front pay may extend until the plaintiff fails to make reasonable efforts to secure substantially equivalent employment or until the plaintiff obtains or is offered such employment.

In addition, in cases involving unlawful intentional discrimination (not disparate impact), the plaintiff may recover compensatory and punitive damages.[71] Compensatory damages include future pecuniary losses, emotional pain, suffering, inconvenience, mental anguish, loss of enjoyment of life, and other non-pecuniary losses. Punitive damages may be recovered for intentional discrimination if the plaintiff demonstrates that the defendant engaged in a discriminatory practice with malice or with reckless indifference to the individual's rights. The sum of the amount of compensatory damages and the amount of punitive damages may not exceed the following: $50,000 for defendants with 15 to 100 employees; $100,000 for defendants with 101 to 200 employees; $200,000 for defendants with 201 to 500 employees; and $300,000 for defendants with more than 500 employees.[72]

CHAPTER ENDNOTES

1. 42 U.S.C. §2000e-2.
2. 42 U.S.C. §2000e-5.
3. 29 CFR §1601.18.
4. 29 CFR §1601.19.
5. 29 CFR §1601.24.
6. 42 U.S.C. §2000e-5(f); 29 CFR §1601.27.
7. 29 CFR §1601.28.
8. 42 U.S.C. §2000e-5(f).
9. 42 U.S.C. §2000e(f).
10. 42 U.S.C. §2000e-2(a)(1).
11. 42 U.S.C. §§2000e, 2000e-2.
12. *Walters v. Metropolitan Educ. Enter., Inc.*, 519 U.S. 202 (1997).
13. See, e.g., *Armbruster v. Quinn*, 711 F.2d 1332 (6th Cir. 1983).
14. 42 U.S.C. §2000e.
15. 42 U.S.C. §2000e(b).
16. 42 U.S.C. §2000e-1(a).
17. 42 U.S.C. §2000e-2.
18. *Tetro v. Elliott Popham Pontiac, Oldsmobile, Buick, and GMC Trucks, Inc.*, 173 F.3d 988 (6th Cir. 1999).
19. 42 U.S.C. §2000e(j).
20. 29 CFR §1605.1.
21. 42 U.S.C. §2000e(j).
22. 29 CFR §1605.2(c).
23. 29 CFR §1605.2(e).
24. 29 CFR §1605.2(d)(1).
25. See *Hafford v. Seidner*, 183 F.3d 506 (6th Cir. 1999); *Chalmers v. Tulon Co. of Richmond*, 101 F.3d 1012 (4th Cir. 1996).
26. See *Phillips v. Martin-Marietta Corp.*, 400 U.S. 542 (1971).
27. 29 CFR §1606.1.
28. 29 CFR §1606.1.
29. *Espinoza v. Farah Mfg. Co.*, Inc., 414 U.S. 86 (1973); 29 CFR §1606.5.
30. 29 CFR §1606.7(a).
31. 29 CFR §1606.7(b).
32. 29 CFR §1606.7(c).
33. 29 CFR §1606.8.
34. 42 U.S.C. §2000e-3(a).
35. 42 U.S.C. §2000e-10.
36. 42 U.S.C. §2000e-8(c).
37. 29 CFR §1602.14.
38. 29 CFR 1602.20(b).
39. 29 CFR 1602.20(c).
40. 29 CFR 1602.7.
41. 29 CFR 1602.13.
42. 42 U.S.C. §2000e-5(b); 29 CFR §1601.9.
43. 29 CFR §1601.12(a).
44. 42 U.S.C. §2000e-5(c).
45. 42 U.S.C. §2000e-5(e).
46. 29 CFR §1601.28(a)(1).
47. 29 CFR §1601.28(a)(2).
48. 42 U.S.C. §2000e-5(e).
49. 411 U.S. 792 (1973).

50. *Reeves v. Sanderson Plumbing Products, Inc.*, 530 U.S. 133 (2000).
51. 490 U.S. 228 (1989).
52. 42 U.S.C. §2000e-2(m).
53. 42 U.S.C. §2000e-5(g)(2)(B).
54. 42 U.S.C. §2000e-6.
55. 401 U.S. 424 (1971).
56. 42 U.S.C. §2000e-2(k).
57. 42 U.S.C. §2000e-2(e).
58. *Dothard v. Rawlinson,* 433 U.S. 321 (1977).
59. 42 U.S.C. §2000e-1(a).
60. 42 U.S.C. §2000e-2(e).
61. 42 U.S.C. §2000e(j).
62. 42 U.S.C. §2000e-2(m).
63. 42 U.S.C. §2000e-5(g)(2)(B).
64. 511 U.S. 352 (1995).
65. *Weaver v. Casa Gallardo Inc.*, 922 F.2d 1515 (11th Cir. 1991); *Fleming v. County of Kane*, 898 F.2d 553 (7th Cir. 1990).
66. 42 U.S.C. §2000e-2(k)(1)(B).
67. 42 U.S.C. §2000e-2(k)(1)(A).
68. 42 U.S.C. §2000e-2(h).
69. 42 U.S.C. §2000e-5(g)(1).
70. 42 U.S.C. §2000e-5(g)(2)(B).
71. 42 U.S.C. §1981a(a)(1).
72. 42 U.S.C. §1981a(b).

Chapter 10

Equal Pay Act

GENERALLY

10-1. What is the Equal Pay Act?

10-2. Who enforces the EPA?

10-3. Who must comply with the EPA?

10-4. Who is protected under the EPA?

10-5. What specifically does the EPA prohibit?

10-6. What is an "establishment" for purposes of the EPA?

10-7. What are "wages" for purposes of the EPA?

10-8. What are "fringe benefits" for purposes of the EPA?

10-9. What record-keeping requirements exist under the EPA?

PROCEDURE FOR FILING A CLAIM UNDER THE EPA

10-10. Does a plaintiff have to file an EEOC charge?

LITIGATION OF AN EPA CLAIM

PRIMA FACIE CASE

10-11. How are EPA claims litigated?

10-12. What constitutes "equal work"?

10-13. What is the "equal skill" test?

10-14. What is the "equal effort" test?

10-15. What is the "equal responsibility" test?

10-16. What is meant by "similar working conditions"?

EMPLOYER DEFENSES

10-17. What defenses are available to an employer once a prima facie case under the EPA is established?

10-18. Are provisions in a collective bargaining agreement establishing unequal pay a defense to an EPA claim?

COMPLIANCE

10-19. Can an employer comply with the EPA by reducing the wages of the higher paid employee?

10-20. May an employer provide certain benefits only to employees of one gender?

10-21. What if it is more expensive to the employer to provide certain benefits to employees of one gender than another?

10-22. May the employer's retirement plan contain any differentials based on gender?

STATUTE OF LIMITATIONS

10-23. What is the statute of limitations under the EPA?

REMEDIES

10-24. What remedies are available under the EPA?

RELATIONSHIP WITH OTHER LAWS

10-25. What is the relationship between the EPA and Title VII of the Civil Rights Act of 1964?

GENERALLY

10-1. What is the Equal Pay Act?

The Equal Pay Act ("EPA") is an amendment to the Fair Labor Standards Act ("FLSA") passed by Congress in 1963. It prohibits unequal wages for women and men who work in the same establishment, on jobs that require equal skill, effort and responsibility, and that are performed under similar working conditions.[1]

10-2. Who enforces the EPA?

The Equal Employment Opportunities Commission ("EEOC") has been charged with enforcement of the EPA since 1979. However, the EEOC has adopted the Department of Labor's procedures for investigation and enforcement under the EPA, as well as its regulations on record-keeping requirements. The EEOC may bring suit on behalf of the aggrieved employee.[2]

The EPA also authorizes individual plaintiffs to file and prosecute civil actions under the EPA.[3]

10-3. Who must comply with the EPA?

The EPA applies to all employers, both public and private, that have employees covered by the EPA.[4] The definition of "employer" in the FLSA is to be used for purposes of EPA claims. The FLSA defines "employer" as any person acting directly or indirectly in the interests of an employer in relation to an employee.[5] (See Q 19-3).

The EPA also applies to labor organizations, which are defined for purposes of the Act as "any organization... in which employees participate and which exists for the purpose, in whole or in part, of dealing with employers concerning grievances, labor disputes, wages, rates of pay, hours of employment, or conditions of work."[6]

10-4. Who is protected under the EPA?

The EPA protects all employees covered by the FLSA.[7] See Q 19-3. Men are protected under the EPA equally with women.[8]

The EPA further applies to executive, administrative and professional employees who are normally exempted from the FLSA.[9]

10-5. What specifically does the EPA prohibit?

The EPA makes it unlawful for an employer to provide unequal wages for men and women who work in the same establishment, on jobs that require equal skill, effort and responsibility, and that are performed under similar working conditions.[10]

The EPA further makes it unlawful for any labor organization to cause or attempt to cause an employer to effect a violation of the EPA.[11]

10-6. What is an "establishment" for purposes of the EPA?

The term "establishment" refers to a distinct physical place where employees work.[12] Each physically separate place of business is ordinarily considered a separate establishment.[13] Accordingly, the obligation to comply with the provisions of the EPA is determined separately with reference to those employees at each particular establishment. Thus, where there are disparities in wage rates among various locations of a single business, the scope of the EPA inquiry will be limited to a single location.

10-7. What are "wages" for purposes of the EPA?

The term "wages" include all payments made to the employee as remuneration for employment. Vacation and holiday pay, premium payments of any kind, and other fringe benefits are also included.[14]

10-8. What are "fringe benefits" for purposes of the EPA?

"Fringe benefits" are considered remuneration for employment under the EPA. Accordingly, it is unlawful to discriminate between men and women performing equal work regarding fringe benefits. Fringe benefits include medical, hospital, accident, life insurance and retirement benefits, profit sharing and bonus plans, leave and

other such benefits.[15] Where an employer conditions benefits to employees and their spouses and families on whether the employee is "the head of the household" or "principal wage earner" in the family, the overall implementation of the plan will be closely scrutinized.[16]

10-9. What record-keeping requirements exist under the EPA?

In addition to all other records required to be maintained by the employer under the FLSA (see Q 19-17), the EPA requires employers to maintain all records relating to the payment of wages, wage rates, job evaluations, job descriptions, merit systems, seniority systems, collective bargaining agreements, description of practices or other matters that describe or explain the basis for payment of any wage differential to employees of the opposite gender in the same establishment, and that may be pertinent to a determination whether such differential is based on a factor other than gender. These records must be preserved for at least two years.[17]

PROCEDURE FOR FILING A CLAIM UNDER THE EPA

10-10. Does a plaintiff have to file an EEOC charge?

No. The employee may, but is not required to, file a charge with the EEOC.[18]

LITIGATION OF AN EPA CLAIM

PRIMA FACIE CASE

10-11. How are EPA claims litigated?

A plaintiff establishes a prima facie case under the EPA by showing that his or her employer is subject to the EPA; that he or she performed work in a position requiring equal skill, effort and responsibility under similar working conditions in the same establishment; and that he or she was paid less than the member of the opposite gender providing the basis of comparison.[19] The jobs, not the skills and qualifications of the incumbents, should be analyzed to establish a prima facie case.[20] A plaintiff must be able to establish which employees of the opposite gender have similar jobs, and how the jobs are similar.[21] However, a plaintiff need only

show discrimination vis-a-vis one employee of the opposite gender.[22]

Once the plaintiff has set forth a prima facie case, the burden shifts to the employer to prove that the unequal pay is made pursuant to:

1. a seniority system;

2. a merit system;

3. a system that measures earnings by quantity or quality of production; or

4. a differential based on any factor other than gender or some combination of these. (See Q 10-17.)

10-12. What constitutes "equal work"?

In determining what constitutes "equal work," actual job content, not job title or description controls.[23] Courts will look to the requirements of the job itself, not to the skills and qualifications of the individual holding the job.[24] The equal work standard does not require that the compared jobs be identical, only that they be "substantially equal."[25]

In determining whether employees perform equal work for purposes of the EPA, the amount of time in which an employee spends in the performance of different duties is not the sole criteria. It is also necessary to consider the degree of difference in terms of skill, effort, and responsibility. These factors are related in such a manner that a general standard to determine equality of jobs cannot be set up solely on the basis of percentage of time. Consequently, finding that one job requires employees to expend greater effort for a certain percentage of their working time than employees performing another job, would not in itself establish that the jobs do not constitute equal work.[26]

Similarly, the performance of jobs on different machines or equipment would not necessarily result in the determination that the work performed is unequal within the meaning of the statute. If the difference in skill or effort required for the operation of such equipment is inconsequential, payment of a higher wage rate to employees of one gender because of a difference in machines or equipment would constitute a prohibited wage rate differential.[27]

Where jobs are performed in different departments or locations within an establishment, such a fact would not necessarily be sufficient to demonstrate that unequal work is involved were the equal pay standard otherwise applies.[28] This is particularly true in the case of retail establishments. Unless the employer can demonstrate that the sale of one article requires a higher degree of skill or effort than the sale of another article, so as to render the equal pay standard inapplicable, it will be assumed for purposes of the EPA that the salesmen and saleswomen concerned are performing equal work.[29]

Three separate tests, i.e., "equal skill" (see Q 10-13), "equal effort" (see Q 10-14), and "equal responsibility" (see Q 10-15) are used to determine whether two jobs constitute "equal work." All three of these criteria must be established for positions to be considered "equal work" for purposes of the EPA.

10-13. What is the "equal skill" test?

Where the amount or degree of skill required to perform one job is substantially greater than that required to perform another job, liability under the EPA will not arise. Skill includes such factors as experience, training, education, and ability.[30] Possession of a skill not needed to meet the requirements of the job cannot be considered in making a determination regarding equality of skill.[31] It is the job that should be scrutinized, rather than the employee. Similarly, the efficiency of the employee's performance on the job is not, in itself, an appropriate factor to consider when evaluating skill.[32]

10-14. What is the "equal effort" test?

The "equal effort" criteria looks to the physical or mental exertion needed for the performance of the job. Where substantial differences exist in the amount or the degree of effort required to be expended in the performance of the job, liability under the equal pay act will not arise. Jobs may require equal effort in performing them even though the effort may be displayed in different ways in two otherwise similar jobs. Differences only in the kind of effort required of the job will not justify wage differentials between employees.[33]

The occasional or sporadic performance of an activity that may require extra physical or mental exertion is not alone sufficient to justify a finding of unequal effort.[34]

10-15. What is the "equal responsibility" test?

This test looks to the degree of accountability required in the performance of the job, with an emphasis on the importance of the job obligation. The additional responsibility must be considerable to justify a pay differential. For instance, a minor responsibility such as turning out the lights in the department at the end of the business day will not justify a pay differential. However, more substantial responsibilities may permit a pay differential. For example, two sales clerks may be engaged primarily in selling identical or similar merchandise. However, one may be given different responsibilities in that one clerk is authorized to determine whether to accept the personal checks of customers, and the other salesperson is not. In this situation, payment of a higher wage rate to this employee would be permissible.[35]

10-16. What is meant by "similar working conditions"?

The term "similar working conditions" encompasses two sub factors: "surroundings" and "hazards." "Surroundings" measures the elements, such as toxic chemicals or fumes, regularly encountered by a worker, and the intensity and frequency of these elements. "Hazards" takes into account the physical hazards regularly encountered, the frequency and the severity of injury they can cause. The phrase "working conditions" does not encompass shift differentials.[36]

EMPLOYER DEFENSES

10-17. What defenses are available to an employer once a prima facie case under the EPA is established?

After the plaintiff has set forth a prima facie case, the burden shifts to the employer to prove that the unequal pay is made pursuant to:

1. a seniority system;

2. a merit system;

3. a system that measures earnings by quantity or quality of production; or

4. a differential based on any factor other than gender or some combination of these.

These exceptions recognize that there are factors other than gender that can be used to justify a wage differential, even as between employees of opposite gender performing equal work on jobs that otherwise meet the test of equal skill, effort, and responsibility, in similar working conditions. An employer who asserts an exception to equal pay has the burden to prove the facts establishing this affirmative defense.

The first three defenses share the requirement that the employer have a "system." A formal written document may not be necessary, but an employer must regularly use an organized and structured procedure with identified criteria to determine wage differences.[37] Employees should be aware of this system and, of course, the system must not be based on gender.[38]

Of the three systems, the merit system defense raises the most problems. Ratings under a merit system must be based on a predetermined criteria applied systematically.[39] An employer must be able to explain how it used its merit system to arrive at each worker's rating and how that rating caused any pay discrepancies among employees doing equal work.[40]

The "factor other than gender" exception applies when an employer can demonstrate both that gender had no part in the wage differential at issue and that the amount of the differential and the wage properly attributable to the factor other than gender are reasonably related. Thus, for example, if a salaried male clerk and a salaried female clerk perform substantially equal work, but one works a forty-hour week while the other works a thirty-five hour week, a wage differential would be permitted so long as the employees were not assigned to their jobs because of their gender and the differential in question was reasonable.

It has been held that, although prior salary alone could not constitute a "factor other than gender" that would justify a wage disparity, prior salary coupled with a higher level of experience could constitute a legitimate "factor other than gender."[41]

The "factor other than gender" exception also has been interpreted to justify certain "red circle" rates, i.e., higher than normal rates that may be paid for various reasons unrelated to gender. For example, an employer may justifiably "red circle" when it transfers an employee who can no longer perform his regular job, due to ill health to a different job that is being performed by opposite gender

employees at a lower rate. Under the "red circle" principle, the employer may justify continuing to pay the employee his pre-transfer rate. Under these circumstances, maintaining the employee's pre-transfer salary is a valid non-discriminatory reason for the differential.[42]

As another example, an employer may require an employee, for a short period, to perform the work of a classification other than the employee's regular classification. If the employee's regular rate is higher than the rate of the classification to which the employee is temporarily assigned, the employer may maintain the employee at the higher rate under the "red circle" principle.[43]

10-18. Are provisions in a collective bargaining agreement establishing unequal pay a defense to an EPA claim?

No. The establishment of provisions in a collective bargaining agreement setting unequal rates of pay will not be a defense for the employer or the bargaining unit. Any such provisions are null and void under law.[44]

COMPLIANCE

10-19. Can an employer comply with the EPA by reducing the wages of the higher paid employee?

No. Compliance with the EPA must be achieved by raising wages paid to underpaid employees.[45] Compliance may not be achieved by lowering the wages paid to higher paid employees of one gender.[46]

10-20. May an employer provide certain benefits only to employees of one gender?

No. An employer may not make available benefits for the spouses or the families of employees of one gender where the same benefits are not made available to the spouses or the families of the opposite gender employee.[47]

10-21. What if it is more expensive to the employer to provide certain benefits to employees of one gender than another?

It is not a defense under the EPA that the cost of benefits is greater with respect to one gender than the other.[48]

10-22. May the employer's retirement plan contain any differentials based on gender?

No. An employer may not have a pension or retirement plan that establishes different optional or compulsory retirement ages based on gender, or that otherwise differentiates benefits on the basis of gender.[49]

STATUTE OF LIMITATIONS

10-23. What is the statute of limitations under the EPA?

A two year statute of limitations applies to the recovery of unpaid wages, except that a willful violation must be commenced within three years after the cause of action occurred.[50]

REMEDIES

10-24. What remedies are available under the EPA?

BACK PAY

Successful litigants under the EPA may recover the difference between the wages they actually received and the average wages paid to opposite gender employees performing equal work during each pay period.[51] Back wages may normally be recovered for a period of two years before the filing of a complaint.[52] The period may be extended to three years when a willful violation is shown.[53]

LIQUIDATED DAMAGES

Because the EPA is part of the FLSA, liquidated damages in an amount equal to the amount of lost earnings and benefits also may be awarded for violations.[54]

However, a "good faith" defense from liquidated damages is available to an employer. If an employer shows to the satisfaction of the court that the act or omission giving rise to the violation was done in good faith and that it had reasonable grounds for believing that its act or omission was not a violation of the EPA, the Court has discretion to award no liquidated damages or to reduce the amount of liquidated damages.[55]

Where an employer could not show that it had any intention of learning and complying with EPA requirements, liquidated damages were awarded.[56] In contrast, when the employer acted in good faith and upon a reasonable belief in the legality of its pay

practices, or when it could not be shown that it knew of and ignored the EPA's requirements, liquidated damages have been denied.[57]

ATTORNEY'S FEES

Reasonable attorney's fees may be awarded to successful EPA claimants in an amount to be established within the court's discretion.[58]

CRIMINAL PROSECUTION

Willful violations of the EPA may be prosecuted criminally and the violator fined up to $10,000. A second conviction for such a violation may result in imprisonment.[59]

RELATIONSHIP WITH OTHER LAWS

10-25. What is the relationship between the EPA and Title VII of the Civil Rights Act of 1964?

COVERAGE

Title VII of the Civil Rights Act of 1964 ("Title VII") covers types of wage discrimination that are not actionable under the EPA.[60] The EPA allows for actions based on unequal wages between the genders only for equal work performed in the same location. Title VII more broadly covers an employment discrimination based on gender, race or religion (see Chapter 9).

DIFFERENCES IN PROOF

A finding of liability under the EPA does not necessarily require a finding of wage discrimination under Title VII. Intent need not be proven under the EPA.[61] However, intent is a necessary element to a finding of liability under Title VII. Similar to the EPA, a Title VII plaintiff must first establish a prima facie case of wage discrimination by showing: (1) that he or she is a member of a protected class; and (2) that the job he or she occupied was similar to higher paying jobs occupied by comparable non-protected class members.[62] Once the plaintiff has established a prima facie case, the burden shifts to the defendant to articulate a legitimate, nondiscriminatory reason(s) for its allegedly discriminatory action.[63] If the defendant is successful in articulating nondiscriminatory reason(s), the burden shifts back to the plaintiff. The plaintiff must then prove that the defendant's articulated reason is a pretext for intentional discrimination.[64] Accordingly, a wage discrimination claim under Title VII will require proof of intentional discrimination.

RECOVERY

A plaintiff may receive recovery under both the EPA and Title VII so long as the plaintiff does not receive duplicative relief for the same wrong. Relief is computed to give each plaintiff the highest benefit in which entitlement under either statute would provide.[65]

CHAPTER ENDNOTES

1. See 29 U.S.C. §206(d) et seq.
2. 29 CFR §1620.33(b).
3. See 29 U.S.C. §216(b); 29 CFR §1620.33(b).
4. 29 U.S.C. §206(d)(1).
5. 29 CFR §1620.8.
6. 29 U.S.C. §206(d)(4).
7. 29 CFR §1620.01.
8. 29 CFR §1620.01(c).
9. 29 CFR §1620.01(a)(1).
10. 29 U.S.C. §206(d)(1).
11. 29 U.S.C. §206(d)(2).
12. 29 CFR §1620.9.
13. 29 CFR §1620.9.
14. 29 CFR §§1620.10, 1620.11.
15. 29 CFR §1620.11(a).
16. 29 CFR §1620.11(c).
17. 29 CFR §1620.32.
18. *County of Washington v. Gunther*, 452 U.S. 161, 175 n.14 (1981).
19. *Jones v. Flagship Intel*, 793 F.2d 714, 722-723 (5th Cir. 1986).
20. *Jones v. Westside-Urban Health Center, Inc.*, 760 F. Supp. 1575, 1578 (S.D. Ga. 1991).
21. *Berg v. Norand Corp.*, 169 F.3d 1140, 1146 (8th Cir. 1999).
22. *EEOC v. White and Son Enterprises*, 881 F.2d 1006, 1009 (11th Cir. 1989).
23. 29 CFR §1620.13(e).
24. See *Mulhall v. Advance Security, Inc.*, 19 F.3d 586, 594 (11th Cir. 1994).
25. 29 CFR §1620.13(a).
26. 29 CFR §1620.14(c).
27. 29 CFR §1620.14(c).
28. 29 CFR §1620.14(c).
29. 29 CFR §1620.14(c).
30. 29 CFR §1620.15(a).
31. 29 CFR §1620.15(a).
32. 29 CFR §1620.15(a).
33. 29 CFR §1620.16(a).
34. 29 CFR §1620.16(b).
35. 29 CFR §§1620.17(b)(2), 1620.17(b)(3).
36. 29 CFR §1620.18.
37. *EEOC v. Aetna Insurance Co.*, 616 F.2d 719, 725 (4th Cir. 1980).
38. See, e.g., *EEOC v. Whitin Mach. Works, Inc.*, 635 F.2d 1095, 1097 (4th Cir. 1980).
39. See e.g., *Ryduchowski v. The Port Authority of New York and New Jersey*, 203 F.3d 135, 142 (2nd. Cir. 2000); *EEOC v. Aetna Insurance Co.*, 616 F.2d 719 (4th Cir. 1980).

40. *EEOC v. Delaware Department of Health and Social Services*, 865 F.2d 1408 (3rd Cir. 1989).
41. *Irby v. Bittick*, 44 F.3d 949, 955 (11th Cir. 1995).
42. 29 CFR §1620.26.
43. 29 CFR §1620.26(b).
44. 29 CFR §1620.23.
45. 29 CFR §1620.25.
46. 29 U.S.C. §206(d).
47. 29 CFR §1620.11(d).
48. 29 CFR §1620.11(e).
49. 29 CFR §1620.11(f).
50. 29 CFR §1620.33(b).
51. See *EEOC v. Liggett & Myers, Inc.*, 690 F.2d 1072, 1076-1078 (4th Cir. 1982).
52. 29 CFR §1620.33(b).
53. 29 CFR §1620.33(b).
54. 29 U.S.C. §216(b); *Soto v. Adams Elevator Equipment Co.*, 941 F.2d 543 (7th Cir. 1991).
55. 29 U.S.C. §260.
56. *EEOC v. White and Son Enterprises*, 881 F.2d 1006, 1012 (11th Cir. 1989).
57. *Peters v. City of Shreveport*, 818 F.2d 1148 (5th Cir. 1987).
58. *Herman v. Roosevelt Fed. Savings & Loan Assoc.*, 569 F.2d 1033, 1036 (8th Cir. 1978).
59. 29 CFR §1620.33(c).
60. 29 U.S.C. §1620.27(a).
61. *Patkus v. Sangamon-Cass Consortium*, 769 F.2d 1251, 1260 (7th Cir. 1985).
62. *Miranda v. B&B Cash Grocery Store, Inc.*, 975 F.2d 1518, 1529 (11th Cir. 1992).
63. *Texas Dept. of Community Affairs v. Burdine*, 450 U.S. 248, 253 (1981).
64. *Saint Mary's Honor Center v. Hicks*, 509 U.S. 502, 526 (1993).
65. 29 U.S.C. §1620.27(b).

Chapter 11

Pregnancy Discrimination Act

GENERALLY

11-1. What is the Pregnancy Discrimination Act?

11-2. What is required by the PDA?

11-3. What is not required by the PDA?

11-4. Who is protected under the PDA?

11-5. Who must comply with the PDA?

11-6. Who is not protected under the Pregnancy Discrimination Act?

11-7. What effect does the Pregnancy Discrimination Act have on state laws?

11-8. What specifically does the Pregnancy Discrimination Act prohibit?

11-9. What sort of pregnancy discrimination by an employer is prohibited under the Pregnancy Discrimination Act?

11-10. What sort of pregnancy discrimination by an employment agency is prohibited under the Pregnancy Discrimination Act?

11-11. What sort of pregnancy discrimination by a labor organization is prohibited under the Pregnancy Discrimination Act?

11-12. In what way does the Pregnancy Discrimination Act prohibit retaliation?

11-13. May an employer limit disability benefits for pregnancy-related conditions to married employees?

11-14. What length of time must benefits for pregnancy-related disabilities be provided?

11-15. Must an employer who provides benefits for long-term or permanent disabilities provide such benefits for pregnancy-related conditions?

11-16. May an employer establish an eligibility waiting period for health insurance coverage of pregnancy-related conditions?

11-17. If an employee is unable to perform the functions of her job for pregnancy-related reasons, does the employer have to provide the employee with an alternative job?

11-18. What procedures may an employer use to determine whether to place a pregnant employee on leave?

11-19. If an employee has been absent from work as a result of a pregnancy-related condition, may her employer require her to remain on leave until after the baby is born?

11-20. If an employee is on leave because of a pregnancy-related condition, does her employer have to hold her job open for her until she returns?

11-21. May an employer use a different policy for seniority and vacation accrual or entitlement to pay raises for an employee on leave for a pregnancy-related condition?

11-22. Can an employer require an employee absent due to a pregnancy-related disability to exhaust her vacation benefits before receiving sick pay or disability benefits?

11-23. If an employer is in compliance with state law requirements for providing leave or disability insurance, does the employer's state law compliance fulfill the employer's obligation under the PDA?

11-24. What are the PDA's requirements regarding employer-provider health insurance coverage?

11-25. Does an employer-provided health insurance plan have to provide coverage for the pregnancy-related conditions of an employee's spouse?

11-26. If an employer offers an employee a choice among several health insurance plans, must each plan offer coverage for pregnancy-related conditions?

11-27. Can an employer discriminate in any way against a woman because she has had an abortion?

11-28. Is an employer required to provide fringe benefits for abortions if fringe benefits are provided for other medical conditions?

11-29. Who enforces the PDA?

11-30. How does the EEOC enforce the PDA?

11-31. How does the United States Department of Justice enforce the Pregnancy Discrimination Act?

11-32. How do individual plaintiffs enforce the PDA?

11-33. Does the PDA have any notice requirements?

11-34. Does the PDA have any record-keeping requirements?

PROCEDURE FOR FILING A PDA CLAIM

11-35. Does a plaintiff have to file an EEOC charge?

11-36. What is the time limit (statute of limitations) for filing an EEOC charge?

11-37. What is a "right to sue" letter?

11-38. What is the time limit (statute of limitations) for filing suit under the PDA?

LITIGATING A PDA CLAIM

11-39. How are PDA claims litigated?

DEFENSES TO PDA CLAIMS

11-40. What procedural defenses exist for PDA claims?

11-41. What statutory defenses exist for PDA claims?

11-42. What are the other defenses to PDA claims?

11-43. What is the "no prima facie case" defense?

11-44. What is the "legitimate, non-discriminatory reason" defense?

11-45. What is the "bona fide occupational qualification" defense?

11-46. Are state employers immune from PDA lawsuits under the Eleventh Amendment?

REMEDIES UNDER THE PDA

11-47. What remedies exist under the Pregnancy Discrimination Act?

GENERALLY

11-1. What is the Pregnancy Discrimination Act?

The Pregnancy Discrimination Act (PDA)[1] amended Title VII (see Chapter 9) to specify that sex discrimination under Title VII includes discrimination based on pregnancy and pregnancy-related conditions. The PDA became law on October 31, 1978. Specifically, it prohibits discrimination "on the basis of pregnancy, childbirth, or related medical conditions...."

Throughout this chapter, these rules regarding discrimination based upon pregnancy, childbirth, or related medical conditions will be referred to as the Pregnancy Discrimination Act or the PDA.

11-2. What is required by the PDA?

The PDA requires that covered employers treat women affected by pregnancy, childbirth, and related conditions the same as other applicants and employees who are similar in their ability (or inability) to work, but who are not affected by pregnancy, childbirth, or related medical conditions.[2]

Specifically, the PDA makes it unlawful to have a policy or practice that excludes from employment applicants or employees because of pregnancy, childbirth, or pregnancy-related medical conditions.[3]

Moreover, the PDA requires employers to treat disabilities caused by or contributed to by pregnancy, childbirth, or pregnancy-related medical conditions the same as disabilities caused by other medical conditions, with respect to:

1.   All fringe benefits;

2.   Employment policies relating to commencement and duration of leave;

3.   Vacation accrual;

4.   Seniority accrual;

5.   Reinstatement; and

6.   All other benefits and privileges of employment.[4]

11-3. What is not required by the PDA?

Although an employer cannot discriminate against workers affected by pregnancy, childbirth, or related medical conditions, the PDA does not require an employer to give more favorable treatment to a workers affected by such conditions.[5]

11-4. Who is protected under the PDA?

Women affected by pregnancy, childbirth, or related medical conditions are protected under the PDA. Abortion is also included among the conditions protected by the PDA.[6]

11-5. Who must comply with the PDA?

The PDA applies to any "employer," as defined by Title VII.

"Employer" under Title VII (see Chapter 9) means any employer, private or public, that "has fifteen or more employees for each working day in each of twenty or more calendar weeks in the current or preceding calendar year, and any agent of such a person....".[7]

The PDA also applies to employment agencies serving such employers[8] and labor organizations that service such employers[9].

The term "employer" does *not* include:

1. The United States or any corporation owned by the United States;

2. An Indian tribe;

3. Any department or agency of the District of Columbia; and

4. A bona fide private membership club (other than a labor organization).[10]

11-6. Who is not protected under the Pregnancy Discrimination Act?

Obviously, male applicants and employees are not protected under the PDA. In addition, female applicants and employees whose current or potential employers do not meet the statutory definition of employer are also not protected under the PDA.

11-7. What effect does the Pregnancy Discrimination Act have on state laws?

The PDA preempts any provision of state law that requires or permits the doing of any act made unlawful by the PDA.[11]

It should be noted, however, that nothing in the PDA exempts or relieves any employer from any liability, duty, penalty, or punishment provided under any state law that makes unlawful a practice that is not unlawful under the PDA.[12]

Accordingly, state and local "fair employment practice" (FEP) laws should be reviewed in conjunction with the PDA for applicability of those laws with respect to pregnancy discrimination.

It should be noted that compliance with state law does not necessarily fulfill an employer's obligations under the PDA (see Q 11-23).[13]

11-8. What specifically does the Pregnancy Discrimination Act prohibit?

The PDA makes unlawful (1) pregnancy discrimination by an "employer" (Q 11-9); (2) pregnancy discrimination by an "employment agency" (Q 11-10); (3) pregnancy discrimination by a "labor organization"(Q 11-11); and (4) retaliation (Q 11-12).

11-9. What sort of pregnancy discrimination by an employer is prohibited under the Pregnancy Discrimination Act?

The PDA generally makes it unlawful for an employer to discriminate against pregnant workers. Specifically, the PDA makes it unlawful to:

1. Fail or refuse to hire or discharge or otherwise discriminate against any individual with respect to her (a) compensation, (b) terms, (3) conditions, or (4) privileges of employment based on her pregnancy, pregnancy-related condition, or because she has had an abortion;[14]

2. Force or require a pregnant employee to take mandatory leave that is not based on her individual ability to perform the essential functions of her position;[15]

3. Fail to hold open a job for pregnancy-related absence for the same length of time that jobs are held open for sick or disability leave absences;[16] and

4. Fail to offer the same fringe benefits, such as (a) disability benefits, (b) sick leave, (c) vacation and seniority accrual, and (d) health insurance to women affected by pregnancy or a pregnancy-related condition as are offered to other employees.[17]

11-10. What sort of pregnancy discrimination by an employment agency is prohibited under the Pregnancy Discrimination Act?

The PDA makes it unlawful for an employment agency (see Q 11-5) to:

1. Fail or refuse to refer for employment, or otherwise to discriminate against; or

2. Classify or refer for employment

any individual based upon such individual's pregnancy or pregnancy-related condition.[18]

11-11. What sort of pregnancy discrimination by a labor organization is prohibited under the Pregnancy Discrimination Act?

The PDA makes it unlawful for a labor organization to:

1. Exclude or expel from its membership, or otherwise discriminate against, any individual because of her pregnancy or pregnancy-related condition;

2. Limit, segregate, or classify its membership, in any way that would deprive (or tend to deprive) any individual of employment opportunities, or would limit such opportunities or otherwise adversely affect her status as an employee or as an applicant for employment, because of pregnancy or a pregnancy-related condition;

3. Classify or fail or refuse to refer for employment any individual, in any way that would deprive (or tend to deprive) any individual of employment opportunities, or would limit such opportunities or otherwise adversely affect her status as an employee or as an applicant for employment, because of pregnancy or a pregnancy-related condition; or

4. Cause or attempt to cause an employer to discriminate against an individual in violation of the forgoing.[19]

11-12. In what way does the Pregnancy Discrimination Act prohibit retaliation?

The PDA prohibits an employer from retaliating against its employees or applicants for employment because they have opposed any unlawful employment practice under the PDA.

Employers are also prohibited from retaliating in any way against an individual who has made a charge, testified, assisted, or participated in any manner in an investigation, proceeding, or hearing under the PDA.

Similar prohibitions apply to employment agencies and labor management committees involved in training programs.[20]

11-13. May an employer limit disability benefits for pregnancy-related conditions to married employees?

No. According to the regulations, an employer may not limit disability benefits for pregnancy-related conditions to married employees, but must also extend them to unmarried women.[21]

11-14. What length of time must benefits for pregnancy-related disabilities be provided?

An employer that provides income maintenance benefits for temporary disabilities must also provide such benefits for pregnancy-related disabilities to the same extent that they are provided for non pregnancy-related temporary disabilities.[22]

11-15. Must an employer who provides benefits for long-term or permanent disabilities provide such benefits for pregnancy-related conditions?

Yes. Benefits for long-term or permanent pregnancy-related conditions must be provided to the same extent as benefits are provided for other conditions resulting in long-term or permanent disability.[23]

11-16. May an employer establish an eligibility waiting period for health insurance coverage of pregnancy-related conditions?

Yes. An employer may require an eligibility period for health insurance coverage of pregnancy-related conditions, but only to the same extent as the eligibility waiting period for other medical conditions.

Additionally, if a health insurance plan excludes benefit payments for pre-existing medical conditions when the coverage becomes effective, it can also exclude benefit payments for medical costs for a pre-existing pregnancy.[24]

11-17. If an employee is unable to perform the functions of her job for pregnancy-related reasons, does the employer have to provide the employee with an alternative job?

It depends on how the employer treats employees temporarily unable to perform their job functions for other reasons.

An employer is required to treat an employee temporarily unable to perform the functions of her job because of a pregnancy-related condition in the same manner as it treats other temporarily disabled employees. Thus, if the employer provides alternative work for employees temporarily unable to perform their job functions for other reasons, it must also provide alternative work to the same extent for employees temporarily unable to perform job functions because of a pregnancy-related condition.[25]

11-18. What procedures may an employer use to determine whether to place a pregnant employee on leave?

An employer may not apply more stringent conditions on pregnant employees. The employer may not single out pregnancy-related conditions for special procedures for making leave decisions. The employer must use the same procedure for making leave decisions for pregnant employees as it uses for any other employee requesting medical leave.[26]

11-19. If an employee has been absent from work as a result of a pregnancy-related condition, may her employer require her to remain on leave until after the baby is born?

No. An employee affected by a pregnancy-related condition must be permitted to work at all times during her pregnancy provided that she is able to perform the functions of her position.

An employer cannot have a rule that prohibits an employee from returning to work for a predetermined amount of time after childbirth.[27]

11-20. If an employee is on leave because of a pregnancy-related condition, does her employer have to hold her job open for her until she returns?

It depends on how the employer treats employees who are on sick or disability leave for non pregnancy-related conditions. An employer must hold the job of an employee who is absent on leave because of a pregnancy-related condition open to the same extent that jobs are held open for employees who are on sick or disability leave for non pregnancy-related conditions.[28]

11-21. May an employer use a different policy for seniority and vacation accrual or entitlement to pay raises for an employee on leave for a pregnancy-related condition?

No. An employer's policy for crediting time for seniority and vacation accrual and pay raise entitlement must be the same as the policy for employees on leave for other reasons.[29]

11-22. Can an employer require an employee absent due to a pregnancy-related disability to exhaust her vacation benefits before receiving sick pay or disability benefits?

It depends on how the employer treats employees absent for other disabling causes. An employer cannot impose a requirement on employees absent due to pregnancy-related disabilities to exhaust vacation benefits before receiving sick pay or disability benefits if employees absent for other disabling causes are not subject to the same requirement.[30]

11-23. If an employer is in compliance with state law requirements for providing leave or disability insurance, does the employer's state law compliance fulfill the employer's obligation under the Pregnancy Discrimination Act?

Not necessarily. For purposes of providing leave or disability insurance, the PDA requires employers to treat employees disabled temporarily by pregnancy the same as employees temporarily disabled for other reasons. Accordingly, if the state law requirement is less than the employer's benefit provided to other temporarily disabled employees, the employer would not fulfill its PDA obligation simply by complying with state law.[31]

11-24. What are the PDA's requirements regarding employer-provider health insurance coverage?

The Pregnancy Discrimination Act requires that an employer must provide health insurance benefits for pregnancy-related conditions to the same extent other medical conditions are covered.

Specifically, an employer-provided health insurance plan must provide the same coverage for pregnancy-related conditions with respect to: (1) deductible provisions; (2) pre-existing condition coverage; (3) reimbursements for expenses; (4) choice of physicians or hospitals; and (5) coverage dollar amount limitations.[32]

11-25. Does an employer-provided health insurance plan have to provide coverage for the pregnancy-related conditions of an employee's spouse?

It depends on how the employer-provided health insurance plan covers employees' spouses for other medical conditions.

If an employer-provided health insurance plan covers the medical expenses of employee's spouses for other medical conditions, it must provide coverage to the same extent for the pregnancy-related conditions of employees' spouses.[33]

Where no coverage is provided for employees' spouses, there is no obligation to provide coverage for the pregnancy-related conditions of employees' spouses.[34]

An employer does not have to provide *spouses* of male employees with the same level of coverage that it provides female *employees*.[35]

An employer *does* have to provide the same as the level of coverage for a pregnancy-related condition of an employee's spouse as are provided for all other medical conditions of employees' spouses. For example, if the employer covers employees for 100% of their reasonable and customary expenses sustained for a medical condition but only covers 50% for dependent spouses, the employer would only be responsible for covering pregnancy-related conditions of male employees' spouses at 50%. An employer does not have to cover the pregnancy-related conditions of other dependents as long as it excludes the pregnancy-related conditions of the dependents of all employees, male and female.[36]

11-26. If an employer offers an employee a choice among several health insurance plans, must each plan offer coverage for pregnancy-related conditions?

Yes. If an employer offers the employee a choice of health insurance plans, all of the offered plans must provide coverage for pregnancy-related conditions, and each plan must treat pregnancy-related conditions the same as other medical conditions covered under the plan.[37]

11-27. Can an employer discriminate in any way against a woman because she has had an abortion?

No. Under the Pregnancy Discrimination Act, an employer cannot: (1) refuse to hire; (2) refuse to promote; (3) discharge; or (4) otherwise discriminate in any of its employment practices against a woman that is considering having or has had an abortion.[38]

11-28. Is an employer required to provide fringe benefits for abortions if fringe benefits are provided for other medical conditions?

Yes and No. All fringe benefits other than health insurance (e.g., sick leave) must be provided for abortions.[39]

In contrast, health insurance coverage does not have to be provided for abortions unless the life of the woman would be endangered if the fetus were carried to term, or where medical complications arise from abortion. If complications arise during an abortion (e.g., excessive hemorrhaging), an employer-provided health insurance plan must cover the additional cost due to the complications attributable to the abortion.[40]

The PDA specifically provides that an employer may voluntarily elect to provide health insurance coverage for abortions; however, the employer must do so in the same manner and to the same degree as it covers other medical conditions.[41]

11-29. Who enforces the PDA?

The Pregnancy Discrimination Act is enforced by the Equal Employment Opportunities Commission (EEOC) (see Q 11-30), the United States Department of Justice (DOJ) (see Q 11-31), and individual plaintiffs (see Q 11-32).

11-30. How does the EEOC enforce the PDA?

The Equal Employment Opportunity Commission (EEOC) is charged generally with the enforcement of Title VII, including the PDA.[42]

The EEOC accepts, processes, and investigates charges of discrimination.

If the EEOC determines, after investigation, that there is probable cause to believe that the law has been violated, it attempts conciliation.

If conciliation attempts fail, the EEOC may file a civil action against the employer in a federal district court, or issue a "notice of dismissal" and a "right to sue" letter to the complaining employee or applicant.[43]

11-31. How does the United States Department of Justice enforce the Pregnancy Discrimination Act?

After the EEOC has finished processing the charge of discrimination, the Justice Department is authorized to file suit in federal district court against state or local government employers charged with discrimination under the PDA.[44]

11-32. How do individual plaintiffs enforce the PDA?

An aggrieved applicant or employee may also file and prosecute civil actions pursuant to Title VII.[45] The individual must have first filed a charge of discrimination with the EEOC (see Q 11-30), however, and have received a "right to sue" letter (see Q 11-37).

11-33. Does the PDA have any notice requirements?

Every employer, employment agency, and labor organization subject to the PDA must post (and keep posted) a notice explaining the rights afforded under the Pregnancy Discrimination Act. The notice must be posted in conspicuous places on the employer's premises where notices to employees, applicants, and members are customarily posted.

The notice must be prepared or approved by the EEOC, and must set forth excerpts from or summaries of the pertinent provisions of Title VII and information pertinent to the filing of a complaint.[46] See Appendix A.

11-34. Does the PDA have any record-keeping requirements?

Every employer, employment agency, and labor organization subject to the PDA (see Q 11-5) is required to (1) make and keep records relevant to the determinations of whether unlawful employment practices have been or are being committed; (2) preserve such records for periods prescribed by the EEOC; and (3) make reports as required by the EEOC.[47]

Some of the most basic records, such as personnel or employment records, must be retained for one year from the date of the record or the employment decision relating to the record, whichever is later.[48]

PROCEDURE FOR FILING A PDA CLAIM

11-35. Does a plaintiff have to file an EEOC charge?

Yes. Before an individual can file a civil suit against an employer or other covered entity under the PDA, the individual must first exhaust her administrative remedies by filing a charge of pregnancy discrimination with the EEOC.

A charge must be made in writing, and under oath or affirmation.[49] Each charge should contain the full name, address, and telephone number of the aggrieved person, or the person making the charge on behalf of the aggrieved person.

A clear and concise statement of the facts, including pertinent dates, constituting the alleged unlawful employment practice (as well as certain additional information) must be included in the charge.[50]

The charge must also indicate, if known by the aggrieved individual, the approximate number of employees of the respondent employer or the approximate number of members of the respondent labor organization, as the case may be.[51]

A statement disclosing whether proceedings involving the alleged unlawful employment practice have been commenced before a state or local agency charged with the enforcement of fair employment practice (FEP) laws must also be included. If such proceedings have begun, the charge must also contain the date when such proceedings commenced, and must identify the state or local agency conducting the proceedings.[52]

Despite the requirement set forth above, a charge will be considered sufficient if the person making the charge provides the EEOC with a written statement that is sufficiently precise to (1) identify the parties; and (2) describe, generally, the action or practices of which the individual wishes to complain.[53]

A charge may be amended to cure technical defects or omissions. Such amendments to the original charge will relate back to the date when the EEOC first received the charge.[54]

If the aggrieved individual resides in a state that has a statute prohibiting pregnancy discrimination and an agency charged with the authority to enforce that statute, then the individual must also file a complaint of discrimination with the state agency. The individual need not, however, pursue her state claims in order to satisfy the state's requirement of state filing. Note that a PDA claimant can file charges with the EEOC and the state agency simultaneously. Note also that if an individual pursues her state claims and state remedies in the state court system, that will foreclose her ability to pursue a claim later in federal court.[55]

11-36. What is the time limit (statute of limitations) for filing an EEOC charge?

In general, an individual must file a charge of unlawful discrimination with the EEOC within 180 days after the alleged unlawful employment practice occurred.

If the aggrieved individual has filed a charge with a state or local agency comparable to the EEOC, the individual can file her EEOC charge within 300 days after the alleged unlawful employment practice occurred, or within 30 days after receiving notice that the state or local agency has terminated its proceedings, whichever is earlier.[56]

Note that, in many states, a charge filed with the state agency is simultaneously filed with the EEOC.

11-37. What is a "right to sue" letter?

Following the filing of a charge, the EEOC conducts an investigation to determine if probable cause exists to believe that unlawful discrimination has occurred.

If the EEOC determines that there is probable cause to believe that illegal discrimination has occurred, the EEOC will attempt conciliation. If conciliation fails, the EEOC may elect to file a lawsuit in federal district court on behalf of the aggrieved individual.

If the EEOC elects not to file a lawsuit on behalf of the individual, the EEOC will issue a "probable cause" finding and a "notice of right to sue," also known as a "right to sue" letter.

In contrast, if the EEOC's investigation shows no probable cause to believe that discrimination occurred, it will dismiss the charge and issue a "right to sue" letter.

The "right to sue" letter gives the individual notice that the EEOC has terminated its investigation, and permits the individual to file a private civil suit.

It is also common for individuals to request a "right to sue" letter prior to the EEOC completing its investigation. A "right to sue letter" will be issued when the aggrieved person requests, in writing, that a notice of right to sue be issued.[57]

Additionally, after the expiration of 180 days from the date of filing of the charge with the EEOC, a right to sue letter may be issued at any time.[58] Prior to the expiration of 180 days from the date of filing of the charge with the EEOC, the issuance may occur at any time so long as a specified EEOC official has determined that it is probable that the EEOC will be unable to complete its administrative processing within 180 days from the filing of the charge. A written certificate stating this must be attached to the notice of right to sue.[59] Such a practice has become more common with an increase in the volume of charges filed with the EEOC.

Generally, the "right-to-sue" letter is required before filing a lawsuit, however, many courts will not dismiss a lawsuit in the absence of a "right to sue" letter but will instead put the case on hold and wait for the plaintiff to obtain such a letter.

11-38. What is the time limit (statute of limitations) for filing suit under the PDA?

A claimant has 90 days after receipt of a "right to sue" letter to file a lawsuit under the PDA.[60]

There is no requirement that the EEOC act within any particular time period. Therefore, an EEOC notice (i.e., a "right to sue" letter) issued any number of years after the alleged discrimination, will, upon its receipt, start the running of the 90-day statute of limitations. So long as the claimant files suit within that 90 days, the action will be timely.

LITIGATING A PDA CLAIM

11-39. How are PDA claims litigated?

The manner in which a PDA claim is litigated depends largely on the type of claim brought.

Discrimination cases under the PDA can be based on either disparate treatment or disparate impact theories.

Claims of discrimination on the basis of pregnancy, childbirth or a related medical condition constitute discrimination based upon sex. Accordingly, it is well settled that such claims of discrimination must be analyzed in the same manner as any sex discrimination case under Title VII.[61]

A PDA claim does have one significant difference from other sex discrimination claims. An individual complaining of discrimination in violation of the PDA *can* compare herself to other females.[62]

For a full discussion on litigation of Title VII claims, see Chapter 9.

DEFENSES TO PDA CLAIMS

11-40. What procedural defenses exist for PDA claims?

As with other Title VII claims, a defendant can attack a plaintiff's PDA claim on a number of procedural grounds related to the filing of an EEOC charge and the statute of limitations by proving a claim is untimely.[63]

For example, a plaintiff must file an EEOC charge prior to filing a lawsuit. If a plaintiff fails to do so, the complaint will likely be dismissed.

Likewise, if a plaintiff fails to file its complaint within 90 days following the issuance of an EEOC "right to sue" letter, then the plaintiff's case will be dismissed.

11-41. What statutory defenses exist for PDA claims?

An employer can raise a number of procedural defenses to defeat a plaintiff's claim of discrimination based on pregnancy, childbirth, or pregnancy-related medical condition under the PDA.

Specifically, a defendant can raise the defense that it is not a covered entity ("employer," "employment agency," or "labor organization," see Q 11-5) as defined by the statute.[64] For example, if a defendant can show that it did not have 15 or more employees for 20 or more weeks in the current or preceding year, then it will not be considered an "employer" under the PDA, and thus not subject to suit.[65]

Moreover, the defendant can raise a specific exclusion under the PDA, such as the bona fide private membership club or Indian tribe exclusions (see Q 11-5).[66]

11-42. What are the other defenses to PDA claims?

Other defenses to PDA claims include the "no prima facie case" defense (see Q 11-43), the "legitimate, non-discriminatory reason" defense (see Q 11-44), and the "bona fide occupational qualification defense" (see Q 11-45).

11-43. What is the "no prima facie case" defense?

Just as with other Title VII claims (see Chapter 9), when defending a disparate treatment claim under the PDA, the defendant may be able to challenge the plaintiff's prima facie case.

For example, in a failure-to-hire case, the employer can argue that the plaintiff is not qualified for the job. In a case where the plaintiff was terminated for misconduct, the employer may be able to show that other employees who engaged in the same misconduct were also terminated.[67]

11-44. What is the "legitimate, non-discriminatory reason" defense?

In a disparate treatment case, once the plaintiff has established a prima facie case, the defendant has the burden of articulating a legitimate, non-discriminatory reason for its action or decision.

For example, if an employee was terminated and the employee claims her termination was because of her pregnancy, childbirth, or pregnancy-related medical condition, the employer may assert that the employee was terminated because she had poor attendance. At that point, the burden would shift to the plaintiff to establish that the employer's reason was not the real reason but a *pretext* for discrimination.[68]

11-45. What is the "bona fide occupational qualification defense"?

The bona fide occupational qualification (BFOQ) defense is another possible defense to a PDA claim.

The PDA provides that it is not an unlawful employment practice for an employer to hire or retain an individual on the basis of her pregnancy or pregnancy-related condition in limited circumstances where pregnancy or a pregnancy-related condition is a bona fide occupational qualification reasonably necessary to the normal operation of that particular business or enterprise.[69]

The BFOQ defense is an affirmative defense, which means that the defendant has the burden of persuasion. A defendant that invokes the BFOQ defense admits, in effect, that it engaged in an action, or made a decision, that ordinarily would constitute unlawful discrimination. If the BFOQ defense is successfully proven, however, the defendant will be insulated from liability.

One area where a BFOQ defense has seen limited success with pregnancy as the BFOQ is where the employee is supposed to be a role model for children and the pregnancy indicates that the employee engaged in premarital sex. A few courts have held that terminating an unmarried employee who became pregnant did not violate the PDA in limited circumstances.[70]

In *Chambers*, the court found that the discharge of the pregnant employee under the "role model rule" served the business

purpose of exposing young girls to positive options in life.[71] The so-called "role model rule" qualified as a BFOQ because the rule was reasonably necessary to the club's purpose and operation.[72]

It should be noted that the EEOC has expressly stated that the BFOQ defense is to be very narrowly construed.[73] For example, a BFOQ based on safety risks to the applicant or employee or to her unborn child has been found to violate the PDA.[74]

Since the BFOQ defense is an affirmative defense, the defendant must prove the defense by a preponderance of the evidence. A defendant invoking the BFOQ defense has the burden of proving that: (1) the pregnancy, childbirth, or related medical condition limit is reasonably necessary to the essence of the business; and either: (2) that all or substantially all individuals excluded from the job involved are in fact disqualified; or (3) that some of the individuals so excluded possess a disqualifying trait that cannot be ascertained except by reference to pregnancy.

11-46. Are state employers immune from PDA lawsuits under the Eleventh Amendment?

No. State and local governments are subject to the PDA in the same way as private employers.[75]

REMEDIES UNDER THE PDA

11-47. What remedies exist under the Pregnancy Discrimination Act?

The remedies available under the PDA are the same as the remedies for violations of Title VII (see Chapter 9).

If the plaintiff proves that the defendant intentionally engaged in or is intentionally engaging in unlawful discrimination, she may be awarded an injunction, reinstatement, or hiring, with or without back pay, attorney's fees, and costs.[76]

MIXED MOTIVE CASES—DECLARATORY OR INJUNCTIVE RELIEF

In a mixed motive case (see Chapter 9), the plaintiff's remedies may be limited to declaratory or injunctive relief, attorney's fees, and costs if the employer proves that it would have taken the same action in the absence of the impermissible motivating factor.[77]

BACK PAY

Back pay is routinely awarded as a remedy where the plaintiff was terminated from employment for an unlawful discriminatory reason. There are, however, limitations on back pay. For example, back pay liability shall not accrue from a date more than two years prior to the filing of a charge with the EEOC. Also, interim earnings or amounts that the plaintiff could have earned through reasonable diligence will reduce a back pay award.

FRONT PAY

Trial courts also award front pay when necessary. Front pay extends until the plaintiff fails to make reasonable efforts to secure substantially equivalent employment or until the plaintiff obtains or is offered such employment.

INTENTIONAL DISCRIMINATION—COMPENSATORY AND PUNITIVE DAMAGES

In addition, in cases involving unlawful intentional discrimination (i.e., disparate treatment, not disparate impact), the plaintiff may recover compensatory and punitive damages.

Compensatory damages include: (1) future pecuniary losses; (2) emotional pain; (3) suffering; (4) inconvenience; (5) mental anguish; (6) loss of enjoyment of life; and (7) other non-pecuniary losses.

Punitive damages may be recovered for intentional discrimination if the plaintiff demonstrates that the defendant engaged in a discriminatory practice with malice or with reckless indifference to the individual's rights.[78]

The sum of the amount of compensatory damages and the amount of punitive damages shall not exceed the following, for each plaintiff:

1. $50,000 for defendants with 15 to 100 employees;

2. $100,000 for defendants with 101 to 200 employees;

3. $200,000 for defendants with 201 to 500 employees; and

4. $300,000 for defendants with more than 500 employees.[79]

CHAPTER ENDNOTES

1. 42 U.S.C. §2000e(k).
2. 42 U.S.C. §2000e(k).
3. 29 CFR Part §1604.10(a).
4. 42 U.S.C. §2000e(k); 29 CFR Part §1604.10(b).
5. See generally, 29 CFR Part §1604 Appendix, A-5.
6. 42 U.S.C. §2000e(k).
7. 42 U.S.C. §2000e(b).
8. 42 U.S.C. §2000e(c).
9. 42 U.S.C. §2000e(d).
10. 42 U.S.C. §2000e(b).
11. 42 U.S.C. §2000e-7.
12. 42 U.S.C. §2000e-7.
13. 29 CFR Part §1604 Appendix, A-19.
14. 42 U.S.C. §2000e-2; 42 U.S.C. §2000e(k); see also 29 CFR §1604, Appendix, A-12; 29 CFR §1604, Appendix, A-34.
15. 29 CFR §1604, Appendix, A-8.
16. 29 CFR §1604, Appendix, A-9.
17. 29 CFR §1604, Appendix, A-5, 29 CFR §1604, Appendix, A-10; 29 CFR §1604, Appendix, A-11; 29 CFR §1604, Appendix, A-15.
18. 42 U.S.C. §2000e-2(b); 42 U.S.C. §2000e(k).
19. 42 U.S.C. §2000e-2(c); see also 42 U.S.C. §2000e(k).
20. 42 U.S.C. §2000e-3(a).
21. 29 CFR §1604, Appendix, A-13.
22. 29 CFR §1604, Appendix, A-15.
23. 29 CFR §1604, Appendix, A-16.
24. 29 CFR §1604, Appendix, A-3; 29 CFR §1604, Appendix, A-28.
25. 29 CFR §1604, Appendix, A-5.
26. 29 CFR §1604, Appendix, A-6.
27. 29 CFR Part §1604, Appendix, A-7; 29 CFR Part §1604, Appendix, A-8.
28. 29 CFR §1604, Appendix, A-9.
29. 29 CFR §1604, Appendix, A-10; 29 CFR §1604, Appendix, A-11.
30. 29 CFR §1604, Appendix, A-18.
31. 29 CFR §1604, Appendix, A-19.
32. See 29 CFR §1604, Appendix, A-25; 29 CFR §1604, Appendix, A-26; 29 CFR §1604, Appendix, A-27; 29 CFR §1604, Appendix, A-28; 29 CFR §1604, Appendix, A-33.
33. 29 CFR §1604, Appendix, A-21.
34. 29 CFR §1604, Appendix, A-21.
35. 29 CFR §1604, Appendix, A-22.
36. 29 CFR §1604, Appendix, A-21; 29 CFR §1604, Appendix, A-22.
37. 29 CFR §1604, Appendix, A-24; 29 CFR §1604, Appendix, A-25.
38. 29 CFR §1604, Appendix, A-34.
39. 29 CFR §1604, Appendix, Introduction; 29 CFR §1604, Appendix, A-35.
40. 29 CFR §1604, Appendix, A-36.
41. 42 U.S.C. §2000e(k); 29 CFR §1604, Appendix, A-37.
42. 42 U.S.C. §2000e-5.
43. 42 U.S.C. §2000e-5.
44. 42 U.S.C. §2000e-6; see also Exec. Order 12068, 43 F.R. 28971, 92 Stat. 2076 (Oct. 31, 1978).
45. 42 U.S.C. §2000e-5(f)(1).

46. 42 U.S.C. §2000e-10. This notice is reproduced in Appendix A.
47. 42 U.S.C. §2000e-8(c).
48. 29 CFR §1602.14.
49. 42 U.S.C. §2000e-5(b); 29 CFR §1601.9.
50. 29 CFR §1601.12(a).
51. 29 CFR §1601.12(a).
52. 29 CFR §1601.12(a).
53. 29 CFR §1601.12(b).
54. 29 CFR §1601.12(b).
55. 42 U.S.C. §2000e-5(d).
56. 42 U.S.C. §2000e-5(e).
57. 29 CFR §1601.28(a)(1).
58. 29 CFR §1601.28(a)(1).
59. 29 CFR §1601.28(a)(2).
60. See 42 U.S.C. §2000e-16(c).
61. *EEOC v. Ackerman Hood & McQueen, Inc.*, 956 F.2d 944, 947 (10th Cir.), cert. denied, 506 U.S. 817 (1992).
62. *Id.* at 948; see also 29 CFR §1604 Appendix, A-14.
63. 42 U.S.C. §2000e-5(e); see generally *EEOC v. South Carolina Nat. Bank*, 562 F.2d 329 (4th Cir. 1977).
64. 42 U.S.C. §2000e(b)(c)(d).
65. 42 U.S.C. §2000e(b).
66. 42 U.S.C. §2000e(b).
67. See, e.g., *Leeker v. Gill Studios, Inc.*, 21 F.Supp.2d 1267 (D. Kansas 1998); see also *Mayberry v. Endocrinology-Diabetes Assoc.*, 926 F.Supp. 1315, 1323-325 (M.D. Tenn. 1996).
68. See, e.g., *Gleklen v. Democratic Congressional Campaign Committee, Inc.*, 199 F.3d 1365, 1367-368; see also *Mayberry v. Endocrinology-Diabetes Assoc.*, 926 F.Supp. 1315, 1323-325 (M.D. Tenn. 1996).
69. 42 U.S.C. §2000e-2(e).
70. *Chambers v. Omaha Girls Club, Inc.*, 834 F.2d 697, 704-05 (8th Cir. 1987); see also *Vigars v. Valley Christian Center of Dublin, Cal.*, 805 F.Supp. 802 (N.D. Cal. 1992).
71. *Id.* at 698, 704-05.
72. *Id.* 705.
73. *International Union, United Auto., Aerospace and Agr. Implement Workers of America, UWA v. Johnson Controls, Inc.*, 499 U.S. 187, 201 (1991).
74. *Id.* at 206-07.
75. 29 CFR §1604, Appendix, A-20.
76. 42 U.S.C. §2000e-5(g)(1).
77. 42 U.S.C. §2000e-5(g)(2)(B).
78. 42 U.S.C. §1981a(b)(1).
79. 42 U.S.C. §1981(b)(3).

Chapter 12

Sections 1981 and 1983

SECTION 1981 GENERALLY

12-1. What is 42 U.S.C. Section 1981?

12-2. Who enforces Section 1981?

12-3. Who is protected under Section 1981?

12-4. Who must comply with Section 1981?

12-5. How does the jurisdiction of Section 1981 differ from the jurisdiction of Title VII?

12-6. What specifically does Section 1981 prohibit?

PROCEDURE FOR FILING A SECTION 1981 CLAIM

12-7. Does a plaintiff have to file an administrative charge before commencing a Section 1981 claim?

12-8. What is the time limit (statute of limitations) for filing a Section 1981 suit?

LITIGATING A SECTION 1981 CLAIM

12-9. How is litigation under Section 1981 similar to litigation of a Title VII race discrimination claim?

12-10. How does litigation of a Section 1981 claim differ from litigation of a Title VII race discrimination claim?

REMEDIES UNDER SECTION 1981

12-11. What remedies exist under Section 1981?

SECTION 1983 GENERALLY

12-12. What is 42 U.S.C. Section 1983?

12-13. Who enforces Section 1983?

12-14. Who is covered by Section 1983?

12-15. Can private employers ever be liable under Section 1983?

12-16. Who is protected by Section 1983?

12-17. What does Section 1983 prohibit with respect to employment practices?

12-18. What are the differences between a discrimination action under Section 1983 and a discrimination action under Section 1981 and/ or Title VII?

12-19. How does Section 1983 protect First Amendment Rights?

12-20. Are the First Amendment rights of independent contractors of covered actors protected by Section 1983?

12-21. What are "property rights" protected by Section 1983?

12-22. How are "property rights" in governmental jobs created?

12-23. Can state law preclude the imposition of a property right?

12-24. How can Section 1983 be used to protect a covered employee's "procedural" rights in employment?

12-25. What "liberty interests" does Section 1983 protect?

PROCEDURE FOR FILING A SECTION 1983 CLAIM

12-26. Does a plaintiff have to file an administrative charge before filing a Section 1983 claim?

12-27. What is the time limit (statute of limitations) for filing a section 1983 suit?

REMEDIES UNDER SECTION 1983

12-28. What remedies exist under Section 1983?

IMMUNITY ISSUES

12-29. Can a public employer ever be immune from liability under Section 1981 or Section 1983?

SECTION 1981 GENERALLY

12-1. What is 42 U.S.C. Section 1981?

42 U.S.C. Section 1981 (Section 1981) was originally enacted as part of the Civil Rights Act of 1866. It provides protection against racial discrimination that is largely congruent with that provided by Title VII.

Section 1981 provides, in material part, that "all persons within the jurisdiction of the United States shall have the same right... to make and enforce contracts... as is enjoyed by white citizens."

For purposes of Section 1981, the terms "make and enforce contracts" includes the "making, performance, modification, and termination of contracts... "[1]

12-2. Who enforces Section 1981?

Section 1981 is enforced by individual plaintiffs.[2]

12-3. Who is protected under Section 1981?

Section 1981 protects against racial discrimination. Discrimination against aliens is covered, if it is racial in character.[3]

Gender discrimination and age discrimination are not covered by Section 1981.[4]

12-4. Who must comply with Section 1981?

With respect to employment claims, Section 1981 specifically applies to all private employers.[5]

The Civil Rights Act of 1991 also amended the coverage of Section 1981 to include conduct "under color of state law."[6]

Most courts now hold that Section 1981 claims may be brought against state and local government employers under some circumstances. Some courts have limited the circumstances under which liability which may be imposed on a government entity for the acts of its employees.[7]

12-5. How does the jurisdiction of Section 1981 differ from the jurisdiction of Title VII?

Unlike Title VII (see Chapter 9), Section 1981 does not exempt any categories of employers from liability. Accordingly, though an employer may be exempt from liability under Title VII, liability could exist under Section 1981.[8]

12-6. What specifically does Section 1981 prohibit?

Section 1981 broadly prohibits racial discrimination in contracts.

With respect to employment law, Section 1981 bans virtually all forms of racial discrimination in the making, performance, enforcement, and termination of employment contracts.[9]

Most courts have now held that Section 1981 also applies to "employment at will."[10]

PROCEDURE FOR FILING A SECTION 1981 CLAIM

12-7. Does a plaintiff have to file an administrative charge before commencing a Section 1981 claim?

No. Section 1981 suits can be maintained in state or federal court without first satisfying the administrative requirements of Title VII.[11]

12-8. What is the time limit (statute of limitations) for filing a Section 1981 suit?

There is no statute of limitations in Section 1981. Prior to 1990, the appropriate state statute of limitations for personal injury actions was used.

In 1990, as part of the Judicial Improvement Act of 1990, Congress enacted a uniform four year statute of limitations for federal civil actions where a statute of limitations is not otherwise provided by law.[12]

Courts are now split as to whether the four year statute of limitations applies, or whether the applicable state statute applies. The majority of decisions have held that the state personal injury statute continues to apply.[13] But see *Nealy v. University Health Services, Inc.*,[14] holding that the federal four year statute of limitations applies.

LITIGATING A SECTION 1981 CLAIM

12-9. How is litigation under Section 1981 similar to litigation of a Title VII race discrimination claim?

The elements of a cause of action under Section 1981 and a cause of action for discriminatory treatment race discrimination under Title VII (see Chapter 9) are virtually identical.[15]

As in Title VII claims, courts will employ a burden shifting analysis, under which the plaintiff has the initial burden of producing a prima facie case of discrimination by a preponderance of the evidence.[16] Accordingly, Section 1981 and Title VII claims are subject to the same burdens of production and burdens of proof.[17]

The issue of liability under a Section 1981 claim is normally conclusive on the issue of liability in a parallel action under Title VII.[18]

12-10. How does litigation of a Section 1981 claim differ from litigation of a Title VII race discrimination claim?

The difference between a Title VII race discrimination claim and a Section 1981 claim is that liability under Section 1981 requires proof of intent to discriminate.[19]

For this reason, no "disparate impact" claims may be brought under Section 1981. See Q 9-19.

REMEDIES UNDER SECTION 1981

12-11. What remedies exist under Section 1981?

The remedies under Section 1981 are compensatory damages, punitive damages, and attorneys fees.

COMPENSATORY AND PUNITIVE DAMAGES

Both compensatory damages and punitive damages may be recoverable under Section 1981.[20]

ATTORNEYS' FEES

Attorneys' fees may be recoverable in a Section 1981 action.[21]

NO DAMAGE CAPS

Unlike a Title VII claim (see Chapter 9), there are no limitations on the damages a plaintiff may recover under Section 1981.[22]

SECTION 1983 GENERALLY

12-12. What is 42 U.S.C. Section 1983?

42 U.S.C. Section 1983 (Section 1983) is a federal law that prohibits the violation, "under color of state law," of all rights, privileges, or immunities secured by the federal Constitution and United States laws.

Section 1983 bans all discrimination, and other constitutional violations by state actors at the state and local level, insofar as the discrimination is based upon constitutionally impermissible factors (race, gender, religion, exercise of First Amendment rights, etc).

Section 1983 also guards the "property rights" of public sector employees at the state and local government levels.

12-13. Who enforces Section 1983?

Individual plaintiffs enforce Section 1983.

12-14. Who is covered by Section 1983?

Section 1983 covers the conduct of all state and local government actors, and all actions taken by persons "under color of state law."

Federal departments and agencies are not covered under Section 1983, because Section 1983 requires action under color of *state* law.[23]

12-15. Can private employers ever be liable under Section 1983?

Yes. A private employer may be subject to employee claims under Section 1983 if the employment action involves state action.

When determining whether a private entity's actions involve state action under Section 1983, the factors that must be considered are:

1. The extent of any public funding;

2. The extent of any public regulation;

3. Whether traditionally public functions have been performed or are involved; and

4. Whether a significant symbiotic relationship exists between the state and the private organization.[24]

As a practical matter, however, claims against private employers are rarely actionable under Section 1983, absent a showing that state or federal action compelled or motivated the employment act in question.

A private employer is not a state actor for Section 1983 purposes simply because it is subject to regulation by a state agency and performs a function which serves the public.[25]

For instance, an employment claim against a private hospital was not found actionable under Section 1983, even though the hospital was regulated by the state and obtained significant state funding, where the employment decision in question was not compelled or influenced by the state.[26]

12-16. Who is protected by Section 1983?

Section 1983 protects all individuals from the deprivation of their federal rights by covered individuals.

12-17. What does Section 1983 prohibit with respect to employment practices?

Section 1983 covers the violation, under color of state law, of all rights, privileges, or immunities secured by the federal Constitution "and laws."[27]

Accordingly, Section 1983 prohibits discrimination and constitutional violations by all state actors. The crucial rights covered include the right not to be deprived of life, liberty, or property without due process of law.

With respect to employment discrimination, Section 1983 bans discrimination by a public employer at the state or local level, insofar as the discrimination is based upon constitutionally impermissible factors (race, gender, religion, exercise of First Amendment Rights, etc.). Section 1983 also protects the property rights of public sector employees in their positions.

Section 1983 would also cover discriminatory treatment on the job by public employers, including sexual harassment already covered by Title VII or gender discrimination not covered by Section 1981.[28]

12-18. What are the differences between a discrimination action under Section 1983 and a discrimination action under Section 1981 and/or Title VII?

DISCRIMINATION BASED UPON RACE

Like Title VII and Section 1981, Section 1983 bans discrimination in employment based upon race. However, Section 1983 only applies to actions by covered individuals, normally state and local government actors. Accordingly, an action for racial discrimination in employment against an actor covered by Section 1983 may be brought under Section 1983, Section 1981, and/ or Title VII. However, an action for racial discrimination against an employer not covered by Section 1983 may be brought only under Section 1981 or Title VII, if applicable.

DISCRIMINATION BASED UPON OTHER "PROTECTED CLASSES"

Unlike a claim brought under Section 1981, a Section 1983 claim may involve discrimination based upon any impermissible factor under Title VII. Accordingly, as against a Section 1983 covered individual, a claim of gender discrimination (including sexual harassment) or religious discrimination may be brought under both Title VII and Section 1983. Such a claim may not be brought under Section 1981, because Section 1981 is limited to racial discrimination.

12-19. How does Section 1983 protect First Amendment Rights?

Any individual who believes that his First Amendment rights have been violated by an individual covered by Section 1983 may bring a claim under Section 1983 (Section 1981 and Title VII are not involved in a First Amendment claim).

In the employment law context, such claims are generally brought by state and local government employees who contend that their employers violated their First Amendment rights.

FIRST AMENDMENT RIGHTS GENERALLY

Public employees who are fired for exercise of First Amendment rights have lost "liberty" without due process of law and can be ordered reinstated.[29]

STANDARD

In order to present a First Amendment claim, the employee must first show that:

1. There was an exercise of First Amendment rights (i.e., the speech was on a matter of public concern); and

2. The activity was a substantial or motivating factor in the decision to take action against the employee.

Once an employee has made this showing, the burden of proof then shifts to defendant-employer to show either:

1. That there was another valid reason was the basis for the discharge, and the employer would have fired the employee even in the absence of protected conduct; or

2. That there was a valid governmental reason for the dismissal or adverse action, even if the adverse action was retaliatory in nature.

PUBLIC CONCERN

The first prong of the employee's prima facie case requires a demonstration that the speech was protected (i.e., was a matter of "public concern").

The test for "public concern" looks to whether the employee is speaking on matters in which the public might be interested, as distinct from wholly personal grievances.[30]

Generally, an employee's complaints about his or her own job, or about the general operation of his or her office, are not a matter of public concern. For instance, a prosecutor's complaint about her own transfer did not qualify as a matter of public concern.[31] However, complaints about police misconduct have been found to be a matter of public concern.[32]

Merely saying "no" to a superior is not a First Amendment exercise, nor is expressing happiness when a superior is fired.[33]

Speech need not be true to be protected. If speech is false, but not recklessly false, as in a libel situation, it is still protected by the First Amendment, and the public employee cannot be fired for such speech.[34]

"SUBSTANTIAL OR MOTIVATING FACTOR"

The employee must also prove that the speech was a "substantial or motivating factor" in the employer's decision to take action against the employee. Proof that the exercise of protected expression was a substantial or motivating factor can be shown by close proximity in time between the exercise of First Amendment rights and the retaliatory action.[35]

BURDEN SHIFTS TO EMPLOYER

If the employee has set forth a prima facie case as described above, the burden shifts to the employer, who must demonstrate that:

1. Another valid reason was the basis for discharge, so that the employee would have been fired even in the absence of protected conduct; or

2. There was a valid governmental reason for the dismissal or adverse action, even if the adverse action was retaliatory in nature.[36]

TERMINATED FOR LEGITIMATE REASON

With respect to the first prong, the employer must show that the employee was, in fact, fired for a valid reason, not in retaliation for the exercise of constitutional rights.[37]

VALID GOVERNMENTAL REASONS FOR TERMINATION

Even if speech is a matter of public concern, the government employer may have a legitimate reason for restricting speech on the job, because of need of government to *promote efficiency* "of the public services it performs through its employees."[38] Thus, if the government need to promote efficiency outweighs the interest of a government employee in speaking out on matters of public concern, restrictions may be imposed on the speech.

For example, a city's interest in maintaining discipline in the police department and establishing a close working relationship with a neighboring sheriff's department outweighed the police chief's First Amendment interest in writing a letter criticizing the sheriff's policy dealing with treatment of persons arrested for DWI.[39]

If speech is *disruptive* of the internal working of the organization, an employee may be fired, even if the speech is on a matter of public concern. The burden is on the employer to show that the speech is disruptive. For example, no liability attaches in situations where an employee's speech against a superior created a disruptive work environment, and the employee was terminated.[40]

OTHER DEFENSES

EMPLOYER'S ERRONEOUS CONCLUSION ABOUT STATEMENTS

If a Section 1983-covered employer erroneously believes that an employee made an unprotected statement, but in fact the statement was protected, the employee can still be fired, so long as the employer's belief was reasonable.[41]

SPOKESMAN FOR OTHERS

If speech is made on orders from a superior and not as a citizen's own views, there is no First Amendment protection for the employee.[42]

12-20. Are the First Amendment rights of independent contractors of covered actors protected by Section 1983?

Even if not technically an employee, an independent contractor or licensee may not lose governmental benefits because of the exercise of his First Amendment rights.[43]

12-21. What are "property rights" protected by Section 1983?

Section 1983 covers property rights.[44] The term "property" includes entitlements, benefits, or expectations created by state law.[45]

Section 1983 has often been used to assert a "property interest" in public employment. The statute is asserted to protect both "substantive" property rights and "procedural" property rights in government employment.

12-22. How are "property rights" in governmental jobs created?

BY LAW

Where state law mandates that a government employee has a right to a job (i.e., he cannot be fired except "for cause"), state law creates "property," which cannot be taken away without procedural due process.[46]

For example, a school employee has a property interest in a job, because state law provided she could only be terminated "for cause." Accordingly, a lack of funding for the position in question could be a basis for terminating the employee. However, this basis must be proven by the employer.[47]

BY REGULATION

Government regulations, such as a city charter or government personnel regulations, may also create a property right in a job.[48]

INFORMAL CREATION OF PROPERTY RIGHTS

A property right in a public position can also be created informally. For example, employee handbooks have, on occasion, been construed as creating a property right in a position, where language has limited the doctrine of employment at will.[49] Further, where an employee's superior orally promises or implies a promise of continued employment, property rights may be created.[50]

PROMISE OF EMPLOYMENT MAY BE UNENFORCEABLE

An explicit promise of a property right in a position may also be unenforceable under some circumstances, such as where state law considers it unenforceable, or where the promise is contrary to state law.[51] It may also be unenforceable where the promise is made by an individual member of a governing entity, but only the governing entity as a whole can bind the county.[52]

12-23. Can state law preclude the imposition of a property right?

Yes. If state law decrees that no rights are granted at all, because a government official has complete discretion whether to grant a benefit or not, then no property interest will be created.[53]

12-24. How can Section 1983 be used to protect a covered employee's "procedural" rights in employment?

Section 1983 claims can also be based on a denial of procedural rights. The "due process" clause of the United States Constitution requires minimum due process protection for Section 1983 covered employees who hold property rights in their jobs.[54] Accordingly, before termination, an employee holding a property right in his or her position must get a pre-termination hearing, where he must be provided:

1. Oral or written notice of the charges;

2. An explanation of the employer's evidence; and

3. An opportunity to present his side of story.[55]

12-25. What "liberty interests" does Section 1983 protect?

APPEARANCE

An employee may have a protected liberty interest in his or her personal appearance, if no state interest justifies restriction. For instance, courts have sometimes protected employees' rights to maintain facial hair.[56]

However, a state interest may justify a restriction on an employee's "liberty" rights. For instance, courts have upheld rules prohibiting beards on a police officer because of the state's interest in uniformity in appearance in a military type organization.[57]

OPPORTUNITY TO CLEAR NAME

Section 1983 has also been interpreted as protecting an employee's "liberty" rights with regard to his or her reputation.

For example, a Section 1983 violation was found where a public employee was fired with stigmatizing charges made in public about him, and he was never given a chance to disprove the charges, which interfered with his right to get another job.[58]

In this type of case, the employee must show that:

1. He was fired;

2. He was stigmatized as a result of the firing process;

3. The charges were made public by the public employer; and

4. He was denied a meaningful hearing to clear his name.[59]

A hearing is not required under any of the following circumstances:

1. Where the employee admitted to the charges;[60]

2. Where the employee is not terminated (i.e, the employee resigns or has some lesser sanction imposed).[61]

POLITICAL ASSOCIATION RIGHTS

Section 1983 also protects the political association rights of non-policymaking and non-confidential employees. Termination of an employee in this classification for his or her political beliefs or associations is a violation of Section 1983. In addition, any adverse employer action taken because of, or in retaliation for, political associational rights, is a violation.[62]

DETERMINING POLICY-MAKING STATUS

In determining whether an employee is protected from adverse employment decisions based upon his or her position, the ultimate inquiry is not what the position is labeled, but rather whether the hiring authority can demonstrate that party affiliation is an appropriate requirement for effective performance of the public office involved.[63]

When determining whether an individual is a policy-maker, consideration may be given to the following factors:

1.   Is the position protected by civil services law?

2.   What degree of competence or expertise is required for the position?

3.   To what degree does the employee exercise control over other employees?

4.   Does the employee make public statements on policy or influence government programs?

5.   Is the employee responsible to partisan politics and political leaders?[64]

Where an employee is exempt from civil service requirements, a presumption is created that the position is unprotected.[65]

"SMALL-OFFICE" EXCEPTION

A limited exception may exist for small offices, because of the need for loyalty within a small group of employees. For example, a sheriff may be permitted to terminate deputies who supported his opponent in an election because of the need for loyalty within the small office.[66]

INDEPENDENT CONTRACTORS ALSO COVERED

Political association protection also applies to independent contractors.[67] For example, a violation of Section 1983 was found where a tow truck operator claimed he was terminated from the city list because he failed to support a political party or its candidate in an election campaign.

PROCEDURE FOR FILING A SECTION 1983 CLAIM

12-26. Does a plaintiff have to file an administrative charge before filing a Section 1983 claim?

No. Section 1983 suits can be maintained in state or federal court without satisfying the administrative requirements of Title VII (see Chapter 9).

12-27. What is the time limit (statute of limitations) for filing a section 1983 suit?

There is no statute of limitations for filing a claim under Section 1983. Accordingly, the appropriate state statute of limitations will be used.[68]

REMEDIES UNDER SECTION 1983

12-28. What remedies exist under Section 1983?

The remedies under Section 1983 are compensatory damages, punitive damages, and attorneys' fees.

COMPENSATORY AND PUNITIVE DAMAGES

Both compensatory and punitive damages are available in a Section 1983 action.[69]

Compensatory damages in a Section 1983 action may include not only out-of-pocket loss and other monetary harms, but also such injuries as impairment of reputation, personal humiliation, and mental anguish and suffering.[70]

ATTORNEYS' FEES

Attorneys' fees may be recoverable under Section 1983.[71]

NO DAMAGE CAPS

As is the case in Section 1981 actions, there are no limits on the damages a plaintiff can recover in a Section 1983 action.

IMMUNITY ISSUES

12-29. Can a public employer ever be immune from liability under Section 1981 or Section 1983?

Yes.

ELEVENTH AMENDMENT

A limited version of the doctrine of "sovereign immunity" is preserved under the Eleventh Amendment to the U.S. Constitution. The Eleventh Amendment bars lawsuits based on federal law unless the state has consented to the suit, or the federal law in question expressly states that immunity shall not apply.

Specifically, the Eleventh Amendment provides that:

> (t)he judicial power of the United States shall not be construed to extend to any suit in law or in equity,

commenced or prosecuted against one of the United States by Citizens of another State, or by Citizens or Subjects of any Foreign State.

Subsequent court decisions hold that, absent consent, a state may also not be sued by its own citizens.[72]

Because Section 1981 and Section 1983 do not expressly state that immunity does not apply, many courts have held that states are immune from the prosecution of lawsuits under Section 1981 and Section 1983.[73]

Further, many courts have held that the Eleventh Amendment immunizes state officials sued in their official capacities from lawsuits under Section 1981 and Section 1983.[74]

QUALIFIED IMMUNITY

The doctrine of qualified immunity may also operate to bar lawsuits against public officials acting in their official capacities.

Under the doctrine of qualified immunity, government officials performing discretionary functions are immune from liability so long as their behavior does not violate "clearly established statutory or constitutional rights of which a reasonable person would have known."[75]

Accordingly, where a public official reasonably could have believed his or her conduct was lawful, qualified immunity may apply.[76]

CHAPTER ENDNOTES

1. 42 U.S.C. §§1981(a), 1981(b).
2. 42 U.S.C. §1981; *Martin v. Airborne Express,* 16 F. Supp. 2d 623, 629 (E.D.N.C. 1996)
3. *St. Francis College v. Al-Khazraji,* 481 U.S. 604 (1987).
4. *Bobo v. ITT, Continental Baking Co.,* 662 F.2d 340, (5th Cir. 1981).
5. 42 U.S.C. §1981(c).
6. 42 U.S.C. §1981(c).
7. See, e.g., *Smith v. Chicago School Reform Board of Trustees,* 165 F.3d 1142 (7th Cir. 1999); *Federation of African American Contractors v. City of Oakland,* 96 F.3d 1204 (9th Cir. 1996).
8. *Crawford v. Willow Oaks Country Club, Inc.,* 66 F. Supp.2d 767 (E.D. Va. 1999).
9. *Mass v. Martin Marietta Corp.,* 805 F.Supp. 1530 (D.Colo. 1992).
10. See, e.g., *Spriggs v. Diamond Auto Glass,* 165 F.3d 1015 (4th Cir. 1999); *Fadeyi v. Planned Parenthood Association of Lubbock, Inc.,* 160 F.3d 1048 (5th Cir. 1998).
11. *Johnson v. Railway Express Agency Inc.,* 421 U.S. 454 (1975).

12. 28 U.S.C. §1658.
13. See, e.g. *Carney v. American University*, 151 F.3d 1090, 1096 (C.A.D.C. 1998); *Roberts v. Roadway Exp., Inc.*, 149 F.3d 1098, 1110 (10th Cir. 1998).
14. *Nealey v. University Health Services, Inc.*, 114 F. Supp. 2d 1358 (S.D. Ga. 2000).
15. See, e.g, *Thomas v. Denny's, Inc.*, 111 F.3d 1506 (10th Cir. 1997); *Freeman v. Chicago Park District*, 189 F.3d 613 (7th Cir. 1999).
16. See, e.g., *Ferrill v. The Parker Group, Inc.*, 967 F. Supp. 472 (N.D. Ala. 1997).
17. *Cross v. Roadway Exp.*, 861 F. Supp. 698 (N.D. Ill. 1994).
18. See *Thomas v. Denny's, Inc.*, 111 F.3d 1506 (10th Cir. 1997).
19. *Melendez v. Illinois Bell Telephone Company*, 79 F.3d 661 (7th Cir. 1996).
20. See, e.g., *Johnson v. Railway Express Agency Inc.*, 421 U.S. 454 (1975); *Mitchell v. Keith*, 752 F.2d 385 (9th Cir. 1985).
21. 42 U.S.C. §1988(b).
22. *Kim v. Nash Finch Co.*, 123 F.3d 1046 (8th Cir. 1997).
23. *Wheeldin v. Wheeler*, 373 U.S. 647 (1963).
24. *Rendell-Baker v. Kohn*, 457 U.S. 830 (1982).
25. *Rendell-Baker v. Kohn*, 457 U.S. 830 (1982).
26. *Beverley v. Douglas*, 591 F.Supp. 1321, 1329 (S.D.N.Y. 1984).
27. See *Maine v. Thiboutot*, 448 U.S. 1 (1980).
28. *Lankford v. City of Hobart*, 73 F.3d 283 (10th Cir. 1996); *Saulpaugh v. Monroe Community Hospital*, 4 F.3d 134 (2nd Cir. 1993).
29. See *Perry v. Sindermann*, 408 U.S. 593 (1972); *Mt. Healthy City School Dist. Bd. of Educ. v. Doyle*, 429 U.S. 274 (1977).
30. *Dishnow v. School Dist. of Rib Lake*, 77 F.3d 194 (7th Cir. 1996).
31. See *Connick v. Myers*, 461 U.S. 138 (1983).
32. *Fikes v. City of Daphne*, 79 F.3d 1079 (11th Cir. 1996).
33. *Berry v. Bailey*, 726 F.2d 670 (11th Cir. 1984); *Yoggerst v. Hedges*, 739 F.2d 293 (7th Cir. 1984).
34. See *Pickering v. Bd. of Education of Township High School Dist. 205*, 391 U.S. 563 (1968).
35. See *Stever v. Independent School Dist. No. 625*, 943 F.2d 845 (8th Cir. 1991); *Martinez v. City of Opa-Locka, Fla.*, 971 F.2d 708 (11th Cir. 1992).
36. *Mt. Healthy City School Dist. Board of Education v. Doyle*, 429 U.S. 274 (1977).
37. See *Bradley v. Pittsburgh Bd. of Education*, 913 F.2d 1064 (3rd Cir. 1990).
38. *Pickering v. Bd. of Education of Township High School Dist. 205*, 391 U.S. 563 (1968).
39. *Tyler v. The City of Mountain Home*, 72 F.3d 568 (8th Cir. 1995).
40. See *Caruso v. De Luca*, 81 F.3d 666 (7th Cir. 1996); *Voigt v. Savell*, 70 F.3d 1552 (9th Cir. 1995).
41. *Waters v. Churchill*, 511 U.S. 661, 676 (1994).
42. *Day v. Johnson*, 119 F.3d 650 (8th Cir. 1997).
43. *Board of County Commissioners, Wabaunsee County, Kansas v. Umbehr*, 518 U.S. 668 (1996).
44. *Lynch v. Household Finance Corp.*, 405 U.S. 538 (1972).
45. *Board of Regents of State Colleges v. Roth*, 408 U.S. 564 (1972).
46. See *Cleveland Bd. of Educ. v. Loudermill*, 470 U.S. 532 (1985).
47. *Goudeau v. Independent School Dist. No. 37 of Oklahoma County*, 823 F.2d 1429 (10th Cir. 1987).
48. *Patrick v. Miller*, 953 F.2d 1240 (10th Cir. 1992); *Perri v. Aytch*, 724 F.2d 362 (3rd Cir. 1983).
49. See *Nicholson v. Gant*, 816 F.2d 591 (11th Cir. 1987).

50. See *McLaurin v. Fischer*, 768 F.2d 98 (6th Cir. 1985).
51. *Ogletree v. Chester*, 682 F.2d 1366, 1371 (11th Cir. 1982).
52. See *Hadley v. County of du Page*, 715 F.2d 1238 (7th Cir. 1983).
53. *Bishop v. Wood*, 426 U.S. 341 (1976).
54. *Cleveland Bd. of Educ. v. Loudermill*, 470 U.S. 532 (1985).
55. *Findeisen v. North East Ind. School Dist.*, 749 F.2d 234 (5th Cir. 1984).
56. See *Nally v. Douglas County*, 498 F. Supp. 1228 (N.D. Ga. 1980); *Pence v. Rosenquist*, 573 F.2d 395 (7th Cir. 1978).
57. See *Kelly v. Johnson*, 425 U.S. 238 (1976).
58. See *Bd. of Regents of State Colleges v. Roth*, 408 U.S. 564 (1972).
59. See, generally, *Watson v. University of Utah Medical Center*, 75 F.3d 569 (10th Cir. 1996).
60. *Codd v. Velger*, 429 U.S. 624 (1977).
61. *Siegert v. Gilley*, 500 U.S. 226 (1991).
62. *Rutan v. Republican Party of Illinois*, 497 U.S. 62 (1990).
63. *Branti v. Finkel*, 445 U.S. 507 (1980).
64. *Vona v. County of Niagara*, 119 F.3d 201 (2nd Cir. 1997).
65. *Stott v. Haworth*, 916 F.2d 134 (4th Cir. 1990).
66. *McBee v. Jim Hogg County*, 730 F.2d 1009 (5th Cir. 1984).
67. *O'Hare Truck Service Inc., v. City of Northlake*, 518 U.S. 712 (1996).
68. *Wilson v. Garcia*, 471 U.S. 261 (1985).
69. *Cunningham v. City of Overland, State of Mo.*, 804 F.2d 1066 (8th Cir. 1986).
70. *Coleman v. Rahija*, 114 F.3d 778 (8th Cir. 1997).
71. 42 U.S.C. §1988(b).
72. *Kimel v. Florida Board of Regents*, 528 U.S. 62, 73 (2000).
73. *Quern v. Jordan*, 440 U.S. 332 (1979); *Hafford v. Seidner*, 183 F.3d 506 (6th Cir. 1999); *Hutsell v. Sayre*, 5 F.3d 996 (6th Cir. 1993); *Rucker v. Higher Educational Aids Board*, 669 F.2d 1179 (1982).
74. *Kentucky, dba Bureau of State Police v. Graham*, 473 U.S. 159 (1985).
75. *Harlow v. Fitzgerald*, 457 U.S. 800 (1982).
76. *Poe v. Haydon*, 853 F.2d 418 (6th Cir. 1988).

HR Survival Guide

Chapter 13

Drug-Free Workplace Act

GENERALLY

13-1. What is the Drug-Free Workplace Act of 1988?

13-2. Who is covered by the Drug-Free Workplace Act?

13-3. What are the requirements of the Drug-Free Workplace Act?

PENALTIES

13-4. What are the penalties for failing to carry out the requirements of the Drug-Free Workplace Act?

13-5. Who makes the determination of whether a contractor or grantee has failed to carry out the requirements of the DFWA?

13-6. What is considered to be a violation of the Drug-Free Workplace Act?

13-7. What procedures govern the conduct of suspension, termination and debarment proceedings?

13-8. What are the procedures contained in the Federal Acquisition Regulation for the suspension or debarment of a contractor?

13-9. What are the procedures contained in Executive Order 12549 for suspension and debarment of grantees?

13-10. Does the head of an agency have the authority to waive a penalty under the Drug-Free Workplace Act?

EXCEPTION

13-11. Is there any exception in the Drug-Free Workplace Act for law enforcement agencies?

DRUG TESTING

13-12. Does the Drug-Free Workplace Act require covered organizations and individuals to implement a drug testing program?

GENERALLY

13-1. What is the Drug-Free Workplace Act of 1988?

The Drug-Free Workplace Act of 1988 ("DFWA"),[1] requires some Federal contractors and all Federal grantees to agree that they will provide drug-free workplaces as a condition of receiving a contract or grant from a Federal agency. The DFWA does not apply to those who do not have or intend to apply for contracts or grants from the Federal government. Also, the DFWA does not apply to subcontractors or subgrantees.

The coverage of the DFWA is dependent upon whether a Federal contract or grant is involved and also whether an individual or organization is the recipient of the Federal contract or grant. Additionally, the requirements of the DFWA vary as to organizations and individuals receiving Federal contracts and grants. Therefore, it is important for employers to determine the DFWA's coverage and requirements on a case-by-case basis.

13-2. Who is covered by the Drug-Free Workplace Act?

The DFWA applies to any organization that is awarded a contract (i.e., contractor) by any Federal agency that is of a value greater than $100,000, other than a contract for the procurement of commercial items.[2] The DFWA defines "contractor" as the department, division, or other unit of a person responsible for the performance under the contract.[3] The DFWA applies to any individual who enters into a contract with a Federal agency.[4] The DFWA also applies to any organization or individual who receives a grant (i.e., grantee) from any Federal agency.[5] The DFWA defines "grantee" as the department, division, or other unit of a person responsible for the performance under the grant.[6]

13-3. What are the requirements of the Drug-Free Workplace Act?

ORGANIZATIONS

For organizations with contracts covered by the DFWA and organizations receiving a grant from a Federal agency, the DFWA requires the organization to do each of the following:

- Publish a statement notifying employees that the unlawful manufacture, distribution, dispensation, possession, or use of a controlled substance is prohibited in the workplace and specifying the actions that will be taken against employees for violations of this prohibition.

- Give employees engaged in the performance of the contract or grant a copy of this statement.

- Notify employees in this statement that they must abide by its terms and report drug convictions for violations occurring in the workplace within five days.

- Notify the contracting or granting agency within ten days after receiving notice of any such conviction.

- Impose a sanction on or require rehabilitation of an employee with a drug conviction.

- Establish a drug-free awareness program to inform employees about the dangers of drug abuse in the workplace, the employer's policy of maintaining a drug-free workplace, any available drug counseling, rehabilitation, and employee assistance programs, and the penalties that may be imposed upon employees for drug abuse violations.

- Make a good faith effort to maintain a drug-free workplace through implementation of the above requirements.[7]

The DFWA defines "employee" as the employee of a contractor or grantee directly engaged in the performance of work pursuant to the provisions of the contract or grant.[8] The DFWA defines "conviction" as a finding of guilt (including a plea of nolo contendere) or imposition of sentence, or both, by any judicial body charged with the responsibility to determine violations of the Federal or State criminal drug statutes.[9] The DFWA defines "drug-free workplace" as a site for the performance of work done in connection with a specific grant or contract of an entity at which employees of such entity are prohibited from engaging in the unlawful manufacture, distribution, dispensation, possession, or use of a controlled substance in accordance with the requirements of the DFWA.[10]

INDIVIDUALS

The DFWA requires an individual who has a contract or grant with a Federal agency to agree that the individual will not engage in the unlawful manufacture, distribution, dispensation, possession, or use of a controlled substance in the performance of the contract and/or in conducting any activity with the grant.[11]

PENALTIES

13-4. What are the penalties for failing to carry out the requirements of the Drug-Free Workplace Act?

A contractor or grantee, whether an individual or an organization, who is covered by the DFWA and who fails to carry out the requirements of the DFWA, can be penalized by:

1. having payments for the contract or grant activities suspended;

2. having a contract or grant suspended or terminated, or

3. both (1) and (2).

Additionally, the contractor or grantee may be prohibited from receiving or participating in any future contracts or grants awarded by any Federal agency for a specified period, not to exceed five years. The latter penalty can be either suspension or debarment.[12]

13-5. Who makes the determination of whether a contractor or grantee has failed to carry out the requirements of the DFWA?

This determination is made by the head of the Federal agency awarding the applicable contract or, in the case of a grant, the head of the Federal agency awarding the grant, or his or her official designee.[13]

13-6. What is considered to be a violation of the Drug-Free Workplace Act?

A contractor or grantee will be penalized for failing to carry out the requirements of the DFWA when the Federal agency head (or for grantees the Federal agency head or his/her official designee) determines, in writing, that: (1) the contractor or grantee has violated one or more of the requirements of the DFWA; or (2) such a number of employees of the contractor or grantee have been convicted of violations of criminal drug statutes for violations occurring in the workplace as to indicate that the contractor or grantee has failed to make a good faith effort to provide a drug-free workplace as required by the DFWA.[14]

13-7. What procedures govern the conduct of suspension, termination and debarment proceedings?

For contractors, the DFWA provides that if a contracting officer determines, in writing, that cause for suspension of payments, termination, or suspension or debarment exists, an appropriate action shall be initiated by a contracting officer of the agency and such action shall be conducted by the agency in accordance with the Federal Acquisition Regulation and applicable agency procedures (See Q 13-8).[15]

With respect to grantees, the DFWA provides that suspension of payments, termination, or suspension or debarment proceedings shall be conducted in accordance with applicable law, including Executive Order 12549 or any superseding Executive order and any regulations promulgated to implement such law or Executive order (See Q 13-9).[16]

13-8. What are the procedures contained in the Federal Acquisition Regulation for the suspension or debarment of a contractor?

The Federal Acquisition Regulation[17] provides that the appropriate official of a Federal agency may suspend or debar a contractor only after following certain due process requirements. The regulation requires that contractors receive notice and an opportunity to present, in person or in writing, or through a representative, information and arguments in opposition to the proposed penalty. If the contractor's submission in opposition raises a genuine dispute over facts material to the proposed penalty, the regulation affords the contractor an opportunity to appear with counsel, submit documentary evidence, present witnesses, and confront any person the agency presents. At this stage, a transcribed record of the proceedings will be made available to the contractor. Where these additional proceedings are necessary, written findings of fact shall be prepared and the official making the decision shall base the decision on the facts as found together with any information and arguments submitted by the contractor and any other information in the administrative record. The contractor is entitled to notice of the agency official's decision.

13-9. What are the procedures contained in Executive Order 12549 for suspension and debarment of grantees?

Executive Order 12549 requires that the appropriate officials follow government-wide criteria and government-wide minimum due process procedures when they act to debar or suspend participants in affected programs. Executive Order 12549 also provides that debarment or suspension of a participant in a program by one Federal agency shall have government-wide effect.

13-10. Does the head of an agency have the authority to waive a penalty under the Drug-Free Workplace Act?

A head of the Federal agency awarding the contract may waive a penalty issued under the DFWA if the agency head determines that the penalty would severely disrupt the operation of the agency to the detriment of the Federal government or the general public.[18]

An agency head may waive a penalty with respect to a grantee if the agency head determines that the penalty would not be in the public interest.[19] The authority of the head of an agency to waive a penalty issued to a contractor or grantee may not be delegated.[20]

EXCEPTION

13-11. Is there any exception in the Drug-Free Workplace Act for law enforcement agencies?

Yes. The DFWA states that, if it is determined by the head of a law enforcement agency that compliance with the DFWA would be inappropriate in connection with the law enforcement agency's undercover operations, then such compliance is not necessary.[21]

DRUG TESTING

13-12. Does the Drug-Free Workplace Act require covered organizations and individuals to implement a drug testing program?

No. The DFWA does not require a covered contractor or grantee to implement a drug testing program. To that end, a federal court has held that the DFWA did not make a public utility a "state actor" for purposes of Constitutional claims asserted by a former employee who was fired following a drug test because the DFWA does not require drug testing.[22]

CHAPTER ENDNOTES

1. 41 U.S.C. §§701-707.
2. 41 U.S.C. §§403(11), 403(12), 701(a)(1).
3. 41 U.S.C. §706(7).
4. 41 U.S.C. §701(a)(2).
5. 41 U.S.C. §702(a).
6. 41 U.S.C. §706(6).
7. 41 U.S.C. §§701(a)(1), 702(a)(1).
8. 41 U.S.C. §706(2).
9. 41 U.S.C. §706(4).
10. 41 U.S.C. §706(1).
11. 41 U.S.C. §§701(a)(2), 702(a)(2).
12. 41 U.S.C. §§701(b)(1), 702(b)(1).
13. 41 U.S.C. §§701(b)(1), 702(b)(1).
14. 41 U.S.C. §§701(b)(1), 702(b)(1).
15. 41 U.S.C. §701(b)(2).
16. 41 U.S.C. §702(b)(2).
17. 48 CFR Chapter 1.
18. 41 U.S.C. §704(a)(1).
19. 41 U.S.C. §704(a)(2).
20. 41 U.S.C. §704(b).
21. 41 U.S.C. §707.
22. See *Parker v. Atlanta Gas Light Co.*, 818 F. Supp. 345 (S.D. Ga. 1993).

Fair Credit Reporting Act

IN GENERAL

14-1. What is the Fair Credit Reporting Act?

14-2. Are all employers subject to the requirements of the FCRA?

14-3. Which federal agency is charged with enforcing the FCRA?

14-4. What are the requirements of the notice and consent provisions of the FCRA?

14-5. What is meant by a "consumer report"?

14-6. What is an "investigative consumer report"?

14-7. What rules apply to investigative consumer reports?

14-8. May medical information be contained in a consumer report?

14-9. What information may not be included in a consumer report?

HR Survival Guide

14-10. What is a consumer reporting agency?

14-11. What is the Consumer Reporting Employment Clarification Act of 1998?

14-12. What is meant by an "adverse action"?

NOTICE REQUIREMENTS

14-13. Must an employer notify an applicant or employee if it intends to take adverse action based upon a consumer report?

14-14. What information must be included in the "pre-adverse action notification"?

14-15. Where can the required description of the individual's rights be obtained?

14-16. What is the purpose of the pre-adverse action notification?

14-17. What may the employer do after furnishing the pre-adverse action notification?

14-18. What information must be contained in the "adverse action notification"?

14-19. How should an applicant or employee dispute inaccurate information contained in the consumer report?

REMEDIES

14-20. What action may be taken against an employer for violating the Fair Credit Reporting Act?

14-21. What is the time limit (statute of limitations) applicable to the FCRA?

14-22. Can employers and CRAs be held criminally liable for violations of the FCRA?

14-23. What remedies are available for "negligent noncompliance" with the FCRA?

14-24. What remedies are available for "willful noncompliance" with the FCRA?

IN GENERAL

14-1. What is the Fair Credit Reporting Act?

The Fair Credit Reporting Act (FCRA) is a federal law, which was originally enacted by Congress in 1970. Its intent is to promote accuracy, fairness and privacy of information in the files of every "consumer reporting agency" (CRA), see Q 14-10. The FCRA provides individuals with specific rights and puts specific obligations on CRAs and "users" of "consumer reports" (e.g., employers).

The text of the FCRA can be found at 15 U.S.C. §1681 et seq. It also can be found at the Federal Trade Commission's website (http://www.ftc.gov).

The FCRA was significantly amended in 1996 (most amendments became effective September 30, 1997) in order to ensure that the information contained in consumer reports is accurate, and to provide a mechanism for individuals to discover and correct inaccurate information.

Generally, in the employment context, the FCRA affects an employer only when the employer hires a third party (the CRA) to gather information and conduct various types of checks on an applicant or employee.

14-2. Are all employers subject to the requirements of the FCRA?

Employers of any size must comply with the requirements of the FCRA when they use the services of a third party (the CRA, see Q 14-10) to conduct background checks on applicants or employees.

14-3. Which federal agency is charged with enforcing the FCRA?

The Federal Trade Commission (FTC) has been given the authority to enforce the requirements of the FCRA. The FTC has procedural, investigative, and enforcement powers, including the power to issue procedural rules and to require the filing of reports, the production of documents, and the appearance of witnesses.[1]

14-4. What are the requirements of the notice and consent provisions of the FCRA?

An employer must disclose to an applicant or employee that it intends to use a third party's services to conduct a background check on the individual. This disclosure must be in writing. If an investigative consumer report (see Q 14-6) and/or medical information are to be obtained, the disclosure must specifically so indicate.

Second, the employer must receive consent from the applicant or employee before authorizing a third party to perform the background check.

This disclosure and authorization may be contained on the same page, but no other information may appear on the disclosure and authorization form. A disclosure and authorization contained within an employment application does not satisfy the requirements of the FCRA.[2]

14-5. What is meant by a "consumer report"?

Generally, "consumer report" means any written, oral, or other communication of any information, provided by a CRA, that bears on an individual's credit worthiness, credit standing, credit capacity, character, general reputation, personal characteristics, or mode of living. For a consumer report to be subject to the provisions of the FCRA, the consumer report must have been prepared by a "consumer reporting agency" (see Q 14-10).[3]

14-6. What is an "investigative consumer report"?

An "investigative consumer report" is a type of consumer report that the CRA creates, based upon personal interviews with an individual's:

1. Neighbors;

2. Friends;

3. Associates; or

4. Others with whom the individual is acquainted,

who may have knowledge concerning the individual's:

1.   Character;

2.   General reputation;

3.   Personal characteristics; or

4.   Mode of living.[4]

14-7. What rules apply to investigative consumer reports?

An employer may not obtain an investigative consumer report (see Q 14-6) concerning an employee unless the employer has clearly and accurately disclosed to the employee that the employer plans to seek such a report.[5] The employer must certify to the consumer reporting agency that it has made this disclosure to the employee.[6]

The disclosure must include a written summary of the rights of the consumer prepared pursuant to 15 U.S.C. §1681g(c).

The disclosure made to the individual must be mailed or delivered to the individual no later than three days after the date on which the report was first requested,[7] and must include a statement informing the individual of his or her right to request additional disclosures.[8]

Specifically, if an individual requests, within a reasonable time, information about the investigative consumer report, the employer must disclose the nature and scope of the investigation that it requested.[9]

The disclosure must be made in writing and mailed or delivered to the individual no later than five days after the request was received or the report was requested, whichever is later.[10]

14-8. May medical information be contained in a consumer report?

A CRA (see Q 14-10) may include medical information only if the applicant or employee specifically consents to the disclosure of such information.[11]

14-9. What information may not be included in a consumer report?

Information that may *not* be included in a consumer report includes:

1. Bankruptcy cases that, measured from the date of entry of the order for relief or the date of adjudication, pre-date the report by more than 10 years;

2. Civil suits, civil judgments, and arrest records that, measured from the date of entry, pre-date the report by more than seven years, or until the governing statute of limitations has expired, whichever is longer;

3. Paid tax liens that, measured from the date of payment, pre-date the report by more than seven years;

4. Accounts placed for collection, or charged to profit and loss, which pre-date the consumer report by more than seven years; and

5. Any other adverse item or information, other than records of convictions or crimes, that pre-date the report by more than seven years.[12]

These exclusions do not apply if the consumer report is to be used in connection with:

1. The employment of any individual whose annual salary may reasonably be expected to equal $75,000 or more;

2. The underwriting of life insurance that may reasonably be expected to involve a face amount of $150,000 or more; or

3. A credit transaction that may reasonably be expected to involve a principal amount of $150,000 or more.[13]

14-10. What is a consumer reporting agency?

A consumer reporting agency (CRA) is defined as any person or entity that:

1. For monetary fees, dues, or on a cooperative nonprofit basis;

2. Regularly engages in the practice of assembling or evaluating information on individuals for the purpose of furnishing consumer reports to third parties; and

3. Who uses interstate commerce for the purpose of preparing or furnishing the reports.[14]

Most CRAs are credit bureaus that gather and sell information about individuals to creditors, landlords, employers, and other types of businesses. Companies that perform various types of background checks for employers on applicants and current employees are also CRAs.

14-11. What is the Consumer Reporting Employment Clarification Act of 1998?

There were several typographical errors and other unclear portions of the amended FCRA. Accordingly, the Consumer Reporting Employment Clarification Act of 1998[15] amended the existing law in several respects.

First, it allows the disclosure and authorization requirements (regarding the procurement of a consumer report for employment purposes) to be handled by oral, written, or electronic means when (1) the consumer involved applies to certain motor carrier employment positions regulated by the Secretary of Transportation or a state transportation agency; and (2) the only interaction at that point between the applicant and the report procurer has been by such means.

Second, it allows a CRA to furnish a consumer report only if the CRA meets certain requirements, including the provision of a summary of the consumer's rights along with the consumer report (See Q 14-15).

Third, it provides national security exemptions from requirements that a CRA disclose to a consumer: (1) the identity of each person that procured a report on that consumer; and (2) that public record information was reported, which is likely to have an adverse effect on a consumer's ability to obtain employment.[16]

Fourth, it allows a CRA to report on criminal convictions beyond seven years.

14-12. What is meant by an "adverse action"?

"Adverse action," for this purpose, includes a denial of employment or any other action or decision taken or made by the employer which adversely affects a current or prospective employee.[17]

NOTICE REQUIREMENTS

14-13. Must an employer notify an applicant or employee if it intends to take adverse action based upon a consumer report?

Yes. If an employer intends to take adverse action against an applicant or employee, based (either in whole or in part) upon information contained in the consumer report, the employer must first provide the applicant or employee with a "pre-adverse action notification."[18]

This pre-adverse action notification must include a copy of the individual's consumer report and a description of the individual's rights under the FCRA.[19]

14-14. What information must be included in the "pre-adverse action notification"?

The pre-adverse action notification should state that the employer intends to take adverse action (e.g., reject the applicant for employment; deny a promotion; etc.), and that adverse action was based, either in whole or in part, upon information contained in the consumer report.

The pre-adverse action notification must inform the applicant or employee of how to make a challenge if he or she disputes the accuracy of the information contained in the consumer report.

Finally, the pre-adverse action notification must also inform the applicant or employee of the name and telephone number of the employer's contact person, should the applicant or employee have any questions.[20]

14-15. Where can the required description of the individual's rights be obtained?

The FTC has developed a document entitled "A Summary Of Your Rights Under The Fair Credit Reporting Act," which is reprinted in Appendix C.

The CRA that prepared the consumer report is required to provide the employer with this summary of rights.

It also can be obtained from the FTC's website: http://www.ftc.gov/bcp/conline/edcams/fcra/summary.htm.

14-16. What is the purpose of the pre-adverse action notification?

The purpose of the pre-adverse action notification is to provide the applicant or employee with an opportunity to see what information was communicated to the employer, so that the he or she may dispute the accuracy of incorrect information.

Congress intended FCRA to prevent negative actions from being taken against an individual because of false or inaccurate information contained in a consumer report.[21]

14-17. What may the employer do after furnishing the pre-adverse action notification?

After providing the pre-adverse action notification, the employer may then take the contemplated adverse action against the individual (e.g., reject the applicant from employment; deny the individual a promotion; etc.).

When it does so, the employer must provide the individual with an "adverse action notification" (see Q 14-18) within three days of taking such action.

14-18. What information must be contained in the "adverse action notification"?

The adverse action notification must inform the applicant or employee of any adverse action that the employer is taking against him or her, and that such adverse action is based, in whole or in part, on a consumer report received from a CRA.

It must inform the applicant or employee of the CRA's name, address, and telephone number.

The adverse action notification must also inform the applicant or employee that the CRA did not make the decision to take the adverse action, and will not be able to provide any specific reasons for the employer's decision.

It must inform the applicant or employee that he or she may obtain a free copy of the consumer report from the CRA, provided that the applicant or employee requests a copy within 60 calendar days. The applicant or employee must also be informed that he or she may dispute the accuracy or completeness of any information in the report with the CRA.[22]

14-19. How should an applicant or employee dispute inaccurate information contained in the consumer report?

In order to dispute information contained in the consumer report, the applicant or employee must first inform the CRA that the consumer report contains inaccurate information.

Once the applicant or employee has notified the CRA that the report may contain inaccuracies, the CRA is required to investigate the disputed item(s), usually within 30 days. After completing its investigation, the CRA must then provide the applicant or employee with a written report of the investigation, and a copy of the report if the investigation results in any change.

If the CRA's investigation does not resolve the dispute, the applicant or employee may add a brief statement to the file. The CRA must normally include a summary of the statement in future reports that are requested.

If an item of information is deleted or a dispute statement is filed, the applicant or employee may request that the CRA notify anyone who has recently received the report of the change.[23]

REMEDIES

14-20. What action may be taken against an employer for violating the Fair Credit Reporting Act?

The aggrieved applicant or employee may sue the employer and/or the CRA in either federal or state court.

The FTC or the chief law enforcement officer of a state (or an official or agency designated by a state) may also bring an action against anyone that violates the FCRA.[24]

14-21. What is the time limit (statute of limitations) applicable to the FCRA?

Generally, an action under the FCRA must be brought within two years from the date on which the liability arises. But in a case where (1) a defendant has materially and willfully misrepresented any information required that the FCRA requires to be disclosed; and (2) such misrepresentation is material to the establishment of the defendant's liability, an action may be brought within two years after the applicant or employee discovers the misrepresentation.[25]

14-22. Can employers and CRAs be held criminally liable for violations of the FCRA?

Yes. The FCRA states that any person who knowingly and willfully obtains information about an individual from a CRA under false pretenses shall be fined and/or imprisoned for up to two years.[26]

Moreover, any officer or employee of a CRA that knowingly and willfully provides information from the CRA's files to a person not authorized to receive such information shall be fined and/or imprisoned for up to two years.[27]

14-23. What remedies are available for "negligent noncompliance" with the FCRA?

An employer that negligently fails to comply with any FCRA requirement may be liable to the applicant or employee in an amount equal to the sum of:

1.   Actual damages sustained;

2.　　Costs of the action; and

3.　　Reasonable attorney's fees.[28]

14-24. What remedies are available for "willful noncompliance" with the FCRA?

An employer that willfully fails to comply with any FCRA requirement may be liable to an applicant or employee in an amount equal to:

1.　　Any actual damages sustained of not less than $100 and not more than $1,000; or

2.　　In the case of a person obtaining a report under false pretenses or knowingly without a permissible purpose, actual damages sustained or $1,000, whichever is greater.[29]

In addition, an employer that willfully fails to comply with any FCRA requirement may be liable for:

1.　　Punitive damages awarded by the court; and

2.　　Costs of the action with reasonable attorney's fees as determined by the court.[30]

Any person who obtains a report from a CRA (1) under false pretenses; or (2) knowingly without a permissible purpose, shall be liable to the CRA for actual damages sustained by the CRA or $1,000, whichever is greater.[31]

Further, the FTC may commence a civil action to recover a civil penalty of up to $2,500 per violation for knowing violations that constitute a pattern or practice of violations of the FCRA.[32]

CHAPTER ENDNOTES

1.　15 U.S.C. §1681s.
2.　15 U.S.C. §1681b.
3.　15 U.S.C. §1681a.
4.　15 U.S.C. §1681a.
5.　15 U.S.C. 1681d(a)(1).
6.　15 U.S.C. 1681d(a)(2).
7.　15 USC 1681d(a)(1)(A).
8.　15 USC 1681d(a)(1)(B).
9.　See 15 U.S.C. §1681d(b).

10. Id.
11. 15 U.S.C. §1681b.
12. 15 U.S.C. §1681c(a).
13. 15 U.S.C. §1681c(b).
14. 15 U.S.C. §1681a.
15. PL 105-347.
16. 15 U.S.C. 1681b(b)(4).
17. See U.S.C. §1681a.
18. 15 U.S.C. §1681b(b).
19. Id.
20. 15 U.S.C. §1681b.
21. 15 U.S.C. §1681, Congressional Findings and Statement of Purpose.
22. See 15 U.S.C. §1681b.
23. 15 U.S.C. §1681i.
24. 15 U.S.C. §1681p; 15 U.S.C. §1681s.
25. See 15 U.S.C. §1681p.
26. 15 U.S.C. §§1681q.
27. 15 U.S.C. §§1681r.
28. 15 U.S.C. §1681o.
29. 15 U.S.C. §1681n.
30. Id.
31. Id.
32. See 15 U.S.C. §1681s(2).

Chapter 15

Polygraph Protection Act

GENERALLY

15-1. What is the Employee Polygraph Protection Act of 1988?

15-2. Who enforces the EPPA?

15-3. Who is protected under the EPPA?

15-4. Who must comply with the EPPA?

15-5. Who is not protected by the EPPA?

15-6. What specifically does the EPPA prohibit?

15-7. Are there exemptions to the EPPA?

15-8. What are the federal government exemptions to the EPPA?

15-9. What are the exemptions available to nongovernmental employers under the EPPA?

15-10. What standards must the polygraph examination meet?

15-11. What restrictions apply to all phases of the polygraph testing?

15-12. What restrictions apply to the pre-test phase?

15-13. What restrictions apply during the actual testing phase?

15-14. What restrictions apply during the post-test phase?

15-15. Are there other miscellaneous restrictions that must be met for the exemption to apply?

15-16. What use can an employer properly make of the polygraph results?

15-17. Does the EPPA have notice requirements?

15-18. Does the EPPA have record keeping requirements?

PROCEDURE FOR FILING AN EPPA CLAIM

15-19. Does a plaintiff have to file a complaint with the DOL?

15-20. How does a plaintiff file a complaint with the DOL?

15-21. What is the civil penalty for violating the EPPA?

15-22. How may a person appeal the assessment of a civil penalty?

15-23. What is the time limit (statute of limitations) for actions under the EPPA?

15-24. Can an employer or applicant waive his or her rights under EPPA in advance?

LITIGATING AN EPPA CLAIM

15-25. What issues are usually litigated in EPPA cases?

REMEDIES UNDER THE EPPA

15-26. What remedies are available for private plaintiffs under the EPPA?

15-27. What remedies are available for the DOL under the EPPA?

15-28. Does the EPPA preempt all state laws?

15-29. Does the EPPA preempt collective bargaining agreements?

GENERALLY

15-1. What is the Employee Polygraph Protection Act of 1988?

The Employee Polygraph Protection Act of 1988 (EPPA) is a federal law that generally prohibits nongovernmental employers from requiring or using "lie detector" devices, either for pre-employment screening or during the course of employment.

Subject to very strict controls and in very limited circumstances, employers can request or require a polygraph test (a type of "lie detector" test), but even in these circumstances, the employer cannot act on the results unless there is additional supporting evidence.[1]

15-2. Who enforces the EPPA?

The Department of Labor (DOL) is charged with the enforcement of the EPPA. The DOL has the authority to issue regulations, and has provided regulations to further carry out the purpose of the EPPA.[2]

The DOL can assess civil penalties for violation of the EPPA, and can file suit in federal court for injunctions and other relief.[3]

The EPPA also authorizes private plaintiffs to file and prosecute civil actions under the EPPA.[4]

15-3. Who is protected under the EPPA?

All employees and prospective employees of covered employers (see Q 15-4) are covered by the EPPA.[5]

The EPPA extends to all employees of covered employers, regardless of the employees' the citizenship status. The EPPA also covers U.S. based employees of foreign corporations.[6]

15-4. Who must comply with the EPPA?

The EPPA applies to all nongovernmental "employers" engaged in interstate commerce. The term "commerce" is interpreted broadly, and, as a practical matter, almost all private employers in the U.S. will be covered by the EPPA.

"Employer" includes any person acting, directly or indirectly, in the interest of the employer in relation to an employee or a prospective employee.[7]

The regulations specifically provide that a polygraph examiner retained for the sole purpose of administering polygraph tests is not deemed to be an "employer" with respect to the examinees.[8] However, some courts have held that a triable issue of facts exists as to whether polygraph examiners become liable as an "employer" when they act on behalf of a employer by providing advice on the EPPA requirements, or, as a matter of economic reality, exert control over the employer's compliance with the EPPA.[9]

15-5. Who is not protected by the EPPA?

Employees of federal, state, and local governments, of any political subdivision of a state or local government, and of any interstate governmental agency are not covered by the EPPA.[10]

While "employees" of governmental entities are not covered, government contractors and employees of government contractors are generally covered by EPPA, subject to the limited exemptions addressed in Q 15-8 and Q 15-9.[11]

15-6. What specifically does the EPPA prohibit?

The EPPA prohibits, either directly or indirectly, most private employers from using lie detector tests, either for pre-employment screening or during the course of employment.[12]

Employers are generally prohibited from requiring, requesting, suggesting, or causing any employee or applicant to take a lie detector test. They are also prohibited from discharging, disciplining, or discriminating against an employee or applicant for refusing to take a lie detector test, or for exercising other rights under the EPPPA.

Employers may not use or inquire about the results of a lie detector test, discharge an employee, or discriminate against an employee or applicant solely on the basis of the results of a lie detector test. Employers may not discharge an employee, or discriminate against an employee or applicant for filing a complaint, or for participating in any proceeding under the EPPA.[13]

An employer who reports a theft or other incident involving economic loss to the proper authorities does not violate the EPPA, if, in the normal course of the subsequent investigation, the authorities conduct a polygraph test of an employee suspected of involvement in the incident. Employers who passively cooperate with police by permitting the police to conduct a polygraph during an employee's normal working hours also do not violate the EPPA. By contrast, an employer who *actively* assists the police by requiring the employee to take the polygraph, reimbursing the police for the cost of the polygraph, or by reviewing the results of the police polygraph does violate the EPPA.[14]

The term "lie detector" is defined as any mechanical or electrical device (including polygraph, deceptograph, voice stress analyzer, and psychological stress evaluator) that is used, or the results of which are used, to render a diagnostic opinion regarding the honesty or dishonesty of a person.[15]

The term "lie detector" does not include medical tests used to determine the presence of controlled substances or alcohol in bodily fluids. The term also does not include written or oral "honesty" tests, or handwriting tests.[16]

15-7. Are there exemptions to the EPPA?

The EPPA establishes several exemptions, which permit certain types of lie detectors to be used in limited circumstances. There are exemptions for the federal government as employer (see Q 15-8), and other exemptions for nongovernmental employers (see Q 15-9).

15-8. What are the federal government exemptions to the EPPA?

The federal government exemptions to the EPPA are the "national defense" exemption, the "security" exemption, and the "FBI contractors" exemption.

NATIONAL DEFENSE EXEMPTION

When conducting a counterintelligence investigation, the federal government may require experts or consultants under contract with the Department of Defense, or employees of Department of Defense contractors to take lie detector tests.[17]

Similarly, when conducting a counterintelligence investigation, the federal government can require experts or consultants under contract with the Department of Energy for atomic energy defense activities, or employees of Department of Energy contractors working on atomic energy matters to take lie detector tests.[18]

SECURITY EXEMPTION

When engaged in intelligence or counterintelligence activity, the federal government may administer lie detector tests to any individual employed by any contractor doing business with the National Security Agency, the Defense Intelligence Agency, the National Imagery and Mapping Agency, or the Central Intelligence Agency.[19]

Similarly, the federal government may administer lie detector tests to any expert or consultant (or the employee of an expert or consultant under contract with the federal government) who has access to top secret information.[20]

FBI CONTRACTORS EXEMPTION

When performing counterintelligence activity, the federal government is permitted to administer lie detector tests to those employees of contractors of the Federal Bureau of Investigation who are engaged in the performance of work under an FBI contract.[21]

15-9. What are the exemptions available to nongovernmental employers under the EPPA?

The exemptions available to nongovernmental employers under the EPPA are the exemption for security services, the limited exemption for ongoing investigations, and the exemption for drug security, drug theft, or drug diversion investigations.

EXEMPTION FOR SECURITY SERVICES

Private employers that have as their primary business purpose:

1. The provision of armored car services;

2. The design, installation, or maintenance of security alarms; or

3. the provision of uniformed or plainclothes security personnel who will protect designated power, water, nuclear, and transportation facilities

can require prospective employees to take polygraph tests provided that they have complied with the other procedural safeguards governing such tests.[22]

EXEMPTION FOR DRUG SECURITY, DRUG THEFT, OR DRUG DIVERSION INVESTIGATIONS

An employer authorized to manufacture, distribute, or dispense controlled substances can administer polygraphs to prospective employees who will have direct access to the controlled substance.

Polygraphs can also be administered to existing employees of such companies, if the test is administered as part of an ongoing investigation involving loss or injury to the manufacturer, distributor, or dispenser of a controlled substance, and the employee being tested had access to the person or property that is subject to the investigation.

All procedural safeguards relating to the polygraph test must be complied with in order for the employer to take advantage of this exemption.[23]

LIMITED EXEMPTION FOR ONGOING INVESTIGATIONS

The EPPA allows private employers to request (but not require) that an employee submit to a polygraph test (but not any other type of lie detector test) if all the following conditions are met:

1. The test is administered in connection with an ongoing investigation involving economic loss or injury to the employer's business;

2. The employee had access to the property that is the subject of the investigation; and

3. The employer has a reasonable suspicion that the employee was involved in the incident or activity under investigation; and

4. The employer executes a statement, provided to the examinee before the test, that:

    a) sets forth, with particularity, the specific incident or activity being investigated and the basis for testing particular employees,

b) is signed by a person (other than a polygraph examiner) authorized to legally bind the employer,

c) is retained by the employer for at least three years, and

d) contains, at a minimum: (i) an identification of the specific economic loss or injury to the employers business, (ii) a statement indicating that the employee had access to the property that is the subject of the investigation, and (iii) a statement describing the basis of the employer's reasonable suspicion that the employee was involved in the incident or activity under investigation.[24]

15-10. What standards must the polygraph examination meet?

Even if an employer meets all the preliminary requirements triggering the ongoing investigation exemption, the test itself must comply with very specific standards. If the employer does not comply with all the standards, the statutory exemption will not apply and the polygraph test will violate the EPPA.[25]

The standards are discussed in Q 15-11 through Q 15-15.

15-11. What restrictions apply to all phases of the polygraph testing?

Throughout all phases of the test:

1. The examinee has the right to terminate the test at any time;

2. The examinee cannot be asked questions in a manner designed to degrade or needlessly intrude on the examinee;

3. The examinee cannot be asked any question concerning—

    a) religious beliefs or affiliations,

    b) beliefs or opinions regarding racial matters,

c) political beliefs or affiliations,

d) any matter relating to sexual behavior, or

e) beliefs, affiliations, opinions, or lawful activities regarding unions or labor organizations; and

4. The examiner cannot conduct the test if there is sufficient written evidence from a physician to indicate that the examinee is suffering from a medical or psychological condition or undergoing treatment that might cause abnormal responses during the actual testing phase.[26]

15-12. What restrictions apply to the pre-test phase?

The prospective examinee must be provided with a written notice at least 48 hours (excluding holidays and weekends) prior to the date of the test. This notice must provide the time and location of the test, and explain the examinee's right to obtain and consult with legal counsel or an employee representative before each phase of the test.

The nature and characteristics of the test and of the instruments involved must also be stated in the pre-test notice.

The prospective examinee must be informed, in writing, whether the testing area contains a two-way mirror, a camera, or any other device through which the test can be observed.

The prospective examinee must also be informed of whether any other device, including any device for recording or monitoring the test, will be used, and that the employer or the examinee may (with mutual knowledge) make a recording of the test.

Prior to taking the test, the examinee must read and sign a written notice, which informs the examinee that:

1. He or she cannot be required to take the test as a condition of employment, and

2. Any statement made during the test may constitute additional supporting evidence for the purposes of an adverse employment action.

This written notice must also inform the examinee of:

1.   The limitations imposed under the EPPA;

2.   His or her legal rights and remedies if the polygraph test is not conducted appropriately; and

3.   The employer's legal rights and remedies under the EPPA.[27]

During the pre-test phase, the prospective examinee must also be provided with an opportunity to review all questions to be asked during the test and must be informed of the right to terminate the test at any time.[28]

The DOL regulations include a standard form, which, if properly completed, will meet the notification requirements of the EPPA.[29] This form is reproduced in Appendix D.

15-13. What restrictions apply during the actual testing phase?

During the actual testing phase, the examiner may not ask the examinee any question "relevant during the test" (i.e., not including "base line" questions) that was not presented in writing for review before the test.

The actual test itself must not be less than 90 minutes in length.[30]

15-14. What restrictions apply during the post-test phase?

Before taking any adverse action, the employer must:

1.   Further interview the examinee on the basis of the results of the test; and

2.   Provide the examinee with—

a) a written copy of any opinion or conclusion rendered as a result of the test, and

b) a copy of the questions asked during the test, along with the corresponding charted responses.[31]

Any opinion or conclusion resulting from the test must be: (1) in writing; and (2) limited solely to an analysis of the polygraph test charts. The written opinion must not include any recommendation concerning employment of the examinee.[32]

15-15. Are there other miscellaneous restrictions that must be met for the exemption to apply?

Yes. The examiner is not permitted to conduct and complete more than five polygraph tests on the calendar day on which the test is given.[33]

In addition, the polygraph examiner must (1) be licensed; and (2) have at least $50,000 of professional liability insurance.[34]

15-16. What use can an employer properly make of the polygraph results?

Information from the polygraph test may only be disclosed to: (1) the person examined; (2) the employer that requested the test; or (3) pursuant to court order, certain governmental agencies and judicial or quasi-judicial bodies.[35]

The employer is also permitted to disclose information from the test to a government agency, if the information is an admission of criminal conduct.[36]

Even if an employer satisfies all the criteria for the exemptions, the results of the polygraph test, or the refusal to take the polygraph, cannot be the sole basis upon which an adverse employment action is taken. Rather, there must be "additional supporting evidence" supporting any adverse action.[37]

ADDITIONAL SUPPORTING EVIDENCE

The additional supporting evidence required to justify an adverse employment action can be the same evidence that created a "reasonable suspicion" of an employee in the first instance—the "reasonable suspicion" that was necessary to meet the ongoing investigation exemption.[38]

The employer may also consider admissions or other statements made before, during, or after the polygraph examination to be the required "additional supporting evidence" that would justify an adverse employment action.[39]

15-17. Does the EPPA have notice requirements?

Yes. The EPPA requires the Secretary of Labor to prepare and distribute a notice describing the EPPA. Employers must post and maintain this notice in conspicuous places where notices to employees and applicants are customarily posted.[40] The notice can be obtained or ordered from the Department of Labor web site:

http://www.dol.gov/dol/esa/public/regs/
compliance/posters/eppa.htm

and is reprinted in Appendix E.

15-18. Does the EPPA have record keeping requirements?

Yes. The polygraph examiner and the employer must maintain all documents related to the polygraph tests, and the documents relating to any investigation and employment action, for three years after the test is administered.[41]

PROCEDURE FOR FILING AN EPPA CLAIM

15-19. Does a plaintiff have to file a complaint with the DOL?

No. An employee can proceed directly against an employer that he or she alleges has violated the EPPA. The individual can sue on his or her own behalf *and* on behalf of all similarly situated employees or prospective employees.[42]

The Secretary of Labor is empowered to file an action in federal court to enjoin alleged violations of the EPPA, and to commence an administrative proceeding to collect a civil penalty.[43]

15-20. How does a plaintiff file a complaint with the Department of Labor?

Any individual can report an alleged violation of the EPPA to the Wage and Hour Division, Employment Standards Administration of the Department of Labor.[44] To the extent practicable, the DOL will attempt to protect the confidentiality of the complainant.[45]

15-21. What is the civil penalty for violating the EPPA?

If, after conducting an investigation, the DOL's Employment Standards Administration determines that the employer or prospective employer violated the EPPA, it will determine the amount of the civil penalty to assess. This civil penalty may be as much as $10,000 per violation.

In making this determination, the DOL will consider any "pertinent" factors, including: (1) the employer's previous compliance record; (2) the gravity of violation; (3) the employer's good faith efforts to comply; (4) the extent to which the employee or prospective employee suffered loss; and (5) the employer's commitment to comply with the EPPA in the future.[46]

15-22. How may a person appeal the assessment of a civil penalty?

Any person against whom a civil penalty is assessed may, within 30 days after receipt of the assessment notice, request a hearing before an administrative law judge (ALJ).[47]

The ALJ's decision can be appealed to the Secretary of Labor within 20 days after the date of the ALJ's decision.[48]

The Secretary of Labor has discretion as to whether to hear the appeal.[49] Applying a clearly erroneous standard of review, the Secretary may modify, vacate, or affirm the administrative law judge's decision.[50]

The Secretary's decision may be appealed to the appropriate United States District Court.[51]

15-23. What is the time limit (statute of limitations) for actions under the EPPA?

EPPA actions must be commenced within three years after date when the alleged violation occurred.[52]

15-24. Can an employer or applicant waive his or her rights under EPPA in advance?

No. An employer or applicant cannot waive or release his or her EPPA rights in advance, for example, as part of a pre-hire employment agreement.

The EPPA provides that any waiver or release may only be part of a written agreement signed by the parties to settle a pending action or complaint.[53]

LITIGATING AN EPPA CLAIM

15-25. What issues are usually litigated in EPPA cases?

Most of the reported cases concerning the EPPA focus on whether the statutory predicates for the exemptions authorizing polygraph testing have been met. Generally, in keeping with the congressional hostility to lie detector tests, the exemptions are narrowly construed.

The major building blocks for the "ongoing investigation" exemption (see Q 15-8): (1) an ongoing investigation; (2) economic loss to the employer's business; and (3) a reasonable suspicion of the specific employee, are extensively described in the regulations.[54]

An "ongoing investigation" must be of a specific incident or activity. Random testing, "fishing exhibitions," and a long lasting continuing "dragnet" investigation do not meet the EPPA standard.[55]

The overall business of the employer must suffer the economic loss or injury—theft committed by one employee against another does not meet the criteria.[56]

"Reasonable suspicion" refers to an observable, articulable basis in fact, which indicates that a particular employee was involved in or responsible for the loss. A general suspicion, or the employee's mere access, standing alone, is not sufficient.[57]

Even if the factual basis justifying the ongoing investigation exemption exists, the employer still violates the EPPA if it does not comply with the EPPA's notification mandates. The required statement to the employee must state, with particularity, the specific incident being investigated, and the basis for testing the particular employee.[58]

Any failure to comply with the factual requirements, the notice requirements, or the substantive manner of conducting the test will nullify the statutory exemption and create a violation of the EPPA.[59]

REMEDIES UNDER THE EPPA

15-26. What remedies are available for private plaintiffs under the EPPA?

Private plaintiffs can recover any appropriate legal or equitable relief, including:

1. Reinstatement;

2. Back pay;

3. Emotional distress damages;

4. Employment; or

5. Promotion.[60]

Courts have discretion to award reasonable costs and attorneys fees to a prevailing private litigant (i.e., not the DOL).[61]

15-27. What remedies are available for the DOL under the EPPA?

The Secretary of Labor may file suit to restrain violations of EPPA. Courts have authority to not only enjoin violations of EPPA, but also to order any appropriate legal or equitable relief, including:

1. Employment;

2. Reinstatement;

3. Promotion; and

4. Lost wages.[62]

The Department of Labor also has the authority to assess a civil penalty upon employers that violate the EPPA. Such civil penalty may be as much as $10,000 per violation (see Q 15-21).[63]

15-28. Does the EPPA preempt all state laws?

No. The EPPA sets the minimum standard of protection. Any state or local law that is more restrictive than the EPPA is still in full force and effect.

Therefore, an employer desiring to conduct polygraph tests must examine not only the exemptions set out in the EPPA, but should also review any applicable state or local law.[64]

15-29. Does the EPPA preempt collective bargaining agreements?

No. As is the case with state or local laws that are more restrictive than the EPPA (see Q 15-28), the EPPA does not preempt the terms of collective bargaining agreements. A collective bargaining agreement that is more restrictive than the EPPA remains in full force and effect.

Thus, before conducting polygraph tests, an employer should not only examine the exemptions set out in the EPPA, but should also review the terms of any applicable collective bargaining agreement.[65]

CHAPTER ENDNOTES

1. See 29 U.S.C. §2001, et seq.
2. See 29 U.S.C. §2004.
3. See 29 U.S.C. §2005.
4. See 29 U.S.C. §2005(c).
5. See 29 U.S.C. §2002.
6. See 29 CFR §801.3.
7. See 29 U.S.C. §2001(2).
8. See 29 CFR §801.2(c).
9. See, *James v. Professionals' Detective Agency, Inc.*, 876 F. Supp. 1013 (N.D. Ill. 1995); *Rubin v. Tourneau, Inc.*, 797 F. Supp. 247 (S.D. N.Y. 1992).
10. See 29 U.S.C. §2006(a), 29 CFR §801.10.
11. See 29 CFR §801.10(d).
12. See 29 U.S.C. §2002.
13. See 29 U.S.C. §2002.
14. See 29 CFR §§801.4(b), 801.4(c).
15. See 29 U.S.C. §2001(3).
16. See 29 CFR §801.2(d)(2).
17. 29 U.S.C. §2006(b)(1)(A).
18. 29 U.S.C. §2006(b)(1)(B).
19. 29 U.S.C. §2006(b)(2).
20. 29 U.S.C. §2006(b)(2)(B).
21. 29 U.S.C. §2006(c).
22. 29 U.S.C. §2006(e).
23. 29 U.S.C. §2006(f).
24. 29 U.S.C. §2006(d).
25. See 29 U.S.C. §2007(b).
26. See 29 U.S.C. §2007(b)(1); 29 CFR §801.22.
27. See 29 U.S.C. §2007(b)(2); 29 CFR 801.23.
28. Id.
29. See 29 CFR 801.23(a)(3), Appendix A.

30. 29 U.S.C. §2007(b)(3); 29 CFR §801.24.
31. See U.S.C. §2007(b)(4), 29 CFR §801.25.
32. See 29 U.S.C. §2007(c)(2)(A).
33. 29 U.S.C. §2007(b)(5).
34. See 29 U.S.C. §2007(c)(1).
35. See 29 U.S.C. §2008.
36. See U.S.C. §2008(c)(2).
37. See 29 U.S.C. §2007(a).
38. See 29 U.S.C. §2007(a)(1); 29 CFR §801.20(b).
39. See CFR §801.20(b).
40. See 29 U.S.C. §2003.
41. See 29 U.S.C. §2007(c)(2)(B).
42. See 29 U.S.C. §2005(c).
43. See 29 U.S.C. §2005(b).
44. 29 CFR §801.7(d).
45. 29 CFR §801.7(e).
46. See 29 CFR §801.42(b).
47. See 29 CFR §801.53.
48. See 29 CFR §801.67(f); 29 CFR §801.69.
49. 29 CFR §801.70(a).
50. See 29 CFR §801.68.
51. See 29 CFR §801.75.
52. See 29 U.S.C. §2005(c)(2).
53. See 29 U.S.C. §2005(d).
54. See 29 CFR 801.12.
55. 29 CFR §801.12(b).
56. See 29 CFR §801.12(c)(3), *Lyle v. Mercy Hospital Anderson*, 876 F. Supp. 157 (S. D. Ohio 1995).
57. See 29 CFR §810.12(f).
58. See 29 CFR §801.12(g)(3).
59. See 29 CFR §801.12(h).
60. U.S. C. §2005(c); see, e.g., *Mennen v. Easter Stores*, 951 F. Supp. 838 (N.D. Iowa 1997).
61. See 29 U.S.C. §2005(c)(3).
62. See 29 U.S.C. §2005(b).
63. See 29 U.S.C. §2005(a)(1).
64. See 29 U.S.C. §2009.
65. See 29 U.S.C. §2009.

Chapter 16

Occupational Safety and Health Administration

IN GENERAL

16-1. What is the Occupational Safety and Health Administration (OSHA)?

16-2. Who is covered by the OSH Act?

16-3. Are there state enforcement programs similar to OSHA?

16-4. What does the OSH Act require?

16-5. What are OSHA's recordkeeping requirements?

OSHA STANDARDS

16-6. What general areas do OSHA standards cover?

16-7. How are OSHA standards created?

16-8. What if an employer disagrees with a new standard or cannot comply with agency requirements?

16-9. Can employers and employees petition OSHA to modify or withdraw standards or requirements?

16-10. Who can file a petition for judicial review?

VARIANCES

16-11. What is a variance? When can an employer request a variance from an OSHA standard?

16-12. What are the types of variances?

16-13. Can an employer continue to operate its worksite while waiting for a decision on a variance application?

ENFORCEMENT

16-14. How does OSHA enforce its standards?

16-15. How does an employer get selected for an OSHA inspection?

16-16. What happens during an OSHA inspection?

16-17. What happens after an OSHA inspection?

16-18. What is in an OSHA citation?

16-19. What are the categories of violations and the types of penalties that OSHA can propose?

16-20. How can an employer challenge the results of an OSHA inspection?

16-21. What defenses can an employer assert to citations and penalties?

16-22. Can an employer petition OSHA for modification of the abatement period?

16-23. Does the OSH Act prohibit an employer from retaliating against employees?

COOPERATIVE PROGRAMS

16-24. What types of cooperative programs are available with OSHA?

IN GENERAL

16-1. What is the Occupational Safety and Health Administration (OSHA)?

The Occupational Safety and Health Administration (OSHA) is an agency of the U.S. Department of Labor. OSHA's sole responsibility is worker safety and health protection. The U.S. Congress created OSHA under the Occupational Safety and Health Act of 1970 (the OSH Act).[1] The OSH Act has been amended a number of times since its enactment. OSHA was established "to assure so far as possible every working man and woman in the Nation safe and healthful working conditions and to preserve our human resources."[2] Prior to 1970, no uniform and comprehensive federal legislation existed to protect against workplace safety and health hazards. The OSH Act also created the National Institute for Occupational Safety and Health (NIOSH), which is the federal research agency for safety and health.[3]

The OSH Act is administered and enforced within the Department of Labor by the Occupational Safety and Health Administration. OSHA is responsible for developing and implementing OSHA's safety and health standards, in accordance with the procedures stated in the OSH Act. OSHA also is responsible for enforcing the OSH Act and its occupational safety and health standards.[4] It does this by using federal agents and the power of the federal government to conduct workplace inspections, and by issuing fines for, and ordering the correction of, any condition that OSHA determines violates the OSH Act or an OSHA safety and health standard. There is no private right of action for violating the OSH Act's safety and health requirements. Individual employees, labor unions and others do not have the legal right to enforce the workplace safety and health requirements of the OSH Act. Only OSHA may do this.

OSHA has its principal office in Washington, D.C. The chief administrator of OSHA is the Assistant Secretary of Labor for Occupational Safety and Health, who reports directly to the Secretary of Labor. OSHA currently has ten regional offices. Each region has several area offices. Each area office is supervised by an area director and is staffed principally by OSHA compliance officers, who conduct workplace inspections, and also by a small number of supervisory compliance officers/assistant area directors.[5]

16-2. Who is covered by the OSH Act?

The OSH Act covers all employers and their employees in the 50 states and all territories and jurisdictions under federal authority. Those jurisdictions include the District of Columbia, Puerto Rico, the Virgin Islands, American Samoa, Johnston Island, the Canal Zone, and the Outer Continental Shelf Lands as defined in the Outer Continental Shelf Lands Act.[6]

OSH Act coverage includes employers and employees in such varied fields as manufacturing, construction, longshoring, shipbuilding, ship repair, agriculture, law and medicine, charity and disaster relief, organized labor, private education, and religious groups to the extent they employ workers for secular purposes.[7] The OSH Act covers employers and employees either directly through federal OSHA or through an OSHA-approved state program.[8]

The OSH Act does not cover the following: (1) the self-employed; (2) immediate members of farming families that do not employ outside workers; (3) employees whose working conditions are regulated by other federal agencies under other federal statutes; (4) public employees in state and local governments.[9]

With regard to federal workers, the OSH Act makes federal agency heads responsible for providing safe and healthful working conditions for their employees. The OSH Act also requires agencies to comply with standards consistent with those OSHA issues for private sector employers.[10] In cases where another federal agency regulates safety and health working conditions in a particular industry, OSHA standards still apply if the other agency's regulations do not address specific working conditions.[11]

16-3. Are there state enforcement programs similar to OSHA?

State plans are OSHA-approved job safety and health programs operated by individual states instead of by federal OSHA. The OSH Act encourages states to develop and operate their own job safety and health plans and precludes state enforcement of OSHA standards unless the state has an approved plan.[12]

Once a state plan is approved under the OSH Act, OSHA funds up to 50% of the program's operating costs. State plans must provide standards and enforcement programs, as well as voluntary compliance activities, that are "at least as effective as" the federal OSHA program.

State plans covering the private sector also must cover state and local government employees. OSHA rules also permit states to develop plans that cover only public sector (state and local government) employees. In these cases, private sector employment remains under federal OSHA jurisdiction. Nearly half the states and two territories operate some form of a state plan.

To gain OSHA approval as a "developmental plan," the first step in the state plan approval process, a state must have adequate legislative authority and must demonstrate that within three years it will provide standards setting, enforcement, and appeals procedures; public employee protection; a sufficient number of competent enforcement personnel; and training, education, and technical assistance programs.

In states with approved plans, OSHA generally limits its enforcement activity to areas not covered by the state and suspends all concurrent federal enforcement. Once the state is operating at least as effectively as federal OSHA and other requirements are met, final approval of the plan may be granted and federal authority will cease in those areas over which the state has jurisdiction.

States with approved state plans respond to accidents and workplace complaints and conduct random unannounced general schedule inspections just like federal OSHA. Citations and proposed penalties are issued under state law and contests are adjudicated by a state review board or other procedure.

Federal OSHA closely monitors state programs. Anyone finding inadequacies or other problems in the administration of a state's program may file a Complaint About State Program Administration (CASPA) with the appropriate OSHA Regional Administrator. OSHA investigates all such complaints and, where complaints are found to be valid, requires appropriate corrective action on the part of the state.

State plans must guarantee the same employer and employee rights as does OSHA. Employer and employee responsibilities in states with their own occupational safety and health programs are generally the same as in federal OSHA states. State safety and health standards under approved plans must either be identical to or at least as effective as federal OSHA standards and must keep pace with federal standards. State plans must adopt standards comparable to federal standards within six months of a federal standard's promulgation. Most state plan standards are very similar to federal standards, but states with approved plans may have different and independent standards.

16-4. What does the OSH Act require?

The OSH Act states an employer's principal obligations:

(a) Each employer -

(1)   shall furnish to each of his employees employment and a place of employment which are free from recognized hazards that are causing or are likely to cause death or serious physical harm to his employees;

(2)   shall comply with occupational safety and health standards promulgated under [the OSH Act].[13]

OSHA may cite an employer under this general duty clause where there is no specific standard that covers the workplace hazard at issue.[14]

Employers must comply with safety and health standards established by OSHA. OSHA safety and health standards are voluminous. They regulate various machines and quipment, practices, operations, and environmental conditions in the workplace. Some are quite vague and general, others are very detailed and specific. Some standards state precisely what conduct is permitted and prohibited. Others put the burden on the employer to evaluate conditions, identify corrective action to be taken and then take it. Some, but not all, standards require one or more of the following: recordkeeping, training, periodic testing and evaluating, and written policies and procedures.

OSHA standards are generally classified under four broad industry groups: general industry (manufacturing, the service sector, health care, government agencies and academia), construction, maritime and longshoring, and agricultural.[15] While there are different standards for each industry group, there is overlap. For example, a construction industry standard may impose the exact same requirements on construction employers as a general industry standard imposes on manufacturers.

Most OSHA safety and health standards are general industry standards.[16] General industry standards apply to all employers covered by the OSH Act, except as follows. First, when a construction, maritime and longshoring or agricultural workplace is involved, a general industry standard does not apply if there is a specific construction, maritime and longshoring, or agricultural standard that applies to a particular situation. Also, some general industry standards, by their terms, are specifically limited to certain types of operations, such as saw mills and bakeries.

16-5. What are OSHA's recordkeeping requirements?

OSHA's recordkeeping requirements consist of the following:

- Employers must maintain records in each establishment of occupational injuries and illnesses as they occur and make those records accessible to employees.

- All employers must report within 8 hours the death of any employee from a work-related incident or the inpatient hospitalization of three or more employees as a result of a work-related incident. Such reports may be made by telephone or in person to the nearest OSHA Area Office or by calling OSHA's emergency tollfree number (1-800 321-OSHA).

- All employers must post during the month of February an annual summary of occupational injuries and illnesses for each establishment.

- All employers must provide, upon request, pertinent recordkeeping records for inspection and copying by any representative of the Secretary of Labor, the Secretary of Health, Education, and Welfare, or the state during any investigation, research, or statistical compilation.[17]

Many specific OSHA standards have additional recordkeeping requirements.

The principal forms needed for recordkeeping are the following:

- *OSHA 200, Log and Summary of Occupational Injuries and Illnesses.* Employers must log each recordable occupational injury and illness on this form within 6 working days from the time the employer learns of it. A complete copy current to within 45 calendar days must be present at all times in the establishment if the employer prepares the log at a central location using automatic data processing equipment. A substitute for the OSHA 200 is acceptable if it is as detailed, readable, and understandable as the OSHA 200.[18]

- *OSHA 101, Supplementary Record of Occupational Injuries and Illnesses.* Each employer must complete the OSHA 101 form within 6 working days from the time the employer learns of the work-related injury or illness. This form asks for more detailed information about each injury or illness. Employers may use a substitute for the OSHA 101 (such as insurance or workers' compensation forms) if the substitute form contains all required information or is supplemented to do so.[19]

Employers with 10 or fewer employees are exempt from maintaining the OSHA log of injuries and illnesses unless the Bureau of Labor Statistics (BLS) or OSHA notifies them that they have been selected to participate in a mandatory data collection.[20]

Certain low hazard industries are exempt from OSHA's recordkeeping and reporting requirement. They are:

- Retail trade, except for SIC 5254, building materials, general merchandise stores, and food stores.

- Service industries, except hotels and other lodging places, repair services, amusement and recreation services, and health services.

- Insurance.

- Real estate.

- Finance.

Employers that are exempt from the recordkeeping and reporting requirements, like nonexempt employers, must comply with requirements to display an OSHA poster and report to OSHA within 8 hours any accident that results in one or more fatalities or the hospitalization of three or more employees and will have to maintain records if OSHA or BLS selects them to participate in a mandatory data collection.[21]

Occupational Injury is defined as any injury such as a cut, fracture, sprain, or amputation that results from a work-related accident or from exposure involving a single incident in the work environment.

Occupational Illness is defined as any abnormal condition or disorder, other than one resulting from an occupational injury, caused by exposure to environmental factors associated with employment. Included are acute and chronic illnesses or diseases that may be caused by inhalation, absorption, ingestion, or direct contact with toxic substances or harmful agents.

All occupational illnesses must be recorded regardless of severity and all occupational injuries must be recorded if they result in: (1) death; (2) one or more lost workdays; (3) restriction of work or motion; (4) loss of consciousness; (5) transfer to another job; or (6) medical treatment (other than first aid).[22]

Employers must log injuries and illnesses on recordkeeping forms and keep the logs current and retained for 5 years at each establishment and make them available for inspection by representatives of OSHA, the Department of Health and Human Services, the Bureau of Labor Statistics, or the designated state agency. The logs also must be updated to reflect any changes that occur.[23]

Employers must keep injury and illness records for each establishment. An employer whose employees work in dispersed locations must keep records at the place where the employees report for work. In some situations, employees do not report to work at the same place each day. In that case, records must be kept at the place from which they are paid or at the base from which they operate.[24] OSHA defines establishment as a "single physical location where business is conducted or where services or industrial operations are performed."[25]

Employers must post copies of the Summary of Occupational Injuries and Illnesses portion of the OSHA 200 no later than February 1 and keep them in place until March 1 of the following year to which the records pertain. If there were no injuries or illnesses during the year, employers must enter zero on the totals line of the form and post it.[26] Employers also must display at each establishment, wherever they normally post notices to employees, the Job Safety and Health Protection workplace poster, or state equivalent, informing employees of their rights and responsibilities under the OSH Act.[27]

Lastly, OSHA requires employers to adhere to the recordkeeping, posting and written program requirements contained in specific standards issued under the OSH Act which apply to the specific employer. Employers can be separately cited by OSHA for failing to adhere to these requirements.

OSHA STANDARDS

16-6. What general areas do OSHA standards cover?

The general areas and some of the particular areas covered by standards in each general area include:[28]

- Walking - Working Surfaces

    - Guarding floor and wall openings and holes

    - Fixed industrial stairs

    - Safety requirements for scaffolding

    - Portable wood ladders

    - Portable steel ladders

    - Fixed ladders

    - Manually propelled mobile ladder stands and scaffolds (towers)

- Means of Egress

  • Employee emergency plans and fire prevention plans

- Powered Platforms, Manlifts, and Vehicle-Mounted Work Platforms

- Occupational Health and Environmental Control

  • Ventilation

  • Occupational noise exposure

- Hazardous Materials

  • Compressed gases (general requirements)

  • Flammable and combustible liquids

  • Spray finishing using flammable and combustible materials

  • Dipping and coating operations

  • Explosives and blasting agents

  • Process safety management of highly hazardous chemicals

  • Hazardous waste operations and emergency response

- Personal Protective Equipment

  • Eye and face protection

  • Respiratory protection

  • Head protection

  • Foot protection

  • Electrical protective equipment

  • Hand protection

- General Environmental Controls

  - Permit-required confined spaces

  - Control of hazardous energy (lockout/tagout)

- Medical and First Aid

- Fire Protection

- Compressed Gas and Compressed Air Equipment

- Materials Handling and Storage

  - Powered industrial trucks (fork lifts)

  - Cranes

- Machinery and Machine Guarding

  - Woodworking machinery requirements

  - Mechanical power presses

- Hand and Portable Powered Tools and Other Hand-Held Equipment

- Welding, Cutting, and Brazing

- Special Industries

  - Pulp, paper, and paperboard mills

  - Textiles

  - Bakery equipment

  - Laundry machinery and operations

  - Sawmills

  - Logging operations

  - Telecommunications

- Electric power generation, transmission, and distribution

- Grain handling facilities

- Electrical

  - Safety related work practices and training

- Commercial Diving Operations

- Toxic and Hazardous Substances

  - Hazardous communication program and training

16-7. How are OSHA standards created?

The Secretary of Labor was empowered until April 28, 1973 to promulgate as OSHA standards any "national consensus standard" or "established Federal standard" without regard to the usual rule-making requirements of the Administrative Procedures Act (APA).[29]

A "national consensus standard" is defined, in part, as:

[A]ny occupational safety and health standard or modification thereof which (1), had been adopted and promulgated by a nationally recognized standards-producing organization under procedures whereby it can be determined by the Secretary that persons interested and affected by the scope or provisions of the standard have reached substantial agreement on its adoption, (2) was formulated in a manner which afforded an opportunity for diverse views to be considered.[30]

Examples of national consensus standards include those promulgated by the American National Standards Institute (ANSI), the National Fire Protection Association (NAPA), the American Society for Testing and Materials (ASTM), and the American Society of Mechanical Engineers (ASME).

An "established Federal standard" is defined to mean:

> [A]ny operative occupational safety and health stan-
> dard established by any agency of the United States
> and presently in effect, or contained in any Act of
> Congress in force on the date of enactment of [the OSH
> Act].[31]

Included among the established federal standards which
became OSHA standards were certain standards under the federal
Construction Safety Act,[32] the Contract Work Hours Safety Standards Act, the Walsh-Healey Public Contracts Act,[33] the Service
Contract Act of 1965,[34] and standards previously promulgated by
a number of federal agencies such as the Atomic Energy Commission, the National Bureau of Standards, the Army Corps of
Engineers, the Coast Guard, and the Departments of Agriculture,
Commerce, Interior and Transportation.

The majority of OSHA standards which exist today are from the
initial package of national consensus standards or established
Federal standards originally adopted by the Secretary of Labor.

OSHA also creates, amends and revokes standards pursuant
to its regular rule-making procedures. First, OSHA develops a plan
to propose, amend, or revoke a standard, either on its own initiative
of in response to petitions from interested parties, such as the
Secretary of Health and Human Resources, NIOSH, state and local
governments, employer or employee representatives, or other
interested parties. OSHA then publishes its intentions in the
Federal Register either as an Advance Notice or as a Notice of
Proposed Rule-Making. Interested parties may submit written
arguments and pertinent evidence with respect to the information
published in the Federal Register and OSHA will schedule a
hearing if requested. After considering public comments, evidence
and testimony, OSHA publishes either the full text of any standard
amended or adopted and the date it becomes effective, along with
an explanation of the standard and the reasons for implementing
it, or a determination that no standard or amendment needs to be
issued.[35]

When the Secretary of Labor determines that employees are "exposed to grave danger from exposure to substances or agents determined to be toxic or physically harmful or from new hazards," and that an emergency standard is necessary to protect employees from such danger, the Secretary may promulgate an emergency temporary standard to take immediate effect upon publication in the Federal Register.[36]

16-8. What if an employer disagrees with a new standard or cannot comply with agency requirements?

An employer who cannot comply with new requirements or anyone who disagrees with a new standard can:

- Petition a court for judicial review;

- Request a permanent, temporary, or experimental variance from a standard or regulation; or

- Apply for an interim order.[37]

16-9. Can employers and employees petition OSHA to modify or withdraw standards or requirements?

Yes. Employers and employees may petition OSHA to modify or revoke standards just as they may petition the agency to develop standards. OSHA continually reviews its standards to keep pace with developing and changing industrial technology.[38]

16-10. Who can file a petition for judicial review?

Anyone who may be adversely affected by a final or emergency standard may file a petition for judicial review. The objecting party must file the petition within 60 days of the rule's publication with the U.S. Court of Appeals for the circuit in which the objector lives or has his or her principal place of business. Filing an appeals petition will not delay enforcement of a standard, unless the Court of Appeals specifically orders it.[39]

VARIANCES

16-11. What is a variance? When can an employer request a variance from an OSHA standard?

A variance is a mechanism through which employers apply for formal permission to deviate from a standard's requirements or time frame. Employers may ask OSHA for a variance from:

- A newly promulgated standard or regulation if they cannot fully comply by the effective date due to shortage of materials, equipment, or professional or technical personnel; or

- The requirements of a standard or regulation if they can demonstrate that their alternative or alternatives provide employees with protection "as safe and healthful" as that provided by the standard or regulation.[40]

16-12. What are the types of variances?

There are temporary, permanent, and experimental variances.[41]

An employer applies for a *temporary variance* if he or she cannot comply with a standard or regulation by its effective date because professional or technical personnel, material or equipment are not available, or because the necessary construction or alteration of facilities cannot be completed in time.

An employer who can prove that working conditions, practices, means, methods, operation, or processes at his or her worksite are as safe and healthful as compliance with the standard may apply for a *permanent variance.*

An employer may apply for an *experimental variance* if he or she is participating in an effort to demonstrate or validate new job safety and health techniques, and either the Secretary of Labor or the Secretary of HHS has approved the experiment.

16-13. Can an employer continue to operate its worksite while waiting for a decision on a variance application?

Employers may apply to OSHA for an interim order so they may continue to operate under existing conditions until OSHA determines whether to grant the variance.[42]

ENFORCEMENT

16-14. How does OSHA enforce its standards?

The OSH Act authorizes OSHA to conduct workplace inspections to enforce its standards.[43] Every establishment covered by the OSH Act is subject to inspection by OSHA compliance safety and health officers.

The OSH Act authorizes OSHA compliance officers to do each of the following:

- Enter any factory, plant, establishment, construction site, or other areas of the workplace or environment where work is being performed;

- Inspect and investigate during regular working hours any such place of employment and all pertinent conditions, structures, machines, apparatus, devices, equipment, and materials;

- Inspect and investigate at other times any such place of employment and all pertinent conditions, structures, machines, apparatus, devices, equipment, and materials; and

- Question privately any employer, owner, operator, agent or employee during an inspection or investigation.[44]

OSHA generally conducts workplace inspections without advance notice. In fact, anyone who alerts an employer in advance of an OSHA inspection can receive a criminal fine of up to $1,000 or a 6-month jail term or both.[45]

There are special circumstances under which OSHA may give advance notice to the employer. Even then, such notice will be less than 24 hours. These special circumstances include:

- Imminent danger situations which require correction as soon as possible;

- Inspections that must take place after regular business hours or that require special preparation;

- Cases where OSHA must provide advance notice to assure that the employer and employee representative or other personnel will be present; and/or

- Situations in which the OSHA Area Director determines that advance notice would produce a more thorough or effective inspection.[46]

Inspections are either safety inspections, designed to find safety violations, or health inspections, designed to find health violations (those related to exposure to hazardous or toxic conditions or substances in the workplace). A safety inspection is conducted by an OSHA safety compliance officer; a health inspection by an OSHA compliance officer who typically also is an industrial hygienist. Safety and health inspections are often conducted together. Further, an industrial hygienist will cite a safety violation if he or she sees one.[47]

OSHA maintains a regular inspection program, inspecting businesses based on either OSHA targeting, employee complaint, or accident. When OSHA inspects, it will determine whether the employer is or is not in compliance with applicable OSHA standards. If the OSHA compliance officer finds a violation, the OSH Act states that "he shall" cite the employer for the violation.[48] Therefore, the OSHA inspector conducting an inspection is not there to warn, provide technical assistance or principally to assure future compliance. Instead, the OSHA compliance officer, by virtue of the way the OSHA law is written and his/her training and background, comes to the employer's place of business with the principal purpose of finding violations of OSHA standards and meeting his/her legal requirement to cite and penalize the employer for any violations found.[49]

16-15. How does an employer get selected for an OSHA inspection?

Inspections by OSHA can be triggered in one of several ways. An inspection may occur as a result of a complaint to OSHA by an employee or a representative of employees who believes that a violation of a safety or health standard exists that threatens physical harm or that an imminent danger exists. The OSH Act requires that the complaint be reduced to writing, set forth with reasonable particularity the grounds for the notice, be signed by the employee or representative of employees (although the identity of the complainant need not be disclosed to the employer), and a copy be given to the employer not later than at the time of the inspection.[50]

An inspection by OSHA also will occur for all job-related fatalities and catastrophes, however they are reported to OSHA. "Fatality" and "catastrophe" are defined as follows:

Fatality. An employee death resulting from an employment accident or illness; in general, from any accident or illness caused by or related to a workplace hazard.

Catastrophe. The hospitalization of three or more employees resulting from an employment accident or illness; in general, from an accident or illness caused by a workplace hazard.[51]

Accidents receiving significant publicity or any other accident not involving a fatality or catastrophe where specific instructions for investigations in connection with a national office special program have been issued also will result in an OSHA inspection. OSHA inspections also may result where an OSHA official observes an open and notorious condition he or she believes violates an OSHA standard (e.g., on an outdoor construction site).

Another way in which an employer is selected for a compliance inspection is as a result of OSHA's programmed inspection of worksites which have been scheduled based upon objective or neutral selection criteria. There are detailed procedures on how OSHA selects worksites for programmed inspections in general industry (safety and health), in the construction industry, in the maritime industry, and for special emphasis programs in what it perceives are high potential injury or illness rate situations which are not covered adequately or at all by its regular scheduling system.[52]

16-16. What happens during an OSHA inspection?

There are four stages of a typical OSHA inspection:

- Presentation of Inspector Credentials

- Opening Conference

- Records Review and Inspection Walkaround

- Closing Conference.[53]

An inspection begins when the OSHA compliance officer arrives at the establishment. He or she displays official credentials and asks to meet an appropriate employer representative. Employers should always insist on seeing the compliance officer's credentials.[54]

An OSHA compliance officer carries U.S. Department of Labor credentials bearing his or her photograph and a serial number that an employer can verify by phoning the nearest OSHA office. Posing as a compliance officer is a violation of the law. Suspected imposters should be promptly reported to local law enforcement agencies. [55]

At the outset of the inspection, the employer should get a clear and precise understanding of exactly what the scope of the investigation will be. The employer either may consent to the inspection or require the OSHA inspector obtain a search warrant. If the employer consents to the inspection, it should make clear to the OSHA inspector that the consent is limited. The employer should set forth the exact parameters of its consent. If the inspector is conducting the inspection pursuant to a warrant, the employer should read the warrant carefully. During the course of the inspection, the employer should permit the OSHA inspector to act only with the limits of its consent or the terms of the warrant.[56]

At the start of an OSHA inspection the inspector holds an "opening conference." At the opening conference, the OSHA inspector will inform the employer of the purpose of the inspection and obtain the employer's consent to include participation of an employee representative when appropriate. The opening conference is brief and normally does not exceed one hour. When the inspection occurs as a result of a complaint, the inspector is required to provide a copy of the complaint(s) to the employer and the employee representative at the beginning of the opening conference.[57]

At the opening conference, the inspector also will determine whether the employer wishes to identify areas in the workplace which contain or might reveal trade secrets. OSHA is required to preserve the confidentiality of all information which might reveal a trade secret.[58]

An OSHA inspection normally will include an examination of injury and illness records employers are required to keep. Also, the OSHA inspector will determine whether the employer has complied with all of OSHA's posting requirements, such as the OSHA poster informing employees or their rights under the OSH Act, the Log and Summary of Occupational Injuries during the month of February, current citations, if any, and petitions for modification of abatement dates.[59]

At some point during the OSHA inspection, the inspector will want to and is entitled to view the condition(s) in the workplace alleged to be hazardous. The employer is entitled to and should accompany and remain with the inspector at all times on his physical inspection of the worksite. In addition, a representative of the employees also must be given an opportunity to accompany the OSHA inspector during the walkaround.[60]

During the walkaround phase of the inspection, the employer should make sure that the OSHA inspector stays within the explicit confines of the employer's original consent to inspect or the express parameters of a warrant if the search is being conducted pursuant to a warrant. The employer should not permit the OSHA inspector to broaden the inspection beyond the scope of the employer's consent or the warrant. OSHA, however, may inspect conditions that are in "plain view" during the course of the inspection, even if beyond the employer's consent or the parameters of a warrant.

Furthermore, the employer should converse with the OSHA inspector about the inspection only to the extent necessary. The employer should not try to persuade or to argue its case to the inspector during the investigation nor provide any information which it is not certain is accurate. On many occasions, employers have tried to win their case during the inspection and in the process have volunteered information which OSHA ends up using against the employer to support the issuance of a citation. The risk of making damaging admissions to an OSHA inspector can be minimized greatly, if not eliminated if the employer simply does not argue the merits of the complaint with the inspector.

During the inspection, the OSHA inspector may request to interview employees. The OSHA regulations provide that such interviews be held in private if they are with non-management employees.

If there are trade secrets the employer wants to protect, it should identify any operation or condition as such to the OSHA inspector. Information obtained in such areas will be labeled specifically as a trade secret and kept confidential. It will not be disclosed by the OSHA inspector except to other OSHA officials concerned with the enforcement of the OSH Act. In fact, there are criminal penalties for federal employees who disclose such trade secret information.[61]

At the conclusion of an inspection, the OSHA inspector will want to conduct a closing conference. An employer can choose not to participate in the closing conference. If one is held, the inspector will describe the apparent violations found during the inspection and the section(s) of the standard(s) which may have been violated. The inspector also will try to obtain input for establishing abatement dates. If abatement is discussed, the employer must be extremely cautious not to say anything which OSHA will attempt to construe as any admission of an OSHA violation. Further, the employer should attempt to obtain clarification of exactly what actions the OSHA inspector contends must be undertaken to abate any alleged violation. The inspector will furnish to the employer at the closing conference the publication "Employer Rights and Responsibilities Following an OSHA Inspection" which explains the responsibilities and courses of action available to the employer if a citation is issued.[62]

16-17. What happens after an OSHA inspection?

Following an inspection, the OSHA Area Director can:

- Issue citations without penalties,

- Issue citations with proposed penalties, or

- Determine that neither is warranted.[63]

16-18. What is in an OSHA citation?

Citations inform the employer and employees of:

- The regulations and standards the employer allegedly violated.

- Any hazardous working conditions covered by the general duty clause of the OSH Act.

- The proposed length of time set for their abatement.

- The classification of the alleged violation and any proposed penalties.

- Informs employers of their rights under the Small Business Regulatory Enforcement Fairness Act of 1996 (SBREFA).

- Explains that OSHA area officers offer assistance and can answer questions about programs and activities.[64]

OSHA will hand deliver or send citations and notices of proposed penalties to the employer by certified mail. The employer must post a copy of each citation at or near the places where the violations occurred for three work days or until the employer abates the violation, whichever is longer.[65]

16-19. What are the categories of violations and the types of penalties that OSHA can propose?

OSHA may cite the following violations and propose the following penalties:[66]

Other-than-Serious. A violation that has a direct relationship to job safety and health, but probably would not cause death or serious physical harm. OSHA may propose a penalty of up to $7,000 for each other-than-serious violation. The agency may adjust a penalty downward for an other-than-serious violation, depending on the employer's good faith (demonstrated efforts to comply with the OSH Act), history of previous violations, and size of business. When the adjusted penalty amounts to less than $100, OSHA does not propose any penalty.

Serious. A violation where there is substantial probability that death or serious physical harm could result and that the employer knew, or should have known, of the hazard. OSHA may propose a mandatory penalty of up to $7,000 for each serious violation. The agency may adjust a penalty for a serious violation downward, based on the employer's good faith, history of previous violations, gravity of the alleged violation, and size of business.

Willful. A violation that the employer intentionally and knowingly commits or a violation that the employer commits with plain indifference to the law. The employer either knows that what he or she is doing constitutes a violation, or is aware that a hazardous condition existed and made no reasonable effort to eliminate it.

OSHA may propose penalties of up to $70,000 for each willful violation, with a minimum penalty of $5,000 for each willful violation. The agency may adjust a proposed penalty for a willful violation downward, depending on the size of the business and its history of previous violations. Usually, OSHA gives employers cited for willful violations no credit for good faith.

In addition to OSHA citations and penalties, the U.S. Department of Justice may bring a criminal action against an employer who willfully violates a standard that results in the death of an employee. If a court convicts such an employer, the offense is punishable by a court-imposed fine or by imprisonment for up to 6 months, or both. The court may impose a fine for a criminal conviction of up to $250,000 for an individual or $500,000 for a corporation.[67]

Repeated. A violation of any standard, regulation, rule or order where OSHA finds a substantially similar violation during a reinspection, OSHA may propose penalties of up to $70,000 for each repeated violation. To be the basis of a repeat citation, the original citation must be final. A citation under contest may not serve as the basis for a subsequent repeat citation.

Failure to Abate. OSHA may propose an additional penalty of up to $7,000 for each day an employer fails to correct a previously cited violation beyond the prescribed abatement date.

Other penalties. Employers also may be assessed penalties for the following:

- Violations of posting requirements can bring a civil penalty of up to $7,000. (OSHA does not fine for failing to post the job safety and health poster).

- Falsifying records, reports, or applications, upon conviction in a court, can bring a criminal fine of $10,000 or up to 6 months in jail, or both.

- Assaulting a compliance officer or otherwise resisting, opposing, intimidating, or interfering with a compliance officer in the performance of his or her duties is a criminal offense. Anyone convicted of such an action is subject to a criminal fine of not more than $5,000 and imprisonment for not more than 3 years.

Violation Categories and Possible Penalties

Type of Violation	Minimum Penalty per Violation	Maximum Penalty per Violation
Other-than-Serious		$7,000
Serious	$100	$7,000
Posting		$7,000
Willful	$5,000	$70,000
Willful with fatality, first conviction		$250,000/$500,000 or 6 months in prison or both
Willful, with fatality, second conviction		$250,000/$500,000 or 1 year in prison or both
Repeated	$5,000	$70,000
Failure to abate		$7,000 per day

16-20. How can an employer challenge the results of an OSHA inspection?

The employer can challenge the results of an OSHA inspection by attempting to informally settle with OSHA or by contesting the citation.

An employer which has been cited has an opportunity to request an informal conference at which time the employer can attempt to settle with OSHA. The informal conference occurs at the OSHA office and must occur before the time to contest the citation(s) expires.[68]

An employer who chooses to contest a citation initially must do two things. First, it must notify the OSHA Area Director in writing of its intent to contest by filing a Notice of Contest. This must be accomplished within 15 working days from the employer's receipt of the citation. Only those issues placed in the Notice of Contest can be heard before the Occupational Safety and Health Review Commission, so care should be exercised in specifying whether the employer is contesting the alleged violations, penalties, abatement dates, or all three. If the employer decides to contest the citation, employers generally contest all aspects of the citation, unless of course, the proposed penalty is zero, in which event the employer can contest only the citation and/or abatement date. If there is more than one citation, the employer should be clear whether it is contesting all aspects of each citation (i.e., alleged violations, penalties, and abatement dates) or just particular portions of one or more citations. If the employer wishes to contest all aspects of all citations, it merely needs to state in its Notice of Contest that it wishes to contest all alleged violations, all penalties, and all abatement dates. OSHA has 15 working days within which to transmit the Notice of Contest to the Review Commission.[69]

After the employer files its Notice of Contest and it has received notice from the Review Commission that the case has been docketed, the employer then must notify its affected employees (and any employee representatives), that the employer is contesting the matter.[70]

After the case is docketed, the Secretary of Labor must file a written complaint with the Review Commission. The employer then must file an answer (or other pleading) within 20 calendar days after receipt of the complaint.[71]

In the time prior to the hearing, the rules of the Review Commission allow for discovery by one of the following methods to occur without leave of the Commission or the Administrative Law Judge: (1) production of documents or things or permission to enter upon land or other property for inspection and other purposes; (2) requests for admissions; and (3) interrogatories. Other discovery, including depositions, may be conducted by agreement or if leave is sought and an order granted permitting the discovery.[72]

The employer should not pass up the opportunity to engage in pre-trial discovery. Often times, an employer's discovery efforts will yield useful information it can use at the trial. An employer's discovery efforts also can narrow the issues and better focus in on OSHA's actual position. Additionally, an employer's discovery efforts can highlight weaknesses in OSHA's case which, in turn, can provide a basis for some type of dispositive motion, settlement, or even dismissal.

At the trial before the Administrative Law Judge (ALJ), the Federal Rules of Evidence (FRE) are applicable.[73] Counsel for the employer should be continually attentive to whether the Secretary of Labor's proffered evidence, including both witness testimony as well as documentary exhibits, constitutes admissible evidence under the FRE. If not, counsel should make whatever objections may be appropriate.

After the trial is over, a transcript is prepared and the parties may submit post trial briefs.[74] After the ALJ issues a written decision, one of the Review Commission members may direct that the ALJ's decision be reviewed by the full Review Commission. This can be done either on a member's own motion or by the losing party filing a petition for discretionary review. If review is granted, there is an opportunity for further briefing.[75] After the decision is final, any adversely affected or aggrieved person may appeal to an appropriate federal court of appeals. Findings of fact must be supported by substantial evidence on the record considered as a whole.[76] Conclusions can be set aside if they are arbitrary, capricious, or constitute an abuse of discretion.[77]

16-21. What defenses can an employer assert to citations and penalties?

There are a number of defenses an employer can raise to contest a citation. Some of the more important or frequently raised ones are discussed below. Rule 8(c) of the Federal Rules of Civil Procedure requires that affirmative defenses be specifically pleaded.

In addition to the specific defenses discussed below, an employer should always remain cognizant that in every case it is the Secretary of Labor's burden of proof to establish all of the specific facts which he contends violate specific elements included in the standard cited and the type of violation alleged, as well as his burden to prove that the employer's employees had access to the hazard and that the employer had knowledge of the violation. The Secretary's failure to prove a basic prima facie case with respect to any one of these critical items should be considered as possible defenses in every case.

Defenses an employer may be in a position to raise include the following:

Impossibility of Compliance. One affirmative defense is impossibility for the employer to comply with the cited standard. As with all affirmative defenses, the burden of demonstrating the "impossibility of compliance" defense is on the employer. For the employer to prevail on the impossibility of compliance defense, it must prove that it would be functionally impossible for it to comply with the OSHA standard at issue or compliance literally would prevent performance of the necessary work.[78] If an employer does not present sufficient evidence demonstrating impossibility or if alternative means of compliance exist, the defense of impossibility will be rejected.[79] Cost to the employer of compliance generally will be of no consequence as far as the impossibility defense is concerned unless genuine economic infeasibility can be demonstrated.[80]

Employee Misconduct. Another affirmative defense to an OSHA citation is that the alleged violation resulted from isolated employee misconduct. The OSH Act does not impose strict liability on employers for isolated and idiosyncratic instances of employee misconduct.[81] To establish the employee misconduct defense, the employer must prove that it had a well-established work rule prohibiting the conduct in question, that it communicated the rule to its employees, and that the rule was uniformly enforced.

Greater Hazard. Another affirmative defense exists where the employer can demonstrate that a greater hazard would exist as a result of compliance with a specific standard. To establish the greater hazard defense, an employer must show (1) that the hazards of compliance are greater than the hazards of non-compliance, (2) that alternative means of protecting employees are unavailable, and (3) the unavailability or inappropriateness of obtaining a variance.[82]

Vagueness and Other Constitutional Challenges. In some cases it may be possible for the employer to raise the argument that the particular standard at issue is unconstitutionally vague. Where OSHA's conduct relating to enforcement does nothing to clarify a vague standard, an employer's ability to raise the vagueness defense will be strengthened.[83] In considering whether an OSHA standard is impermissibly vague, the standard is considered not only on its face, but also in light of the conduct to which it is applied in the particular case.[84] So long as there is reasonable warning of the prescribed conduct in light of common understanding and practices, it generally will be found to pass constitutional muster.

16-22. Can an employer petition OSHA for modification of the abatement period?

When a citation is issued, a date by which the alleged violation must be remedied or abated is specified in the citation. This period is stayed if the employer files a notice of contest to the alleged violation. It is not stayed if the employer only contests the amount of the proposed penalty or the abatement period.[85]

If a notice of contest is not filed, the employer still may need and can request additional abatement time after the 15-working-day contest period has passed to abate by filing a petition for modification of abatement (PMA).[86]

PMAs must be filed in writing with the Area Director who issued the citation no later than the close of the next working day after the date on which abatement originally was required. A PMA must include all of the following information:

(1)   All steps taken by the employer and the date of such action, in an effort to achieve compliance within the prescribed abatement;

(2)   The specific additional abatement time necessary to achieve compliance;

(3)   The reasons additional time is necessary, including the unavailability of professional or technical personnel, or of materials or equipment, or because necessary construction or alteration of the facilities cannot be completed prior to the original abatement date;

(4)   All available interim steps being taken to safeguard the employees against the cited hazard during the abatement period; and

(5)   A certification that a copy of the PMA has been posted and served upon any employee representatives.

If objections to the PMA are raised either by OSHA or by the affected employees, the matter is docketed for a hearing under OSHA's expedited hearing procedures.

16-23. Does the OSH Act prohibit an employer from retaliating against employees?

Yes. The OSH Act gives employees the right to seek safe and healthful conditions on the job without fear of punishment.[87]

Employees may exercise such rights as:

- Voicing concerns to an employer, union, OSHA, any other government agency, or others about job safety or health hazards;

- Filing safety or health grievances;

- Participating in a workplace safety and health committee or in union activities concerning job safety and health;

- Participating in OSHA inspections, conferences, hearings, or other OSHA-related activities; and

- Refusing to work when a dangerous situation threatens death or serious injury where there is insufficient time to contact OSHA and where the employee has sought from his or her employer and been unable to obtain a correction of the dangerous conditions.

An employer may not retaliate if an employee exercises these or any other rights under the OSH Act. This means that an employer may not fire, demote, take away seniority or other earned benefits, transfer to an undesirable job or shift, or threaten or harass any worker who complains about safety and health conditions or participates in job safety-related activities.

COOPERATIVE PROGRAMS

16-24. What types of cooperative programs are available with OSHA?

OSHA has the following types of cooperative programs: Consultation, Voluntary Protection Programs, and OSHA Strategic Partnership Programs. Each is discussed below.

Consultation. Besides helping employers identify and correct specific hazards, OSHA's consultation service provides free onsite assistance in developing and implementing effective workplace safety and health programs that emphasize preventing worker injuries and illnesses. In addition, OSHA has available in its regional offices individuals to provide assistance on issues related to compliance, ergonomics, bloodborne pathogens, and small business. OSHA's comprehensive consultation assistance includes an appraisal of all mechanical systems, physical work practices, and environmental hazards of the workplace, as well as all aspects of the employer's present job safety and health program.

Largely funded by OSHA, consultation programs are run by state agencies at no cost to the employer who requests it. OSHA does not propose penalties or issue citations for hazards identified by the consultant. The employer's only obligation is to correct all serious hazards and potential safety and health violations that OSHA identifies. OSHA provides consultation assistance to the employer with the assurance that his or her name and firm and any information about the workplace will not be routinely reported to OSHA enforcement staff.[88]

Voluntary Protection Programs. Voluntary Protection Programs (VPP) represent a part of OSHA's effort to extend worker protection beyond the minimum required by OSHA standards. These programs-along with others such as expanded onsite consultation services and full service area offices, and OSHA's Strategic Partnership Program (OSPP)-are cooperative approaches which, when coupled with an effective enforcement program, expand worker protection to help meet the goals of the OSH Act.

OSHA reviews an employer's VPP application and conducts an onsite review to verify that the employer's safety and health programs are operating effectively at the site. OSHA conducts onsite evaluations on a regular basis, the timing of which depends upon the employer's level of participation. Each February, all participants must send a copy of their most recent annual site evaluation to their OSHA regional office. This evaluation must include their injuries and illnesses for the past year. Sites participating in a VPP are not scheduled for regular, programmed inspections. OSHA, however, handles any employee complaints, serious accidents, or significant chemical releases that may occur according to routine enforcement procedures.[89]

OSHA Strategic Partnership Programs. These strategic partnerships are alliances among labor, management, and government to foster improvements in workplace safety and health. These partnerships are voluntary, cooperative relationships between OSHA, employers, employee representatives, and possibly others-trade unions, trade and professional associations, universities, and other government agencies. OSPPs are the newest member of OSHA's cooperative programs.

These partnerships encourage, assist, and recognize the efforts of the partners to eliminate serious workplace hazards and achieve a high level of worker safety and health. Whereas OSHA's Consultation Program and VPP entail one-on-one relationships between OSHA and individual worksites, most strategic partnerships seek to have a broader impact by building cooperative relationships with groups of employers and employees. There are two major types of OSPPs:

- Comprehensive, which focus on establishing comprehensive safety and health programs at partnering worksites.

- Limited, which help identify and eliminate hazards associated with worker deaths, injuries, and illnesses, or have goals other than establishing comprehensive worksite safety and health programs.[90]

CHAPTER ENDNOTES

1. 29 U.S.C. §§651-678.
2. 29 U.S.C. §651(b).
3. 29 U.S.C. §671.
4. 29 U.S.C. §651(b).
5. *All About OSHA*, OSHA Pub. 2056.
6. 29 U.S.C. §653.
7. 29 CFR Parts 1910-1928.
8. 29 U.S.C. §667.
9. 29 U.S.C. §652(5).
10. 29 U.S.C. §668.
11. *All About OSHA*, OSHA Pub. 2056.
12. 29 U.S.C. §667(b); 29 CFR Parts 1902, 1952, 1953, 1954; *All About OSHA*, OSHA Pub. 2056.
13. 29 U.S.C. §654.
14. 29 U.S.C. §666.
15. 29 CFR Parts 1910, 1915-1922, 1926.
16. 29 CFR Part 1910.
17. *All About OSHA*, OSHA Pub. 2056.
18. 29 CFR §1904.2.
19. 29 CFR §1904.4.
20. 29 CFR §1904.15.
21. 29 CFR §1904.8; *All About OSHA*, OSHA Pub. 2056.
22. *All About OSHA*, OSHA Pub. 2056.
23. 29 CFR §1904.6.
24. 29 CFR §1904.14.
25. 29 CFR §1904.12(g).
26. 29 CFR §1904.5.
27. 29 CFR §1903.2.
28. These general industry standards are found at 29 CFR Part 1910. Employers should consult these regulations to determine if and how particular standards in these general areas apply to their specific operations. There are also standards for the construction industry set forth in 29 CFR Part 1926, for the maritime industry set forth in 29 CFR Parts 1915-1918, and for agriculture set forth in 29 CFR Part 1928.
29. 29 U.S.C. §655(a).
30. 29 U.S.C. §652(9).
31. 29 U.S.C. §652(10).
32. 40 U.S.C. §333.
33. 41 U.S.C. §35.
34. 41 U.S.C. §351).
35. 29 U.S.C. §655(b); *All About OSHA*, OSHA Pub. 2056.
36. 29 U.S.C. §655(c).
37. 29 U.S.C. §655; 29 CFR Part 1905; *All About OSHA*, OSHA Pub. 2056.
38. 29 U.S.C. §655; 29 CFR Part 1911; *All About OSHA*, OSHA Pub. 2056.
39. 29 U.S.C. §655(f); *All About OSHA*, OSHA Pub. 2056.
40. 29 U.S.C. §655; 29 CFR Part 1905; *All About OSHA*, OSHA Pub. 2056.
41. 29 U.S.C. §655; 29 CFR Part 1905; *All About OSHA*, OSHA Pub. 2056.
42. *All About OSHA*, OSHA Pub. 2056.
43. 29 U.S.C. §657.
44. *All About OSHA*, OSHA Pub. 2056.
45. 29 U.S.C. §666(f); *All About OSHA*, OSHA Pub. 2056.

46. 29 CFR §1903.6, *All About OSHA*, OSHA Pub. 2056.
47. 29 CFR Part 1903.
48. 29 U.S.C. §658(a).
49. 29 CFR §1903.14.
50. 29 U.S.C. §657(f).
51. OSHA's Field Inspections Reference Manual, Chapter II, B.
52. OSHA's Field Inspections Reference Manual, Chapter I, B.
53. *All About OSHA*, OSHA Pub. 2056.
54. *All About OSHA*, OSHA Pub. 2056.
55. *All About OSHA*, OSHA Pub. 2056.
56. 29 CFR §1903.4.
57. 29 CFR §1903.11.
58. 29 U.S.C. §664; 29 CFR §1903.9.
59. 29 U.S.C. §657; 29 CFR §1903.3.
60. 29 U.S.C. §657; 29 CFR Part 1903.
61. 29 CFR §1903.9.
62. 29 CFR §1903.7.
63. 29 CFR §1903.14; *All About OSHA*, OSHA Pub. 2056.
64. 29 CFR §§1903.14, 1903.15; *All About OSHA*, OSHA Pub. 2056.
65. 29 CFR §1903.16; *All About OSHA*, OSHA Pub. 2056.
66. 29 U.S.C. §666; *All About OSHA*, OSHA Pub. 2056.
67. 18 U.S.C. §3571.
68. 29 CFR §1903.20.
69. 29 U.S.C. §659.
70. 29 CFR §2200.7.
71. 29 CFR §2200.34.
72. 29 CFR §§2200.52-2200.56.
73. 29 CFR §2200.71.
74. 29 CFR §§2200.66, 2200.74.
75. 29 CFR §§2200.91, 2200.92, 2200.93.
76. 29 U.S.C. §660.
77. *Advance Bronze, Inc. v. Dole*, 917 F.2d 944 (6th Cir. 1990).
78. See e.g., *Mato, Inc.*, 12 BNA OSHC 1512 (1985).
79. *Donovan v. Williams Enter., Inc.*, 11 BNA OSHC 2241 (D.C. Cir. 1984); *Fabsteel of La., Inc.*, 11 BNA OSHC 1712 (1983).
80. See e.g., *Mercury Metal Prod., Inc.*, 11 BNA OSHC 1704 (1983).
81. *Pennsylvania Power & Light Co. v. OSHRC*, 737 F.2d 350 (3d Cir. 1984).
82. *True Drilling Co. v. Donovan*, 703 F.2d 1087 (9th Cir. 1983).
83. See, e.g., *Transcontinental Drilling Co., Inc.*, 11 BNA OSHC 1045 (1982).
84. *Vanco Constr., Inc. v. Donovan & OSHRC*, 723 F.2d 410 (5th Cir. 1984).
85. 29 CFR Part 1903.
86. 29 CFR §1903.14a.
87. 29 U.S.C. §660(c); 29 CFR Part 1977; *All About OSHA*, OSHA Pub. 2056.
88. 29 CFR Part 1908; *All About OSHA*, OSHA Pub. 2056.
89. *All About OSHA*, OSHA Pub. 2056.
90. *All About OSHA,* OSHA Pub. 2056.

Chapter 17

Immigration and Employment Authorization

EMPLOYMENT ELIGIBILITY VERIFICATION

17-1. Can an employer hire a foreign national for employment in the United States?

17-2. What is employment for purposes of the employment eligibility verification rules?

17-3. Do citizens and nationals of the U.S. need to prove to their employers that they are eligible to work?

17-4. Does an employer need to complete a Form I-9 for everyone who applies for a job with the employer?

17-5. What steps should an employer follow to properly complete Form I-9?

17-6. Can an employer fire an employee who fails to produce the required documents within three business days?

17-7. What is the employer's responsibility concerning the authenticity of documents presented to it?

17-8. May an employer accept a photocopy of a document presented by an employee?

17-9. What happens if an employer properly completes a Form I-9 and the INS discovers that the employee is not actually authorized to work?

17-10. What must an employer do when an employee's work authorization expires?

17-11. For how long must the employer retain the Form I-9 for an employee?

EMPLOYMENT-BASED NONIMMIGRANT VISAS

17-12. What is a nonimmigrant visa?

17-13. What is the filing fee for an employment-based nonimmigrant visa?

17-14. What is the processing time for an employment-based nonimmigrant visa petition?

17-15. What status is available to the spouse and children of a nonimmigrant employee?

H-1B NONIMMIGRANT VISAS

17-16. What are the general requirements for petitioning the INS to hire a nonimmigrant in an H-1B specialty occupation?

17-17. Does the employer need to demonstrate that there is a shortage of qualified U.S. workers?

17-18. Are there special fees for an H-1B visa?

17-19. For how long is an H-1B visa valid?

17-20. May an H-1B employee transfer to a different geographic location of the employer?

17-21. May an employer hire a foreign national who is already in the U.S. under H-1B status with another employer?

17-22. Must an H-1B visa holder be working at all times?

17-23. What liability does the employer have if the employer discharges an H-1B worker before the end of the period of authorized H-1B status?

17-24. May the H-1B nonimmigrant employee also seek permanent immigrant status?

17-25. Is there an annual limit on the number of H-1B visas issued nationally?

TN VISAS

17-26. What are the requirements for a TN nonimmigrant visa for Canadian and Mexican professionals?

17-27. What are the procedures for Canadian citizens?

17-28. What are the procedures for Mexican citizens?

17-29. Is the TN visa category limited to specific professions?

17-30. Is there a limit on the number of times a TN visa can be renewed?

17-31. May a TN nonimmigrant also seek permanent immigrant status?

L-1 VISAS

17-32. What is an L-1 intracompany transferee visa?

17-33. What are the requirements for an L-1 nonimmigrant visa?

17-34. What are the procedures for petitioning for an L-1 intracompany transferee?

17-35. For how long is an L-1 visa valid?

17-36. May an L-1 intracompany transferee also seek permanent immigrant status?

OTHER EMPLOYMENT-BASED NONIMMIGRANT CATEGORIES

17-37. What other types of employment-based nonimmigrant visas are available to foreign nationals?

EMPLOYMENT-BASED PERMANENT IMMIGRANT VISAS

17-38. What is an immigrant visa?

17-39. How does an employer petition for an employment-based immigrant visa for a foreign worker?

17-40. What are the processing times for obtaining an employment-based immigrant visa?

17-41. What are the filing fees for employment-based immigrant visas?

17-42. What are the procedures for obtaining labor certification (for those employment-based immigrant categories requiring labor certification)?

17-43. What are the requirements for the EB-1 extraordinary ability employment-based immigrant visa category?

17-44. What are the requirements for an EB-1 outstanding professor or researcher?

17-45. What are the requirements for an EB-1 multinational manager or executive?

17-46. What are the requirements for an EB-2 classification for "members of the professions holding advanced degrees" or foreign nationals of "exceptional ability in the sciences, arts, or business"?

17-47. What are the requirements for an EB-3 third preference employment-based immigrant visa?

EMPLOYMENT ELIGIBILITY VERIFICATION

17-1. Can an employer hire a foreign national for employment in the United States?

Pursuant to the Immigration and Nationality Act, it is unlawful for an employer to hire, or to recruit or refer for a fee, for employment in the United States a foreign national knowing the foreign national is unauthorized for such employment. An employer establishes an affirmative defense that it has not violated this law by complying in good faith with the requirements for completing an Employment Eligibility Verification form (Form I-9) for each employee.[1]

17-2. What is employment for purposes of the employment eligibility verification rules?

Employment is any service or labor performed by an employee for an employer within the United States. Employment does not include casual employment by individuals who provide domestic services in a private home that is sporadic, irregular, or intermittent.[2] The term "employee" means an individual who provides services or labor for an employer for wages or other remuneration, but does not include independent contractors.[3] The term "independent contractor" includes individuals or entities who carry on independent business, contract to do a piece of work according to their own means and methods, and are subject to control only as to results.[4]

17-3. Do citizens and nationals of the U.S. need to prove to their employers that they are eligible to work?

Yes. While U.S. citizens and nationals are automatically eligible for employment, they too must provide proof of employment eligibility and complete Form I-9.[5]

17-4. Does an employer need to complete a Form I-9 for everyone who applies for a job with the employer?

No. An employer needs to complete Form I-9 only for people it actually hires for employment. For purposes of Form I-9, a person is hired when the person actually begins to work for the employer for wages or other remuneration.[6]

17-5. What steps should an employer follow to properly complete Form I-9?

Employers should follow the instructions for completing Form I-9 provided in the Handbook for Employers published by the Immigration and Naturalization Service (INS). The instructions detail the following steps (also set forth in INS regulations):

- Newly-hired employees must complete Section 1 of Form I-9 and sign and date the form.

- Employees must present to the employer an original document or documents that establish identity and employment eligibility within three business days of the date employment begins. Some documents establish both identity and employment eligibility. These documents are listed on List A of the Handbook and in regulations.[7] Other documents establish identity only (List B) or employment eligibility only (List C).[8] The employer must examine one document from List A or one from List B and one from List C. The employer may not specify which document or documents an individual is to present.[9]

- The employer must fill in Section 2 of the I-9 Form indicating the document title, issuing authority, document number and expiration date (if any).[10]

17-6. Can an employer fire an employee who fails to produce the required documents within three business days?

Yes. An employer can terminate an employee who fails to produce the required documents, or a receipt for replacement documents (in the case of lost, stolen or destroyed documents), within three business days of the date employment begins. However, the employer must apply these practices uniformly to all employees. If an employee has presented a receipt for a replacement document, he or she must produce the actual document within 90 days of the date employment begins.[11]

17-7. What is the employer's responsibility concerning the authenticity of documents presented to it?

The employer must examine the documents and, if they reasonably appear on their face to be genuine and to relate to the person presenting them, the employer must accept them. To do otherwise could be an unfair immigration-related employment practice. If a document does not reasonably appear on its face to be genuine and to relate to the person presenting it, the employer must not accept it.[12]

17-8. May an employer accept a photocopy of a document presented by an employee?

No. Employees must present original documents. The only exception is a certified copy of a birth certificate.[13]

17-9. What happens if an employer properly completes a Form I-9 and the INS discovers that the employee is not actually authorized to work?

Obviously, the employer cannot continue to employ the unauthorized employee. The employer will have a good faith defense against the imposition of penalties for hiring an authorized alien unless the government can prove that the employer had actual knowledge of the unauthorized status of the employee.[14]

17-10. What must an employer do when an employee's work authorization expires?

When an employee's work authorization expires, the employer must reverify the employee's employment eligibility. Reverification on the Form I-9 must occur not later than the date work authorization expires.[15] The employer may fill in Section 3 of the Form I-9 or use a new Form I-9 if needed.[16]

17-11. For how long must the employer retain the Form I-9 for an employee?

The employer must retain the Form I-9 for three years after the date employment begins, or one year after the person's employment is terminated, whichever is later.[17]

EMPLOYMENT-BASED NONIMMIGRANT VISAS

17-12. What is a nonimmigrant visa?

A nonimmigrant visa allows a foreign national to enter the United States for a limited period of time for a specific purpose, such as tourism, business meetings, or employment by a U.S. employer. There are several distinct employment-based nonimmigrant categories, including H-1B specialty occupations, TN professions for Canadian and Mexican citizens, and L-1 multinational executive, managerial or "specialized knowledge" positions, the requirements for which are outlined in the questions that follow.

17-13. What is the filing fee for an employment-based nonimmigrant visa?

Generally, a U.S. employer petitions for a nonimmigrant visa using INS Form I-129, which requires a filing fee of $110. Certain visas require additional fees. After the INS approves a petition, the employee must apply at a U.S. consulate abroad for the visa. The fee for the visa depends on the particular consulate, but it is normally about $45.

17-14. What is the processing time for an employment-based nonimmigrant visa petition?

The processing time is normally 30 to 60 days after the INS regional service center receives the petition.

17-15. What status is available to the spouse and children of a nonimmigrant employee?

The spouse and unmarried minor children of a nonimmigrant employee are entitled to apply for a nonimmigrant visa allowing admission to the U.S. for the same period as the nonimmigrant employee. The spouse and children may not accept employment in the U.S. unless they independently qualify for an employment-based nonimmigrant category and are the beneficiaries of an employment-based visa petition.

H-1B NONIMMIGRANT VISAS

17-16. What are the general requirements for petitioning the INS to hire a nonimmigrant in an H-1B specialty occupation?

The first step is to file a Labor Condition Application (Form ETA 9035) with the U.S. Department of Labor. On this application, the employer must state the wage or salary to be paid to the foreign national and must attest that this wage is greater than or equal to the "prevailing wage" and the "actual wage" paid to other employees in the same position.

- The prevailing wage is the average wage paid to similarly employed workers in the geographic area where the nonimmigrant will be employed as of the time of filing the application.[18] The prevailing wage can be determined through a private wage survey or through a state employment agency wage publication.

- The actual wage is the average wage paid to other employees in the same position with similar experience and qualifications in the employer's organization.[19]

The employer must attest on the Labor Condition Application (LCA) that its employment of H-1B nonimmigrants will not adversely affect the working conditions of workers similarly employed.[20]

The employer must also attest on the LCA that there is not a strike or lockout in the course of a labor dispute in the occupational classification at the place of employment.[21] If the job is unionized, the employer must provide the bargaining representative with a copy of the LCA. If the job is not unionized, the employer must post a notice of the intent to hire and the wage to be paid to the foreign national in two conspicuous places at the work site for ten consecutive days.[22]

Within one business day of filing the LCA, the employer must establish a public access file that may be viewed by any person. This file must include a copy of the filed LCA, a copy of the notice provided to a bargaining representative or posted in the workplace, the source of the prevailing wage determination, and a memo from the employer explaining the actual wage determination.[23]

The Department of Labor's processing time for the LCA is about seven days. Once the LCA is approved, the employer may file the H-1B petition with the INS. The employer must fill out INS Form I-129 and the H Supplement to Form I-129, and provide supporting documentation. The employer must present evidence that the following two requirements are met:

1. The position offered is in a specialty occupation, meaning that it requires at least the equivalent of a U.S. Bachelor's degree.[24] The petition and letter in support should carefully define and describe the position. The employer should provide supporting documentation such as company literature, product literature, financial information and a position description to demonstrate to the INS the economic viability of the company as well as the requirements for the position.

2. The foreign national qualifies for the position. The employee must have the equivalent of a U.S. Bachelor's degree in a field of study relating to the position.[25] Generally, diplomas and transcripts should be submitted. If the foreign national does not have a four-year degree, he or she can demonstrate through work experience or a combination of college education and experience that he or she has the equivalent of a Bachelor's degree. There are private credentials evaluation firms that will evaluate an employee's education and employment experience and certify whether it constitutes the equivalent of a U.S. Bachelor's degree. If work experience is used, the INS requires letters from former employers stating the length of employment and describing the foreign national's job duties and skills. Generally, three years of work experience is equal to one year of college.

17-17. Does the employer need to demonstrate that there is a shortage of qualified U.S. workers?

No. Unlike most categories of employment-based permanent immigrant visa petitions, the employer does not need to show that it cannot find U.S. workers for nonimmigrant positions; the employer must only demonstrate that it will pay the foreign national at least as much as the prevailing wage for U.S. workers.

17-18. Are there special fees for an H-1B visa?

Yes. The INS charges the normal nonimmigrant visa petition filing fee of $110 plus a recently-enacted additional $1,000 fee that must be paid by the employer as a mandatory donation to a U.S. worker training fund. Certain employers are exempt from paying the $1,000 fee, including universities, primary and secondary schools, and certain research institutions and non-profit organizations. All petitioners must now file a separate Form I-129W stating whether the employer is paying the $1,000 fee or qualifies for the exemption.

17-19. For how long is an H-1B visa valid?

The initial petition is valid for a maximum of three years, and the maximum authorized stay in the U.S. in H-1B status is six years at a time. Therefore, an employer who wishes to employ a nonimmigrant beyond three years will need to petition for an extension of stay before the first three-year period expires. After six years, the foreign national must remain outside the U.S. for at least one year before another H-1B petition can be approved.[26]

17-20. May an H-1B employee transfer to a different geographic location of the employer?

Yes, but the employer must first file and receive an approved Labor Condition Application certifying that the salary is at least as much as the prevailing wage in the new geographic location.

17-21. May an employer hire a foreign national who is already in the U.S. under H-1B status with another employer?

Yes, but the employer must first file a new Labor Condition Application and H-1B petition for that employee. Once the new employer files a non-frivolous H-1B petition, the employee may begin work for the new employer without having to return to his or her home country to obtain a new visa stamp. For I-9 compliance, the employer should attach a copy of the receipt notice for the pending petition along with a copy of the foreign national's I-94 card showing previous H-1B status.

17-22. Must an H-1B visa holder be working at all times?

As long as the employer/employee relationship exists, an H-1B nonimmigrant is still in status. The H-1B nonimmigrant may work part-time or be on vacation, sick leave, maternity/paternity leave or on strike and still be in status.

17-23. What liability does the employer have if the employer discharges an H-1B worker before the end of the period of authorized H-1B status?

The employer will be liable for the reasonable costs of return transportation to the foreign national's home country.[27]

17-24. May the H-1B nonimmigrant employee also seek permanent immigrant status?

Yes. The H-1B nonimmigrant category is one of the few nonimmigrant categories where the nonimmigrant may have dual intent to enter the U.S. on a temporary basis and at the same time apply for permanent residency. The assumption is that if the nonimmigrant does not obtain permanent residency, he or she will return to his or her home country upon expiration of the nonimmigrant visa.

17-25. Is there an annual limit on the number of H-1B visas issued nationally?

Yes. Congress has set the cap for the years 2001, 2002 and 2003 at 195,000 H-1B visas. Certain petitions are exempt from the cap, including petitions by institutions of higher learning and nonprofit or government research organizations.

TN VISAS

17-26. What are the requirements for a TN nonimmigrant visa for Canadian and Mexican professionals?

The TN visa is similar in requirements to the H-1B visa. TN visas provide for the admission of Canadian and Mexican citizens who will be engaged in "business activities at a professional level" in the U.S., which are defined as those jobs that require at least a Bachelor's degree or appropriate credentials demonstrating status as a professional in a profession set forth in Appendix 1603.D.1 of the North American Free Trade Agreement (NAFTA).[28] The INS regulations also specify which professions qualify for TN status.[29] The following documentation is needed to obtain a TN visa:

- A letter from the U.S. employer confirming an offer of employment and outlining the nature of the professional job; the anticipated length of stay, the beneficiary's educational credentials and professional qualifications, compliance with any applicable state licensure requirements, and arrangements for the beneficiary's salary.

- Diplomas and transcripts (if the degree is not from the U.S., Canada or Mexico, it must be evaluated).

- Licenses and professional memberships, if applicable.

- Proof of Canadian or Mexican citizenship.[30]

17-27. What are the procedures for Canadian citizens?

Canadian citizens can present this documentation at a port of entry or pre-clearance station at an airport. They do not need to present a petition approved by the INS, or a Labor Condition Application.[31] They will be given an I-94 card valid for multiple entries over one year.[32] Once in the U.S., the TN visa holder can apply for an extension at the INS Northern Service Center.[33] A new TN petition is required for a change of employer.[34]

17-28. What are the procedures for Mexican citizens?

For Mexican citizens, the employer must petition for a TN visa at the INS Northern Service Center, and must present an approved Labor Condition Application in addition to the documents listed in Q 17-26.[35] Mexican citizens must obtain the TN visa at a U.S. consulate; they cannot obtain the visa at the border like Canadians can.[36]

17-29. Is the TN visa category limited to specific professions?

Yes. Unlike the H-1B visa, the TN visa is limited to a specific (but rather extensive) list of professions. The list can be found in Appendix 1603.D.1 of NAFTA and in regulations.[37]

17-30. Is there a limit on the number of times a TN visa can be renewed?

No. TN visas can be renewed each year for an indefinite number of years.[38]

17-31. May a TN nonimmigrant also seek permanent immigrant status?

No. Unlike the H-1B visa, the TN visa is not a dual intent visa. A person on a TN visa cannot pursue permanent residency.[39]

L-1 Visas

17-32. What is an L-1 intracompany transferee visa?

An L-1 intracompany transferee visa is a nonimmigrant visa available to a foreign national coming to work in the U.S. for an employer that is affiliated with a company for which the foreign national worked prior to entering the U.S.[40]

17-33. What are the requirements for an L-1 nonimmigrant visa?

The nonimmigrant must have had at least one continuous year of full-time employment abroad with a qualifying organization within the three years preceding the filing of the petition.[41]

The foreign company and the U.S. company must be "qualifying organizations," meaning that the U.S. and the foreign company must have the relationship of a parent, subsidiary or branch, or have common majority ownership, or, where there is less than majority ownership, common control by the same person or entity.[42]

The foreign national must be coming as an executive, manager or "specialized knowledge" employee. Executives and Managers are granted L-1A status. Specialized knowledge employees are granted L-1B status.

- An "executive" is one who directs the management of the organization or a major component or function of the organization, establishes the goals and policies of the organization or function, exercises wide latitude in discretionary decisionmaking, and receives only general supervision or direction from higher level executives, the board of directors, or stockholders of the organization.[43]

- A "manager" manages the organization, a department, or a function of the organization; supervises and controls the work of other supervisory, professional, or managerial employees, or manages an essential function within the organization, or a department or subdivision of the organization; has the authority to hire and fire employees, or functions at a senior level within the organizational hierarchy; and exercises discretion over the day-to-day operations of the activity or function over which he or she has authority.[44]

- A "specialized knowledge" employee must have special knowledge of the organization's products, service, research, equipment, techniques, management or other interests and its application in international markets, or expertise in the organization's processes and procedures.[45]

17-34. What are the procedures for petitioning for an L-1 intracompany transferee?

The employer must fill out INS form I-129 and the L Supplement to Form I-129 and send it along with a letter in support, supporting documentation, and filing fee to the regional INS service center with jurisdiction over the location of the U.S. company. The letter in support should provide a detailed explanation of the "qualifying relationship" between the U.S. company and the foreign company and a detailed description of the transferee's current job duties, prospective job duties and employment history. The supporting documentation should include company literature, financial information, organizational charts, and the beneficiary's resume.

17-35. For how long is an L-1 visa valid?

Executives and managers may stay in L-1A status for up to seven years. The initial petition is valid for three years and then a petition for an extension of stay is required. Specialized knowledge employees may stay in L-1B status for up to five years.[46]

17-36. May an L-1 intracompany transferee also seek permanent immigrant status?

Yes. Like the H-1B nonimmigrant category, L-1 nonimmigrants may have dual intent to work in the U.S. on a temporary basis and at the same time apply for permanent residency.[47] The EB-1 multinational manager/executive category for employment-based permanent residency closely resembles the L-1A visa category. The permanent immigrant visa petition requires a showing of all of the same evidence. The main additional requirement is that the U.S. operation be in existence for at least a year.

OTHER EMPLOYMENT-BASED NONIMMIGRANT CATEGORIES

17-37. What other types of employment-based nonimmigrant visas are available to foreign nationals?

Some other types of employment-based nonimmigrant visas available to foreign nationals include the following:

- F-1 student visas. Foreign students may be employed by a U.S. employer for up to 12 months before or after graduation in order to obtain "optional practical training" before they return to their home country. U.S. employers often hire recent graduates authorized to work under an F-1 visa and then petition for a change of status to another nonimmigrant visa category such as an H-1B. The employer does not petition for F-1 employment authorization. The student must first obtain a recommendation from the school and then apply to the INS for employment authorization prior to accepting employment.[48]

- H-1B classification for fashion models who are of distinguished merit and ability and who are coming to the U.S. to perform services which require a fashion model of prominence.[49]

- H-2A visas for temporary or seasonal agricultural workers.[50]

- H-2B visas for temporary nonagricultural workers. The employer's need must generally be one year or less and can be a one-time occurrence, seasonal need, peakload need, or intermittent need.[51]

- H-3 visas for temporary trainees for admission to training programs not designed primarily to provide productive employment.[52]

- O-1 visas for foreign nationals who have "extraordinary ability in the sciences, arts, education, business, or athletics" which have been demonstrated by sustained national or international acclaim. Examples of O-1 nonimmigrants who may be employed temporarily in the U.S. are Nobel-Prize-winning scientists and internationally acclaimed athletes, artists or entertainers.[53]

- P-1 classification for internationally known athletes, individually or as part of a group or team, and entertainment groups (not individuals).[54]

- P-2 visas for artists under the auspices of a reciprocal exchange program.[55]

- P-3 visas for culturally unique artists or entertainers.[56]

- R religious visas for foreign members of a religious denomination having a bona fide non-profit religious organization in the United States to work in the United States as a minister or other professional capacity for the religious organization for a period not to exceed five years.[57]

EMPLOYMENT-BASED PERMANENT IMMIGRANT VISAS

17-38. What is an immigrant visa?

An immigrant visa (also known as a green card) authorizes a foreign national to live and work permanently in the United States. Generally, immigrant visas can be obtained in two ways: (1) based on family ties or marriage to a U.S. lawful permanent resident or citizen; or (2) based on an offer of employment by a U.S. employer.

There are five categories of employment-based immigrant visas:

- First preference (EB-1 priority workers): (1) Foreign nationals with extraordinary ability; (2) outstanding professors and researchers; and (3) certain multinational executives and managers. There are 40,000 visas available each year for this category.

- Second preference (EB-2 workers with advanced degrees or exceptional ability): (1) Foreign nationals who are members of the professions holding advanced degrees or their equivalent; and (2) foreign nationals who because of their exceptional ability in the sciences, arts, or business will substantially benefit the national economy, cultural, or educational interests or welfare of the United States. There are 40,000 visas available each year to be allotted between these two subcategories.

- Third preference (EB-3 professionals, skilled workers, and other workers): (1) Foreign national with at least two years of experience as skilled workers; (2) professionals with a Bachelor's degree; and (3) others with less than two years experience, such as an unskilled worker who can perform labor for which qualified workers are not available in the United States. There are 40,000 visas allotted each year for these three subcategories, but only 10,000 of those are available for unskilled workers.

- Fourth preference (EB-4 special workers such as those in a religious occupation or vocation): Foreign national who, for at least two years before applying for admission to the United States, has been a member of a religious denomination that has a non-profit religious organization in the United States, and who will be working in a religious vocation or occupation at the request of the religious organization. There are 10,000 visas available each year for this classification.

- Fifth preference (EB-5 immigrant investors): Foreign nationals who establish a business, invest one million dollars in the business, and create full-time employment for at least ten U.S. workers. There are 10,000 visas available each year for this category.

17-39. How does an employer petition for an employment-based immigrant visa for a foreign worker?

The first step for most employment-based immigrant visa categories is to obtain a labor certification from the Department of Labor certifying that there are no qualified U.S. workers available to fill the position offered. The labor certification requirement applies to all workers in the EB-3 category and most workers in the EB-2 category. Foreign nationals in the EB-1 preference category are exempt from the labor certification requirement. After labor certification is obtained (if required), the employer may then file the immigrant visa petition on Form 1-140 along with supporting documentation to the regional INS Service Center. Once the petition is approved, and a visa number is issued by the State Department, the foreign national then applies for the actual visa (the "green card").

17-40. What are the processing times for obtaining an employment-based immigrant visa?

Depending on the state, the labor certification process (if required) can take one year or more. Then, the employer may file the I-140 Petition, which can take up to six months for the INS to process, depending on the regional INS Service Center. Then, the employee, if already in the U.S., may apply for adjustment to permanent resident status using Form I-485, which can take the INS up to a year and a half to process. If the employee is not already in the U.S., he or she applies for the visa at a consulate, which can take up to six months. Therefore, the entire process can take two to three years. If a labor certification is not needed, the I-140 Petition and the subsequent visa application can take one to two years.

17-41. What are the filing fees for employment-based immigrant visas?

There is no fee for the labor certification application. The filing fee for the I-140 petition is $115. The filing fee for the I-485 adjustment application is $220.

17-42. What are the procedures for obtaining labor certification (for those employment-based immigrant categories requiring labor certification)?

Labor certification is an attestation to the Department of Labor that there are no available qualified U.S. workers for the position in which the employer seeks to hire a foreign national on a permanent basis. The employer must submit the Department of Labor Application for Alien Employment Certification, Form ETA-750, Parts A and B. The initial filing is with a state employment service agency (SESA). The application requires a statement of the qualifications of the foreign national, signed by the foreign national, and a description of the job offer, including documentation that:

1. the job opportunity is being described without unduly restrictive job requirements (i.e., the requirements shall be those normally required for the job in the U.S., shall be those defined for the job in the Dictionary of Occupational Titles, and shall not include requirements for a language other than English);

2. the employer's other efforts to recruit U.S. workers have been unsuccessful;

3. no unions were able to refer U.S. workers (if unions are customarily used as a recruitment source in the industry);

4. the employer's requirements for the job as described represent the employer's actual minimum requirements for the job and it is not feasible to hire workers with less training or experience than that required by the employer's job offer; and

5. if U.S. workers have applied for the job, they were rejected solely for lawful job-related reasons.[58]

As soon as the Labor Certification is filed with the SESA, the employer must post a notice of the filing and the job offer in a conspicuous place at the work site for at least ten days, as on-site recruitment. If there is a union or bargaining representative, notice must be given to it.

When the SESA receives the application, it determines the prevailing wage for the job opportunity and compares it to the wage offered. If the wage offered is below the prevailing wage, the SESA will advise the employer to increase the wage offer or the application will be denied.[59]

Once the SESA determines that the Labor Certification Application is satisfactory, the SESA will supervise a period of recruitment for the position for a period of 30 days. (This SESA-supervised recruitment can be avoided only if the employer can submit a detailed summary of legitimate recruitment efforts during the previous six months.[60] The SESA will place a job order in the regular Employment Service recruitment system.[61] Further, the employer must place an advertisement for the job opportunity in a newspaper of general circulation or in a professional or trade publication, whichever is appropriate to the occupation and most likely to bring responses from able, willing, qualified and available U.S. workers. The advertisement shall describe the job opportunity with particularity and direct applicants to apply with the SESA for referral to the employer. If published in a newspaper of general circulation, it must be published for at least three consecutive days.[62]

The employer must provide to the SESA a written report of the results of all recruitment efforts during the 30-day recruitment period. The report shall identify each recruitment source; state the number of U.S. workers responding to the employer's recruitment; state the names, addresses, and provide resumes of the U.S. workers interviewed; and explain the lawful job-related reasons for not hiring each worker interviewed.[63]

If no qualified U.S. workers are recruited, the SESA will forward the application to the Department of Labor Regional Certifying Officer. The Certifying Officer will either approve the application or issue a "Notice of Findings" that it intends to deny the application because of a defect. Faced with a Notice of Findings, the employer can either cure the defect and start the recruitment process again or attempt to rebut the finding that there is a defect. Adverse decisions may be appealed to the Board of Alien Labor Certification Appeals.

17-43. What are the requirements for the EB-1 extraordinary ability employment-based immigrant visa category?

Foreign nationals that qualify for this category are those with extraordinary ability in the sciences, arts, education, business or athletics, which has been demonstrated by sustained national or international acclaim and whose achievements have been recognized in the field through extensive documentation. The foreign national must be one of "that small percentage who have risen to the very top of the field of endeavor." People who have received a major internationally recognized award, such as a Nobel Prize, will qualify for an EB-1 classification. If the foreign national has not received an award of that caliber, a foreign national may qualify if he or she can show at least three of the following ten types of evidence:

1. receipt of lesser nationally or internationally recognized prizes or awards for excellence in the field of endeavor;

2. membership in associations in the field which require outstanding achievement of their members;

3. published material about the foreign national in professional or major trade publications or other major media;

4. evidence that the foreign national has participated, either individually or on a panel, as a judge of the work of others in the same field for which classification is sought;

5. evidence of the foreign national's original scientific, scholarly, artistic, athletic, or business-related contributions of major significance in the field;

6. evidence of the foreign national's authorship of scholarly articles in professional or major trade publications, or other major media;

7. evidence that the foreign national's work has been displayed at artistic exhibitions or showcases;

8. evidence that the foreign national has performed in a leading or critical role in distinguished organizations;

9. evidence that the foreign national commands a high salary or other significantly high remuneration in relation to others in the field; or

10. evidence of commercial success in the performing arts, as shown by box office receipts, record sales, etc.[64]

Labor certification is not required for this category. Further, unlike the other two EB-1 subcategories, the EB-1 worker of extraordinary ability may petition for himself or herself. (The employer must file the petition for most other employment-based visas.)

17-44. What are the requirements for an EB-1 outstanding professor or researcher?

Outstanding professors and researchers must be recognized internationally as outstanding in a particular academic field. In addition, an outstanding professor or researcher must have at least three years experience in teaching or research in the academic field, and enter the U.S. in a tenure-track teaching or comparable research position at a university or other institution of higher education. If the employer is a private company rather than a university or educational institution, the department, division, or institute of the private employer must employ at least three persons full time in research activities and have achieved documented accomplishments in an academic field. Evidence that the professor or researcher is recognized as outstanding in the academic field must include documentation of at least two of the following:

1. receipt of major prizes or awards for outstanding achievement;

2. membership in associations that require their members to demonstrate outstanding achievements;

3. published material in professional publications written by others about the foreign national's work in the academic field;

4. participation, either on a panel or individually, as a judge of the work of others in the same or allied academic field;

5. original scientific or scholarly research contributions in the field;

6. authorship of scholarship books or articles (in scholarly journals with international circulation) in the field.[65]

Labor certification is not required for this category.

17-45. What are the requirements for an EB-1 multinational manager or executive?

Similar to the requirements for an L-1A nonimmigrant visa, a multinational manager or executive is eligible for EB-1 permanent immigrant status if he or she has been employed outside the U.S. in the three years immediately preceding the filing of the petition for at least one year in a managerial or executive capacity by a firm or corporation and seeks to enter the U.S. to continue employment with that organization or an affiliate or subsidiary of the organization. If the foreign national is already in the U.S. working for the same employer or affiliate by which the foreign national was employed overseas, the foreign national must have been employed by the entity abroad for at least one year in a managerial or executive capacity in the three years preceding entry as a nonimmigrant. The petitioner must be a U.S. employer, doing business for at least one year, that is an affiliate, a subsidiary, or the same employer as the firm, corporation, or other legal entity that employed the foreign national abroad.[66] Labor certification is not required for this category.

17-46. What are the requirements for an EB-2 classification for "members of the professions holding advanced degrees" or foreign nationals of "exceptional ability in the sciences, arts, or business"?

EB-2 petitions must generally be accompanied by an approved, individual labor certification from the Department of Labor on Form ETA-750 (the procedures for which are in Q 17-42). For workers with exceptional ability in the sciences, arts, or business, the foreign national may apply to waive the labor certification requirement if such a waiver would be in the national interest. A petition for a foreign professional holding an advanced degree may be filed when the job requires an advanced degree (beyond a Bachelor's degree) and the foreign national possesses such a degree or the equivalent. The petition must include documentation such as an official academic record showing that the foreign national has a U.S. advanced degree or a foreign equivalent degree, or an official academic record showing that the foreign national has a U.S. Bachelor's degree or a foreign equivalent degree and letters from current or former employers showing that the foreign national has at least five years of progressive post-baccalaureate experience in the specialty.

An EB-2 petition for a foreign national having exceptional ability in the sciences, arts, or business must include documentation of at least three of the following:

1. An official academic record showing the foreign national has a degree, diploma, certificate or similar award from a college, university or other institution of learning relating to the area of exceptional ability;

2. Letters documenting at least ten years of full-time experience in the occupation being sought;

3.   A license to practice the profession or certification for a particular professional or occupation;

4.   Evidence that the foreign national has commanded a salary or other remuneration for services which demonstrates exceptional ability;

5.   Membership in professional associations;

6.   Recognition for achievements and significant contributions to the industry or field by peers, government entities, professional or business organizations.

If the above standards do not apply to the occupation, other comparable evidence of eligibility is also acceptable.[67]

17-47. What are the requirements for an EB-3 third preference employment-based immigrant visa?

All petitions filed in the EB-3 category require a job offer and a labor certification (the requirements for which are discussed in Q 17-42). There are three EB-3 categories — professionals who hold a Bachelor's degree, skilled workers, and other workers (unskilled workers.)[68]

- Professionals who hold a Bachelor's degree. Like the H-1B non-immigrant category, the position must require a Bachelor's degree and the foreign national must hold a U.S. Bachelor's degree or its foreign equivalent. Unlike the H-1B nonimmigrant category, the foreign national is not able to make up for a lack of education through experience.

- Skilled workers. The position offered must require at least two years' training and experience and the foreign national must possess the requisite training and experience. The training requirement may be met through relevant post-secondary education.

- Other workers. This category covers "unskilled labor," which is work that takes less than two years of higher education, training or experience to perform. The petition must be accompanied by evidence that the foreign national meets any training or educational requirements of the job. There is an extreme backlog in visa numbers for this category, which has an annual limit of 10,000 visas. Currently, the backlog is about six years.

CHAPTER ENDNOTES

1. 8 U.S.C. §1324a(a)(3).
2. 8 CFR §274a.1(h).
3. 8 CFR §274a.1(f).
4. 8 CFR §274a.1(j).
5. *Handbook for Employers*, INS Pub. M-274.
6. 8 CFR §274a.1(c); *Handbook for Employers*, INS Pub. M-274.
7. 8 CFR §274a.2(b)(1)(v)(A).
8. 8 CFR §§274a.2(b)(1)(v)(B), 274a.2(b)(1)(v)(C).
9. 8 CFR §274a.2(b)(1)(v).
10. 8 CFR §274a.2(b)(1)(iii).
11. *Handbook for Employers*, INS Pub. M-274.
12. *Handbook for Employers*, INS Pub. M-274.
13. *Handbook for Employers*, INS Pub. M-274.
14. *Handbook for Employers*, INS Pub. M-274.
15. 8 CFR §274a.2(b)(1)(vii).
16. *Handbook for Employers*, INS Pub. M-274.
17. 8 CFR §274a.2(b)(2)(i); *Handbook for Employers*, INS Pub. M-274.
18. 20 CFR §655.731(a)(2).
19. 20 CFR §655.731(a)(1).
20. 20 CFR §655.732.
21. 20 CFR §655.733.
22. 20 CFR §§655.730, 655.734.
23. 20 CFR §655.760.
24. 8 CFR §214.2(h)(4)(iii)(A).
25. 8 CFR §214.2(h)(4)(iii)(C).
26. 8 CFR §214.2(h)(13)(iii).
27. 8 CFR §214.2(h)(4)(iii)(E).
28. 8 CFR §214.6(b).
29. See 8 CFR §214.6(c).
30. 8 CFR §214.6(d); 8 CFR §214.6(e).
31. 8 CFR §214.6(e)(2).
32. 8 CFR §214.6(f)(1).
33. 8 CFR §214.6(h)(2).
34. 8 CFR §214.6(i)(2).
35. 8 CFR §214.6(d).
36. 8 CFR §214.6(f)(2).
37. 8 C.F.R. §214.6(c).
38. 8 CFR §214.6(h).
39. 8 CFR §214.6(b).
40. 8 CFR §214.2(l).
41. 8 CFR §214.2(l)(3)(iii).
42. 8 CFR §214.2(l)(1)(ii)(G).
43. 8 CFR §214.2(l)(1)(ii)(C).
44. 8 CFR §214.2(l)(1)(ii)(B).
45. 8 CFR §214.2(l)(1)(ii)(D).
46. 8 CFR §214.2(l)(12).

47. 8 CFR §214.2(l)(16).
48. 8 CFR §214.2(f)(10); 8 CFR §214.2(f)(11).
49. 8 CFR §214.2(h)(4)(i)(C).
50. 8 CFR §214.2(h)(5).
51. 8 CFR §214.2(h)(6).
52. 8 CFR §214.2(h)(7).
53. 8 CFR §214.2(o).
54. 8 CFR §214.2(p)(1)(ii)(A).
55. 8 CFR §214.2(p)(1)(ii)(B).
56. 8 CFR §214.2(p)(1)(ii)(C).
57. 8 CFR §214.2(r).
58. 20 CFR §656.21(b).
59. 20 CFR §656.21(e).
60. 20 CFR §656.21(i)).
61. 20 CFR §656.21(f).
62. 20 CFR §656.21(g).
63. 20 CFR §656.21(j)(i).
64. 8 CFR §204.5(h).
65. 8 CFR §204.5(i).
66. 8 CFR §204.5(j).
67. 8 CFR §204.5(k).
68. 8 CFR §204.5(l).

Chapter 18

WARN

GENERALLY

18-1. What is the Worker Adjustment and Retraining Notification Act?

18-2. Who enforces the WARN Act?

18-3. Who must comply with the WARN Act?

18-4. Who is protected by the WARN Act?

18-5. What qualifies as an "employment loss" for purposes of the WARN Act?

18-6. Who is not protected by the WARN Act?

18-7. What triggers the notice requirements of the WARN Act?

18-8. What is a "single site of employment"?

18-9. Do states and local governments have WARN Act-like laws?

WARN ACT NOTICE

18-10. What does the WARN Act require?

18-11. When must the WARN Act notice be given?

18-12. What are the exceptions to the notice requirements of the WARN Act?

18-13. Who must give the WARN Act notice?

18-14. Who should receive the WARN Act notice?

18-15. How should the WARN Act notice be provided?

18-16. What information must a WARN Act notice contain?

18-17. What information must be contained in a WARN Act notice to the representative of the affected employees?

18-18. What information must be contained in a WARN Act notice to affected employees who do not have a representative?

18-19. What information must be contained in a WARN Act notice to the state dislocated worker unit and the chief elected official of local government?

18-20. What are "bumping rights"?

18-21. Are there exceptions to the 60-day notice requirement?

18-22. What is the "faltering" company exception to the 60-day notice requirement?

18-23. What is the unforeseeable business circumstances exception to the 60-day notice requirement?

18-24. What is the natural disaster exception to the 60-day notice requirement?

18-25. When should the notice period be extended?

LITIGATING WARN ACT CLAIMS

18-26. How are claims for violation of the WARN Act pursued?

18-27. What is the time limit (statute of limitations) for filing a WARN Act claim?

18-28. What are the elements of a prima facie case under the WARN Act?

18-29. How are WARN Act claims litigated?

DEFENSES TO WARN ACT CLAIMS

18-30. What procedural defenses exist for WARN Act claims?

18-31. What statutory defenses exist for WARN Act claims?

18-32. What judicial defenses exist for WARN Act claims?

18-33. Are state employers immune from WARN Act lawsuits under the Eleventh Amendment?

REMEDIES UNDER THE WARN ACT

18-34. What remedies exist under the WARN Act?

GENERALLY

18-1. What is the Worker Adjustment and Retraining Notification Act?

The Worker Adjustment and Retraining Notification (WARN) Act is a federal law passed by Congress to protect workers, their families, and the community from sudden and unexpected job losses caused by plant closings and mass layoffs.

The WARN Act generally requires employers to provide 60 calendar days notice in advance of plant closings and mass layoffs.

The WARN Act took effect on February 4, 1989.[1]

18-2. Who enforces the WARN Act?

An employee, his or her representative, or a local government official may sue in a United States District Court to enforce the WARN Act.

A local union may also have standing to file a lawsuit on behalf of its members, if it can demonstrate an interest in the litigation other than the benefit of its members.[2]

The Department of Labor (DOL) has no enforcement powers under the WARN Act, but it does have the authority to promulgate regulations thereunder.[3]

18-3. Who must comply with the WARN Act?

The WARN Act applies to any employer that:

1. Employs 100 or more employees, excluding part-time employees; or

2. Employs 100 or more employees, including part-time employees, who, in the aggregate, work at least 4,000 hours per week (not including hours of overtime).[4]

To determine whether the 100-employee requirement has been met, employees on temporary layoff or on leave, and who have a reasonable expectation of being recalled, are counted as employees.[5]

An employee has a "reasonable expectation" of recall when there is an understanding, either through industry practice or through employer notification, that the employment with the employer has been temporarily interrupted and the employee is subject to recall to the same or similar job.[6]

"Employer" includes nonprofit organizations, public entities, and quasi-public entities that engage in commercial business.[7]

Governmental entities are not covered by the WARN Act unless they (1) engage in commercial business; (2) are separately organized from the regular government; (3) have their own governing bodies; and (4) have independent authority to manage their personnel and assets.[8]

Generally, independent contractors and wholly or partially owned subsidiaries of a parent company are treated as separate employers or as part of the parent or contracting company, depending on the degree of their independence from the parent.[9]

18-4. Who is protected by the WARN Act?

The WARN Act protects "affected employees," which are defined as employees who may reasonably be expected to experience an employment loss as a consequence of a proposed plant closing or mass layoff by their employer.[10]

This definition includes white-collar and managerial employees as well as employees in a skilled trade and other blue-collar occupations, but does not include business partners.[11]

Employees who are likely to lose their jobs because of "bumping rights" (see Q 18-20) or other factors should be given notice to the extent that such workers can be identified at the time that notice must be given.[12]

When in doubt, the DOL suggests that the employer provide notice.[13]

18-5. What qualifies as an "employment loss" for purposes of the WARN Act?

An "employment loss" is defined as any of the following:

1.   An employment termination, other than a discharge for (a) cause, (b) voluntary departure, or (c) retirement;

2.   A layoff exceeding six months; or

3.   A reduction in hours of work of more than 50% during each month of any six month period.[14]

An "employment loss" does not occur where the employer transfers or rehires an employee into another position or with a new company; nor does an employment loss occur where an employee is reassigned or transferred to employer-sponsored retraining or job search activities.[15]

Likewise, no employment loss occurs where the closing or layoff is the result of the relocation or consolidation of all or part

of the employer's business, and, prior to the closing or layoff, the employer offers:

1. To transfer the employee to a different site of employment, within a reasonable commuting distance, with no more than a six month break in employment; or

2. To transfer the employee to any other site of employment, regardless of distance, with no more than a six month break in employment, and which the employee accepts within 30 days of the offer or the closing or layoff, whichever is later.[16]

18-6. Who is not protected by the WARN Act?

Part-time employees are not entitled to notice under the WARN Act.[17]

An employee is designated as "part-time" if he or she averages fewer than 20 hours per week, or has been employed fewer than six of the 12 months preceding the date on which notice would otherwise be required.[18] Thus, full-time employees who have worked fewer than six months are designated as part-time employees for purposes of the WARN Act notice.

Seasonal employees may also be considered part-time employees.[19]

18-7. What triggers the notice requirements of the WARN Act?

Two situations trigger the notice requirements of the WARN Act: a plant closing or a mass layoff.[20]

PLANT CLOSING

A plant closing occurs when there is (1) any permanent or temporary shutdown at a single site of employment; (2) which results in an employment loss; (3) during any 30 day period; (4) for 50 or more employees (not including part-time employees).[21]

A temporary shutdown triggers the notice requirement only if there are a sufficient number of terminations, layoffs exceeding six months, or another employment loss, as defined by the statute.[22]

MASS LAYOFF

A mass layoff is a reduction in force that is not caused by a plant closing, but results in an employment loss.

A mass layoff occurs when there is a loss of employment during any 30 day period of at least 33% of the employees at a single site of employment, unless that percentage affects fewer than 50 employees. In some cases, therefore, the laying off of 50 workers does not automatically trigger a mass layoff, if those workers comprise less than 33% of the workforce. However, if at least 500 employees are affected, a mass layoff is presumed, regardless of the percentage of the workforce affected. Under either scenario, part-time employees are not counted.[23]

18-8. What is a "single site of employment"?

The term "single site of employment" can refer to either a single location or a group of contiguous locations.[24]

For example, a campus, industrial park, or separate facilities across the street from one another may be considered a "single site of employment" for purposes of the WARN Act.[25] Additionally, separate buildings or areas that are not directly connected or in immediate proximity may be considered a single site of employment if they (1) are in reasonable geographic proximity; (2) are used for the same purpose; and (3) share the same staff and equipment.[26]

Non-contiguous sites in the same geographic area which do not share the same staff or operational purpose should not be considered a single site.[27]

Similarly, contiguous buildings owned by the same employer which (1) have separate staff or management; (2) produce different products; and (3) have separate workforces are not considered single sites of employment.[28]

Employees whose primary duties involve work outside the employer's regular employment sites (e.g., sales persons and bus drivers) are assigned to the home base from which work is assigned for this purpose.[29]

Foreign sites of employment are not covered by the WARN Act, but they are counted in determinning whether the employer is subject to the WARN Act.[30]

18-9. Do states and local governments have WARN Act-like laws?

Many states have passed their own plant shutdown or layoff laws. Further, state law claims have occasionally been asserted to challenge complete or partial plant closings. Many local governments also have laws that address plant closings or mass layoffs, but these laws may violate state home rule provisions.

The WARN Act expressly permits concurrent laws to regulate on this matter. State "WARN" laws have survived a challenge that the Employee Retirement Income Security Act (ERISA) and the National Labor Relations Act (NLRA) preempt state regulation of plant closings.[31]

WARN ACT NOTICE

18-10. What does the WARN Act require?

The WARN Act requires a covered employer to give at least 60 days advance notice of certain plant closings and mass layoffs (see Q 18-7). This advance notice must be given to the appropriate state and local government officials, and to the affected employees or their union representative.[32]

Congress has expressed a preference that notice be given whenever possible, even if not required by the WARN Act.[33]

18-11. When must the WARN Act notice be given?

Unless an exception applies (see Q 18-12), the WARN Act notice must be given at least 60 calendar days prior to any planned plant closing or mass layoff.[34]

If the employee terminations occur on different dates, the date of the first individual termination within the statutory periods triggers the 60-day notice requirement.[35]

A worker's last date of employment is considered the date of that worker's layoff.[36]

Looking ahead 30 days and behind 30 days, the employer should determine whether employment actions (both taken and planned) will, in the aggregate, for any 30-day period, reach the

minimum numbers required to constitute a plant closing or mass layoff, and thus trigger the notice requirement.[37]

Likewise, looking ahead 90 days and behind 90 days, the employer should determine whether employment actions (both taken and planned), each of which is not separately of sufficient size to trigger WARN, will, in the aggregate, for any 90-day period, reach the minimum numbers required to constitute a plant closing or mass layoff, and thus trigger the notice requirement.[38]

Notice is not required where the employer can demonstrate that the separate employment losses are the result of separate and distinct actions and causes, and are not an attempt to evade the WARN Act requirements.[39]

18-12. What are the exceptions to the notice requirements of the WARN Act?

No notice is required in the following situations:

1.   Certain cases involving transfers, which are discussed at Q 18-5;[40]

2.   Where there is a closing of a temporary facility, or if the closing or layoff is the result of the completion of a particular project or undertaking, and the affected employees were hired with the understanding that their employment was limited to the duration of the facility or project or undertaking;[41] and

3.   Where there is a strike or lockout, and a plant closing or mass layoff occurs for reasons related to the strike or lockout, and which are not intended to evade the requirements of the WARN Act.[42]

18-13. Who must give the WARN Act notice?

The WARN Act prohibits an employer from closing a plant or causing a mass layoff until the end of a 60-day period after the employer serves written notice of such action. Thus, the employer must provide the appropriate notice.[43]

It is the employer's responsibility to determine who, within the employer's organization, should prepare and deliver the notice.[44]

Usually, the person who actually gives the notice is the plant manager, local personnel director, or a labor relations officer.

If a short-term layoff—of six months or less—is extended beyond six months due to business circumstances not reasonably foreseeable at the time of the initial layoff, the employer must provide notice as soon as it becomes reasonably foreseeable that the extension is necessary.[45]

A short-term layoff extended beyond six months for any other reason shall be treated as an employment loss from the date of its commencement.[46] Accordingly, an employer who is uncertain as to the length of a layoff should provide notice to avoid potential liability under the WARN Act.

In the case of the sale of part or all of a business, the seller is responsible for providing notice of any plant closing or mass layoff that takes place up to and including the effective date of the sale, and the buyer is responsible for providing notice of any plant closing or mass layoff that takes place thereafter.[47]

If the buyer has definite plans to carry out a plant closing or mass layoff within 60 days of purchase, the buyer may authorize the seller to give notice to affected employees as the buyer's agent. Whether or not the seller gives notice, the responsibility for giving the notice remains with the buyer.[48]

The regulations suggest that the prudent course may be for the buyer and seller to determine whether a mass layoff or plant closing is a likely impact of the sale, and to arrange for advance notice to be given to the appropriate parties.[49]

18-14. Who should receive the WARN Act notice?

An employer must provide the notice to:

1. Each representative of the affected employees (determined as of the time of the notice);

2. In the absence of a representative, to each affected employee;

3. The state or entity designated by the state to receive such notice (e.g., the state dislocated worker unit); and

4.   The chief elected official of the local government where the closing or layoff is to occur.[50]

18-15. How should the WARN Act notice be provided?

Any reasonable method of delivery to the necessary parties which is designed to ensure receipt of notice at least 60 days before separation is acceptable (e.g., first class mail, or personal delivery with optional signed receipt).[51]

While insertion of a specific notice into pay envelopes will suffice, a preprinted notice that is regularly included in each employee's pay check or pay envelope will not satisfy the WARN Act requirements.[52]

18-16. What information must a WARN Act notice contain?

A WARN Act notice must contain certain information, based upon whether it is sent to (1) the representative of the affected employees (see Q 18-17); (2) affected employees who do not have a representative (see Q 18-18); or (3) the state dislocated worker unit and chief elected official of local government (see Q 18-19).

In addition to the requirements of the specific notices, a WARN Act notice will be invalid unless it meets all of the following requirements:

1.   The notice must be specific;[53]

2.   The notice may be conditional upon the occurrence or nonoccurrence of an event such as the renewal of a major contract, but only when the event is definite and the occurrence or nonoccurrence will necessarily lead to a plant closing or mass layoff less than 60 days after the event;[54] and

3.   The information in the notice shall be based upon the best information available to the employer at the time the notice is served.[55]

18-17. What information must be contained in a WARN Act notice to the representative of the affected employees?

A WARN Act notice to the representative of affected employees must contain the following:

1. The name and the address of the employment site where the plant closing or mass layoff will occur;

2. The name and telephone number of a company official to contact for further information;

3. A statement as to whether the planned action is expected to be permanent or temporary, and whether the entire plant is to be closed;

4. The expected date of the first separation and the anticipated schedule for making separations; and

5. The job titles of positions to be affected, and the names of the workers currently holding affected jobs.[56]

This notice may also include additional information useful to employees, such as information available on dislocated worker's assistance, and, if the planned action is expected to be temporary, the estimated duration, if known.[57]

18-18. What information must be contained in a WARN Act notice to affected employees who do not have a representative?

A WARN Act notice to each affected employee who does not have a representative must be written in language understandable to the employee, and must contain:

1. A statement as to whether the planned action is expected to be permanent or temporary, and, if the entire plant is to be closed, a statement to that effect;

2. The expected date when the plant closing or mass layoff will commence, and the expected date when the individual employee will be separated;

3. An indication of whether "bumping rights" (see Q 18-20) exist;

4. The name and telephone number of a company official to contact for further information.[58]

The notice may also include additional information useful to the employee.[59] See Q 18-17.

18-19. What information must be contained in a WARN Act notice to the state dislocated worker unit and the chief elected official of local government?

A separate notice must be provided to both the state dislocated worker unit and the chief elected official of the applicable unit of the local government. It may be either the standard notice form or the alternative notice form.

STANDARD NOTICE FORM

The standard notice must contain:

1. The name and the address of the employment site where the plant closing or mass layoff will occur;

2. The name and telephone number of a company official to contact for further information;

3. A statement as to whether the planned action is expected to be permanent or temporary, and whether the entire plant is to be closed;

4. The expected date of the first separation and the anticipated schedule for making separations;

5. The job titles of positions to be affected, and the number of affected employees in each job classification;

6. An indication as to whether "bumping rights" (see Q 18-20) exist;

7. The name of each union representing affected employees; and

8. The name and address of the chief elected officer of each union.[60]

The notice may include additional information useful to the employees.[61] See Q 18-17.

ALTERNATIVE NOTICE FORM

In the alternative, an employer may give notice to the state dislocated worker unit and to the chief elected official of the applicable unit of local government by providing them with a written notice stating:

1.   The name and address of the employment site where the plant closing or mass layoff will occur;

2.   The name and telephone number of a company official to contact for further information;

3.   The expected date of the first separation; and

4.   The number of affected employees.

An employer opting for notice under this provision must have the other information normally required available on the plant site and readily accessible.[62]

18-20. What are "bumping rights"?

Collective bargaining agreements between the employer and its employees' representative (union) often contain provisions for "bumping rights." Where such bumping rights exist in a union contract, senior employees who are scheduled to be layed off may displace or "bump" less senior employees in other job classifications. The individual collective bargaining agreement will address the scope of such bumping rights, and any conditions or limitations on their operation.

18-21. Are there exceptions to the 60-day notice requirement?

By statute, there are three exceptions to the requirement that notice be given 60 days in advance of the plant closing or mass layoff: (1) the "faltering" company exception (see Q 18-22); (2) the unforeseeable business circumstances exception (see Q 18-23); and (3) the natural disaster exception (see Q 18-24).[63]

18-22. What is the "faltering" company exception to the 60-day notice requirement?

The "faltering" company exception applies only to plant closings (not mass layoffs).[64]

Under the faltering company exception, an employer may order the shutdown of a single site of employment before the end of the 60-day period if the employer was actively seeking capital at the time notice was required.[65]

This capital must be of the sort that, if obtained, would have enabled the employer to avoid or postpone the shutdown.[66]

Specifically, the employer must have been seeking financing or refinancing through the arrangement of loans, the issuance of stocks, bonds, or other methods of internally generating financing; or the employer must have been seeking additional money, credit, or business through any other commercially reasonable method.[67]

The employer must be able to identify specific actions taken to obtain capital or business and must show that there was a realistic opportunity to obtain the financing or business sought.[68]

Additionally, the employer must have had a reasonable, good faith, belief that giving the required notice would have precluded the employer from acquiring the needed capital or business.[69]

18-23. What is the unforeseeable business circumstances exception to the 60-day notice requirement?

The unforeseeable business circumstances exception applies to plant closings and mass layoffs caused by business circumstances that were not reasonably foreseeable at the time that the 60-day notice would otherwise have been required.[70]

Business circumstances that were not reasonably foreseeable are often characterized by some sudden, dramatic, and unexpected action outside the employer's control.[71]

For example, the sudden and unexpected termination of a major contract, a strike at a major supplier, or an unanticipated major economic downturn might qualify under this exception.[72]

In addition, a government-ordered closing of an employment site that occurs without prior notice also may be an unforeseeable business circumstance.[73]

The employer must exercise commercially reasonable business judgment, as compared with a similarly situated employer, in

predicting the demands of its particular market.[74] However, the employer is not required to adequately predict general economic conditions that may affect demand for its products or services.[75]

18-24. What is the natural disaster exception to the 60-day notice requirement?

The natural disaster exception applies to plant closings and mass layoffs resulting from any type of natural disaster, such as floods, earthquakes, droughts, storms, tidal waves, and similar effects of nature.[76]

To qualify for this exception, the employer must be able to demonstrate that its plant closing or its mass layoff is the direct result of a natural disaster.[77]

Even if the natural disaster fully prevents any advance notice, notice must nonetheless be given as soon as practicable.[78]

Plant closings or mass layoffs occurring as an indirect result of a natural disaster may qualify under the unforeseeable business circumstances exception.[79]

18-25. When should the notice period be extended?

Rolling notice (i.e., routine periodic notice) is prohibited.[80] However, additional notice *is* required when the date or schedule of dates of a planned plant closing or mass layoff is extended beyond the date or the ending date of any 14-day period announced in the original notice.

If the postponement is for a period of less than 60 days, the notice need only contain:

1. Reference to the earlier notice;

2. The date to which the planned action is postponed; and

3. The reasons for the postponement.[81]

If the postponement extends for 60 days or more, an additional notice is required.[82]

LITIGATING WARN ACT CLAIMS

18-26. How are claims for violation of the WARN Act pursued?

Anyone to whom a WARN Act notice must be given has standing to sue for himself or herself, or for other similarly situated persons.[83]

A local union may also have standing to file a lawsuit on behalf of its members, if it can demonstrate an interest in the litigation other than the benefit of its members.[84] Class actions are anticipated and expected by the WARN Act.[85]

The Department of Labor (DOL) has no enforcement powers under the WARN Act, but is authorized to promulgate regulations.[86]

18-27. What is the time limit (statute of limitations) for filing a WARN Act claim?

The WARN Act does not contain a specific time limit or statute of limitations. Courts will look to the most appropriate state law limitations period for application to WARN Act claims.[87] Therefore, the statute of limitations for filing a WARN Act claim varies from state to state, with many courts applying terms ranging from two to six years.[88]

18-28. What are the elements of a prima facie case under the WARN Act?

In order to establish a prima facie case under the WARN Act, the following factors must be established by the party bringing suit:

1.   The employer must be an employer that is required to comply with the WARN Act (see Q 18-3);

2.   An act has occurred that "triggers" a WARN Act notice (see Q 18-7); and

3.   There must have been an "employment loss" (see Q 18-5).

18-29. How are WARN Act claims litigated?

Federal courts have jurisdiction over WARN Act suits, and they may be brought "in any district in which the violation is alleged to have occurred, or in which the employer transacts business."[89]

The WARN Act has been interpreted to allow trial by jury, because the remedies afforded by the WARN Act are primarily legal, rather than equitable.[90]

DEFENSES TO WARN ACT CLAIMS

18-30. What procedural defenses exist for WARN Act claims?

A number of procedural defenses may be raised to defeat a claim of a WARN Act violation.

The court may simply lack jurisdiction over a WARN Act claim, if a defendant can show that it is not an employer as defined by the statute. For example, if a defendant can show that it did not employ 100 or more employees, excluding part-time employees, then it will not be considered an employer under the WARN Act and thus will not be subject to suit.[91] In addition, even if the defendant employs more than 100 employees, but the employees, in the aggregate, work fewer than 4,000 hours per week, exclusive of overtime hours, the defendant still is not considered an employer under the WARN Act.[92]

Conversely, a defendant can defend itself procedurally under the WARN Act by demonstrating that the plaintiff is not protected by the WARN Act. For example, the defendant may show that: (1) fewer than 50 employees were affected by a plant closing; (2) less than 33% of the total work force was affected by a mass layoff; or, (3) if more than 50 employees were affected, all of the affected employees came from different employment sites, making the total number of affected employees from each site fewer than 50.[93]

Additional procedural defenses may include the statute of limitations. As explained in Q 18-27, the WARN Act does not contain a statute of limitations, so the most analogous state law statute of limitations is used.[94]

18-31. What statutory defenses exist for WARN Act claims?

The WARN Act does provide statutory exceptions, which may be considered "affirmative defenses." Such defenses would include the statutory exceptions discussed more fully at Q 18-12.

18-32. What judicial defenses exist for WARN Act claims?

Courts have recognized other "defenses" to WARN Act claims. These defenses include:

1. The exclusion of business partners, consultants, contract employees of other employers, and self-employed persons from the "affected employee" category;[95]

2. The "small employer" exception;[96]

3. The allocation of notice obligations between buyers and sellers;[97]

4. The salutary effects of (a) "bumping" under collective bargaining agreements, (b) recall within six months, or (c) job transfers, retraining, or job search activities;[98]

5. The exclusion of foreign sites from the WARN Act;[99]

6. Creative interpretations of what constitutes a "single site of employment";[100] and

7. Pay in lieu of notice compliance.[101]

18-33. Are state employers immune from WARN Act lawsuits under the Eleventh Amendment?

The WARN Act does not apply to federal, state, and local governmental employers, unless they (1) engage in commercial business; (2) are separately organized from the regular government; (3) have their own governing bodies; and (4) have independent authority to manage their own personnel and assets.[102]

REMEDIES UNDER THE WARN ACT

18-34. What remedies exist under the WARN Act?

The following remedies exist under the WARN Act. The remedies provided in the WARN Act are exclusive.[103]

INJUNCTION TO PREVENT PLANT CLOSING OR
MASS LAYOFF UNAVAILABLE

The first remedy that aggrieved employees may be inclined to pursue is injunctive relief to prevent the closing of the plant or the mass layoff. However, the WARN Act expressly provides that a "Federal court does not have authority to enjoin a plant closing or mass layoff."[104]

Plants can be ordered reopened when unfair labor practices have been committed.[105] For example, an employer might close a plant that is only a part of its entire operations, rather than bargain with a labor organization that has been certified by the NLRB as the bargaining agent for a group of employees. A plant closing under these circumstances violates the National Labor Relations Act (NLRA) and the duty to bargain in good faith. On the other hand, if the employer completely shuts down its entire operation and goes out of business, then no bargaining obligation exists, even though the WARN Act may apply.

BACK PAY

Failure to comply with the WARN Act can result in back pay liability for the employer, up to a 60-day period for each affected employee, and include the value of any lost benefits under ERISA-covered employee benefit plans.[106] In such a situation, with respect to a medical benefit plan, the employee is entitled to reimbursement only for medical expenses actually incurred.[107]

CIVIL PENALTIES

The employer is also subject to a fine of not more than $500 a day, up to a total of 60 days, for failing to provide notification to the appropriate local unit of government.[108] This provision is excused if the employer pays each affected employee the amount for which the employer is liable under the WARN Act within three weeks from the date when the employer orders the plant shutdown or mass layoff.[109]

If the employer can demonstrate objective good faith in its attempt to comply with the WARN Act, it may qualify for a reduction in damages.[110]

PUNITIVE DAMAGES

Punitive damages are not available under the WARN Act.[111]

ATTORNEYS FEES

The prevailing party may be awarded reasonable attorneys fees as part of the costs.[112]

CHAPTER ENDNOTES

1. See 29 U.S.C. §2101 et seq.
2. See *United Food & Commercial Workers Union Local 751 v. Brown Group, Inc.*, 517 U.S. 544 (1996).
3. See 29 U.S.C. §2107; 20 CFR §639.1(d).
4. See 29 U.S.C. §§2101(a)(1)(A), 2101(a)(1)(B).
5. See 20 CFR §639.3(a)(1).
6. See 20 CFR §639.3(a)(1).
7. 20 CFR §639.3(a)(1).
8. 20 CFR §639.3(a)(1).
9. See 20 CFR §639.3(a)(2).
10. See 29 U.S.C. §2101(a)(5).
11. See 20 CFR §639.3(e).
12. See 20 CFR §639.3(e).
13. 20 CFR 639.1(c).
14. See 29 U.S.C. §2101(a)(6).
15. See 20 CFR §639.3(f).
16. See 29 U.S.C. §2101(b)(2); 20 CFR 639.3(f).
17. See 20 CFR §639.3(h).
18. See 29 U.S.C. §2101(a)(8).
19. See 20 CFR §639.3(h).
20. See 29 U.S.C. §§2101(a)(2), 2101(a)(3).
21. See 29 U.S.C. §2101(a)(2).
22. See 29 U.S.C. §§2101(a)(2), 2101(a)(3), 2101(a)(6).
23. See 29 U.S.C. §2101(a)(3).
24. See 20 CFR §639.3(i)(1).
25. See 20 CFR §639.3(i)(2).
26. See 20 CFR §639.3(i)(3).
27. See 20 CFR §639.3(i)(4).
28. See 20 CFR §639.3(i)(5).
29. See 20 CFR §639.3(i)(6).
30. See 20 CFR §639.3(i)(7).
31. See *Fort Halifax Packing Co. Inc., v. Coyne*, 482 U.S. 1 (1987).
32. See 20 CFR §§639.1(a), 639.2.
33. See 29 U.S.C. §2106.
34. See 29 U.S.C. §2102.
35. See 20 CFR §639.5(a).
36. See 20 CFR §639.5(a).
37. See 20 CFR §639.5(a)(1)(i).
38. See 20 CFR §639.5(a)(1)(ii).
39. See 20 CFR §639.5(a)(1)(ii).
40. 20 CFR §639.5(b).
41. 20 CFR §639.5(c).
42. 20 CFR §639.5(d).
43. 29 U.S.C. §2102(a).
44. See 20 CFR §639.4(a).
45. See 20 CFR §639.4(b).

46. See 20 CFR §639.4(b).
47. 20 CFR §639.4.
48. Id.
49. Id.
50. See 29 U.S.C. §2102(a); 20 CFR §639.6.
51. See 20 CFR §639.8.
52. See 20 CFR §639.8.
53. 20 CFR §639.7(a)(1).
54. 20 CFR §639.7(a)(2).
55. 20 CFR §639.7(a)(3).
56. See 20 CFR §639.7(c).
57. Id.
58. See 20 CFR §639.7(d).
59. Id.
60. See 20 CFR §639.7(e).
61. Id.
62. See 20 CFR §639.7(f).
63. 29 U.S.C. §2102(b).
64. See 20 CFR §639.9(a).
65. See 29 U.S.C. §2102(b)(1).
66. See 29 U.S.C. §2102(b)(1); 20 CFR §639.9(a)(3).
67. See 20 CFR §639.9(a)(1).
68. See 20 CFR §§639.9(a)(1), 639.9(a)(2).
69. See 20 CFR §639.9(a)(4).
70. See 29 U.S.C. §2102(b)(2)(A); 20 CFR §639.9(b).
71. See 20 CFR §639.9(b).
72. See 20 CFR §639.9(b)(1).
73. See 20 CFR §639.9(b)(1).
74. See 20 CFR §639.9(b)(2).
75. See 20 CFR §639.9(b)(2).
76. See 29 U.S.C. §2102(b)(2)(B); 20 CFR §639.9(c).
77. See 20 CFR §639.9(c)(2).
78. See 20 CFR §639.9(c)(3).
79. See 20 CFR §639.9(c)(4).
80. See 20 CFR §639.10(b).
81. 20 CFR §639.10(a).
82. 20 CFR §639.10(b).
83. See 29 U.S.C. §2104(a)(5).
84. See *United Food & Commercial Workers Union Local 751 v. Brown Group, Inc.*, 517 U.S. 544 (1996).
85. 29 U.S.C. §2104(a)(5).
86. See 29 U.S.C. §2107; 20 CFR §639.1(d).
87. See *North Star Steel Co. v. Thomas*, 515 U.S. 29 (1995).
88. *Id.*
89. See 29 U.S.C. §2104(a)(5).
90. See *Bentley v. Arlee Home Fashions, Inc.*, 861 F. Supp. 65 (E.D. Ark. 1994). See 20 CFR §639.1(d).
91. See 29 U.S.C. §2101(a)(1).
92. See 29 U.S.C. §2101(a)(1)(B).
93. See 29 U.S.C. §2101(a)(2).
94. See *North Star Steel Co. v. Thomas*, 515 U.S. 29 (1995).
95. See 29 U.S.C. §2101(a)(5); see also Employment law Checklists and Forms § 6-5.8 (D)(3), (4).

96. See 29 U.S.C. §2101(a)(1)(A), (B).
97. *Burnsides v. M.J. Optical, Inc.*, 128 F.3d 700 (8th Cir. 1997).
98. *United Mine Workers International Dist. 28 v. Harman Mining Corp.*, 780 F. Supp. 375 (W.D. Va.1991), recall within six months, *Martin v. AMR Services Corp.*, 877 F. Supp. 108, 117 (E.D.N.Y. 1995), job transfers, *Alter v. SCM Office Supplies, Inc.*, 906 F. Supp. 1243, 1250 (N.D. Ind. 1995), or retraining or job search activities, Employment Law Checklists and Forms § 6-5.8 (E)(2).
99. Employment Law Checklists and Forms § 6-5.8 (H)(7).
100. *Teamsters Local Union 413 v. Dirver's, Inc.*, 101 F.3d 1107 (6th Cir. 1996); Employment Law Checklists and Forms § 6-5.8 (H).
101. *Williams v. Phillips Petroleum Co.*, 23 F.3d 930, 936-37 (5th Cir. 1994).
102. See 20 CFR §639.3(a)(1).
103. See 29 U.S.C. §2104(b).
104. 29 U.S.C. §2104(b).
105. See *Monongahela Steel Co.*, 265 NLRB No. 262 (1982).
106. See 29 U.S.C. §§2104(a)(1)(A), 2104(a)(1)(B).
107. See 29 U.S.C. §2104(a)(1)(B).
108. See 29 U.S.C. §2104(a)(3).
109. See 29 U.S.C. §2104(a)(3).
110. See 29 U.S.C. §2104(a)(4).
111. See *Finnan v. L.F. Rothschild & Co.*, 726 F.Supp. 460, 464-65 (S.D.N.Y. 1989).
112. See 29 U.S.C. §2104(a)(7).

Chapter 19

The Fair Labor Standards Act

In General

19-1. What is the purpose of the Fair Labor Standards Act?

19-2. Who enforces the FLSA?

19-3. Who is covered by the FLSA?

19-4. What employees are exempt from the requirements of FLSA?

Requirements

19-5. What are the basic requirements of the FLSA?

Minimum Wage

19-6. What is the minimum wage?

19-7. What categories of employees may be paid less than minimum wage?

19-8. What other considerations apply to minimum wage calculation?

OVERTIME

19-9. What constitutes work under the FLSA?

19-10. What is the "regular rate" used for overtime calculation?

19-11. What payments are included in calculating the regular rate?

19-12. What payments may be excluded from the regular rate?

19-13. How is overtime calculated?

19-14. Can an employer allow an employee time off in lieu of overtime pay?

19-15. Can an employee voluntarily waive overtime pay?

CHILD LABOR

19-16. What are the restrictions on child labor?

RECORD-KEEPING

19-17. What records must an employer keep under FSLA?

IN GENERAL

19-1. What is the purpose of the Fair Labor Standards Act?

The Fair Labor Standards Act (FLSA), originally enacted in 1938, regulates the hours and wages of employees engaged in interstate commerce.[1] Specifically, the FLSA requires employers subject to its provisions to pay a minimum hourly wage, and to pay overtime compensation for hours worked over the statutory maximum.[2] The FLSA also includes provisions prohibiting oppressive child labor.[3]

The FLSA does not regulate issues such as pay raises, vacation, holiday, severance or sick pay, or premium pay for holiday or weekend work. These may be covered by applicable state or local law. If so, the employer must comply with the state or local law, since the FLSA does not preempt state and local laws that provide greater benefits to employees.[4]

19-2. Who enforces the FLSA?

The FLSA is administered by the Wage and Hour Division within the U.S. Department of Labor (DOL). The Wage and Hour division has one chief Administrator primarily responsible for enforcing the FLSA. The Administrator is appointed by the President and confirmed by the Senate.[5] The Wage and Hour division has regional offices around the country. The DOL may directly sue an employer for violations, but individual employees may also sue. There is a two year statute of limitations on suits for back wages, unpaid overtime, or liquidated damages, but if the violation was willful, the statute of limitations is extended to three years.[6]

INDIVIDUAL PLAINTIFFS

An individual employee, or group of employees, may sue an employer to recover back wages and overtime compensation as well as an additional, equal amount in liquidated damages. Individual plaintiffs may join together in a collective action. Employees must choose to opt into an FLSA suit to be bound by the judgment. The decision to opt in must be filed with the court.[7]

The FSLA also prohibits retaliation against an employee for filing a complaint or asserting his rights under the FLSA. The U.S. Tenth Circuit Court of Appeals has ruled that an employee discharged in retaliation for complaining about FLSA violations was entitled to back pay and liquidated damages.[8]

THE SECRETARY OF LABOR

When the Secretary of Labor sues an employer directly, civil penalties may be assessed. These penalties can be up to $1000 per violation against a repeated or willful violator of the minimum wage or overtime provisions of the FSLA. Violations of the child labor provisions of the FSLA can bring civil penalties of up to $10,000 per employee who was the subject of the violation. In determining the size of the civil penalties, the size of the employer and the gravity of the violation are considered. The Secretary can also pursue an action to enjoin an employer from violating the FSLA, and can pursue remedies, such as back wages, on behalf of the employee. If the Secretary files suit, the individual employee's right to action terminates, unless the Secretary later dismisses the action.[9]

19-3. Who is covered by the FLSA?

The FLSA provides two basic means of coverage. It provides for coverage of individual employees, and it provides "enterprise" coverage for all the employees in a business who are not otherwise exempt. If the enterprise coverage applies, individual employee coverage is irrelevant. The following provisions set forth the basics for making coverage determinations.

COVERED ENTERPRISE

Any employee of an enterprise is covered as long as the enterprise has annual sales of at least $500,000. An enterprise is defined as an entity with a common business purpose, engaged in commerce or the production of goods in interstate commerce, or which has employees handling, selling, or otherwise working on such goods or materials. Certain entities may qualify as covered enterprises even if they do not meet the dollar sales standard. These include enterprises engaged in operation of a hospital, institution for the care of the sick, aged or mentally ill, a school for handicapped or gifted children, a preschool, elementary or secondary school, an institution of higher learning, or the activity of a public agency.[10]

INDIVIDUAL EMPLOYEES

The FLSA also provides for coverage of an employee on an individual basis, without regard for the nature of the enterprise. If an employee is engaged in interstate commerce, or in the production of goods for interstate commerce, he is covered by the FLSA, even though other employees of the same employer are not.[11]

This is very broad coverage. An employee may be engaged in commerce because he uses instrumentalities of interstate commerce, which would include bridges, ships and roads, even if that use is confined to one state. If an employee's work involves handling goods that will travel or have traveled in interstate commerce, he is covered.[12] The Supreme Court has said that the test is "whether the work is so directly and vitally related to the functioning of and instrumentality or facility of interstate commerce as to be, in practical effect, a part of it, rather than isolated, local activity."[13]

The definition of "production" of goods for commerce is also broad. Even steps in preparation of a product for commerce, or functions "closely related or directly essential" to production are considered production. Employees in small businesses that do interstate business are therefore usually covered. Indeed, employees of such enterprises who do not do direct production work, but whose work is related to production, are usually covered. This is generally seen to include workers in maintenance, custodial and clerical functions.[14]

EMPLOYEE DEFINED

The FLSA definition of an employee is very simple, and very broad: "any individual employed by an employer."[15] The FSLA goes on to include specifically certain employees of the U.S. government, U.S. Post Office, and certain state employees. The FLSA does not require a formal employment relationship; any time an employer "suffers or permits" an individual to work, an employment relationship results.[16] This is true even if the parties never intended an employment relationship.[17]

An employer's labeling a worker as an *independent contractor* is not enough to remove the person from FLSA protection, if the FLSA test of employee status is met. This test involves balancing a number of factors, including:

1. the employer's right to control the worker's activities,

2. the degree to which the worker's opportunity for profit depends on his own managerial skill,

3. whether the worker has invested in his own equipment or hired helpers,

4. whether the service rendered requires special skill,

5. the degree of permanence of the working relationship, and

6. whether the service rendered is an integral part of the alleged employer's business, or an ancillary function.[18]

A person who works without any compensation agreement and voluntarily works for his or her own advantage in order to learn a skill or trade is a *trainee*, and not an employee. The DOL has set up a six part test to determine if a worker is a trainee or an employee:

1. whether the training is similar to that of a vocational school,

2. whether the training is for the benefit of the trainees,

3. whether the trainees displace regular employees and work under their observation,

4. whether the employer derives any advantage from the training,

5. whether the trainees are entitled to a job at the end of the training, and

6. whether the employer and the trainee understand that the trainee is not entitled to wages during the training.

These factors are not all inclusive, and the totality of the circumstances should be considered in determining whether an individual should be treated as a trainee.[19]

EMPLOYER DEFINED

The FLSA's definition of an employer is "anyone directly or indirectly acting in the interest of an employer in relation to an employee." Public agencies are expressly included, but labor organizations and their officers are excluded (other than in relation to employees of the union itself). This definition is general enough to include corporate officers as individuals, providing they control employee working conditions and company policy.[20]

A single individual may be an employee of more than one employer at the same time. Whether the employment is a joint employment depends on the facts of each case. If the various employers are entirely independent, they may disregard work performed for the other employers during the workweek. However, if the employers are not completely disassociated, all work in the workweek must be considered as one employment. This means that hours from all joint employers must be added together to determine total hours for the week for overtime purposes.[21]

19-4. What employees are exempt from the requirements of FLSA?

All of the previous discussion in this chapter involved the rules for employers and employees covered by the FSLA. The FLSA also provides for numerous exemptions.[22] If an employee is exempt from the FSLA by the nature of his work, the employer need not pay minimum wages and overtime. The U.S. Supreme Court has held that the employer has the burden of proving the exemption, and that the exemptions are to be narrowly construed.[23]

WHITE COLLAR EXEMPTIONS

Employees who are employed in a "bona fide executive, administrative or professional capacity" are exempt from the requirements of the FSLA. These are perhaps the most common exemptions. In order to qualify for any of these three exemptions, the employee must be paid a specified minimum amount on a salary basis, and his work must consist of specified categories of duties. The fact that an employee is well paid or holds a special job title will not qualify him or her for the exemption.[24] For each of the exemptions, if the employee is paid over $250 per week in salary, a "short test" may be applied.

Executive employees. An exempt executive employee is one who is paid over $155 per week and: (1) manages the enterprise, or a customarily recognized department or subdivision of it; (2) directs the work of two or more people; (3) has the authority to hire and discharge; (4) regularly uses discretionary power in the job; and (5) devotes no more than 20% (40% if in a retail or service enterprise) of the workweek to activities not described above. This final requirement means that employers must monitor the amount of "nonexempt" work done by employees for whom they claim the exemption.[25]

Administrative employees. An exempt administrative employee is paid over $155 per week and: (1) performs nonmanual or office work directly related to management policies or business operations; (2) customarily and regularly uses discretion and independent judgment in performing the job; (3) regularly and directly assists a proprietor or executive, or performs technical work or special projects with only general supervision; and (4) devotes no more than 20% of the workweek to activities not described above. The critical issue in administrative exemptions is often whether the employee does office or nonmanual work, as opposed to production work.[26]

Professional employees. An exempt professional is an employee paid at least $170 per week salary, whose duties consist of: (1) work requiring knowledge customarily acquired over a prolonged course of specialized instruction and study; creative work in an artistic endeavor; teaching or tutoring; or theoretical or practical application of highly specialized computer knowledge; (2) consistent use of discretion or judgment; (3) work that is predominately intellectual, and cannot be standardized in terms of output over time; and (4) no more than 20% nonexempt work in a given workweek.[27]

Combination exemptions. The employer may combine exempt duties from more than one "white collar" category to create a combination exemption for an employee. For example, an employee whose primary duties include both professional and administrative work, who may not qualify for either exemption alone, may receive a combination exemption. Employees may also be exempt by combination of "white collar" duties with duties from other types of exemptions, but if the salary and duties tests are different, they must qualify for the stricter of the two requirements.[28]

"Short test" for exemption. White collar employees paid a salary of over $250 per week may qualify for exemption based on a "short test." The short test simplifies the analysis of the duties of the employee. For executive exemptions, the employee need only manage the enterprise, or a customarily recognized department or subdivision of it, and direct the work of two or more employees. For administrative exemptions, the employee must perform nonmanual office work directly related to management policies or business operations, and exercise discretion and independent judgment. For professional exemptions, the employee be engaged in work requiring knowledge customarily acquired by a prolonged course of study, or work involving theoretical or practical application of highly specialized knowledge of computer systems.[29]

"Salary basis" requirement. Under either the long test or the short test, an employee must be paid on a salary basis. This means that the employee must receive a predetermined amount constituting all or part of his compensation, which is not subject to reduction based on the quality or quantity of work performed. Deductions for absences of less than a full day violate the definition of salary basis, and can cause the employer to lose the exemption. The Supreme Court has held that an employee is not paid on a salary basis if the employer takes improper deductions in actual practice, or if it has a policy that creates a significant likelihood of such deductions.[30] DOL regulations do allow for a "window of correction" where an employer who has inadvertently made an improper deduction may reimburse the employee and not lose the exemption.[31]

OTHER EXEMPTIONS

The FLSA provides for a long list of less common exemptions. An exhaustive review of all of these provisions would be outside the scope of this chapter, but a brief summary of some relatively common ones follows.

Computer systems employees. Computer analysts, program-mers, and software engineers who meet either the white collar professionals salary requirement or are paid an hourly rate over $27.63 may be exempt. To qualify the computer professional must be engaged in either (1) the application of systems analysis techniques and procedures to determine hardware, software or system functional specifications; (2) the design, development, documentation, analysis, creation or testing of computer systems or programs; or (3) some combination of those duties.[32]

Retail and service employees. If a retail or service establish-ment employee's regular rate of pay is greater than 1.5 times the statutory minimum wage, and more than half of the employees compensation comes from commissions, the employee may be exempt from the FSLA's general overtime provisions.[33]

Outside salespeople. Outside salespeople, as defined in DOL regulations, are exempt from the FSLA's overtime and minimum wage provisions.[34] The regulations define an exempt outside salesperson as any employee who: (1) is employed for the purpose of, and who is customarily and regularly engaged away from his or her employer's place of business in making sales or obtaining orders or contracts for services; and (2) whose hours spent in work other than the above do not exceed 20% of the hours worked in the workweek by nonexempt employees of the employer. The regula-tion also specifies that work incidental to and in conjunction with the employee's own outside sales activity is regarded as exempt work.[35]

Hospital employees. Hospital and residential care enterprises may, pursuant to a prior agreement with their employees, use a fixed work period of 14 consecutive days in lieu of the workweek for overtime calculation. They must pay time and one half the regular rate for hours over 8 in a workday and 80 in the 14 day period.[36]

Miscellaneous exemptions. Finally, specific exemption rules exist for the following categories of employees, the details of which are beyond the reach of this chapter:

•   Transportation employees, including employees of common carriers, taxicab drivers and rail and air carrier employees.[37]

•   Domestic service employees, including babysitters and companion services workers.[38]

- Newspaper and communications industry employees, including telephone operators, certain radio and television employees, and newspaper delivery employees.[39]

- Fishing and seafood industry employees involved in catching or harvesting aquatic products, or the processing or packing of such products.[40]

- Forestry employees of small forestry and logging enterprises.[41]

- Employees receiving remedial education from the employer are exempt for up to 10 hours per workweek from the overtime provisions of the FSLA. This applies only to employees who lack a high school diploma or eighth grade education, where the employer is providing remedial basic education, not job specific training.[42]

REQUIREMENTS

19-5. What are the basic requirements of the FLSA?

The FLSA has three basic requirements: (1) that employees be paid a statutory minimum wage, (2) that employees be paid an overtime premium for hours over a statutory maximum, and (3) restrictions on oppressive child labor. These requirements are subject to a variety of exceptions, and certain categories of employees are exempt from the requirements altogether.

MINIMUM WAGE

19-6. What is the minimum wage?

Beginning September 1, 1997, the federal minimum wage became $5.15 per hour. Some states, however, have their own minimum wage laws, and employers must comply with these state laws if they provide for a higher minimum wage. Certain exceptions to minimum wage provisions of FLSA allow workers to be paid a subminimum wage. The subminimum wage provisions give discretion to the Secretary to approve such arrangements.

19-7. What categories of employees may be paid less than minimum wage?

Certain students, handicapped employees, and new hires may be paid less than the minimum wage.

Students. A full time student working in a retail or service establishment, agriculture or institution of higher learning may be paid at 85% of the statutory minimum wage.[43] The Secretary of Labor must issue a certificate authorizing the arrangement. The employer may apply for the certificate at a regional office of the Wage and Hour Division.[44] Generally, the student may not work at this rate more than 20 hours per week when school is in session, or 40 hours per week when school is not in session.[45]

Handicapped employees. Where an employee's disability reduces his work performance, the employer may receive a certificate to pay less than the minimum wage.[46] In the case of handicapped employees, the employer must pay one and one half times the regular rate for hours over 40 in a week, unless the Secretary issues a certificate relieving the employer from the overtime pay obligation.[47]

New hires. Employees under the age of 20 may be paid not less than $4.25 per hour for the first 90 days on the job. Employers may not displace regular employees to employ a worker at this wage.[48]

19-8. What other considerations apply to minimum wage calculation?

Generally, employers may not make deductions other than local, state and federal payroll taxes from employee pay that would reduce the employee's regular wage below the statutory minimum. Tipped employees may be paid a separate, lower minimum wage, and given credit for their tips. The following considerations apply to minimum wage calculations.

Costs for uniforms. If the wearing of a clean uniform is required by law, by the employer or by the nature of the job, the cost of furnishing or maintaining uniforms may not be deducted from the employee's pay, if it would reduce the wages below the statutory minimum for overtime or minimum wages.[49]

Tip Credit. The FLSA sets the cash wage to be paid tipped employees at a set amount, then allows the employer to apply a credit toward the minimum wage for tips received. If the employee's tips plus the cash wage do not equal the minimum wage, the employer is required to make up the difference. The employer bears the burden of proving the amount of tips received for purposes of the credit.[50] A "tipped employee" is any employee engaged in an occupation where he or she customarily receives more than $30 per month in tips.[51] A compulsory charge for service, such as a restaurant charging a percentage of the bill, does not count as a tip. Employees must be allowed to retain all tips, either individually or through a tip pooling arrangement.[52]

Cost of food and lodging. The FLSA allows the employer to take a credit for the reasonable cost of food and lodging provided by the employer. This is generally interpreted to mean that the employer may not earn a profit on these credits. DOL regulations require the employer to give the employee a choice before taking the deduction.[53]

Maximum hours/overtime pay. The FLSA requires that employees who are not covered by an exemption be paid one and one half times their "regular rate" for all hours worked in excess of 40 in a workweek.[54] The definitions of the regular rate, hours worked and the workweek are further defined by the statute, regulations and case law. These definitions are critical in determining if an obligation to pay overtime has arisen, and how overtime is calculated.

OVERTIME

19-9. What constitutes work under the FLSA?

The U.S. Supreme Court has adopted a two part test to determine whether an activity is work covered by the FLSA. Under this analysis, an activity is work if it is: (1) controlled or required by the employer, and (2) pursued necessarily and primarily for the benefit of the employer and its business.[55] Since the FLSA defines "employ" to include "to suffer or permit to work," any time an employee is doing unrequested work with the knowledge of the employer, the employee is involved in worktime under the FLSA.[56] This rule also applies to work away from the employee's normal worksite, such as homework done with the employer's knowledge.[57] Under this rule, it is the employer's duty to stop the employee from doing work the employer doesn't want done.[58]

Bona fide meal periods are not worktime, as long as the employee is relieved completely from duty during the meal period. The FLSA does not mandate a particular length for meal periods, but DOL regulations suggest that 30 minutes or more is long enough to be a bona fide meal period.[59]

The FSLA does not require employees to be paid for absences from work for holidays, vacations or illnesses. These payments are a matter of agreement between the employer and the employee. These absences, even if paid, need not be counted as worktime for FLSA purposes.

On duty periods spent waiting for work are counted as worktime. Examples include a firefighter on duty at a station house, waiting for a call to come in, or an assembly line worker waiting for parts needed to perform his job.[60]

Preliminary and postliminary activities: commuting time. The Portal to Portal Act of 1947,[61] supplements the FLSA by providing that activities "preliminary" (before) or "postliminary" (after) the principal work activity the employee was hired to perform are not worktime except in two situations: (1) such activities are compensable by custom or practice, or (2) they are indispensable to the performance of the principal activity.

Under the Portal to Portal Act, time spent commuting to work is not worktime, but time spent traveling as part of the principal activity is.[62] For instance, where an employee is required to report to a central location to pick up tools and receive his assignment, the travel from that designated place to the worksite is work time.[63] One exception to this rule occurs when an employee who has gone home after completing a day's work is subsequently called out on an emergency basis. The employee should receive credit for all time traveling to the emergency work site.[64] Similarly, travel from home to work on a one day assignment to another city is work time. In this situation, the employer may deduct the amount of time the employee normally spends commuting, or the time spent traveling from home to a travel depot such as an airport or train station.[65]

Travel away from the employee's home community that cuts across the employee's workday is work time. The employee is simply substituting travel for other principal duties. DOL regulations also require employers to count travel away from the employee's home community on nonworking days as worktime if it occurs during the hours corresponding to the employee's regular work hours. For instance, an employee who works from 9 a.m. to 5 p.m. Monday through Friday, but is required to travel away from his community during these hours on Saturday must have the travel time credited as working hours.[66] If an employee requests permission to drive his personal vehicle instead of a public conveyance, the employer may count as hours worked either the time spent driving the personal car or the time the employee would have spent traveling on the public conveyance during working hours.[67]

The Portal to Portal Act was amended in 1996 to allow employers and employees to agree on the use of company vehicles for commuting without the commute being considered worktime.[68]

Attendance at lectures, meetings, training programs. Attendance at lectures, meetings, and training programs is not worktime if (1) it is in fact voluntary, (2) it is outside the employee's regular hours, (3) it is not directly related to the employee's job, and (4) the employee does not perform productive work for the employer during the meeting. If the employer requires attendance, even indirectly, or if training is designed to make the employee more effective in his job, attendance is compensable.[69]

19-10. What is the "regular rate" used for overtime calculation?

The FLSA requires that employees be paid overtime compensation at a rate of one and one half times their "regular rate" for hours worked over 40 in a workweek. The regular rate is initially defined as "all remuneration for employment paid to, or on behalf of, the employee."[70] This definition has been further defined by the Supreme Court as an hourly rate actually paid the employee for the normal, nonovertime workweek for which the employee is employed.[71] The workweek is defined by DOL regulation as any "fixed and regularly occurring period of 168 hours - seven consecutive 24 hour periods."[72] The regular rate, then, is a rate per hour for normal hours. This does not mean that employees must be paid per hour, only that a salary or other pay basis must be broken down to an hourly rate to calculate overtime. This is normally done by simply dividing the employee's total pay for a workweek by the number of hours worked during that workweek.[73] Hours may not be averaged across workweeks to avoid the 40 hour limit for regular pay.[74]

Certain types of payments to employees are to be included in deriving the regular rate (see Q 19-11), and others are excluded (see Q 19-12).

19-11. What payments are included in calculating the regular rate?

The following are included in calculating the regular rate.

Bonus and lump sum payments. Where a bonus payment is a lump sum payment paid without regard to hours worked, but considered part of an employee's regular pay, it must be added to the total remuneration for the workweek in calculating the regular rate. Examples of bonuses normally added to the regular rate include production bonuses, attendance bonuses, bonuses for taking undesirable work assignments, and bonuses for completing work quickly.[75]

Meals, lodging, and similar services. Meals, lodging, and services provided primarily for the employee's benefit and convenience must also be added to the regular rate at a reasonable cost basis.[76]

19-12. What payments may be excluded from the regular rate?

The following payments may be excluded from the regular rate.

Employee benefits. Employer payments to a pension plan or for life, accident or health insurance are not included in the regular rate calculation, as long as the plan has been formally adopted according to DOL regulations, and employees have notice of the plan.[77]

Vacations, leave and other hours not worked. Payments for hours not worked are generally excluded from the regular rate calculation, as long as they are approximately equal to the employee's normal earnings for comparable time periods.[78]

Expense reimbursement. Repayments to employees of expenses incurred by the employee on the employer's behalf, such as travel expenses, or expenses for work supplies for the employer, are not included in the regular rate computation.[79]

Employer gifts. Gifts, or payments in the nature of gifts' are excluded as long as they are not: (1) geared to wages or hours, (2) so substantial that employees consider the gift a payment of wages, or (3) paid pursuant to contract.[80]

Discretionary bonuses. Bonus payments in recognition of work performed may be excluded if the employer retains discretion over the amount to be paid and whether payment is made at all, the decision to pay is made near the end of the bonus period, and the employees have no contractual right to expect the payments regularly.[81]

Premium payments. Premium payments used to compensate employees for working beyond the normal workday or workweek may be excluded from the regular rate, and in fact may be taken as a credit towards overtime pay if the employee qualifies for overtime in that workweek.[82]

19-13. How is overtime calculated?

The FLSA does not mandate that employees be paid by the hour, or by any other particular method. Employers and employees are free to contract for the full gamut of possible pay methods, as long as the employer complies with the FSLA's overtime requirements. The calculation of overtime pay, however, varies with the pay method.

Hourly rate. If an employee is paid an hourly rate for regular hours, overtime calculation is very straightforward: hours over 40 must be paid at 1.5 times the regular hourly rate.[83]

Piece rate. When an employee is paid on a piece rate basis, the calculation becomes somewhat more cumbersome. Any of three methods may be used: (1) time and one half of the employee's regular rate, (2) piece and one half, meaning one and one half the piece rate for work performed during overtime hours, or (3) an average hourly rate, agreed upon by the employer and employee, representing a fair estimate of the employees actual average hourly earnings.[84]

Fixed salary: specified number of non overtime hours. If the pay method calls for a fixed salary for a certain number of non overtime hours, the regular rate is determined by dividing the fixed salary by the number of hours it intends to compensate. In an overtime workweek that regular rate is paid for the first forty hours and multiplied by 1.5 for all hours over forty.[85]

Fixed salary: fluctuating number of hours. Where the employer and employee agree that a fixed salary shall cover all hours worked in a week, no matter how many, the salary constitutes straight time compensation for all hours in the week. The employer must then pay at least one half the regular rate in addition for all hours worked over forty. The employer must also be careful that the fixed salary compensates the employee at a rate equal to or greater than the applicable minimum wage. In this pay scheme, the employee's regular rate will vary from week to week depending on the hours worked.[86]

Commissions. When an employee is paid commissions weekly, those commission payments are added to all other earnings for the workweek, and the total is divided by the number of hours worked to derive the regular rate. Overtime is then paid at a rate of one half that regular rate for hours over forty.[87] If commission payments cannot be allocated to particular workweeks, the employer may allocate the amount equally to each week or to each hour worked in the period for which the commission is paid.[88]

19-14. Can an employer allow an employee time off in lieu of overtime pay?

Generally, the FLSA requires overtime compensation to be paid on the regular payday covering the workweek in which the overtime was worked.[89] Except under certain very narrow circumstances, an employer may not give an employee time off in lieu of overtime. For most employers compensatory time off may only be permitted when it is taken in the same pay period in which the overtime was earned. Because overtime must be offset within a pay period, compensatory time is never allowed for employees paid weekly. Because an employer may never owe an employee overtime pay, time off plans require careful record keeping. Employees must have individual accounts showing the amount of overtime owed and the time credited to the account.[90]

19-15. Can an employee voluntarily waive overtime pay?

An employee covered by the Act may not waive his right to overtime or to minimum wage. Even individual employment contracts or collective bargaining agreements do not alter employees' basic rights under the FLSA.[91]

CHILD LABOR

19-16. What are the restrictions on child labor?

The FLSA contains the basic federal law against "oppressive child labor."[92] But child labor restrictions are different for agricultural and nonagricultural employment. The FSLA allows children over 16 to be employed in any non hazardous nonagricultural job. Hazardous nonagricultural jobs may not be performed by children under 18. DOL regulations define a lengthy list of hazardous occupations, ranging from mining to machine operations, logging and many more.[93]

14 and 15 year old children may work in certain jobs, as specified by the Secretary of Labor.[94] The positions must be nonhazardous as determined by the Secretary. The employment is allowed under four conditions: (1) employment must be outside regular school hours, except if the child is enrolled in a work training program; (2) the child may not work more than three hours on any school day and not more than eight hours on a nonschool day; (3) the child may not work more than 18 hours during a school week and 40 hours when school is not in session; and (4) all work must be performed between 7:00 a.m. and 7:00 p.m. during the school year. From June 1 to Labor Day the evening hours are extended to 9:00 p.m.[95]

Agricultural positions may be held by children under 16 outside of school hours. Generally, hazardous occupations such as driving a tractor are limited to those over 16. However, if the child is employed by a parent or a person standing in the place of a parent, on a farm owned by the parent, he may work in hazardous occupations despite his age.[96]

RECORD-KEEPING

19-17. What records must an employer keep under FSLA?

The FLSA requires every employer subject to its minimum wage and overtime provisions to make, keep and preserve certain records on employees. In addition, the employer must keep records on exempt employees so that the employer can prove the validity of the exemption. The FLSA does not dictate any particular format of record keeping, but the required information must clearly and accurately be recorded so that government inspectors can understand it. The records must generally reflect:

1. The employee's full name as used in Social Security records.

2. The employees current home address, including ZIP code.

3.   For employees under 19 years of age, the date of birth. For employees 18 years of age and younger, an age certificate, work certificate, or other proof of the employee's age.

4.   The sex of each employee and his or her occupation.

5.   The definition of the employee's normal workweek.

6.   Indication of the employee's regular rate for any week where overtime is owed.

7.   The number of hours for each workday and workweek.

8.   Total wages or earnings due for each workweek.

9.   The total additions to and deductions from the wages paid to each employee for each pay period.

10.   The total wages paid for each pay period.

11.   The date of any payments made and the pay period covered by those payments.[97]

Most of these records must be kept for at least three years. "Supplementary" records such as wage rate tables and "basic employment and earnings records," and records of deductions and additions to pay must be kept for two years.[98]

CHAPTER ENDNOTES

1.   29 U.S.C. §201 et seq.
2.   29 U.S.C. §§206, 207.
3.   29 U.S.C. §212.
4.   29 U.S.C. §218(a).
5.   29 U.S.C. §204(a).
6.   29 U.S.C. §255(a).
7.   29 U.S.C. §216(b).
8.   *Brown v. Pizza Hut of Am., Inc.*, 113 F.3d 1245 (10th Cir. 1997).
9.   29 U.S.C. §§216, 217.
10. 29 U.S.C. §§203(r), 203(s).
11. 29 U.S.C. §§206(a)(1), 207(a)(1).
12. 29 CFR §§776.10, 776.11.
13. *Mitchell v. C.W. Vollmer & Co. Inc.*, 349 U.S. 427, 429 (1955).
14. 29 U.S.C. §203(j).
15. 29 U.S.C. §203(e).
16. 29 U.S.C. §203(g).
17. *Usery v. Pilgrim Equip. Co. Inc.*, 527 F.2d 1308 (5th Cir. 1976).

18. *Real v. Driscoll Strawberry Assoc. Inc.*, 603 F.2d 748 (9th Cir. 1979).
19. *Reich v. Parker Fire Protection Dist.*, 992 F.2d 1023 (10th Cir. 1993).
20. 29 U.S.C. §203(d).
21. 29 CFR §791.2.
22. 29 U.S.C. §213.
23. *A.H. Phillips v. Walling Inc.*, 324 U.S. 490 (1945).
24. 29 CFR §541.
25. 29 CFR §541.1.
26. 29 CFR §541.2.
27. 29 CFR §541.3.
28. 29 CFR §541.600.
29. 29 CFR §§541.1(f), 541.2(e), 541.3(e).
30. *Auer v. Robbins*, 519 U.S. 452 (1997).
31. 29 CFR §541.118(a).
32. 29 U.S.C. §213(a)(17); 29 CFR §541.303(b).
33. 29 U.S.C. §207(ii).
34. 29 U.S.C. §213(a).
35. 29 CFR §541.5.
36. 29 U.S.C. §207(j), 29 CFR §778.601.
37. 29 U.S.C. §§213(b)(1), 213(b)(2).
38. 29 U.S.C. §213(a)(15).
39. 29 U.S.C. §§213(a)(8), 213(a)(10), 213(b)(9).
40. 29 U.S.C. §213(a)(5).
41. 29 U.S.C. §213(b)(28).
42. 29 U.S.C. §207(q); 29 CFR §778.603.
43. 29 U.S.C. §214(b).
44. 29 CFR §§519.3, 519.13.
45. 29 CFR §§519.6(j), 519.16(e).
46. 29 U.S.C. §214(c).
47. 29 CFR §525.12(e).
48. 29 U.S.C. §206(g).
49. 29 CFR §§531.3(d)(2), 531.35.
50. 29 U.S.C. §203(m), 29 CFR §531.53.
51. 29 U.S.C. §203(t).
52. 29 CFR §§531.52, 531.55.
53. 29 CFR §531.30.
54. 29 U.S.C. §207.
55. *Armour & Co. v. Wantock*, 323 U.S. 126 (1944).
56. 29 CFR §785.11.
57. 29 CFR §785.12.
58. 29 CFR §785.13.
59. 29 CFR §785.19.
60. 29 CFR §785.15.
61. 29 U.S.C. §§251-262.
62. 29 CFR §785.35.
63. 29 CFR §785.38.
64. 29 CFR §785.36.
65. 29 CFR §785.37.
66. 29 CFR §785.39.
67. 29 CFR §785.40.
68. 29 U.S.C. §254(a).
69. 29 CFR §§785.28, 785.29.
70. 29 U.S.C. §207.

71. *Walling v. Youngerman-Reynolds Hardwood Co. Inc.*, 325 U.S. 419 (1945).
72. 29 CFR §778.105.
73. 29 CFR §778.109.
74. 29 CFR §778.104.
75. 29 CFR §§778.209, 778.210.
76. 29 CFR §§778.216, 778.217.
77. 29 CFR §778.215.
78. 29 CFR§778.218.
79. 29 CFR §778.217.
80. 29 CFR §778.212.
81. 29 U.S.C. §207(e)(3)(a).
82. 29 CFR §§778.201, 778.206.
83. 29 CFR §778.110.
84. 29 CFR §§778.111, 778.418, 548.306.
85. 29 CFR §778.113.
86. 29 CFR §778.114.
87. 29 CFR §778.118.
88. 29 CFR §778.120.
89. 29 CFR §778.106.
90. 29 CFR §516.2.
91. *Brooklyn Sav. Bank v. O'Neil*, 324 U.S. 697 (1945).
92. 29 U.S.C. §212(c).
93. 29 CFR §570.31 et seq.
94. 29 U.S.C. §203(l).
95. 29 CFR §570.35(a)(1).
96. 29 U.S.C. §213(c)(2).
97. 29 CFR §516.1 et seq.
98. 29 CFR §§516.5, 516.6.

Chapter 20

National Labor Relations Act

In General

20-1. What is the National Labor Relations Act?

20-2. What is the NLRB?

20-3. What does the NLRB do?

20-4. Who is protected under the National Labor Relations Act?

20-5. Who is not covered under the National Labor Relations Act?

20-6. Who is a supervisor under the NLRA?

Unfair Labor Practices

20-7. What are unfair labor practices committed by employers?

20-8. What are unfair labor practices committed by unions?

20-9. How are unfair labor practice cases processed?

20-10. What remedies can be enforced against employers found guilty of committing an unfair labor practice?

20-11. What authority does NLRB have to secure injunctive relief from a court?

20-12. What defenses exist for unfair labor practice charges?

Union Organizing Under NLRA

20-13. How does a union organize a group of employees?

20-14. After losing an election, how soon can a union come back and try again?

20-15. What type of employer conduct is unlawful during a pending union representation election?

20-16. Once employees elect a union to represent them, how can they get rid of the union?

Union Representation and Collective Bargaining

20-17. What are the duties of an employer and a union under the NLRA with regard to collective bargaining?

20-18. What subjects must employers and unions address in negotiations?

20-19. What duty does an employer have to provide information requested by the union?

20-20. What type of conduct constitutes a violation of the duty to bargain?

20-21. What happens if both parties cannot reach an agreement?

IN GENERAL

20-1. What is the National Labor Relations Act?

The National Labor Relations Act (NLRA), which developed from three congressional enactments, is a federal law governing relations between labor unions and businesses engaged in inter-state commerce.[1] Initially, the Wagner Act of 1935 outlawed only employer unfair labor practices - such as interference with employ-ees' freedom to organize and bargain collectively, employer domi-nation of employee unions, anti-union discrimination, and refusal to bargain in good faith. The Taft Hartley Act of 1947, also known as the Labor Management Relations Act, added prohibitions against certain union conduct such as intimidation of employees, coercion or restraint of employees, refusal to bargain in good faith, and certain types of strikes, picketing and secondary boycotts. In 1959, the NLRA as we now know it was amended by the Landrum-Griffin Act, also known as the Labor-Management Reporting & Disclosure Act. The Landrum-Griffin Act was enacted to correct union abuses of the law, regulate internal union affairs, and ensure employees the right to decline to form, join or assist unions.

Overall, the NLRA establishes the right of employees to orga-nize and to bargain collectively with their employers or to refrain from all such activity. With its consolidated laws and their amend-ments, the NLRA was enacted to encourage the practice and procedure of collective bargaining in an attempt to reduce inter-ruptions in commerce caused by industrial strife. The historical roots and procedural results of the NLRA have led to the belief by many employers that the NLRA has a distinct "pro-union" slant - giving advantages to those wishing to unionize over those employ-ees who wish to refrain from doing so.

20-2. What is the NLRB?

The National Labor Relations Board is an independent federal agency created by the Wagner Act of 1935 to administer the National Labor Relations Act. The agency has two major, separate components. The Board itself has five members and primarily acts as a quasi-judicial body in deciding cases on the basis of formal records in administrative proceedings. Board members are ap-pointed by the President of the United States, with the consent of the Senate, to 5-year terms, with the term of one member expiring each calendar year. The General Counsel, also appointed by the President to a 4-year term with Senate consent, is independent from the Board and is responsible for the investigation and prosecution of unfair labor practice cases and for the general supervision of the NLRB field offices in the processing of such cases. Each regional office is headed by a regional director who is responsible for making the initial determination in cases arising within the region's geographical area.[2]

20-3. What does the NLRB do?

The NLRB has two principal functions: (1) to determine, through secret-ballot elections, whether appropriate groupings of employees wish to be represented by a union in dealing with their employer and if so, by which union; and (2) to prevent and remedy unlawful acts, engaged in by either employers or unions. The agency does not act on its own motion in either function. It processes only those charges of unfair labor practices and petitions for employee elections that are filed with the NLRB in one of its 52 regional, subregional, or resident offices. However, employers should be aware that once the General Counsel of the NLRB begins to investigate an unfair labor practice charge, the General Counsel is authorized to investigate like or similar conduct that occurred in the six months before the filing of the charge even though that conduct was not specifically mentioned in the charge as originally filed.[3]

20-4. Who is protected under the National Labor Relations Act?

The NLRA guarantees employees the right to organize and join unions, to bargain collectively through representatives chosen by a majority of employees in an appropriate bargaining unit, and to engage in other concerted activities for the purpose of collective bargaining or other mutual aid or protection or to refrain from any such activities.[4]

20-5. Who is not covered under the National Labor Relations Act?

Only "employees" are afforded coverage and protection under the NLRA. An employee is any individual who is employed by an employer who affects interstate commerce. However, the NLRA's definition of "employee" specifically excludes:

- Agricultural laborers;

- Domestic servants;

- Any individual employed by a parent or spouse;

- Independent contractors;

- Supervisors;

- Government employees; and

- Individuals employed by an employer subject to the Railway Labor Act - typically airline and railroad employees.[5]

20-6. Who is a supervisor under the NLRA?

The term "supervisor" means any individual who has the authority, in the interest of the employer, to hire, transfer, suspend, layoff, recall, promote, discharge, assign, reward, or discipline other employees, or responsibly to direct them, or to adjust their grievances, or effectively to recommend any such action as long as the exercise of such authority is not merely routine or clerical in nature, but requires the use of independent judgment.[6]

The actions of an employer's supervisor towards or involving a statutory employee or a labor organization constitutes a basis upon which the employer can be found to have committed an unfair labor practice, and for which the employer can be required to remedy the violation.

UNFAIR LABOR PRACTICES

20-7. What are unfair labor practices committed by employers?

The NLRA makes it an unfair labor practice for an employer to interfere with, restrain or coerce employees in the exercise of their rights under the NLRA to organize and join unions, to bargain collectively, and to engage in other concerted activities for the purpose of collective bargaining or other mutual aid or protection.[7] Types of employer conduct which violate this provision include: interrogating employees concerning union sympathies and activities, surveilling employees who are engaged in union activities, threatening reprisal for employees who engage in union activities or who support a union, promising benefits to employees who refrain from union support or union-related activity, or retaliating against employees for engaging in any protected activity.

It is an unfair labor practice for an employer to dominate or interfere with the formation or administration of a union or to contribute financial or other support to it.[8] This provision prohibits, among other things, the creation of a labor organization by the employer, as well as, employer formation of employee committees for the purpose of dealing with that committee concerning terms and conditions of employment.

The NLRA prohibits employers from discriminating against an employee to encourage or discourage union membership, activity, or support.[9] Typical violations under this provision include: discharging or disciplining union supporters because they are union supporters, providing benefits to employees who refrain from union activities or support, and any other discrimination in regard to hire or tenure of employment, or any term or condition of employment based on union support, activity, or refraining from such support.

Employers are prohibited from discriminating against an employee who files a charge or gives testimony under the NLRA.[10] Typical retaliatory employer conduct under this provision includes the discharge or discipline of employees who file unfair labor practice charges with the NLRB or give testimony to the NLRB or its agents.

Employers are also prohibited from refusing to bargain in good faith with the representative of its employees with regard to wages, hours, and other terms and conditions of employment, including the failure to timely provide information concerning any such matter that has been requested by a bargaining agent.[11]

20-8. What are unfair labor practices committed by unions?

The NLRA prohibits unions from restraining or coercing employees in the exercise of their right to join or assist a labor union or to refrain from doing so. Such prohibited conduct includes: physical or verbal threats of violence, actual violence, and threats to or action that does adversely affect an employee's job status or benefits the employee exercising a NLRA right. The NLRA also prohibits a labor organization from restraining or coercing an employer in the selection of its representative for collective bargaining or adjustment of grievances.[12]

Labor organizations are prohibited from causing or attempting to cause an employer to discriminate against an employee.[13] Such violations under this provision may include: union agreements with employers which unlawfully condition employment or job benefits on union membership, illegal hiring hall agreements and practices, or causing an employer to terminate or to reduce an employee's seniority or benefits because he engaged in any activity protected by the NLRA.

A union is prohibited from refusing to bargain in good faith with an employer about wages, hours and other conditions of employment if it is the representative of that employer's employees.[14] A union bargaining agent also has the obligation to provide an employer, upon the employer's specific request, information and/or data that is relevant to the bargaining process and/or to the processing of a grievance pursuant to a labor agreement with that employer.

The NLRA prohibits a labor organization from engaging in certain strikes or boycotts or taking other specified action in order to accomplish certain unlawful purposes or objectives.[15] Specifically, a union is prohibited from engaging in or inducing or encouraging any individual employed by any person (whether or not an "employer" under the NLRA) engaged in commerce or in an industry affecting commerce to engage in a strike, work stoppage or boycott. Also, a union is prohibited from threatening, coercing, or restraining any person engaged in commerce or in an industry affecting commerce where in either case an object is:

(1)   to force or require any employer or self-employed person to join any labor or employer organization or to enter into any agreement to cease or refrain from handling a product of or doing business with another employer;

(2)   to force or require any person to cease using, selling, handling, transporting, or otherwise dealing in the product of any other producer, processor, or manufacturer, or to cease doing business with any other person, or force or require any other employer to recognize or bargain with a labor organization as the representative of its employees unless such labor organization has been so certified under the NLRA;

(3)   to force or require any employer to recognize or bargain with a particular labor organization as the representative of its employees if another labor organization has been certified under the NLRA as the representative; and

(4)   to force or require any employer to assign particular work to employees in a particular labor organization or in a particular trade, craft, or class rather than to employees in another trade, craft, or class, unless such employer is failing to conform to an appropriate Board order or certification.

Unions are prohibited from requiring employees to pay excessive or discriminatory membership fees.[16]

The NLRA prohibits labor unions from causing or attempting to cause an employer to pay or agree to pay money or other things of value for services which are not performed or are not to be performed.[17]

Lastly, a labor organization that is not currently certified as the employees' representative is prohibited from picketing or threatening to picket an employer with a goal of obtaining recognition from the employer.[18]

20-9. How are unfair labor practice cases processed?

When an unfair labor practice charge is filed, the appropriate NLRB field office conducts an investigation to determine whether there is reasonable cause to believe the NLRA has been violated. If the Regional Director determines that the charge lacks merit, it will be dismissed if the charging party does not withdraw the charge. A dismissal may be appealed to the General Counsel's office in Washington, D.C. If the Regional Director finds reasonable cause to believe an unfair labor practice has been committed, a formal complaint is issued unless a voluntary settlement has first occurred.

If settlement efforts fail, the case goes to hearing before an NLRB Administrative Law Judge. The Administrative Law Judge holds an evidentiary hearing and thereafter issues a written decision that may be appealed to the five-Member Board in Washington for a final agency determination. The Board's decision is subject to review in a U.S. Court of Appeals. Depending upon the nature of the case, the General Counsel's goal is to complete investigations and, where further proceedings are warranted, issue complaints within 7 to 15 weeks from the filing of the charge. Of the total charges filed each year (about 35,000), approximately one-third are found to have merit as to one or more portions of the charged matters. Over 90% of the cases deemed to have merit are settled at one stage or another short of a final Board decision.[19]

20-10. What remedies can be enforced against employers found guilty of committing an unfair labor practice?

The NLRB has broad remedial authority under the NLRA, including the power to issue cease and desist orders, reinstate employees with or without back pay, reimburse employees for lost benefits, force an employer to post a notice, and force an employer to recognize and to bargain with the union.[20] Remedial authority of the Board under the NLRA also includes judicial injunctive relief in various situations. The remedial task of the NLRB is to take measures designed to restore the relationships that would have been had there been no unfair labor practice committed.[21] Because the NLRA is considered essentially remedial, however, the Board's remedies may not be punitive in nature.[22]

20-11. What authority does NLRB have to secure injunctive relief from a court?

The NLRA empowers the Board to petition a federal district court for an injunction to temporarily prevent unfair labor practices by employers or unions and to restore the status quo, pending the full review of the case by the Board.[23] In determining whether this provisions is appropriate in a particular case, the principal question is whether injunctive relief is necessary to preserve the Board's ability to effectively remedy the unfair labor practice alleged, and whether the alleged violator would otherwise reap the benefits of its violation.[24]

Under NLRB procedures, after deciding to issue an unfair labor practice complaint, the General Counsel may request authorization from the Board to seek injunctive relief. After considering documents submitted by the General Counsel, the Board votes on whether to authorize injunctive proceedings. If a majority votes to do so, the General Counsel, through his regional staff, files the case in the appropriate federal district court. The court may grant such temporary relief as it deems "just and proper." The order, subject to an appeal to a Court of Appeals, remains in effect while the Board fully adjudicates the merits of the unfair practice complaint or until the case is settled.

A mandatory duty is imposed on the NLRB to seek appropriate injunctive relief whenever a complaint is issued alleging certain forms of union misconduct, typically involving "secondary boycotts" and "recognitional picketing."[25] Finally, the Board may ask a Court of Appeals to enjoin conduct that the Board has found to be unlawful.[26]

20-12. What defenses exist for unfair labor practice charges?

There are numerous and varied defenses which can be utilized by an employer to avoid the determination that an unfair labor practice has been committed. The most common defense arises in response to an unfair labor practice charge alleging discrimination in regard to the hire or tenure of employment or any term or condition of employment to encourage or discourage membership in a labor organization.[27] In such a case, the employer's reason for the alleged discrimination will determine whether or not an unfair labor practice has been committed. Specifically, discrimination which is motivated by union animus or an anti-union purpose and has the foreseeable effect of either discouraging or encouraging union support or membership will likely constitute an unfair labor practice.

However, where it can be proven that employer conduct is motivated by legitimate and substantial business reasons and not by anti-union feelings, such conduct will not constitute an unfair labor practice. This is true even where the employer conduct does in fact encourage or discourage union membership or support. The NLRB has held that where the General Counsel makes a prima facie showing that protected employee conduct was a substantial or motivating factor in the employer's decision, the employer must prove that the same action would have been taken even absent the protected conduct.[28]

Under this approach, the General Counsel's prima facie case must show the existence of protected activity, that the employer had knowledge of such protected activity, and union animus. Once these elements are proven, the employer may rebut the prima facie case by showing that its actions were not based on prohibited motivations. Otherwise, the employer will have to demonstrate that the same employment action would have occurred for legitimate business reasons regardless of the employee's protected activity. This approach is applied in all cases alleging violations described above which are based on employer motivation.

An additional employer defense to unfair labor practice charges is the statutory six-month limitations period. The NLRA provides that "no complaint shall issue based on any unfair labor practice occurring more than six months prior to the filing of the charge with the Board."[29] This six month limit commences when notice of an adverse employment action is clearly and unequivocally communicated to the affected employee. Therefore, any conduct which occurred more than six months prior to the filing of a charge cannot be found to be an unfair labor practice. However, in appropriate situations evidence of those activities that occurred more than six months prior to the filing of a charge may be utilized to "explain" conduct that did occur within the time frame covered by the charge.

UNION ORGANIZING UNDER NLRA

20-13. How does a union organize a group of employees?

Once a union begins an organizing drive seeking to represent a particular group of employees, the entire process can take less than two months to unfold completely to a conclusion. In other instances, due to prolonged organizing, litigated issues involving the appropriate bargaining unit and/or the question of whether various individuals are supervisors, confidential employees or guards and the filing of unfair labor practice charges which can delay an election, the entire process could take years to resolve. The categories below outline the representational process from start to finish.

BARGAINING UNIT DETERMINATION

Under the NLRA, representatives selected for the purposes of collective bargaining by a majority of employees in a unit appropriate for such purposes, must be the exclusive representatives of all the employees in such unit.[30] The NLRB is primarily responsible for determining whether a bargaining unit is appropriate. The underlying concept historically used by the Board in determining if a unit is appropriate is "community interest" (i.e., those employees who share similar terms and conditions of employment). The typical criteria considered in making unit determinations are similar wages, benefits, working conditions, employee transfers and interchange, supervisors, integration of work product, and geographical location. The NLRB is not required to determine "the *only* appropriate unit, or the *ultimate* unit, or the most appropriate unit; the NLRA requires only that the unit be 'appropriate.'"[31]

Although the NLRA contains no set criteria outlining how determinations of appropriate bargaining units should be decided, the Board has made bargaining unit determinations by examining numerous factors, including:

- Extent and type of union organization of the employees;

- Bargaining history in the industry;

- Similarity of duties, skills, interests, and working conditions of the employees;

- Organizational structure of the company; and

- Desires of the employees.

Congress imposed some specific limitations relative to bargaining unit determinations:

- Professional employees may not be included in a unit with other employees unless a majority of the professionals vote for inclusion in the unit.[32]

- The Board may not decide that any craft unit is inappropriate on the ground that prior Board determinations established a different unit.[33]

- Guards may not be included in a unit with other employees, and any organization representing guards may not be affiliated with any other organization that admits other employees to membership.[34]

- The extent of union organization shall not be controlling in determining whether a unit is appropriate.[35]

TYPICAL BARGAINING UNITS

A brief listing of some common types of bargaining units follows:

- *Production and Maintenance Unit.* This is the kind of unit usually found in manufacturing facilities and is favored by the NLRB in industrial and similar establishments. Plant clerical employees who work with production employees are ordinarily included in this unit.

- *Craft Unit.* A craft unit is composed of a distinct and homogeneous group of skilled craftsmen, working as such, together with their apprentices and/or helpers.

- *Technical Unit.* It is composed of employees whose work is of a technical nature. These employees use specialized training, ordinarily obtained either in colleges or in technical schools.

- *Department Unit.* The NLRA sanctions a department unit within a plant where the work involved has been traditionally regarded as similar to crafts even though not requiring craft skills. Several examples of this type unit are foundry workers and powerhouse operators.

- *Office Clerical Unit.* The NLRB has consistently held that the interests of office clerical employees are different from those of other employees.

- *Guards.* The NLRA prohibits including in a unit any individual employed as a guard. Thus, guards must be in a separate unit limited to guards, and their bargaining agent is limited to a labor organization whose membership is limited to only guards.

- *Single v. Multi-Plant Units.* The NLRB relies upon the presumption that one plant of a multi-plant operation may be an appropriate unit. A unit may cover the employees in one plant of an employer, or it may cover employees in two or more plants of the same employer if the evidence overcomes the presumption.

A bargaining unit can include only persons who are employees as defined by the NLRA. In addition, the NLRB, as a matter of policy, excludes from bargaining units employees who act in a confidential capacity to a person or persons who exercise managerial functions in the field of labor relations. Examples of such matters include contract negotiations, disposition of grievances, rate changes and instructions regarding overtime allowances and earning adjustments.

SHOWING OF INTEREST THROUGH AUTHORIZATION CARDS

In order for a union to involve NLRB action in a representation election process, it must establish a "showing of interest." That showing of interest must establish that at least 30% of the total number of employees in the proposed bargaining unit that the union wishes to represent desires to be represented by the union. This procedure ensures that questions of representation brought in front of the NLRB are in fact serious enough to justify the expenditure of Board resources in processing a union's request for representation. The Board follows this procedure stringently, and such determinations concerning a union's showing of interest are done administratively and usually are not subject to litigation before the Board or Court review.

Most unions utilize authorization cards signed by interested employees to prove they have the 30% showing of interest necessary to move forward with the representation process. These authorization cards generally contain language stating that the employee who signs the card is authorizing the union to represent that employee for the purposes of collective bargaining. A "dual purpose" or membership card will contain additional language stating that the employee who signs the card is also applying for membership with the union. Once these cards are signed by employees, they do not go stale for one full year. During this time the union may continue to accumulate additional cards until they reach the necessary 30% level which will enable the union to trigger the NLRB election procedures.

Although 30% of cards is the minimum number for a showing of interest, most unions will not involve the NLRB until they have a 65%-75% level of cards signed. This higher number helps ensure that the union can successfully win an NLRB conducted election. However, once a union has obtained signed authorization cards from over 50% of the employees in an appropriate bargaining unit, it can demand recognition from the employer either verbally or in writing, and offer to prove its majority standing via a check of the cards. An employer is under no obligation to accept that demand for recognition. In order to avoid accidentally recognizing the union as the representative for any group of employees, it is important that all of an employer's managers and officials are aware that they should never examine nor accept any union proffered documentation, including authorization cards, to prove the union's recognition request. Accepting such documentation would likely eliminate the need for the union to win a NLRB conducted election.

During an organizing campaign, some employees will want to revoke signed authorization cards. While the union is under no obligation to return an authorization card if requested, an employee can neutralize the effect of the card by mailing (return receipt requested) or personally delivering a dated revocation letter to the union which specifically revokes the employee's authorization and/or application for membership. In case the authorization cards have already been taken to the NLRB, an employee should also send an identical letter to the appropriate NLRB office. However, it should be noted that it is an unfair labor practice for an employer to solicit or specifically request an employee to take such action or to provide clerical assistance to an employee for that purpose. Such a revocation letter may help relieve the employee of the responsibility and legal exposure which attaches to union membership.

VOLUNTARY RECOGNITION OR PETITION

Voluntary recognition is the process whereby an employer accepts the union as the representative of its employees without the benefit of an election to determine whether or not employees wish to be represented. This approach can only be utilized by an employer if the union has provided the Company with evidence - normally in the form of signed cards designating the union as their bargaining agent - that the union has been selected by more than 50% of the employees in a bargaining unit.

The more typical method to gain recognition is for a union to file an RC-Certification of Representation petition. The petition must be accompanied by documentary proof (usually authorization cards) showing that at least 30% of the employees in the proposed bargaining unit support the petition. The showing of interest submitted by the union is held in strict confidence by the NLRB, which is solely responsible for evaluating the sufficiency and validity of a union's showing of interest. An employer may question the validity of a showing of interest by alleging, for example, that the authorization cards were obtained by fraud, have forged signatures, or are from persons who are not employed by the Company. The Regional Director will investigate the charges and administratively determine, without a hearing, whether the employer's allegations are valid. The Region's decision on the showing of interest is not appealable.

An employer also may file a petition with the NLRB, referred to as an RM-Representation (Management Petition). An RM petition may be filed only after a union has made a demand upon the employer to be recognized as the employees' bargaining representative. When the employer files an RM petition, no showing of interest by the union is required.

HEARING OR CONSENT AGREEMENT

Once a petition is filed, the NLRB determines whether a question concerning representation exists, whether there is jurisdiction over the employer, whether a contract bar exists, whether the petitioning union is a bona fide labor organization, whether the petition for bargaining unit is an appropriate one, whether there are any substantial disputes concerning which employees are in the proposed unit, whether there are disputes as to who is eligible to vote, and whether an agreement to hold an election can be achieved promptly. A hearing to take evidence on any contested matters is scheduled immediately so that the petition can be processed promptly should the parties not reach overall agreement on the holding of an election.

A representation hearing is considered a non-adversarial investigatory proceeding, open to the public, at which evidence is presented by the parties on these issues in dispute. A verbatim transcript is made and each party to the proceeding has the right to appear in person, by counsel or by some other representative. Once the hearing is closed and if there are contested issues which have been developed during the hearing, the parties are given the opportunity to submit a post-hearing brief on the contested issues. The hearing officer thereafter submits a report to the Regional Director which consists of a summary of the evidence and an analysis of the issues presented. Thereafter, the Regional Director will issue a decision, or, in rare instances where a novel or an extremely complex issue is involved, transfer the matter to the NLRB itself for a decision. The decision will set forth the finding of facts and the conclusions of law involved and either direct that an election be held in the near future or dismiss the petition. The Regional Director's decision is subject to a discretionary, not mandatory, review by the NLRB which is generally limited to those rare instances where a novel issue is involved.

A hearing will not be necessary, of course, if the parties are able to reach agreement and resolve their differences. There are two different kinds of such agreements: one is called an Agreement for

Consent Election (Consent), and the other is called a Stipulation for Certification upon Consent Election (Stipulation). Both agreements resolve the wording of the ballot, the payroll period eligibility date, the election date, hours and location, and the appropriate bargaining unit. The Consent, however, vests final authority with the Regional Director (with limited review by the Board) to investigate and rule upon challenged ballots and objections to the conduct of the election. The Stipulation, by contrast, provides that the Board shall determine all election questions, including challenges and objections to the conduct of the election. Even where there is a Stipulation, however, the Regional Director will investigate a dispute for the Board and may issue a report and recommendations with respect to the disposition of the issues in question which is subject to a party's right to be reviewed by the NLRB. In either case, the election will be supervised by the regional office.

VOTER ELIGIBILITY LIST

Within seven days after the direction of an election has issued or the execution of an election agreement, the employer must furnish the NLRB with an alphabetical list of the employees eligible to vote and their home addresses. This list, known as the Excelsior list, should not include job classifications, titles, phone numbers, rates of pay, seniority or any other information. The list is made available to the union for use during its election campaign. An election will not be held any sooner than 10 days after the Excelsior list is received, and failure to furnish the list is a basis for setting aside an election.

NOTICE OF ELECTION

Shortly before employees are scheduled to vote, the NLRB will mail to the employer a Notice of Election. This is a blue and white poster that must be posted in a conspicuous location for at least 3 full workdays before 12:01 a.m. of the day of the vote. Failure to properly post this notice may be grounds for setting aside the results of an election in which the union has lost.

THE ELECTION

The election itself is conducted by an NLRB agent and varies in length depending on the number of eligible voters and the number of shifts involved. Each party to the election designates the specified number of observers allowed that party during the election. Under Board policy, the observers must be employees but do not have to be voters. Supervisors cannot be an observer.

The NLRB agent conducting the election will instruct the observers about their duties - identifying voters, checking names against the Excelsior list, challenging individuals if necessary, and assisting in counting the ballots. If an employee is ineligible to vote, he or she must be challenged when asking for a ballot. The NLRB agent will then permit the challenged employee to vote, but the ballot will be placed in an envelope and sealed, its status to be determined later, if necessary. If a prospective voter is not on the eligibility list, the NLRB agent should automatically challenge that individual, but if the agent fails to do so, the parties' election observers should do so.

TALLY OF BALLOTS AND CERTIFICATION

Unless it is decided before the election that the results must be sealed pending a Board or court determination, the ballots will be counted immediately after the polls close. To win representation rights, the union must receive a majority of the valid votes cast.

After counting the ballots, two documents will be prepared. One is a Tally of Ballots showing the results of the count, and a statement that the tabulation was accurate. The Tally will be signed and a copy will be served upon all parties. The Board agent will also prepare a Certification on Conduct of Election to be signed by the parties' observers. The Certification states that the election was conducted fairly and the secrecy of the ballot was preserved. If there is any question about the way in which the election was conducted, the Certification should not be signed. However, signing the Certification does not preclude a party from thereafter filing objections.

Finally, if the number of challenged ballots is sufficient to affect the results of the election, then the eligibility of the challenged voters will have to be resolved before the outcome can be ascertained. Some challenged ballots can be easily resolved at the tally by proving a voter's eligibility to cast a ballot. Other more complex challenges may have to be resolved at a later date.

OBJECTIONS

Within seven days after the Tally of the Ballots has been prepared, any objections to the election must be filed with the Regional Director, with copies served to the other parties. Objections may be based on the manner in which the election was held, or based on conduct which affected the results of the election. If the objections are sustained, the election will be set aside, and a new one will be conducted.

The Regional Director has the authority to conduct an investigation into the objections. If substantial factual issues exist, he may order a hearing. After completion of the investigation, the Regional Director's actions are determined by whether the election was a directed election, a Stipulation, or a Consent. Essentially, the Board or the Regional Director will resolve the objections and/or challenges. In either case, a decision will be rendered overruling the objections and certifying the results, or sustaining the objections, in whole or part, and setting the election aside.

If the union wins the election, the NLRB will certify it as the bargaining representative for the employees in the designated appropriate bargaining unit. There is no direct court review of the NLRB's representation determination. The employer may, however, refuse to bargain with the union, thereby committing an unfair labor practice which can then be reviewed by a United States Court of Appeals. If, on the other hand, the union loses the election, the NLRB will issue a Certification of Results.

20-14. After losing an election, how soon can a union come back and try again?

A union that files a petition for an election and subsequently withdraws that petition after a stipulated agreement or a decision and direction of election has been entered into, may not petition for an election in that same bargaining unit of employees for the following six months. However, when a union loses an election whose results have been certified, the NLRA will not permit another election to be conducted in the same bargaining unit within twelve months following the date of the first election. This "election bar rule" does not, however, preclude a union from attempting to organize employees, obtain signed authorization cards, or file a petition for an election during that same twelve month period.

20-15. What type of employer conduct is unlawful during a pending union representation election?

Once a union files a petition for a representation election, the time frame occurring after that petition is filed until the voting period ends on the election day is considered the "critical period." During this time frame, the employer's and the union's behavior can be raised as an objection to the election and potentially result in the election results being set aside. Specifically, conduct that would qualify as an unfair labor practice under the NLRA during this critical period would be a basis to invalidate the election. In addition, other less serious conduct which might not rise to the level of being an unfair labor practice will nevertheless be found to improperly affect the election results, and constitute a basis for rerunning the election.

The following are just a few examples of conduct which routinely are found to be election interference:

- announcing wage or benefit improvements when it is not the normal time frame for such improvements or the size of the improvement is greater than normal.

- promising or indicating that employees will receive new or better wages or benefits if the union is rejected.

- making a campaign speech on company time to assembled employees where any part of the speech occurs within the 24 hour period immediately before the time when the election polls are scheduled to open.

- using forged documents which voting employees are unable to recognize the propaganda for what it really is.

- reproducing any document that purports to be a copy of the Board's official ballot, other than one which is completely unmarked and unaltered in form and content and is clearly marked on its face as a sample ballot.

- permitting the circulation of anti-union propaganda at the company while rigidly enforcing a no-solicitation rule against the union.

- taking pictures or other forms of surveillance of employees engaged in receiving or distributing union literature or other union activity.

- a union waiving initiation fees for employees provided they sign authorization cards before election day.

- company officials/supervisors visiting employees at their homes.

- electioneering by any party to an election at or near the polling place including extraneous conversations with employees in the polling area engaged in by either union or company observers.

The NLRA does provide that employers may express their views, arguments and opinions regarding unions or representation by a union and such conduct shall not constitute an unfair practice if the employer's expressions do not contain any threat of reprisal or force, or promise of benefit.[36] In order for employer "expressions" to fall within this scope, they must not contain expressed or veiled threats of reprisal, or force or promise of benefit.

Thus, statements of historical fact with respect to benefits and conditions of employment already in place prior to the union's appearance are permissible. Also permitted are observations concerning prior activities of the union such as strikes, failed efforts to reach agreement on a labor agreement, rejection by other groups of employees to have or to continue to have this union be their representative, examples of specific restrictive agreement provisions the union has agreed to with other employers, the provisions of the union's constitution and by-laws to discipline and fine its members, the amount of periodic dues, fees and initiation fees charged by the union and other similar factual information.

20-16. Once employees elect a union to represent them, how can they get rid of the union?

The process which employees may follow when they no longer wish to be represented by a union is called decertification. Similar to the representation process, decertification requires a showing of interest of 30% of the employees in the bargaining unit who indicate that they no longer wish to be represented by their current union. Once this showing of interest is presented to the Board, a decertification petition may be filed and the Board will conduct a decertification election among the bargaining unit.

This decertification process can be very difficult for employees to utilize for several reasons. First, decertification petitions can only be filed during a specific window period preceding the expiration of a labor contract or after a labor agreement has expired with no written extension but prior to the execution of a new agreement. The window period for health care employees is between 120 days and 90 days before a contract expires; in all other industries, the window period falls between 90 days and 60 days before a contract expires. Decertification petitions filed outside of this window will not be processed by the NLRB.

Secondly, decertification is difficult because the NLRA forbids employers from assisting employees through this process. There-fore, employers may not obtain signatures for the showing of interest, file the paperwork with the NLRB, or otherwise help employees maneuver through the legal process of the decertifica-tion. Any such assistance on the part of the employer may invalidate a decertification petition. For these reasons, although many employees are unhappy with their union representation, successful decertification elections are less common than most people may expect.

Union Representation and Collective Bargaining

20-17. What are the duties of an employer and a union under the NLRA with regard to collective bargaining?

Under the NLRA, an employer and the certified representative of that employer's employees have an obligation to bargain in good faith.[37] This duty encompasses the duty to meet at reasonable times, confer in good faith with respect to wages, hours, and other terms and conditions of employment, and to reduce the negotiated agreement to writing upon request of either party. However, this duty does not require either party to agree to proposals or make any concessions.[38]

What does this duty to "bargain in good faith" really mean? There have been numerous and varying court decisions addressing the specific duties that employers and unions must fulfill. Al-though the NLRA does not specify how often or for what duration parties must meet, parties must negotiate with the view and intent of reaching an agreement if possible.[39]

20-18. What subjects must employers and unions address in negotiations?

Three categories of bargaining subjects exist: mandatory, permissive, and illegal. The NLRA compels collective bargaining with respect to mandatory subjects, those set out as "rates of pay, wages, hours of employment, or other conditions of employment," or as "wages, hours, and other terms and conditions of employment."[40]

Permissive subjects are those which the parties are free to bargain over if they wish even though they fall outside the category of mandatory subjects. Specifically, permissive subjects include the definition of the bargaining unit, the selection of a bargaining representative, the recognition clause, interest arbitration clauses, and clauses dealing with internal union affairs. Neither party can be forced to negotiate to an impasse over any permissible subject of bargaining.

Illegal subjects of bargaining include provisions for a closed shop, hiring hall provisions that would give preference to union members, or any clauses that would cause discrimination among employees or cause the union to breach its duty to represent employees.

20-19. What duty does an employer have to provide information requested by the union?

The duty to provide requested information to the union only exists once that union becomes the certified representative for a group of employees. Once a union is the chosen representative for employees, the collective bargaining process requires that an employer supply requested information to the union regarding the subjects at issue in negotiations or contract administration.[41]

This obligation, which applies to both employers and unions, includes the duty to promptly furnish to the requesting party pertinent and relevant bargaining information including all information which is relevant and necessary to the intelligent performance of a party's collective bargaining and contract administration duties.[42] The relevant and necessary standard is very liberally construed, typically encompassing all information directly related to the union's function as bargaining representative and appearing reasonably necessary for the performance of this function. Overall, requested information must be provided unless it plainly appears irrelevant. Information that is clearly relevant and necessary includes any information regarding wages, hours and working conditions of employees in the bargaining unit.

One employer defense for an unfair labor practice charge alleging a failure to provide requested information is that the union has waived its right to the information. The duty to furnish information exists independent of an agreement between the parties, but a union may waive its right to relevant and necessary information in a collective bargaining agreement. For such a waiver to be valid, however, the union must clearly and unmistakably bargain away its right to such information - waiver will not be established merely by silence in a collective bargaining agreement.

20-20. What type of conduct constitutes a violation of the duty to bargain?

Certain conduct can lead to a determination that one or both parties has committed an unfair labor practice by refusing to bargain. One example of prohibited conduct involves unilateral changes in wages, hours, working conditions and other terms of employment made by an employer during the course of collective bargaining or during the life of a collective bargaining agreement where such unilateral action has not been specifically granted to the employer under the terms of the collective bargaining agreement. Such changes, committed without negotiating with the union, are normally regarded as per se refusals to bargain.[43]

The exceptions to the unilateral employer action violation include impasse, necessity, and waiver. The impasse exception may be utilized when exhaustive good faith bargaining fails to completely resolve differences between the parties and the parties' positions become stalemated. Thereafter, the employer is free to make unilateral changes in working conditions consistent with its final offer that the union has rejected.[44] The necessity exception to a violation for unilateral changes is a narrow exception which applies to the issuance of particular work rules which effect the "protection of the core purposes" of the employer's business. In order to qualify for the exception, the unilaterally enacted rule must be "(1) narrowly tailored in terms of substance, to meet with particularity only the employer's legitimate and necessary objectives, without being overly broad, vague, or ambitious; and (2) appropriately limited in its applicability to affected employees to accomplish the necessarily limited objectives."[45] The waiver exception applies when a union is put on notice of an intended change and does not seek to bargain with the employer about that change.

Another per se violation of the duty to bargain occurs when an employer attempts to bargain directly with employees, which is referred to as "direct dealing." The NLRB has held that direct dealing evidences a lack of good faith in the duty to bargain. Other kinds of bargaining violations include a refusal to execute a written contract that has been agreed upon, or to confer or meet at reasonable times and places, and by insisting on bargaining over nonmandatory subjects.

20-21. What happens if both parties cannot reach an agreement?

In cases where exhaustive good faith bargaining fails to completely resolve differences between the parties and the parties' positions become stalemated, then an impasse occurs. Although there is no set standard in determining whether or not an impasse has been reached, the existence or non-existence of an impasse normally arises after negotiations have taken place for an extended period of time, and it becomes obvious that the negotiations have reached the point of a stalemate. Once an impasse occurs, the employer is free to make unilateral changes in working conditions consistent with its final offer that the union has rejected.[46]

Some factors enumerated by the NLRB in determining whether or not an impasse has been reached include:

- the good faith of the parties in negotiations;

- the length of the negotiations and the quantity of negotiation sessions conducted within that period;

- the importance of the issue or issues remaining;

- the contemporaneous understanding of the parties as to the state of the negotiations;

- the continuation of bargaining;

- anti-union sentiment evidenced by prior or concurrent acts; and

- the length of hiatus between bargaining meetings.

When an impasse is reached, the duty to bargain is suspended but not permanently terminated. Any changed condition making possible renewed successful negotiations will renew the parties' duty to bargain. For example, any change in the bargaining position of either party, a strike, or significant business change will signal a break in the impasse and reinstate the parties' duty to bargain with one another. Therefore, although an impasse in bargaining may lead to a strike, once the strike begins the parties are under a renewed duty to go back to the bargaining table. If it is then determined that even with the changed condition of the strike that the parties are still at impasse, the impasse will relieve the parties of their duty to bargain until another change in the bargaining position of either party makes possible renewed successful negotiations.

CHAPTER ENDNOTES

1. 29 U.S.C. §141 et seq.
2. *Fact Sheet on the National Labor Relations Board.*
3. *Fact Sheet on the National Labor Relations Board.*
4. 29 U.S.C. §157.
5. 29 U.S.C. §§152(2), 152(3).
6. 29 U.S.C. §152(11).
7. 29 U.S.C. §158(a)(1).
8. 29 U.S.C. §158(a)(2).
9. 29 U.S.C. §158(a)(3).
10. 29 U.S.C. §158(a)(4).
11. 29 U.S.C. §158(a)(5).
12. 29 U.S.C. §158(b)(1).
13. 29 U.S.C. §158(b)(2).
14. 29 U.S.C. §158(b)(3).
15. 29 U.S.C. §158(b)(4).
16. 29 U.S.C. §158(b)(5).
17. 29 U.S.C. §158(b)(6).
18. 29 U.S.C. §158(b)(7).
19. *Fact Sheet on the National Labor Relations Board.*
20. 29 U.S.C. §§160(a), 160(c).
21. *Franks v. Bowman Transp. Co. Inc.*, 424 U.S. 747 (1976).
22. See *Phelps Dodge Corp. v. NLRB*, 313 U.S. 177 (1941).
23. 29 U.S.C. §160(j).
24. *Fact Sheet on the National Labor Relations Board.*
25. 29 U.S.C. §160(l).
26. 29 U.S.C. §160(e).
27. See 29 U.S.C. §158(a).
28. *Wright Line, Wright Line Div.*, 251 NLRB 1083 (1980).
29. 29 U.S.C. §160(b).
30. 29 U.S.C. §159(a).
31. *Morand Bros. Beverage Co.*, 91 NLRB 409, 418 (1950) (emphasis original).
32. 29 U.S.C. §159(b)(1).
33. 29 U.S.C. §159(b)(2).
34. 29 U.S.C. §159(b)(3).
35. 29 U.S.C. §159(c)(5).
36. 29 U.S.C. §158(c).

37. 29 U.S.C. §158(d).
38. *NLRB v. Tomco Communications, Inc.*, 567 F.2d 871 (9th Cir. 1978).
39. *NLRB v. Highland Park Mfg. Co.*, 110 F.2d 632 (4th Cir. 1940).
40. 29 U.S.C. §§159(a), 158(d).
41. *NLRB v. Truitt Mfg. Co.*, 351 U.S. 149 (1956).
42. *NLRB v. Acme Indus. Co.*, 385 U.S. 432 (1967).
43. *NLRB v. Katz*, 369 U.S. 736 (1962).
44. *NLRB v. Katz*, 369 U.S. 736 (1962).
45. *Peerless Publications*, 283 NLRB 334 (1987).
46. *NLRB v. Katz*, 369 U.S. 736 (1962).

Equal Employment Opportunity is

THE LAW

Employers Holding Federal Contracts or Subcontracts

Applicants to and employees of companies with a Federal government contract or subcontract are protected under the following Federal authorities:

RACE, COLOR, RELIGION, SEX, NATIONAL ORIGIN

Executive Order 11246, as amended, prohibits job discrimination on the basis of race, color, religion, sex or national origin, and requires affirmative action to ensure equality of opportunity in all aspects of employment.

INDIVIDUALS WITH DISABILITIES

Section 503 of the Rehabilitation Act of 1973, as amended, prohibits job discrimination because of disability and requires affirmative action to employ and advance in employment qualified individuals with disabilities who, with reasonable accommodation, can perform the essential functions of a job.

VIETNAM ERA AND SPECIAL DISABLED VETERANS

38 U.S.C. 4212 of the Vietnam Era Veterans Readjustment Assistance Act of 1974 prohibits job discrimination and requires affirmative action to employ and advance in employment qualified Vietnam era veterans and qualified special disabled veterans.

Any person who believes a contractor has violated its nondiscrimination or affirmative action obligations under the authorities above should contact immediately:

The Office of Federal Contract Compliance Programs (OFCCP), Employment Standards Administration, U.S. Department of Labor, 200 Constitution Avenue, N.W., Washington, D.C. 20210 or call (202) 219-9430, or an OFCCP regional or district office, listed in most telephone directories under U.S. Government, Department of Labor.

Private Employment, State and Local Government, Educational Institutions

Applicants to and employees of most private employers, state and local governments, educational institutions, employment agencies and labor organizations are protected under the following Federal laws:

RACE, COLOR, RELIGION, SEX, NATIONAL ORIGIN

Title VII of the Civil Rights Act of 1964, as amended, prohibits discrimination in hiring, promotion, discharge, pay, fringe benefits, job training, classification, referral, and other aspects of employment, on the basis of race, color, religion, sex or national origin.

DISABILITY

The Americans with Disabilities Act of 1990, as amended, protects qualified applications and employees with disabilities from discrimination in hiring, promotion, discharge, pay, job training, fringe benefits, classification, referral, and other aspects of employment on the basis of disability. The law also requires that covered entities provide qualified applicants and employees with disabilities with reasonable accommodations that do not impose undue hardship.

AGE

The Age Discrimination in Employment Act of 1967, as amended, protects applicants and employees 40 years of age or older from discrimination on the basis of age in hiring, promotion, discharge, compensation, terms, conditions or privileges of employment.

SEX (WAGES)

In addition to sex discrimination prohibited by Title VII of the Civil Rights Act (see above), the Equal Pay Act of 1963, as amended, prohibits sex discrimination in payment of wages to women and men performing substantially equal work in the same establishment.

Retaliation against a person who files a charge of discrimination, participates in an investigation, or opposes an unlawful employment practice is prohibited by all these Federal laws.

If you believe that you have been discriminated against under any laws, you immediately should contact:

The U.S. Equal Employment Opportunity Commission (EEOC), 1801 L. Street, N.W., Washington, D.C. 20507 or an EEOC field office by calling toll free (800) 669-4000. For individuals with hearing impairments, EEOC's toll free TDD number is (800) 800-3302.

Programs or Activities Receiving Federal Financial Assistance

RACE, COLOR, NATIONAL ORIGIN, SEX

In addition to the protection of Title VII of the Civil Rights Act of 1964, Title VI of the Civil Rights Act prohibits discrimination on the basis of race, color or national origin in programs or activities receiving Federal financial assistance. Employment discrimination is covered by Title VI if the primary objective of the financial assistance is provision of employment, or where employment discrimination causes; or may cause discrimination in providing services under such programs. Title IX of the Education Amendments of 1972 prohibits employment discrimination on the basis of sex in educational programs or activities which receive Federal assistance.

INDIVIDUALS WITH DISABILITIES

Section 504 of the Rehabilitation Act of 1973, as amended, prohibits employment discrimination on the basis of disabilities in any program or activity which receives Federal financial assistance. Discrimination is prohibited in all aspects of employment against disabled persons who, with reasonable accommodation, can perform the essential functions of a job.

If you believe you have been discriminated against in a program of any institution which receives Federal assistance, you should contact immediately the Federal agency providing such assistance.

*U.S. GOVERNMENT PRINTING OFFICE 1994-0-368-769

Your Rights
Under The
Family and Medical Leave Act of 1993

FMLA requires covered employers to provide up to 12 weeks of unpaid, job-protected leave to "eligible" employees for certain family and medical reasons.

Employees are eligible if they have worked for a covered employer for at least one year, and for 1,250 hours over the previous 12 months, and if there are at least 50 employees within 75 miles.

Reasons For Taking Leave:

Unpaid leave must be granted for *any* of the following reasons:

• to care for the employee's child after birth, or placement for adoption or foster care;

• to care for the employee's spouse, son or daughter, or parent, who has a serious health condition; or

• for a serious health condition that makes the employee unable to perform the employee's job.

At the employee's or employer's option, certain kinds of *paid* leave may be substituted for unpaid leave.

Advance Notice and Medical Certification:

The employee may be required to provide advance leave notice and medical certification. Taking of leave may be denied if requirements are not met.

• The employee ordinarily must provide 30 days advance notice when the leave is "foreseeable."

• An employer may require medical certification to support a request for leave because of a serious health condition, and may require second or third opinions (at the employer's expense) and a fitness for duty report to return to work.

Job Benefits and Protection:

• For the duration of FMLA leave, the employer must maintain the employee's health coverage under any "group health plan."

• Upon return from FMLA leave, most employees must be restored to their original or equivalent positions with equivalent pay, benefits, and other employment terms.

• The use of FMLA leave cannot result in the loss of any employment benefit that accrued prior to the start of an employee's leave.

Unlawful Acts By Employers:

FMLA makes it unlawful for any employer to:

• interfere with, restrain, or deny the exercise of any right provided under FMLA:

• discharge or discriminate against any person for opposing any practice made unlawful by FMLA or for involvement in any proceeding under or relating to FMLA.

Enforcement:

• The U.S. Department of Labor is authorized to investigate and resolve complaints of violations.

• An eligible employee may bring a civil action against an employer for violations.

FMLA does not affect any Federal or State law prohibiting discrimination, or supersede any State or local law or collective bargaining agreement which provides greater family or medical leave rights.

For Additional Information:

Contact the nearest office of the Wage and Hour Division, listed in most telephone directories under U.S. Government, Department of Labor.

U.S. Department of Labor
Employment Standards Administration
Wage and Hour Division
Washington, D.C. 20210

WH Publication 1420
June 1993

U.S. GOVERNMENT PRINTING OFFICE:1996 171-169

A Summary of Your Rights Under the Fair Credit Reporting Act

The federal Fair Credit Reporting Act (FCRA) is designed to promote accuracy, fairness, and privacy of information in the files of every "consumer reporting agency" (CRA). Most CRAs are credit bureaus that gather and sell information about you — such as if you pay your bills on time or have filed bankruptcy — to creditors, employers, landlords, and other businesses. You can find the complete text of the FCRA, 15 U.S.C. 1681-1681u. The FCRA gives you specific rights, as outlined below. You may have additional rights under state law. You may contact a state or local consumer protection agency or a state attorney general to learn those rights.

- **You must be told if information in your file has been used against you.** Anyone who uses information from a CRA to take action against you — such as denying an application for credit, insurance, or employment — must tell you, and give you the name, address, and phone number of the CRA that provided the consumer report.

- **You can find out what is in your file.** At your request, a CRA must give you the information in your file, and a list of everyone who has requested it recently. There is no charge for the report if a person has taken action against you because of information supplied by the CRA, if you request the report within 60 days of receiving notice of the action. You also are entitled to one free report every twelve months upon request if you certify that (1) you are unemployed and plan to seek employment within 60 days, (2) you are on welfare, or (3) your report is inaccurate due to fraud. Otherwise, a CRA may charge you up to eight dollars.

- **You can dispute inaccurate information with the CRA.** If you tell a CRA that your file contains inaccurate information, the CRA must investigate the items (usually within 30 days) by presenting to its information source all relevant evidence you submit, unless your dispute is frivolous. The source must review your evidence and report its findings to the CRA. (The source also must advise national CRAs — to which it has provided the data — of any error.) The CRA must give you a written report of the investigation, and a copy of your report if the investigation results in any change. If the CRA's investigation does not resolve the dispute, you may add a brief statement to your file. The CRA must normally include a summary of your statement in future reports. If an item is deleted or a dispute statement is filed, you may ask that anyone who has recently received your report be notified of the change.

- **Inaccurate information must be corrected or deleted.** A CRA must remove or correct inaccurate or unverified information from its files, usually within 30 days after you dispute it. **However, the CRA is not required to remove accurate data from your file unless it is outdated (as described below) or cannot be verified.** If your dispute results in any change to your report, the CRA cannot reinsert into your file a disputed item unless the information source verifies its accuracy and completeness. In addition, the CRA must give you a written notice telling you it has reinserted the item. The notice must include the name, address and phone number of the information source.

- **You can dispute inaccurate items with the source of the information.** If you tell anyone — such as a creditor who reports to a CRA — that you dispute an item, they may not then report the information to a CRA without including a notice of your dispute. In addition, once you've notified the source of the error in writing, it may not continue to report the information if it is, in fact, an error.

- **Outdated information may not be reported.** In most cases, a CRA may not report negative information that is more than seven years old; ten years for bankruptcies.

- **Access to your file is limited.** A CRA may provide information about you only to people with a need recognized by the FCRA — usually to consider an application with a creditor, insurer, employer, landlord, or other business.

- **Your consent is required for reports that are provided to employers, or reports that contain medical information.** A CRA may not give out information about you to your employer, or prospective employer, without your written consent. A CRA may not report medical information about you to creditors, insurers, or employers without your permission.

- **You may choose to exclude your name from CRA lists for unsolicited credit and insurance offers.** Creditors and insurers may use file information as the basis for sending you unsolicited offers of credit or insurance. Such offers must include a toll-free phone number for you to call if you want your name and address removed from future lists. If you call, you must be kept off the lists for two years. If you request, complete, and return the CRA form provided for this purpose, you must be taken off the lists indefinitely.

- **You may seek damages from violators.** If a CRA, a user or (in some cases) a provider of CRA data, violates the FCRA, you may sue them in state or federal court.

The FCRA gives several different federal agencies authority to enforce the FCRA:

FOR QUESTIONS OR CONCERNS REGARDING	PLEASE CONTACT
CRAs, creditors and others not listed below	Federal Trade Commission Consumer Response Center- FCRA Washington, DC 20580 * 202-326-3761
National banks, federal branches /agencies of foreign banks (word "National" or initials "N.A." appear in or after bank's name)	Office of the Comptroller of the Currency Compliance Management, Mail Stop 6-6 Washington, DC 20219 * 800-613-6743
Federal Reserve System member banks (except national banks, and federal branches/ agencies of foreign banks)	Federal Reserve Board Division of Consumer & Community Affairs Washington, DC 20551 * 202-452-3693

FOR QUESTIONS OR CONCERNS REGARDING	PLEASE CONTACT
Savings associations and federally chartered savings banks (word "Federal" or initials "F.S.B." appear in federal institution's name)	Office of Thrift Supervision Consumer Programs Washington D.C. 20552* 800- 842-6929
Federal credit unions (words "Federal Credit Union" appear in institution's name)	National Credit Union Administration 1775 Duke Street Alexandria, VA 22314 * 703-518-6360
State-chartered banks that are not members of the Federal Reserve System DC 20429 * 800-934-FDIC	Federal Deposit Insurance Corporation Division of Compliance & Consumer Affairs Washington,
Air, surface, or rail common carriers regulated by former Civil Aeronautics Board or Interstate Commerce Commission	Department of Transportation Office of Financial Management Washington, DC 20590 * 202-366-1306
Activities subject to the Packers and Stockyards Act, 1921	Department of Agriculture Office of Deputy Administrator-GIPSA Washington, DC 20250 * 202-720-7051

U.S. DEPARTMENT OF LABOR

EMPLOYMENT STANDARDS ADMINISTRATION

Wage and Hour Division
Washington, D.C. 20210

NOTICE

EMPLOYEE POLYGRAPH PROTECTION ACT

The Employee Polygraph Protection Act prohibits most private employers from using lie detector tests either for pre-employment screening or during the course of employment.

PROHIBITIONS

Employers are generally prohibited from requiring or requesting any employee or job applicant to take a lie detector test, and from discharging, disciplining, or discriminating against an employee or prospective employee for refusing to take a test or for exercising other rights under the Act.

EXEMPTIONS*

Federal, State and local governments are not affected by the law. Also, the law does not apply to tests given by the Federal Government to certain private individuals engaged in national security-related activities.

The Act permits *polygraph* (a kind of lie detector) tests to be administered in the private sector, subject to restrictions, to certain prospective employees of security service firms (armored car, alarm, and guard), and of pharmaceutical manufacturers, distributors and dispensers.

The Act also permits polygraph testing, subject to restrictions, of certain employees of private firms who are reasonably suspected of involvement in a workplace incident (theft, embezzlement, etc.) that resulted in economic loss to the employer.

EXAMINEE RIGHTS

Where polygraph tests are permitted, they are subject to numerous strict standards concerning the conduct and length of the test. Examinees have a number of specific rights, including the right to a written notice before testing, the right to refuse or discontinue a test, and the right not to have test results disclosed to unauthorized persons.

ENFORCEMENT

The Secretary of Labor may bring court actions to restrain violations and assess civil penalties up to $10,000 against violators. Employees or job applicants may also bring their own court actions.

ADDITIONAL INFORMATION

Additional information may be obtained, and complaints of violations may be filed, at local offices of the Wage and Hour Division, which are listed in the telephone directory under U.S. Government, Department of Labor, Employment Standards Administration.

THE LAW REQUIRES EMPLOYERS TO DISPLAY THIS POSTER WHERE EMPLOYEES AND JOB APPLICANTS CAN READILY SEE IT.

The law does not preempt any provision of any State or local law or any collective bargaining agreement which is more restrictive with respect to lie detector tests.

U.S. DEPARTMENT OF LABOR

EMPLOYMENT STANDARDS ADMINISTRATION

Wage and Hour Division
Washington, D.C. 20210

WH Publication 1462
September 1988

Notice to Examinee

Section 8(b) of the Employee Polygraph Protection Act, and Department of Labor regulations (29 CFR 801.22, 801.23, 801.24, and 801.25) require that you be given the following information before taking a polygraph examination:

1. (a) The polygraph examination area does __ does not __ contain a two-way mirror, a camera, or other device through which you may be observed.

   (b) Another device, such as those used in conversation or recording, will __ will not __ be used during the examination.

   (c) Both you and the employer have the right, with the other's knowledge, to record, electronically, the entire examination.

2. (a) You have the right to terminate the test at any time.

   (b) You have the right, and will be given the opportunity, to review all questions to be asked during the test.

   (c) You may not be asked questions in a manner which degrades, or needlessly intrudes.

   (d) You may not be asked any questions concerning: Religious beliefs or opinions; beliefs regarding racial matters; political beliefs or affiliations; matters relating to sexual preference or behavior; beliefs, affiliations, opinions, or lawful activities regarding unions or labor organizations.

   (e) The test may not be conducted if there is sufficient written evidence by a physician that you are suffering from a medical or psychological condition or undergoing treatment that might cause abnormal responses during the examination.

(f)   You have the right to consult with legal counsel or other representative before each phase of the test, although the legal counsel or other representative may be excluded from the room where the test is administered during the actual testing phase.

3.   (a)   The test is not and cannot be required as a condition of employment.

(b)   The employer may not discharge, dismiss, discipline, deny employment or promotion, or otherwise dis criminate against you based on the analysis of a polygraph test, or based on your refusal to take such a test without additional evidence which would support such action.

(c)   (1)   In connection with an ongoing investigation, the additional evidence required for an employer to take adverse action against you, including termination, may be

    (A)   evidence that you had access to the property that is the subject of the investigation, together with

    (B)   the evidence supporting the employer's reasonable suspicion that you were involved in the incident or activity under investigation.

    (2)   Any statement made by you before or during the test may serve as additional supporting evidence for an adverse employment action, as described in 3(b) above, and any admission of criminal conduct by you may be transmitted to an appro priate government law enforcement agency.

4.   (a)   Information acquired from a polygraph test may be disclosed by the examiner or by the employer only:

    (1)   To you or any other person specifically designated in writing by you to receive such information;

(2)   To the employer that requested the test;

(3)   To a court, governmental agency, arbitrator, or mediator that obtains a court order;

(4)   To a U.S. Department of Labor official when specifically designated in writing by you to receive such information.

(b)   Information acquired from a polygraph test may be disclosed by the employer to an appropriate governmental agency without a court order where, and only insofar as, the information disclosed is an admission of criminal conduct.

5.   If any of your rights or protections under the law are violated, you have the right to file a complaint with the Wage and Hour Division of the U.S.Department of Labor, or to take action in court against the employer. Employers who violate this law are liable to the affected examinee, who may recover such legal or equitable relief as may be appropriate, including, but not limited to, employment, reinstatement, and promotion, payment of lost wages and benefits, and reasonable costs, including attorney's fees. The Secretary of Labor may also bring action to restrain violations of the Act, or may assess civil money penalties against the employer.

6.   Your rights under the Act may not be waived, either voluntarily or involuntarily, by contract or otherwise, except as part of a written settlement to a pending action or complaint under the Act, and agreed to and signed by the parties.

I acknowledge that I have received a copy of the above notice, and that it has been read to me.

_____

(Date)

_____

(Signature)

Index

Index

Index

Index

Index

Index

RISK FREE FOR 30 DAYS

Use this form to order additional books. If you are not completely satisfied, return them within 30 days for a full refund.

Four Easy Ways to Order:
1. Call **1-800-543-0874** to order and ask for Operator **BB**.
2. Fax your order to **1-800-874-1916.**
3. Visit our website at **www.nationalunderwriter.com** to see our complete line of products and order online.
4. Complete and mail the attached postage paid reply card.

PAYMENT INFORMATION

Add shipping and handling charges to all orders as indicated. If your order exceeds total amount listed in chart, call 1-800-543-0874 for shipping and handling charge. Any order of 10 or more or $250.00 or over will be billed for shipping by actual weight, plus a handling fee. Unconditional 30 day guarantee.

SHIPPING & HANDLING
(Additional)

Order Total	Shipping & handling
$20.00 to $39.99	$6.00
40.00 to 59.99	7.00
60.00 to 79.99	9.00
80.00 to 109.99	10.00
110.00 to 149.99	12.00
150.00 to 199.99	13.00
200.00 to 249.99	15.50

Shipping and handling rates for the continental U.S. only. Call 1-800-543-0874 for overseas shipping information.

SALES TAX
(Additional)

Sales tax is required for residents of the following states:

CA, DC, FL, GA, IL, KY, NJ, NY, OH, PA, WA.

The
NATIONAL UNDERWRITER Company
PROFESSIONAL PUBLISHING GROUP

Orders Dept #2-BB
P.O. Box 14448 · Cincinnati, OH 45250-9786

2-BB

_____ Copies of *The HR Survival Guide to Labor & Employment Law* (#2330001) $65.00
_____ Copies of *Benefits Facts* (#6020002) $50.00

❑ Check enclosed* ❑ Charge my VISA/MC/AmEx (circle one)

*Make check payable to The National Underwriter Company. Please include the appropriate shipping & handling charges and any applicable sales tax.

Card # _____ Exp. Date _____

Signature _____

Name _____Title _____

Company _____

Street Address _____

City _____ State _____ Zip _____

Business Phone (_____) _____ Fax (_____) _____

E-mail_____